How We Love

Discover Your Love Style, Enhance Your Marriage

Workbook Included!

Milan & Kay Yerkovich

WATERBROOK
PRESS

Trade Paperback ISBN 978-1-4000-7299-6
eBook ISBN 978-0-307-45733-2

Copyright © 2006, 2008 by Milan and Kay Yerkovich
Illustrations copyright © 2006 by Tom Clark

Published in association with the literary agency of Alive Communications Inc., 7680 Goddard Street, Suite 200, Colorado Springs, CO 80920, www.alivecommunications.com.

Published in the United States by WaterBrook, an imprint of the Crown Publishing Group, a division of Penguin Random House LLC, New York.

WATERBROOK® and its deer colophon are registered trademarks of Penguin Random House LLC.

The Library of Congress has cataloged the hardcover edition as follows:
Yerkovich, Milan.
    How we love : a revolutionary approach to deeper connections in marriage / Milan and Kay
Yerkovich. — 1st ed.
        p. cm.
    Includes bibliographical references.
    ISBN 978-1-4000-7298-9
    1. Marriage—Psychological aspects. 2. Man-woman relationships—Psychological aspects. 3. Attachment behavior. 4. Interpersonal conflict. I. Yerkovich, Kay. II. Title.
    HQ801.Y47 2006
    646.7'8—dc22

                                                2006016877

Printed in the United States of America
2016

20

rigorous, original, and understandable. If you want to strengthen and enrich your marriage, as well as grow personally, I strongly encourage you to read and digest this material. The effect on all your relationships will be powerful."

—Dr. Jim Masteller, executive director of the Center for Individual
and Family Therapy

"Through Milan and Kay's candid stories you will learn your own love style, find how to connect more deeply with your spouse, and ultimately realize who you were meant to be at the core of your being."

—Greg Campbell, retired business executive

"Forget everything external you think defines you. The quality of your relationships and your contributions to them are what make life great or miserable. This book is a key to a world of insight into intimacy only *you* can bring to your relationships. With each page, I felt Milan and Kay had seen my movie! My marriage is different today because of the simple, profound help I discovered in these pages."

—Kenny Luck, author of *Risk* and *Every Man, God's Man,* men's pastor
at Saddleback Church, and founder of Every Man Ministries

"The Yerkoviches have taken important developmental and psychological concepts and given them to us in a user-friendly fashion. They give us a peek into their personal journey and the countless people they have helped move from young hurts toward more meaningful intimate attachment. *How We Love* helps us see ourselves more clearly and understand our roles in the impasses of our relationships.… A practical and impactful read for all!"

—Jill Hubbard, PhD, clinical psychologist, cohost of *New Life Live!*
national radio program, speaker, and full-time mom

"I am excited that Milan and Kay have given us the guiding principles of a successful marriage. With candor and uncommon insight they have demystified the issues in relationships that cause so many couples to get stuck. This book will get the wheels rolling and provide a destination filled with hope, healing, and fulfillment."

—Dr. Mick Ukleja, president of LeadershipTraq and chair of the
Governing Council of the Ukleja Center for Ethical Leadership

To our four children, who effortlessly exposed every character flaw we didn't even know we had:

To our firstborn son, Kevin, and his wife, Stephanie, (and grandpups Gretzky and Gidget). Kevin, you continue to bring new meaning to the word enthusiastic, and we have always loved your passion for life.

To Amy, our first daughter, and her husband, Steve, and our adorable grandchildren, Reece and Roxy. Amy, your sweet spirit and generous heart touch all who know you.

To our son, John, his wife, Gable, and our delightful granddaughter, Penelope. John, your free spirit and love for the arts teach all of us to appreciate each moment and make the most of it.

To Kelly, our daughter, last but not least. Your love for learning is an inspiration. Your maturity and wisdom continue to amaze us. May your choice of life partner be as wonderful as Stephanie, Steve, and Gable.

We are grateful that each of you has taught us, loved us, and helped us redefine *how we love.*

We love you,
Mom and Dad

Contents

Workbook

Foreword

Talk is cheap, real cheap—until it comes to paying for marriage counseling. That kind of help can be quite expensive by the hour—hour after hour, week after week, month after month. Furthermore, *bad* marriage counseling can cost you more than money. It can cost you your marriage. A counseling degree doesn't guarantee quality help.

Of course I am a firm believer in good, solid counseling for individuals as well as couples. But when it comes to marriage counseling these days, a whole lot of time and money are wasted. After all, improving your marriage is not just about learning to communicate better or listen more closely. It involves much more than formulaic prescriptions, and sometimes it takes a marriage falling apart before you fully realize how rare good advice and wise counsel can be.

Through the years I have worked with hundreds of marriage counselors in a variety of capacities. I have even sought marriage counseling for myself from no less than ten therapists. Some were excellent, and some were nothing short of horrible. I believe all their motives were well placed and their desire to help, strong. But the results I'd hoped for never materialized. Desperate and willing to try anything, I implemented what they suggested, but nothing helped. In one particular case, a very overrated counselor gave advice that was very, very damaging. I do not blame any of these well-meaning professionals for my problems. They did the best they could. But the money and time I spent did not help my marriage.

You may have had a similar experience. You too may have found yourself in a claustrophobic office, talking to a clinician who didn't say much, and desperately wanting hope to surface somewhere, somehow. Often I felt as if we were chatting over a cup of tea in the parlor while my house was burning down. Counselor after counselor seemed to major on minor issues, to focus on topics that didn't seem all that helpful—and usually weren't helpful at all.

When my marriage was most vulnerable, I still had a thousand answers for everyone else, but I didn't know what to do to turn things around in my own relationship. I was like a plumber who spent his days under someone else's sink while his own pipes at home were leaking. And no matter where I turned, no one had a wrench that fit the pipes in my house. Eventually those pipes just disintegrated.

Since those dark days I have learned many lessons that have changed me in profound ways. Pain does that. It breaks you and then it makes you, and my life could have been so different if I'd learned those lessons earlier. Now I hope others can learn some of these lessons without having to go through the "graduate school of pain" that is now my alma mater.

Some of the most valuable lessons I learned came from Milan and Kay Yerkovich. During the long process of my healing, a wonderful woman suggested that perhaps a visit with Milan would be helpful. While working at a church for a number of years, she had watched many people meet with Milan and had never heard anything but rave reviews. She had also seen great transformations in lives and marriages. I was willing to do anything, even go see a guy with the last name of Yerkovich.

From the moment I met him, I knew God would use him greatly in my life. I knew he was a man full of God's wisdom who knew how to apply it to real-life situations. He was kind and caring, but he immediately confronted me about the pity party I was throwing for myself. He also required that I stop participating in my favorite pastime—the blame game. And I learned that understanding how to communicate more effectively doesn't matter if you don't first work on how you love. I continued to meet with Milan on a regular basis, I read what he and Kay had written, and then I spent time with both of them. To say that my contact with them was life changing is an understatement. Everything totally changed when I discovered how I loved, accepted the downsides of being that way, and then moved out (fearfully) to live life and to love in a different way.

I learned that for many reasons—like genetics, family environment, personal choices, and conditioned reactions—there was an "imprint of intimacy" within me dictating decisions about love. I wanted to believe I was loving and caring, but I was actually living out a pattern of avoiding intimacy. With the help of Milan and Kay, I was able to see the walls I was building, walls that every avoider like me feels entitled to build.

Another remarkable discovery for me was that my avoider type is attracted to vacillators, and that this sets up a core pattern of unfulfilled expectations. I'm still astounded that this pattern is so predictable. How could the Yerkoviches understand my past so well, accurately describe my current problems, and even predict what my future would be if I did not make some changes? That was the best part of my experience with Kay's and Milan's teaching. You *can* make changes. You *can* change the course of your own history-in-the-making. With their direction and combined wisdom, I began to put into practice the concepts presented in this book, and my life began to change—and yours can too.

You may not share my particular love style or pattern of relating, but you will find yourself and your type in this book, and it will amaze you how well Milan and Kay know your patterns. Their insights will open your eyes to both who you are and why you do some of the things you do. The ideas in these pages will also help you see the real people behind the facades presented by some people close to you. And once you understand those folks, rather than infecting their wounds, you just might find yourself helping to heal them even as you experience healing yourself.

I love this book, and I think you are going to like it too. Rarely is there a book everybody ought to stop and read for their own sakes as well as for the sakes of everybody around them. *Mere Christianity* by C. S. Lewis and *Boundaries* by Dr. Henry Cloud and Dr. John Townsend are two of those books. *How We Love* also falls into that category. Whether you want to change the way you love or want to better understand those you love, this book will be of great help to you. In fact, if you don't agree, e-mail your address to me at sarterburn@newlife.com and I will refund the price of the book. Your investment is secure. Now read on to understand and experience the transformation of a lifetime.

—STEPHEN ARTERBURN

P.S. You can hear Milan on our radio program *New Life Live!* at www.newlife.com or on SIRIUS satellite radio and XM Satellite Radio.

Preface

When something is broken you cannot repair it unless you understand how it works. People who understand hardware and software fix computers. Mechanics who understand how an engine works fix your car. Some of us try to fix our marriages without ever taking a look at how they work. We were stuck in our marriage in the same old frustrating place for fourteen years. When we each backed up and looked at our first lessons in love from our families of origin, we immediately recognized the unseen forces governing how we loved. For the first time, we understood the source of our frustrations and why we were stuck. Deep change was possible at last.

Writing this book has taken many years, much trial and error, and countless hours, and it certainly could not have been written before the midpoint of our lives. The sort of insight we offer has come from making many mistakes and praying through many years for wisdom. One of our greatest hopes is to save you from some of the struggles we have known.

When we present this information at seminars, our aim is to be transparent about our own failures, and we write about our journey with candidness. The concepts we share here are not completely original, but we've found that they are what work. Some of these concepts are based on attachment theory, and we are grateful to the many researchers whose study of bonding and attachment has made this book richer. (A synopsis of the current research is included in the "For Further Study" section on pages 292–94.) The Judeo-Christian outlook and applications are our own.

The corresponding workbook is essential to applying what you'll learn in these pages. It includes many specific ideas and exercises that will help you engage with the principles in this book, and it is designed to be used by individuals and couples as well as in group settings. Because the greatest growth happens when we have feedback and accountability, it is our hope that you'll use this material—at least for the first time—in a group setting. And because the cost of therapy is quickly grow-ing beyond the reach of many people, we are excited to share so much of what we do in marriage counseling sessions for just the cost of a book and workbook.

We appreciate your sincere desire to invest the time and energy your marriage deserves, and we pray this book will help you achieve your goal of deeper intimacy. We wish you many happy years of continued growth.

Part
1

What Determines How You Love

Chapter 1

Why Every Marriage Gets Stuck

I f we all naturally knew *how* to love, this book would be unnecessary, and Milan and I would each be out of a job as counselors. All of us who have been married more than a few years will admit it is a bit more challenging than we anticipated on our wedding day.

Every marriage has nagging problems calling for our attention. Many people end up thinking their relationship is difficult because they married the wrong person. But the fact that many people are on to their second and third marriages proves that no marriage is tension free. Sometimes our marriages seem to run fairly smoothly—until we hit a crisis or face difficult circumstances. Stress always makes underlying problems more apparent.

Over the years many couples have come to us for help with their problems. We routinely ask several standard questions no matter what situation they describe. Recently, for instance, when Hannah and Robert came in for their initial session, I said to them, "Tell me about the chronic irritations in your relationship. Perhaps it's the same old fight that never gets resolved. Maybe it's a pattern of relating that occurs again and again. Where do you get stuck?"

Hannah looked at Robert, and they laughed. "That's easy," she smiled. "It happened in the car on the drive to your office. I'm always the one bringing up the problems, so Robert is always telling me I am controlling. I was mad at him because he didn't know what he wanted to talk about in our counseling session. He's too passive. I want him to initiate more and try harder."

Robert chimed in, "I do try. It's just never enough for you, Hannah."

Hannah looked at me. "See? Now he will pout and withdraw, and nothing will get resolved."

I summarized, "So no matter what problem you want to discuss, this is your same old dance, the pattern that happens over and over. Is that correct?"

Robert and Hannah both nodded. They had pinpointed their core pattern.

Some couples who are just dating can already describe their core pattern. A core pattern is the predicable way you and your spouse react to each other that leaves each of you frustrated and dissatisfied. Some are married a few years before it is apparent, but sooner or later couples can readily identify the same old place where they get stuck. Maybe it's the same complaints that come up again and again without ever getting resolved or a familiar pattern of fighting, no matter what the topic. Milan and I are no different. We were married in 1972, and by 1976 we had discovered the classic scene that would play itself out over and over for ten more years of our marriage.

We would put the kids to bed and collapse on the couch. I would pick up a magazine and began to thumb through it, and Milan would sit quietly watching me. This was a familiar feeling; I knew he was taking my emotional temperature. I was hoping he would pick up the remote and turn on the television.

"How are you doing?" he would ask. "Did you have a good day?"

I would feel myself getting annoyed. "Why do you keep asking me that? You already asked me that question two times since you came home from work. It's the same answer: I'm fine."

We were starting the wearisome dance that would send us both to bed angry and frustrated. So I would try to derail the invitation. "I think there's a game on TV tonight."

But Milan was always undeterred. "If you're fine, then why did it bother you when I hugged and kissed you when I came home from work? I'm happy to see you, and you act like it's a chore to give me a little affection. You've been distant all evening. What's going on?"

Then came my loud sigh. *I wish you would go away and let me read my magazine,* I would think.

But for some reason, I would begin to explain, knowing it wouldn't help. "I've had kids hanging on me all day. When you got home, I was in the middle of cooking dinner and supervising homework, and you want me to drop everything. Why do you always have to make such a big deal?" The next steps of the dance were predictable. Milan would give me examples of my lack of affection and attentiveness, and I would tell him he was too needy and made me feel smothered.

If you have been married for a few years, you can probably describe your own recurring fight, the discussion you've had repeatedly that never gets settled. You can probably also describe the ways you avoid dealing with problems, and they may be some of the same lines we hear in our offices every day:

- "I try hard to make you happy, but you are never satisfied."
- "I feel like I'm walking on eggshells with you."
- "I've told you over and over what I need, and you just won't do it."
- "Why can't you be more spontaneous and passionate?"
- "If you would listen and do what I ask, I wouldn't be angry."
- "I'm happy with the way things are. You're the one who is always bringing up problems."
- "You say you're sorry, but nothing changes."

Are any of these steps in your same old dance?

Maybe, like us, you find yourself locked in the same tiring dance. Maybe you've tried to change your marriage and have been disappointed with the results. Much marriage advice focuses on treating symptoms and surface issues. You think, *If it were possible to simply stop certain behaviors and do something different, it would be that easy.* But trying to change the things on the surface misses the underlying issues. Occasionally, the adjustment brings good results, and the annoying problem dies down. But it always comes back because there are source patterns guiding those bumbling steps, and until you address them, the dance won't get any better.

Marriage is the most challenging relationship you will ever have, and to think otherwise is to live in denial. When you are with someone day in and day out, you can't hide. Your weaknesses become quite visible, and old feelings from the distant past are stirred. The physical nearness of your mate triggers old feelings as you look to him or her to meet many of the needs your parents were originally supposed to meet.

Milan and I spent the first fourteen years of our marriage trying to change our destructive patterns, but we were only addressing the obvious issues that constantly surfaced. We listed the problems and searched for solutions. After fourteen years, though, a huge change took place when we discovered the unseen forces that determined *how we loved*. We realized our lessons in love didn't start in marriage. They started in infancy and lasted all the years we lived with our parents. Our experiences growing up, good and bad, left a lasting imprint in our souls that determined our beliefs and expectations about how to give love and receive love. Milan and I had different lessons about love, which resulted in different imprints, and without realizing it, we were dancing to different tunes. No wonder we were stepping on each other's toes! Lasting change became possible when we made that revolutionary discovery.

The Revolutionary Truth

What are these imprints—these earlier dance lessons that, healthy or not, form our beliefs and expectations about love? All of us have an imprint of intimacy, the sum of our learning how to love.[1] Our imprint determines our love style—how we interact with others when it comes to love. For a few of us, our early love lessons were ideal, and our love style is healthy and positive. Most of us, though, had some hurtful experiences resulting in a harmful imprint and impaired love style. Have you ever considered the unseen forces governing how you love? Like Milan and me, you will most likely identify with one of five common, ineffective love styles resulting from less-than-ideal imprints.

I first learned how definable these love styles were when I was in graduate school. I had a wonderful supervisor and mentor named Dae Leckie. She taught me the importance of our first lessons about love and introduced me to attachment theory.[2] I was amazed that I could easily identify my own love style as well as Milan's. For the first time I could see how our different styles collided and were at the root of the destructive core pattern that had frustrated us for fourteen years. This new knowledge provided the most profound revelations about how we loved—and why it wasn't working.

Milan: Being cautious about some aspects of psychology, I found it interesting to see that in the New Testament the Greek word for "soul" is *psuche,* which means "inner person" in its broadest sense.[3] The word *psychology* uses the same Greek root and literally means "the study of the soul," giving rise to our concept of the spiritual that resides within. Attachment theory, simply put, is based on a child's bond with his or her primary caregiver. God designed us to need connection, and our relationships with our parents is the first place this happens—or doesn't happen. Attachment theory outlines specifically what can go wrong and looks at how our ability to love is shaped by our first experiences with our parents and caregivers during our early years. These early experiences leave a lasting imprint on our souls that is still observable in our adult relationships.

Kay: Of course, none of us are shaped perfectly during our formative years. Our world is less than ideal, and our ability to love is marred as a result. Attachment theory helps us recognize this by simply describing observable behavioral patterns, some that are helpful and some that are harmful when it comes to forming healthy, loving relationships. Milan and I had no idea what was driving us to respond to each other in the damaging ways we were. All we could see were the frustrating symptoms we had tried for years to resolve. Locked in this repetitive dance, we followed different rhythms and threw each other off balance, neither of us understanding where we learned the songs we danced to. It was definitely a destructive duet!

As we came to understand the harmful aspects of our imprints and the resulting love styles, Milan and I were finally able to understand that the frustrating core pattern that had plagued our marriage for years was a result of our individual imprints colliding. No wonder it felt like we were dancing with four left feet! Attachment theory explained the root of Milan's pursuing and my distancing, the sparks behind countless arguments in our marriage. Attachment theory revealed why his "niceness" was annoying and why connection was so difficult for me. And it explained the root of both Milan's anxiety and my depression.

We also learned where our original melodies came from and what each of us was contributing to our destructive duet. For example, we've heard so many couples say, "I never felt this frustrated by anybody before. Only my spouse makes me feel this way, so it must be his or her fault." Actually, the opposite is true. Primary relationships cause our *own* injurious imprints and resulting love styles to come fully into the light. In fact, our marriage relationships will shine the spotlight on our old attachment injuries. The good news is, marriage offers an opportunity for you and your mate to be each other's healer as you face these wounds together. When you discover the roots of your relational struggles, you can change how you love each other.

Milan: Attachment theory is valuable, life-changing information, and it is not difficult to understand. Simply put, what bothers you most about your spouse is undoubtedly related to painful experiences from his or her childhood and a lack of training in addressing the true challenges of marriage. Your marriage problems did not begin in your marriage! You and your spouse are doing the dance steps you learned in childhood. For each of you, a pattern of relating was set in motion long before you met, causing you to relate to each other in certain ways. Most of us learn how to love from our parents, but occasionally a grandparent, aunt, uncle, or baby-sitter has a lot of influence. Unaware of the powerful influence of our early years in predetermining our dance, we aren't able to understand our reactions or make changes.

The fact is, we can never truly know our mates until we understand their childhood experiences. As I began to share detailed memories of my past, Kay began to understand me in a deeper way. I'd been raised in a Christian home that had many positive qualities, but love meant being overprotected in some ways and underprotected in other ways. I didn't understand some of my parents' emotions and relational stresses, so I developed separation anxiety at an early age. When Kay learned the origin of my fear, she began to understand why her tendency to distance was so agitating to me. Kay was able to become more patient and loving when my anxiety was triggered, and I understood myself better.

Then, as I listened to Kay's memories, I began to understand why she seemed so detached and distant at times. I felt less rejected and anxious when this happened once I understood this was a response she had learned as a child. Much of the irritation we had toward each other began to be replaced with a new compassion.

The Same Old Dance

Kay and I grew up in the fifties (What's a "shoo bop bop"?) and were teenagers in the sixties, and our lives and music are virtually inseparable. For our second date I asked Kay to a concert, and over the years we have enjoyed many styles of music. While many songs are about the blissful beginnings or the sorrowful endings of relationships, not many songs are written about the hard work of change or the rewards of persevering through relational challenges.

In my office I have a painting of a couple dancing titled "Dance Me to the End of Love" by Jack Vettriano. In it, a beautifully poised couple stands at the edge of a dance floor prepared for a ballroom dance competition. (My wife thinks they are dancing on the beach, but being a man, I see a competitive scene.) Consider this scene metaphorically. With other couples softly faded beyond them, these two individuals are ready to take their turn upon the dance floor of life. How will they fare? What challenges lie ahead? Will the whimsical currents and turns of fate sweep them along uncontrollably, finally ripping them apart, or will they navigate the passages of life and emerge on the other side more deeply in love and still dancing?

Their success will be determined by their willingness to persevere when the dance becomes awkward and they start leading in different directions. Sooner or later, every couple will struggle. They will have to acknowledge that they are out of step and be ready to grow as individuals in order to find a new rhythm and a new dance that brings them close again. But some people choose to say good-bye when the dance gets difficult. Many other couples want to improve their relationship, but they do not know where to begin.

In my work as a pastoral counselor doing marriage therapy and in Kay's work as a licensed marriage and family therapist, we have talked with hundreds of couples. Often, these hurting people want a quick fix. But what if they make a real effort and it still doesn't work out? There is no guarantee. Life and relationships are uncertain, and Garth Brooks sings about the latter in his signature song, "The Dance":

I could have missed the pain
But I'd have had to miss the dance.

He's right. Love *is* like a dance. Yet many of the couples we see in our offices would disagree with Garth. Sitting in the pain of divorce and looking back at the marriage, they would rather have skipped the dance altogether than to find themselves wounded and exhausted at the end of a dusty, bumpy road that has led them to this relational dead end.

Kay: The truth is, every marriage has areas of pain and distress, but we think the pain can be constructive. It's like a red light on the dashboard of a car signaling us that the engine needs attention. It is uncomfortable to be stuck, and it is uncomfortable to change. We might as well choose the discomfort that is productive— and change! Is the red light in your marriage flashing? We hope to help you see the cause of the discord and give you tools to do whatever needs to be done, from adjusting the timing to overhauling the engine.

You Can Learn a New Dance!

Milan: Learning about loves styles (attachment theory) has helped us immensely, and we believe that it can help you too. Stop for a minute and ask yourself a few questions. Are family relationships more difficult than you thought they would be? Would you like less conflict and more intimacy in your marriage? Have you been married long enough to observe that the same fights occur again and again? Is unresolved conflict eroding intimacy in your marriage? Have you lost some of the affection you used to enjoy? Are you and your spouse on opposite poles when it comes to sexual desire? Do you have trouble providing each other comfort and nurture? Do you feel like you are simply roommates, busily pursuing life and tending to family needs and occasionally stopping in the hall to exchange pleasantries, sometimes with undertones of resentment? If you answered yes to any of these questions, this book could be an insightful catalyst for change in your relationship.

Couples and families entering our offices for help come with myriad issues. No matter what the surface problems, though, Kay and I have discovered that when we focus on deepening a couple's bond and connection by addressing each person's love style, the initial symptoms often resolve themselves. We rarely see anything new. Instead we see familiar and predictable patterns created by five common imprints, and that is good news. *Why is that good news?* you might be thinking. Well, what would you rather hear from a doctor—"I've seen thirty of these cases this week" or "This is so rare, I need to look it up in a medical journal"? When there is ready recognition of a problem more common than we realized, we usually feel optimistic that our condition is treatable. We breathe a sigh of relief and listen attentively as the doctor explains the prognosis and recommends a course of treatment. Even though something is wrong with us, when the physician reassures us that it is not rare and is quite treatable, we feel optimistic the problem will eventually be rectified.

Kay: The same is true with harmful imprints. Each imprint is recognizable, and when different imprints collide, the resulting patterns are predictable. We hope and pray that once you understand your individual part of the marriage dance, you will begin to experience a mental shift and feel inspired to learn a new rhythm so you are no longer stepping on your spouse's toes. This book can change how you love by giving you a clear diagnosis of and remedy for your marital problem. (We should also mention that our companion workbook offers more practical ways to facilitate change.) But, most of all, we want to share with you our passion about the revolutionary principles we'll share, because our marriage and hundreds of others have been literally transformed by the power and application of this information.

We invite you to discover the source of your relational difficulties once and for all as we unveil the following:

- how your formative years created your relational love style
- what your problematic imprint can do inside a marriage
- why your imprint creates a core pattern with your spouse's
- where to find the skills that will have you doing a whole new dance in your marriage

It has been nineteen short years since God brought us the people who helped us uncover the roots of our marital struggles. We believe these people were an answer to our prayer, the one that has been spoken in our house more often than any other. It consists of four simple words: "Lord, give us wisdom." It's a handy little prayer that fits into every day, because we need wisdom for big and small

Chapter 2

The Revealing Question You Need to Answer

For years, Milan and I danced through marriage, each with two left feet, tripping each other and stepping on each other's toes. Little did we know we were each moving to songs we knew by heart—and the melodies didn't match.

Had we known the significant impact one little question about our early lives would have on our marriage, we might have avoided a lot of problems and made some important changes a lot sooner. We call it the comfort question. It is not a question about your marriage, but its answer can accurately pinpoint the relative difficulties you're currently experiencing. We have asked this question to thousands of people when we speak together at seminars. People often tell us the question haunted them for weeks. We've asked it of couples and their family members when we do counseling. We've asked it of friends in everyday conversation. But we started by asking it of ourselves. The question is simple: can you recall being comforted as a child after a time of emotional distress?

Your answer to that question could potentially reveal more about your relationships than any other insight you might uncover. Realize here we aren't talking about when you fell down and scraped your knee or got sick with the flu. We are looking for a time when you were significantly upset and a parent offered consolation and relief. You might think, *I had a happy childhood. I can't remember needing comfort.* But the fact is, we all experienced something emotionally upsetting during the first eighteen years of life. It didn't have to be a major trauma. Maybe your best friend moved away or you were disappointed because you didn't make the baseball team. Perhaps a good friend hurt or betrayed you. You may have faced something serious like a learning disability, a divorce, a death, or verbal or physical abuse that left you confused, upset, and in need of comfort. Whatever happened to you, at a specific time during your childhood, you experienced either comfort for your pain or the stark absence of it, and that representative memory influences your current relationships in untold ways.

Sometimes people who haven't experienced real, soul-level comfort have trouble understanding what exactly it is. Awhile back, I spoke with a group of people who have chronic or terminal illnesses. When I asked them the comfort question, only one person in the entire group had a memory to share. "I remember my grandma bringing me soup when I was sick in bed," she said. "I was sick a lot. My grandma was very sweet and kind."

"That's nice. Did your grandma hug you or sit and talk?" I asked.

She thought about that for a moment. "No," she finally said. "She just brought soup and left."

Bringing food to a sick child is certainly a nurturing act, but it alone lacks the ingredients of comfort that would have really connected to the heart of a child. Perhaps Grandma could have stroked the little girl's hair. She might have asked about any special events she was missing by being sick, consoled her, or soothed her concern about other family members becoming ill. Maybe her parents should have been looking at their family situation to see if stress was undermining her health.

Related to the comfort question is this: How was conflict handled in your family? For example, was there a time when you were not getting along with one of your parents or when stress or a specific problem caused a lot of tension in the family? Did disagreement leave you feeling alone and disconnected to your parent or family? If you were fortunate enough to be a part of a family that acknowledged problems and successfully resolved them, you learned an important lesson: when conflict ruptures a relationship, repairing it brings relief.[1] If, when you were young, you experienced the relief that comes with resolving disagreements, you will seek that same experience in your marriage as an adult. If not, when things go wrong in your relationships, you may have difficulty expressing yourself, finding solutions, and feeling relief.

If distressful feelings were soothed or problems were resolved when you were a child, you experienced comfort and relief. You therefore know what comfort feels like; you understand its depth on an intuitive level. If you have a memory of comfort, you may not struggle in your relationship the way others do who cannot understand the importance of the three components that make up this unique emotional state.

See if you recall receiving any of these three critical ingredients of comfort.

TOUCH

Significant studies have shown the incredible importance of touch on a baby's development.[2] If you have a memory of comfort, was your parent hugging you or holding you? Was there tenderness, and were you soothed? Some parents touch and hold babies and toddlers but then stop offering nurturing physical contact as their children get older. Yet touch is and remains a vital component of true comfort. When I asked one of my friends the comfort question, she said, "I don't like to be touched. I wouldn't want anyone touching me when I was upset." She went on to explain how her mom was often cold and critical, and her dad left the family when she was only five. She undoubtedly received physical comfort as a baby and toddler, but as an adult she didn't have conscious memories of soothing touch to help her know her need for this kind of comfort.

The fact is, we all need touch—it's a necessary part of comfort.

LISTENING

Second, was at least one of your parents able to listen and help you talk about what was upsetting to you? Parents who are good listeners ask questions so they can understand what is going on in their child's heart and mind. Some parents only ask questions when their kids are in trouble. "Did you clean your room?" "Who ate the ice cream?" "What did you do to your brother?" Hopefully there were also inquiries about what was happening in your heart. "You look sad. What's bothering you?" "I know you don't want to go, but help me understand why not." These kinds of requests tell us someone is interested in our hearts. It's even better when the feelings we then share are confirmed as appropriate, reasonable, or understandable. If your parent said something like "Now I can see why you are so sad" or "I would be mad too if that happened to me," they validated your feelings. In your memory of comfort, did your parent ask questions, listen, and accept your feelings?

We often offer reassurance and miss the opportunity to really listen. A man in my office was trying to comfort his wife who was crying about their rebellious teen. He told her several times, "It will be okay. He'll grow out of it." He was trying to help, but it never occurred to him to ask questions to find out more about how she felt or to validate her tears. I asked him to hold her and tell her it was okay to cry, because this was a tough time for her as a parent. With arms of comfort and permission to feel, she cried harder. After she quieted down, I helped him ask some questions that clarified what was most upsetting to her. They both left feeling better.

RELIEF

Finally, did you feel relief? When we were children, if someone noticed we were having a hard time and offered us a safe place to share our troubles, we felt seen and valuable. Being touched and being listened to brings relief. If we felt sad and our parents listened to what was troubling us and held us as we cried, we were soothed. If we were able to express our frustration and someone listened and responded, we felt relief. If a parent assured us that someone bigger and stronger would keep us safe, we were undoubtedly comforted.

Comfort is not possible unless an emotional connection was made. If you have memories of being consoled, it is safe to assume that your family both encouraged you to express your feelings and then responded when you were hurting. Talking about your inner emotions and experiences helped your parents know you, but there is another benefit. It also helped you know *yourself*.[3] When a parent listens to us and asks questions, we have an opportunity to reflect and put words to what's going on inside us. The self-awareness that comes from learning to reflect gives us the ability to understand our reactions, behaviors, needs, and inner conflicts when we're adults. And, as we will see, this ability is one of the most important skills to bring to a marriage.

WHAT IF YOU DON'T HAVE A MEMORY OF COMFORT?

If you can't recall a specific memory of being comforted, you're in good company. Our work with struggling couples tells us that roughly 75 percent of the adults we surveyed do not have a single memory of receiving comfort from a primary care-giver when they were children. Of course, we may have been comforted during our early years and can't remember those times. But if we don't have a conscious mem-ory of comfort from our childhoods and if we rarely experienced relief from our families who taught us to relate to people, then we are missing some important experiences to take into marriage. Milan and I believe this common comfort deficit is pervasive and far-reaching, causing countless difficulties in people's relationships, communication, and daily lives.

Milan has few memories of comfort growing up, and I have no specific mem-ory. That's not to say we don't have some wonderful memories of times with our parents and siblings. But in asking ourselves the comfort question, we're evaluat-ing our families' ability to emotionally connect. Our early experiences taught us how important—or unimportant—our feelings and the feelings of others are in any given relationship. For Milan and me, our lack of experience with emotional connection when we were growing up made it difficult to find deep intimacy and satisfaction within marriage. And we've found this to be, unfortunately, a common experience.

If your parents had difficulty noticing and soothing your distress, you proba-bly grew up in a family with little emotional connection. Without realizing it, your mom or dad most likely discouraged the expression of certain emotions or re-sponded poorly to your feelings. (If that's the case, your parents probably didn't enjoy meaningful emotional connections within their own families growing up.) When emotional connection is lacking, you learn to restrict emotions and mini-mize what's bothering you, and you will not expect relationships to offer comfort.

After all, it's hard to expect something you've never experienced. Most people who grew up with a lack of emotional connections have no idea what they're missing.

It is important to say here that we are not trying to turn you against your parents or give you a target at which you can shoot arrows of blame. Most of our parents did the best they could and were simply working with the tools they had. Our parents did not receive all they needed growing up either. Your goal is not to find fault but to gain a realistic picture of what went right and what went wrong in your early life so you can begin the healing journey toward growth and maturity.

WHAT YOUR ANSWER REVEALS

You might be wondering, *What's the big deal? Why is this question so important?* Actually, your answer to the comfort question reveals a great deal about certain aspects of your relationships. If your parents touched you, listened to you, helped you express what was going on in your soul (we call them "soul words"), accepted your feelings, and resolved problems well, you'll have a healthy view of relationships. Such positive experiences growing up are like great dance lessons that teach us how to successfully navigate relationships later in life. Good parenting leaves on a child a secure imprint of intimacy that forms positive beliefs and healthy expectations about all future relationships. Memories of comfort are a strong indicator you were imprinted by your early experiences to express feelings, seek connection, and expect relief when life gets bumpy and you hit the potholes of life. Now, when you are upset, you won't think twice about seeking relief through relationships. It is natural for you to go to your mate for comfort.

Of course, no family offers comfort perfectly all the time, but if it happened often enough, you will take healthy skills into your marriage. Even experiences outside your family—experiences with teachers, neighbors, or coaches—can provide valuable lessons and skills. A positive impression from any source creates an inner sense of confidence about what relationships offer.[4] When people experience comfort during their childhood, they know a deeper level of bonding and intimacy.

Whatever one's childhood experience, the resulting imprint of intimacy creates a way of relating called a love style.[5] Our love style is the way we approach relationships. People with a secure love style are comfortable making emotional connections, and they have the ability to form close bonds with others in a way that feels natural. They often choose mates with whom vulnerability is relatively easy and safe. When looking for a marriage partner, they feel something missing with someone who does not have soul words to express the many emotions and thoughts inside.[6] When someone leaves home with an ideal imprint, we call them a secure connector. Chapter 4 will take a closer look at what kind of parenting produces this imprint and identify the traits and characteristics of an adult who is a secure connector.

Answers to the comfort question also reveal why some people are so good at communicating while others have such difficulty. We are not born knowing how to understand and express what is inside our souls. That kind of knowing ourselves requires contemplation and reflection. We have to learn to notice and be aware of our internal experiences, to search our hearts and find words for what is inside us. Being fully known and understood requires that we say *aloud* to someone else what is going on within our souls.

Were you taught to identify and express those feelings? Hopefully, you received healthy attention and people expressed a genuine interest in you in a variety of ways as you grew. If you trusted your parents and felt safe enough to share your inner self with them, you likely learned some soul words for expressing your feelings and became able to relate to people on a deep level. Soul words allow you to express all that is going on in your heart and mind. If your parents were able to provide you with opportunities to express your emotions in this way, they equipped you with both an awareness of and the ability to communicate deep emotion. We'll spend more time discussing soul words later because of their foundational importance to intimacy.

YOUR SECRET SONG

Did you think your first dance was in junior high? Actually, it was way back in childhood with your parents—and you memorized the steps. We all dance through life to a tune so familiar that most of us don't even hear it. Our first experience of dependence leaves an impression that determines how we relate to everyone around us, how we dance through life.

Once you begin to see how bonding and emotional attachment operate within a family, you start realizing just how important this concept of early imprinting really is. The word *imprint* is defined as "a pattern, design, or mark made by pressing something down on, or into, something else."[7] But this concept didn't really crystallize for me until several years ago when I met an accomplished artist named Antje (if you are German, you can pronounce her name). One day while we were in her ceramics studio, she handed me a ball of soft clay and said, "Make something." It was more fun than I could have imagined, and in a few minutes I was hooked.

She decided to encourage my new passion by attending a class with me in which a well-known artist would demonstrate several different techniques. When we went, the instructor had gathered several interesting objects with which to make impressions into her small rectangles of wet clay before carefully firing them. After seeing the interesting designs the stamps created, Antje and I began making stamps with everything—buttons, leaves, jewelry, even random household items. Each stamp left a unique impression in the clay that, when fired, became indelible. I realized that each of us was once a wet lump of clay in the hands of our parents and that we all experienced the inevitable molding and stamping that determined how we would respond in future relationships.

"Crybabies Never Win"

When I asked my friend Rebecca about memories of comfort, she stared at me blankly. "Why would I need comfort?" she asked.

I rephrased the question. "When you were growing up, what happened when you cried?"

"My mom always told me to go to my room if I was going to cry. I hardly ever cry, but if I do, I still go to my room or take a drive in my car. I don't like to cry in front of anyone. It's embarrassing." Imprinted to hide her feelings, Rebecca does not seek relief through relationships. Also, having learned to conceal her feelings, she does not have soul words to describe them. So Rebecca is unable to receive comfort from another person. In fact, she moves away from people when she is sad.

Was your experience like Rebecca's? Was it safe for you to show all your feelings when you were growing up? When such emotional connection is missing, children often discover that it is *unsafe* to expose their feelings. At one of our seminars, a young man told us about his experience. "I remember missing a fly ball at a Little League baseball game when I was ten years old, and my dad was watching," he said. "We lost the game when I dropped the ball. I held back my tears until we got in the car, but eventually I broke down. My dad looked at me and said, 'Crybabies never win games.' Since then I've never shown him any feelings at all."

This man had carried that shame with him his entire life. When he needed comfort from his father, he'd gotten only more pain. His dad probably didn't realize he was imprinting his son, but he did. When feelings of sadness or fear are forced underground, sometimes anger becomes the only acceptable emotion because it is *not* vulnerable. I asked the man if he struggled with anger now as an adult. He looked surprised. "Well, it's sort of a problem in my marriage, and it is definitely a problem when it comes to dealing with my kids. How did you know?"

Anger may be the only emotion this man felt safe to express since it had not been acceptable to reveal his sadness when he was growing up. Unfortunately, like many men, this man learned early on not to express vulnerable feelings because they had been too difficult for someone else to handle. So anger effectively blocked his awareness of "unacceptable" feelings. Our baseball player did not allow himself sadness. He had no ability to express the emotion because doing so had been prohibited. In order for this man's soul to heal more fully, his marriage needed to be a safe haven where all feelings were acceptable, especially the ones he was discouraged from showing as a child.

"You're Too Sensitive"

When parents are either unaware of their own feelings or unable to express them appropriately, they will struggle to form a healthy emotional connection with their children. Case in point. Gina was a highly sensitive child with powerful emotions.

Whenever she became upset, her mother grew anxious and uncomfortable. If Gina's feelings persisted, her mom became irritated and called Gina a drama queen. By doing so, she was communicating a powerful message to Gina: "You feel things too deeply. There is something wrong with you."

Gina's imprint led her to believe she was bad for having deep feelings. Now as an adult, she works hard to diminish her emotions and often apologizes for her feelings because she believes emotions are bothersome and frustrating to others. Rebecca, the baseball player, and Gina all carry damaged imprints. They have learned to hide feelings and avoid vulnerability. They don't know how to seek relief through relationships. And damaged imprints create problematic love styles.

In part 2, we'll look at the five love styles that arise from damaged imprints like these. Each one was formed in an environment characterized by a lack of comfort, and each one resulted in an invisible barrier to love. Each style is the sum of our negative relational experiences and determines the degree we will risk emotional vulnerability with others.

DISCOVERING THE PROBLEM

Like everyone else we've met, Milan and I entered marriage wanting to do our best and succeed. The problem was, we didn't know what the problems were! We were completely unaware of the invisible roadblocks to success. Looking back, we can sadly say that our parents did not learn from their own parents how to express emotions or find relief in their relationships. As a result, they were limited in their abilities to pass this skill on to Milan and me.

Since we didn't know the problem, we didn't understand that soul words, comfort, and relief were missing in our marriage and our parenting. Occasionally we did a passable job at resolving conflict, but we ignored a lot and avoided problems far more often than we solved them. We couldn't employ (let alone teach our kids) a skill we didn't have. Like most people, we desired to be the best partners possible—but it *wasn't* possible. Not until fourteen years down the marriage road did we discover that we were missing some important abilities.

Our first discovery was that we both avoided unpleasant feelings. Having come to believe that Christians are supposed to have "joy, joy, joy, joy down in our hearts," we both resisted negative emotions. I never saw Milan cry one time during the first fifteen years of our marriage, and I rarely cried, but if I did, I made sure I was alone. Also, we both feared anger and avoided it altogether. And fear or anxiety meant we were not trusting God. We never did learn to *feel and deal* with a wide variety of emotions. And this whole unhealthy situation was perfectly normal to us because it was what we'd always known. This was how the grownups we knew operated.

When our fourth child was a baby and the older three were in elementary and junior high school, we realized our family was missing something. We didn't do feelings! And have you ever noticed how hard it is to have an emotional connection when no emotions are apparent? We started to remedy this situation by taping a list of feeling words to the refrigerator to help us learn to describe what was going on inside us. The feeling might have been about anything—friends, work, school, church, sports, or siblings. The point was to learn to identify the feeling and then manage it appropriately. Our only rule was that every emotion had to be talked about. We began to call this process of discovery "feeling and dealing," and if this exercise did nothing else, it made a huge difference in our marriage. The change didn't happen overnight, and at first dealing with feelings was very awkward and even uncomfortable. But we figured any change is like that—and it certainly beat the alternative of not changing! After many trials and test runs, we began to see results. We became aware and respectful of one another's emotions and felt our relationships deepen as that invisible barrier began breaking down. And we sincerely believe that if we could do it, so can you.

THE KEY TO INTIMACY

Are you beginning to see the importance of genuine emotional connection within your marriage? And had you ever considered comfort such a key ingredient in marriage? The ability to console and bring relief to your spouse when he or she is upset and agitated is foundational to a close, emotional bond. But for the first fourteen years of our married life, we were unable to do this—and *all* the couples and families who come to us for help struggle with it as well. This book is our response to the overwhelming difficulty so many people are experiencing in their relationships due to a lack of healthy emotional connection. We want to first help you identify your problematic imprint and love style and then give you tools for creating a new imprint that will mean a deeper, richer bond with your spouse.

Because understanding your childhood experience is foundational to discovering your imprint and resulting love style, we'll spend a little time examining what exactly went on in your past. As counselors we have encountered surprisingly powerful resistance from people about this. Many people who lacked deep emotional connection as children resist looking back, some of them even to the point of denying that the past is significant. Yet, in many cases, the stronger the resistance to looking back, the greater that need actually is. If your childhood was a battlefield, you may be fighting your own war against the past. We've found that before we can begin discussing the different imprints, we need to explain that moving beyond the past is the goal here. In fact, that's the entire point of our work as counselors, teachers, and therapists: to put the past in the past so we can get on with our present lives. But the simple fact is that before we can learn how to love correctly, we need to see clearly how the past has shaped us.

So without further qualification, let's look at how we can uncover our early imprints of intimacy.

Chapter 3

Imprints of Intimacy
from Our First Lessons in Love

When she was eighteen years old, Tina came to Milan and me for help. She was desperate for close connections, but she often felt misunderstood, which made her angry. She was frustrated by her inner turmoil and told us, "Something is wrong, but I don't understand exactly what the problem is or how to change it."

In our first session I asked Tina to explore the feelings beneath her anger. She was quiet for a while, considering the matter for the first time ever. "Uneasy," she finally said. "It's a yucky feeling, like something is wrong, and I want someone to make that feeling go away. Then I get irritable because it won't." She looked up at me with big eyes. "Wow, I never really thought how anxious I feel before I get angry. Or I just never put words to it."

As we continued talking, I discovered that Tina's feelings of anger and anxiety were intense. She could see that she often overreacted and that little things set her off. Often this intensity tells me that the past is flooding into the present. Yet nothing in Tina's memories seemed to fit. We revisited numerous childhood experiences, yet nothing seemed to explain the cause of her current emotions.

Then finally, in his gracious way, God intervened. During a conversation with her mother, Tina was surprised to hear her mom describe a serious car accident that had taken place when Tina was only ten months old. Tina's car seat had protected her from injury, yet at the scene, her seat—with Tina it—had been placed to the side of the road while injured passengers were tended to. The atmosphere was one of total chaos. Police came. An ambulance arrived. Tina watched as para-medics removed her mother from the car and took her away in their big, noisy van. Tina didn't see her mother after that for an entire week while her mother recovered in the hospital from a broken pelvis. The uninterrupted care Tina had experienced for the first ten months of her life had vanished in a flash.

When her mother arrived home after a week in the hospital, she was shocked that Tina wouldn't look at her or come to her. Even worse, Tina's mom was not allowed to pick her up or hold her until her injuries fully healed.

Imagine what this experience had done to young Tina even though she remembered none of it consciously. After listening to her story, I asked Tina to describe what she might have felt at the time of the accident and afterward. "Scared. No…terrified," she said. "Like my mom was never coming back." She paused. "I sort of still feel like that all the time, and it's so strong. When someone leaves, I feel like that person won't come back, and I get scared." She continued, "When my mom came back, I didn't want to look at her because I was mad that she'd left. And I was afraid she might leave again." Tina began to cry. "I still have these feelings all the time. Every time my boyfriend leaves. It's the exact same feel-ing. I'm not crazy. I really did feel all this. I still feel it."

In the preceding chapter I mentioned that an imprint is like a song we know by heart. It plays over and over in our relationships, and unless we take the time to learn to hear it, we'll remain unable to do anything about it. Many people have told us, "I can't remember much of my childhood. How could it have such a strong impact on my relationships today?"

I'll let Dr. Daniel Siegel help me explain. In his book *The Developing Mind*, Dr. Siegel presents a fascinating description of how we recall our early years as he discusses two types of memory: explicit, which requires language, and implicit, which is preverbal. "Explicit memory is what most people mean when they refer to the generic idea of memory.… When explicit recollections are retrieved, [one has] the internal sensation of 'I am remembering.'… Explicit memory is often communicated to ourselves and to others in the form of descriptive words or pic-tures communicating a story or sequence of events."[1] If we asked you to share a sad childhood memory, you would tell a story from your past and be aware that the sad feeling is linked to the event you are recalling. You would know you are "remembering," and you would know why you are sad.

Implicit memories, however, are our preverbal "baby memories." As an infant and toddler, you experienced your environment through facial expressions, voice tones, feelings, and bodily sensations when you responded to your parents and surroundings, always learning what to expect. These feelings and sensations (good and bad) are implicit memories, and "by a child's first birthday, these repeated patterns of implicit learning are deeply encoded in the brain."[2]

We adults are influenced by these preverbal, implicit memories when they are activated in current relationships. We experience them as a flood of feelings, but without the awareness that we are remembering anything. Dr. Siegel clarifies, "Implicit memory involves parts of the brain that do not require conscious processing during encoding or retrieval."[3] Also, as implicit memories are recalled, there is no sensation that something is being recollected. Milan and I think of these as "feeling memories" that are formed by experiences and relationships during our preverbal years. And when our negative implicit memories go unnoticed, they can wreak havoc on relationships.

Remembering Your Clearest Picture of the Past

Are you surprised that such an early experience can affect a person for so many years? Tina was exceptionally bright, perceptive, and sensitive from birth, but a specific trauma had interrupted her attachment to her mother and shattered her secure base of comfort. Connecting that past event to her present troubles flipped the switch for Tina. Suddenly she understood the reason for her reactivity. And after hearing her mother's account of the experience, Tina realized that her mother had been a victim of the situation as well. Tina's deeper awareness and resulting healing confirm the remarkable truth that "knowing about implicit memory allows us the opportunity to free ourselves from the prison of the past."[4]

Milan and I believe that identifying our own childhood imprints really can help us overcome present problems in our relationships. But to uncover those relational "dance steps" we learned from our parents, we must first be willing to form a picture of our early years. Most of us have plenty of memories from which to draw. But asking relatives for their recollections can sometimes be helpful too, especially when we're asking about our infancy.

I asked my mom what I was like as an infant, and her answer stunned me. "Oh, you were glum," she said, "and you never smiled. I remember telling your dad I thought there was something wrong with you, and he just laughed at me. When you were ten months old, you broke your collarbone trying to crawl into your twin sister's crib. You lay on the floor for a month and wouldn't move or smile. And every time I picked you up, you cried." I remember being totally shocked. In those few sentences, my mom had given me the key to my lifelong bouts of depression: it had begun during my first year of life.

Even though such important realizations as Tina's and mine can come from looking back, many people still hold the opinion that the past is in the past so we should just move on. The past can't be changed, so why dwell on it? Though simply talking about past events can move important discoveries toward the surface, some people resist, claiming they have no childhood memories—or at least none of consequence.

I vividly remember my early sessions with Lee and Karen. Lee was an angry man, and his wife had told me privately that their three-year-old daughter, Stacie, seemed afraid of him. In our third therapy session, Lee finally released what had been obvious to me at my initial encounter with him. He'd been pleasant and actually quite charming during our first meeting. I was sure he left feeling good about the headway he thought he'd made in convincing me that the marriage problems centered on the shortcomings of his petite, extroverted wife. But Lee had no idea how much he'd given away during our initial phone conversation before he ever walked into my office. In my experience, wives are generally the initiators when it comes to making counseling appointments. When a man calls, it often means one of two things: he's either desperate or controlling. And Lee was definitely not the desperate kind.

Lee sat in front of me as the storm inside him began rumbling out. His jaw was tight, and there was an intensity and hardness in his dark eyes. His body was tense, and he held his arms tightly at his sides, his fists clenched. My own childhood training had outfitted me with built-in radar for these signs of inner rage, and my radar screen began to beep wildly.

Karen's sideways glances at Lee while she spoke confirmed my caution. As she was telling me about their difficulty in dealing with young Stacie, Karen was obviously weighing how much she should give away, her own radar beeps growing louder and more persistent. I decided to stoke the fire. "Lee," I said, turning to him, "tell me your best and worst childhood memory."

Lee shot a glare at his wife and then at me. "What does that have to do with our marriage? We came here for marriage counseling, which is probably a waste of time. Let's stick to the topic."

I looked steadily at Lee. I flashed on an image of a tomb where a boy's tender heart had been covered over with heaping shovels of anger. His intimidating ways guarded the entrance so effectively that I was certain he had no idea he was defending an inner chamber. I also had no doubt that the success or failure of their marriage therapy depended upon getting Lee to guide us to that subterranean world.

"Lee, what would greatly help us understand the problems in your marriage is for me to learn about what you experienced as a child and what it was like to live in your family growing up. You told me last session your dad used to take you fishing. Is that right?"

"Yeah. But that has nothing to do with my marriage. Like I said before, let's stick to the topic. That was a long time ago. It doesn't matter."

"Well, Lee, I disagree. You lived there for approximately eighteen years. That is where you first experienced relationships and how they work or don't work. As the old saying goes, more is caught than taught. Your family was like a classroom continually teaching you what to do with your feelings and your needs. And all families have their strengths and weaknesses."

Lee interrupted me. "It was fine. I had a good childhood. My dad took me fishing, and my mom cooked and cleaned. We were just a normal family in middle-class America."

"Well, then, it shouldn't be too hard for you to answer this next question. Tell me about comfort in your family. Share a specific memory of a time one of your parents comforted you when you were upset, when you were scared or sad for some reason."

"Oh, I'm sure there were lots of times," Lee said.

"Share just one," I coaxed.

Looking up at the ceiling, Lee searched the panorama of his childhood for an answer that would qualify him for dismissal from my "unrelated" prying. I knew it would be an agonizing search. I have rarely had an angry man answer this question with a concrete, positive memory.

"I remember a time when my dad was mad and kind of went off. Mom came into my room and told me it would be okay. She sort of apologized. Maybe gave me a hug or something."

"I see," I said, pausing for a moment. Lee's lips pulled tight.

"I'm wondering what your dad did to prompt your mother's visit. What caused him to be so upset?"

Lee laughed. "Anything and everything! I probably forgot to put a tool back in the toolbox. That happened more than once."

"Exactly what happened when he went off? If I had been an observer in your home, what would I have seen?"

Lee laughed again. "A red face. A contorted, berserk red face! Mom came up to my room after he yelled at me from the garage. I always knew I was going to get it bad when I could hear him from there. He threw a few tools around, and a wrench dinged his prize, red convertible. He turned purple."

"What happened next?"

"Oh, that one got me the belt. He took it off and started swinging. I deserved it, though. He had told me to put the tools away plenty of times."

"How old were you?"

"You ask too many questions. I don't know. Seven or eight? Is this interrogation over yet?"

"Not yet, Your Honor. My client, eight-year-old Lee, has not been fully represented. I think he deserves a fair hearing." I smiled. "I am now addressing Lee, the eight-year-old. Were you afraid of your dad?"

"Sure, but what's the big deal? Aren't all kids scared of their old man?"

"I'm not sure." I paused. "Is Stacie afraid of you?" Lee looked out the window, and I hurried on. "So, what did your mom do while all this was going on?"

"She was smart enough to stay clear."

"What did she do when she went up to your room?"

"Just like I said before: Told me she was sorry. Probably gave me a hug."

"Exactly what was she sorry for? What did she *do*?"

"She always thought Dad was too hard on us. She felt bad, I guess. She always waited until things settled down. Then she would come and try to smooth things over. She'd tell us he didn't mean it."

"Did she ever speak up and tell your father that she felt he was too harsh?"

"No way! Everyone knew not to get in Dad's way. Even Mom." Lee looked at his watch. He seemed like a caged animal. I was the sole defender of the child he once was, his adult self having joined his father's side. I launched a careful maneuver to try to take out Lee's defenses.

"Let me summarize what I am hearing, Lee. Your story makes me very sad. When you made mistakes, your father reacted with fits of anger. If you ever reacted in the same way, you would have been severely punished, which seems like a double standard. Your mother was like a child herself and couldn't protect you. She made the apologies your dad should have made. You seem to have forgotten the fear that little boy must have felt, almost as if you are speaking about someone else. I'm sure your dad did the best he could, Lee, but I wonder how much better your current relationships might be if your father had been more patient and tender."

Lee is like many people who want a good marriage but believe looking back at their childhood is a waste of time. He doesn't see how inextricable his past experience is from his present problems. The past defines nearly everything about us: our emotions, beliefs, desires, and preferences. We are the sum of our history. To ignore it is to be blind to the currents that sweep us along through life.

THE CURRENTS OF THE PAST

Kay and I live in Southern California, and we like to go to the beach. When the waves are good, I like to bodyboard at T-Street in San Clemente. One day I entered the water by the stairs that descend from a bridge over the railroad tracks. The waves were huge that day. After catching a bunch of tubular curls, I sat watching the horizon for the next big set. Suddenly I heard the lifeguard's voice over the loudspeaker. "Attention, bodyboarder! You are too close to the pier!" *Wonder who he's talking to,* I thought. Fortunately, I looked up toward the beach, scanned the area, and realized he was talking to me! Somehow I had drifted a quarter mile from the stairs and was in an entirely different place than I'd thought.

Sometimes life is like that. Focused on other things, we can't see our own position in the present situation. Left alone, we might remain unaware of the riptide of our childhood pulling us perilously closer to danger. Yet many of us *are* aware that currents are there, and still we choose to ignore them. Why do so many of us resist looking back?

The answer is twofold. First, *we want to believe that our present conflict is the issue.* Like Lee, we think if we can just fix the present conflict, we can continue on with our lives. Yet Lee's anger didn't grow so big and strong in a vacuum. Ironically, his anger (along with Karen's passive response) was at the very heart of the current marriage problem. But, left to his own conclusions, Lee would never have considered the idea that his history had any effect on his relationship with Karen.

Second, *all we want is to get rid of the pain.* We've all been trained to look for the quick fix when we're stressed out, in pain, or fed up with life. The last thing we want to do is dig up more pain to pile on top of what we're already feeling. Besides, the present carries much more weight on our daily to-do lists. When we're faced with marital unhappiness, we tend to want to deal with it the way we do with heartburn: "Just give me relief!"

A client recently told me, "My childhood was a prison of pain. I escaped when I was seventeen, and I closed the door. I'm never going back there." Many of us are like this, totally unwilling to acknowledge the deep wounds we've suffered. If looking back is likely to be painful, we want to be sure there will be some real benefits.

LOOKING BACK TO FIND COMPASSION

After fourteen years of marriage, I thought I knew Milan. And he believed he knew me. We did know some things about each other's upbringing. It didn't take me long to realize his family had had different foods, cars, appliances, holiday traditions...you name it! They also had different ideas about things like how many times you use a towel before you throw it in with the dirty clothes (more than once, right?). We'd handled many of those natural adjustment issues that new couples are supposed to deal with. What we'd never done, though, was listen to specific childhood memories and consider how those experiences had affected us growing up.

One of the greatest benefits of talking about our history was the compassion it gave us for each other. In fact, it even helped us understand ourselves better. As I saw Milan's past in a realistic light, his current behavior made much more sense. I also remember the night he asked about my parents' divorce. He'd known about the event since our dating days, but I had never explained details. I'd never discussed my feelings about the day my sisters and I first heard that my dad was leaving, let alone the aftermath of the weeks and months that followed. As I shared, I realized what a caring, compassionate listener can do to help us discover the impact of an event on our lives. I learned much about myself during that conversation. Significantly, I realized I carried a core distrust of men. That was indeed a problem, since I was married to one.

Just as my compassion for Milan had grown when he talked about his past, he began to have more compassion for that part of me that struggled to allow myself to need him. Interestingly, the more he listened, the more my trust grew and the closer to him I felt. Slowly, his compassion melted away that distrust.

Slowly I was seeing my spouse and my marriage in a whole new light.

And the same thing happened with Karen. Her relationship with Lee was a real roller coaster. But one week, after discussing their families of origin for several months, Karen came in alone, explaining that Lee was sick. "Tell me about the week, Karen," I said.

"It was terrible!" she said.

"What made it so terrible for you?"

She stared at the floor with tears forming in her eyes and let out a deep sigh. "Lee's behavior is so unpredictable. One minute he seems like he wants to be close, and then he gets angry at the smallest thing. He seems so hypersensitive...so extreme...so all-or-nothing... It's almost as though he sabotages intimacy on purpose."

"How does it make you feel?"

"I want out!" she snapped. "I can't take it anymore."

I nodded, but I was thinking about a way to salvage the situation. Karen was feeling like any of us would when faced with the overwhelming thought of continuing on in the confusion and frustration of the past few years.

I asked her to lean back in the sofa and close her eyes. "Now," I said, "reflect back on what you learned in last week's session when we discussed Lee's childhood fears of his father. Picture him at that park having just run from his house to escape his father's drunken rage. What does Lee look like?"

Karen was silent for several minutes. Finally, she said, "I see a little boy, eight years old. He's out of breath from running. His heart is pounding, and his forehead is sweating, and he is sitting alone on a swing crying. He's staring at the sand below his feet, and every now and then he looks over his shoulder in the direction of his house to see if anyone's coming. He looks worried. He wants someone to come find him. Anyone except his dad. He is scared."

"That's a great picture, Karen," I said, urging her on. "What else do you see, hear, and smell?"

After pausing for a while, she said, "I hear him crying softly, and I can see his clothes are grubby...stains on his shirt. His face is smudged with dirt, and the tears wash clean streaks down his cheeks." She smiled with her eyes still closed. "He smells like our puppy dog. His face is slowly changing. He clenches his teeth. He kicks the sand, gets up. He throws handfuls of sand as hard as he can, over and over. He drops to his knees and stares at the sand, running his hands through it slowly and alternately looking up into the late afternoon sky. The sand and the sun are his only comfort."

I was impressed with Karen's ability to visualize the scene—and disappointed

Lee wasn't there to hear her. "Karen, I want you to imagine what he's feeling on the inside at this moment."

Her answer was faster this time. "So many feelings going on all at once… He is confused. He is probably overwhelmed and can't even begin to make sense of them. I'm sure he hurts deeply."

"You're right. He really does hurt. Now pretend you're on a park bench nearby and tell me how what you've seen makes you feel."

She softened even more, her closed eyes squinting. "I just want to go over and pick him up and put him on my lap and hug him." Tears rolled down her cheeks.

As our hour drew to a close, I asked Karen a final question. "Karen, do you feel differently about Lee than when you first walked in tonight?"

She opened her eyes and looked at me, her face more relaxed now. She took a deep breath. "I do feel different, I guess." A wry smile crossed her face. "I do. I see him with more compassion."

Karen had moved to a new place. No longer ignoring the root of her problems, she was beginning to build an empathetic base from which to view Lee's struggles. And her situation is not uncommon. Many of the traits in our spouses that we might find especially irritating had their origins in the difficulties they experienced as children. Lee's struggle with trust, his vacillating behavior, and his outbursts of anger were understandable once Karen took the time to get to know the little child inside her mate.

The following week I was delighted to learn that Karen had told Lee all about our session. As she described both her picture of Lee as a child and the compassion she felt toward him, he began to cry. They hugged and experienced the sadness of Lee's childhood together. Later she told us, "That is the closest I have ever felt to Lee. It gave me new hope our marriage can change."

CHANGING THE TUNE YOU DANCE TO

Old tunes from the past can so completely shape our beliefs that we don't see that our current problems arise from old lessons we learned about how to handle feelings, needs, conflicts, gender roles, and communication. Our early experiences are so deeply woven into the fabric of our being that they determine how we respond in all our future relationships. And until we're willing to go back and hear those old songs for what they are, we remain locked in our familiar but unhealthy, unproductive dances.

Many of our clients believe they grew up in normal American families. Yet when they look closer, they see patterns that negatively influence the present, and many realize they need to learn compassion not only for their mates but also for themselves. This realization is the first step forward in the process of bonding with your spouse in healthy ways. Our companion workbook offers a guide to help you think about your early history and recognize the influence of your past.

Now let's look at some of the hallmarks of close, secure relationships. We'll also see what teaches children how to love in healthy ways, preparing them to have the positive imprint of the secure connector.

Chapter 4

Ideal Love Lessons: The Secure Connector

As we've seen, our experience of being comforted is an essential element of our ability to bond with another person. But exactly how does a successful bond take place? In the next few pages, we're going to look at some important things parents do to send their children into adulthood with the skills they'll need to connect with their spouses. Like trying to tango when you've never had a dance lesson, you won't have the intuitive skills for navigating the challenges of marriage unless your parents helped you form a deep, secure bond with them. So think about your own experiences, as well as those of your spouse, as you read the next section.

PARENT AND CHILD BONDING

Secure attachment might best be represented as a circular series of steps that create a secure love style. Beginning from the top, we follow the progression of events through the experience of developing a close emotional connection (please see the diagram on page 39).

IF YOU GOT IT, YOU CAN GIVE IT

Our friends Tracie and Trevor are giving their toddler son, Cole, skills that will help him relate well to his future spouse. At nineteen months old, Cole already has all the signs of a close, secure bond with his parents. Sitting at a restaurant with them,

Cole watched a baby crying. He looked back and forth between Tracie and the crying toddler. "Baby crying!" he said. "Baby crying!"

"Yes," said Tracie, "the baby is sad."

The baby kept wailing, and Cole asked, "Baby okay? Baby okay?"

"His mommy is trying to help him calm down," Tracie explained.

Cole was looking for help making sense of the experience. His mother was attentive and gave Cole words for the baby's feelings and, by extension, for his own feelings. These soul words (introduced in chapter 2) are the first step in describing our feelings.

Notice, though, that at just nineteen months, Cole was already able to see the needs of those around him. This indicates Cole's own needs had been recognized, welcomed, and attended to many times. He could give because he had received. He was responsive because his parents had responded to him. Someday when Cole marries, he'll notice when his wife is upset and say, "Wifey okay? Wifey sad?" She will love his sensitivity!

In our marriages, it's difficult to give something we never got. Did you have parents who were compassionate and tuned in to your feelings? If not, could that be why you and your spouse have difficulty responding to each other?

Did Your Parents Get to Know All of You?

When Mark, one of my (Kay's) clients, asked his mother what he was like as a baby, she said, "Oh, I'm so glad you were the second. Your brother was such a handful, and I could put you in the playpen for hours, and you were happy and content."

It made sense, then, that Mark's wife, Kim, complained that he didn't need her for anything. He seemed content watching television by himself. Mark had certainly learned early on not to expect much from others. Because he had a compliant nature, he was left to himself. No one took the time to get to know Mark or respond to him. So he didn't expect or want that in his marriage. He also didn't know how to get to know his wife on a deep level.

Kids come into the world dancing to their own tunes, with different temperaments, different likes and dislikes. Parents need to get to know their infants and find out what works and what doesn't. Naturally extroverted children don't require much prodding to connect, whereas reserved children may benefit from gentle encouragement and good timing. It takes more effort to get to know and understand a quiet child. Some children who are a whirlwind of activity demand their parents' attention, whereas those who prefer to sit and read a book may miss out on being noticed and listened to. Did your parents learn that you liked a lot of interaction or that you were easily overstimulated and quickly worn out by noise and commotion?

In an optimal home environment, parents notice and respond to their child's unique traits. They get to know their baby, and they create time to interact in a way that brings their little one pleasure and relief. If your parents were able to respond in a sensitive way most of the time, they helped you progress toward a secure bond because you felt known and understood.[1]

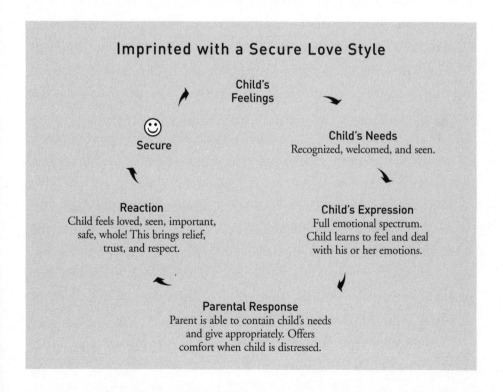

Imprinted with a Secure Love Style

Child's Feelings

😊
Secure

Child's Needs
Recognized, welcomed, and seen.

Reaction
Child feels loved, seen, important, safe, whole! This brings relief, trust, and respect.

Child's Expression
Full emotional spectrum. Child learns to feel and deal with his or her emotions.

Parental Response
Parent is able to contain child's needs and give appropriately. Offers comfort when child is distressed.

Did You Learn to Trust?

I think we would all agree that trust is a very important ingredient in a healthy marriage. We cannot feel close to someone if we don't trust that person. By the time we marry, many experiences have taught us how much we can or cannot trust other people to understand us and meet our needs. In fact, before we could even talk, our parents were teaching us whether we could rely on them.

How exactly do we learn to trust? We learn to trust if something happens consistently over and over again. When I'm driving, for instance, I trust the light to turn red after it is yellow. It happens every time. I don't feel anxious and unsure when I see a yellow light, because I know what it means, and I know how to respond.

Our parents teach us about trust in the same way. The learning process begins when we are babies, and it repeats itself daily, weekly, and monthly, thousands of times. After all, as a baby, you were a bundle of needs. When you were hungry or uncomfortable, you cried and screamed to tell your parents, "Get over here and figure out what I need and give it to me." Any kind of soothing touch—nursing, cuddling, bathing, burping—helped bring you relief. If Mom and Dad appreciated your unique temperament and responded to it in soothing ways, you also felt known and accepted. If these attentive responses were reinforced by repetition, you formed an inner core of trust and learned you could depend on relationships to bring fulfillment and security. In turn, this positive experience freed you to trust again.

Infancy is all about learning to deal with pain and need. If babies learn from the very beginning that their passionate needs will be met, they also learn that Mom and Dad bring relief. Trust is built on the replication of this experience over weeks and months and years. We think of it as a circle of comfort because when a parent meets a child's needs and brings relief, this frees them to need again and again, and so the circle repeats.

Consider the impact on a marriage relationship if infant bonding didn't go well. Mary was the last of five children, all born in a seven-year span. Mary's dad left just before she was born, and her mom had to assume all the family responsibilities. They moved into Grandma's house so Mary's mother could get a job. When they were adults, the older children remembered Grandma as mean and impatient, and Mary's older sister recalled feeling sorry for Mary because she was left in her crib to cry for much of the day. When Mary was older, she remembered feeling like a nuisance to people. "I don't trust *anybody*!" she said, during a session when she had explained that she avoided relying on her husband. As a result, her marriage suffered.

If the ability to trust is solidly formed during our early years, it will help us enjoy a strong marriage later on. Now let's consider another important aspect of maintaining healthy relationships that we learn growing up.

DID YOU LEARN RESPECT?

Ideally in the preschool years (one to six years old), the bonding that began at birth continued, but with an important addition. Hopefully, Mom and Dad were also teaching manners. Whereas you could only scream at first, you later learned words and gestures to help your mom and dad know what you wanted. Eventually you were taught to add "please" and "thank you" to your requests, and with any luck, you didn't forget this when you were a teenager. And now how are your manners in your marriage?

Did your parents teach you to take turns and to acknowledge the needs of others? How many times did they have to repeat that lesson before it sank in? Over and over, right? Again and again you were instructed to respectfully share your feelings and needs as well as to recognize the feelings and needs of others. And as you learned to wait your turn, you also learned to be patient. Of course, when it comes to respect and taking turns, the learning is more caught than taught. Parents who try to teach this behavior without modeling it in their marriage don't get far in imparting the value to their children.

And that may be why so many people these days struggle with respect and taking turns in their marriages. For example, Ted never remembers having to do anything that wasn't exactly what he wanted to do when he was a child. His dad was never home, and his mom lost control of him when he was two. He often mouthed off to his mom in condescending ways, and now he's struggling in his marriage as a result. He has incredible difficulty accommodating his wife's desires when they're different from his own. He speaks down to her in exactly the same way he spoke to his mother as he was growing up.

DID YOUR PARENTS UNDERSTAND YOUR BEHAVIOR?

Children under five show their feelings through their behavior because most of these little people don't yet have the words to express their feelings. So wise parents ask, "What is my child saying through this behavior that he can't express in words?" The tendency, however, is to react to irritating behavior rather than try to understand. But children must learn words for their feelings, and that takes time. At first, all children can do to communicate is act fussy or irritable. As Mom or Dad offer understanding and teach their children words for their feelings, the children develop an understanding of the feelings underlying their behavior. The absence of such understanding during childhood can surface later in marriage. Some adults still act out their feelings, because they never learned to put words to what's inside.

In one such example, I discovered that Carla's parents were rigid and controlling. To them, good manners meant Carla was to be compliant and quiet, never questioning their requests. To this day they proudly describe how they took her feisty temperament and taught her "first-time obedience." They never considered their daughter's feelings important. Today it's no surprise that Carla struggles in her marriage to assert her needs and that her husband is frustrated because she won't make choices or decisions. "She's there," he says, "but nobody's home."

WERE YOUR FEELINGS ALLOWED?

Some seemingly minor emotions in an adult feel huge to a child, so an important part of loving a child is trying to remember what it was like to be small and that new feelings are intense and overwhelming. The way a parent handles a child's fear, shame, anger, sadness, and jealousy is critical.

Parents must help children learn to label what they're feeling and to manage the emotion in increasingly sophisticated ways. Many parents erroneously believe the goal is to eliminate uncomfortable feelings ("Don't be sad/mad") rather than to teach the child to handle them. As children learn to feel and then deal with their emotions, they are learning one of life's—and marriage's—most important skills: to process emotion and manage stressful situations.

Does marriage make you feel things you never felt before? If you're having trouble managing your emotions in marriage, you may have missed a few lessons about how to feel and deal as a child.

DID YOUR PARENTS TEACH YOU TO FEEL AND DEAL?

Emotions are like ice cream. They come in a wide variety. If your parents helped you develop a secure connection early on, they undoubtedly honored and respected your feelings. As you were growing up, were you taught to successfully manage an assortment of emotions? How well do you and your mate feel and deal in your marriage relationship? Do you manage your emotions—or do they manage you? To be emotionally healthy, you have to be able to accept and respond to emotion. But you can't pass this skill on to your own children if you yourself don't know how to do it. Feeling and dealing is a critical lesson parents teach children. The relatively few adults who were taught this lesson have a greater understanding of their emotions and can pass that on to their children.

Imagine a mom telling a typical six-year-old—after offering a ten-minute warning—"Susie, it's time for your friends to go home." Susie first ignores her mom, and when Mom begins to show her friends to the door, Susie throws a tantrum. After the friends leave, the lesson begins.

Now Mom could say, "How dare you throw a fit in front of your friends! No playmates for the rest of the week!" Or Mom could say, "You should be grateful that I allow your friends over to play, but instead you act like a brat. Don't you *ever* do that again." But instead this wise and healthy mom says, "I see you're angry and sad because playtime is over and you wanted to play more. It's okay to feel mad when playtime ends, but you need to learn to control your emotions and express them in good ways. I know you really like your friends, and you're not happy that they have to leave. But a tantrum is not the right way to handle your frustration. You need to sit here quietly until you're ready to talk about it."

Reactive statements (like the first two Mom options above) would demand that Susie get rid of her feelings. By demonstrating understanding (option three), Susie will know Mom cares about her feelings when Mom sets limits. When Mom accepts and respects Susie's feelings beneath the tantrum, Mom lets her know that her emotions are both understandable and controllable.

Throughout this book we will see why the ability to appropriately express a full spectrum of emotions is so important. The fact is that, when Susie marries, she will have a huge advantage over those people who didn't learn to feel and deal when they were growing up. Susie will know how to manage rather than avoid painful emotions. Children raised in homes like Susie's learn through their experiences to have good listening skills and to draw out the opinions and feelings of others. As adults, they are open, vulnerable, and comfortable with disclosure. They have interpersonal skills and are able to negotiate mutually satisfying solutions to problems.

Were You Allowed to Be the Kid?

Were your parents able to manage their own internal stress so that your needs could remain the focus most of the time, or did you have to become the parent to one of your parents? Many times children wind up taking responsibility for a parent's feelings.

Linda, for example, didn't realize until she got married just how much she took the role of the parent. When she was young and her mom was stressed, she would complain to Linda, her oldest child, "The kids are giving me a headache. I'm going to bed." Feeling scared, lonely, and uncertain as to when Mom might reappear, Linda tried to help. Even though she was a child herself, it was up to Linda to take care of her siblings. When Linda got married, she was overly responsible and had difficulty playing and enjoying free time with her spouse. Every job had to be done before she could leave the house.

Tony, an eight-year-old boy I worked with, had parents who fought. When Tony sensed a fight brewing, he coaxed his dad to watch television with him to forestall the argument between his parents. When they were growing up, neither Linda nor Tony learned to manage their feelings. Instead they learned to manage and subdue the reactivity of their parents. When parents notice, understand, and manage their own emotions, children are free to be children.

Often our clients are far better at describing or guessing the feelings of those around them than they are at identifying their own feelings. Frequently the reason is that they grew up caring for their parents. Kids who are caretaking their parents don't have anyone to ask about their feelings. Consequently these kids don't realize their feelings are important.

When parents are stressed, children need to understand it isn't their fault so they won't be unnecessarily burdened. But of course children can do this only if their parents know how to feel and deal with their emotions and verbalize them. Were your parents able to feel and deal with their own emotions? Could they take care of their own emotional needs, or was that your job? Think back and ask yourself if you were free to be the kid in your house growing up or if you had to grow up too fast. What about your spouse?

Did You Learn How to Fill Your Tank?

Good parenting takes a lot of time and energy. That's why good parents schedule time for self-care. One way to find renewed energy to parent our children is by fostering friendships that meet our physical, spiritual, and emotional needs.

Cynthia was a client who was always on the edge of losing it with her two children. She was always busy, and she kept her kids in constant activities. When I (Milan) asked Cynthia what she did for herself to recharge, she was bewildered. "Who has time for that?" she replied.

"Do you have time put gas in your car?"

"Well, you have to do that, or it wouldn't run." She paused for a moment and laughed. "I get your point."

As it turned out, Cynthia desperately missed quiet time to read. She decided to take the hour her children were in preschool to go to the coffee shop and read. She knew if she stayed home, she would end up finding work to do. When I saw her again several weeks later, she was delighted. "I have so much energy on those days to give to my kids. It does renew me."

What did your parents do to manage their stress levels? What are you doing to manage stress in your marriage?

Did You Learn Independence and Dependence?

Part of being secure is being comfortable with both connection and separateness. Babies make their first venture toward independence when they learn to crawl. For the first time, they can move away from Mommy by their own choice, but they'll still want her within sight for many months (and mommies are usually obliging). As children grow, they learn to separate further with statements like "No, mine!" or "I'll do it myself!" Parents need to be comfortable with their children's ventures toward independence, or problems will ensue. When parents force dependence on their sons and daughters, they inhibit their children's growth toward autonomy and maturity.

Parents need to both encourage exploration and allow children to assert their need for comfort. Adults who are being fed emotionally in their own relationships have the easiest time allowing this sort of back-and-forth movement. The alternating cycles of separation and connection begin early and continue toward adulthood. If Mom and Dad are modeling healthy connection and separation in their marriage, children often experience a good balance of dependence and independence. An overemphasis on either connection or independence can cause a harmful imprint. More on this later.

Did You Learn to Take Turns?

Secure connectors have learned how to both give and receive. Sound simple? Yet we often observe an imbalance as people tend to favor one or the other. Good givers are aware of the feelings and needs of others, and they confidently extend themselves as listeners and comforters. Good receivers are aware of and communicative about their emotions, and they possess the vulnerability to admit their need to others.

In Christian circles, giving is often viewed as the more spiritual role. Pastor Tom may be considered the king of givers—kind, encouraging, attuned to every need. But he's so fatigued. When asked to identify people he receives from, he comes up empty. "I receive a lot of joy in helping others," he says.

Tom frequently feels overwhelmed and lonely. He's ashamed to share his struggles, not wanting to acknowledge any negative emotions. But over time he'll need to learn to accept his feelings as indicators of his natural needs. If he can begin to acknowledge and release these suppressed emotions and find comfort, he may recover his vitality. You will recognize Tom's love style in the chapters ahead. To become a secure connector, Tom will need to learn to receive.

CAN YOU ACCEPT GOOD AND BAD?

The ability to accept good and bad is intrinsic to having a sense of security. And the fact is that, just as everyone has strengths and weaknesses, we all have good days and bad days, successes and failures. People who know this and can allow others this same latitude don't have the difficulties that come with requiring perfection and devaluing themselves as well as others for not measuring up. When disappointments happen, the secure person simply logs the experience as a lesson and presses on with life. Often, people who were raised in perfectionist households obsess over failures and are unable to focus on growing into the future. Conversely, adults with a secure imprint have an awareness of their limitations and can accept disappointment when failure occurs. They focus on their strengths and find the motivation to try again because they were taught that their worth is based on more than performance.

DO YOU KNOW HOW TO WAIT?

A secure imprint allows us to delay gratification. When we wait for what we want, we are accepting that we have needs, but also that we are not the center of the universe. We don't devalue our experiences and needs, but we know there is an appropriate time to express our emotions and desires, and we are able to put others first.

We can take moments for ourselves, but we are also aware of others' needs and are able to give thoughtful consideration to them. Having wants and desires brings a sense of vitality to life, and the secure adult balances wanting with waiting, and receiving with giving.

OTHER HALLMARKS OF A SECURE CONNECTOR

Do You Know How to Say No?

When secure adults find themselves around unhealthy or demanding people, they are able to say no and set limits on those destructive relationships. They don't deliberate over unreasonable requests or when they know that saying yes will overextend them. Even when setting a limit causes others to be annoyed, adults with a secure imprint do not obligate themselves simply to avoid being seen in a negative light.

Can You Take Risks?

Secure connectors enter into adulthood with a healthy sense of adventure and an eagerness to try new things. Being confident of their abilities, they are not frightened or overwhelmed by change, they don't view mistakes as deadly, and they aren't burdened by crippling shame. So secure adults are able to approach new activities or unfamiliar situations with curiosity and interest.

Can You Ask for Help?

Adults with a secure love style are able to ask for help. They understand that their need for assistance is not a sign of weakness. They have a basic sense of trust that relationships will offer support and comfort, and that sense allows them to seek people out when needs arise. While we may think of secure people as self-reliant (and they are!), they also know when to depend on others.

Can You Work Toward Compromise?

Conflict happens, and secure adults do not avoid or ignore problems. Instead, they address problems openly, seeking fairness, and using their learned negotiation skills. They are not willing to continually give in to someone, nor do they need to be in constant control, always demanding their own rights. Secure people see the benefit of compromise and the value of agreeing to disagree. Different points of view are not only tolerated, but respected.

Can You Say You're Sorry?

Truly secure people are not defensive. In fact, the ability to admit mistakes and apologize for errors is an indicator of a person's security. The ownership of their own shortcomings makes it easy for secure people to forgive others when they are wronged. Many individuals who visit our offices have not yet learned the importance of extending heartfelt apologies when they are in the wrong.

BARRIERS TO BONDING

Most of us enter adulthood thinking we had normal childhoods. After reading about ideal love lessons, you may be thinking, *I missed out on some important training when I was growing up.* As my (Milan) good friend Joey O'Connor says, " 'Normal' is just a setting on your dryer." Now that we've seen how optimal parenting helps a child enter adulthood as a secure connector, let's consider what happens when things aren't as normal as we thought. What happens when we have no memories of comfort and when the parenting we received was less than ideal?

Human beings are not that inventive, and the ways we struggle in relationships are surprisingly predictable. *There are five harmful love styles: the avoider,*[2] *pleaser,*[3] *vacillator,*[4] *controller,*[5] *and victim.*[6] They are harmful because they have programmed us to respond and behave in ways that hinder us from bonding and finding the intimacy that God designed us to enjoy. Knowing how these love styles differ is crucial since they are responsible for all of the complicated challenges people face when connecting with one another.

In fact, you can think of your love style as your way of relating that runs counter to intimacy. The love styles that arise from our damaged imprints have the power to ruin any marriage. Yet in recognizing your and your spouse's styles of relating, you will see what you can do to grow toward a more secure style and, ultimately, toward a deeper knowledge of your spouse. And, as we know from years of experience, a more fulfilling romance will be the happy result.

Essentially, all of our barriers to bonding arise from a few common sources in our early experiences. Let's look at the starting point of these harmful imprints and why they keep us stuck in detrimental patterns in our marriages. Then we will move on and discover the distinctive traits of the five love styles, each of which blocks intimacy and makes it difficult to enjoy a close connection with our spouses.

Anxiety

Secure imprints come from good parenting, from families where Mom and Dad bond with their children in ways that produce a core of trust and respect. Stress, trauma, and inadequate parenting cause children to feel anxious about how to get what they need, so an anxious core forms instead of a core of trust. Since none of us had perfect parents and we all live in a stressful world, each one of us has an anxious core to some degree. Positive childhood experiences result in low levels of anxiety that are manageable. Remember, the secure connector learned as a child to feel and deal, so they have the skills to deal with upsetting feelings in a constructive way. Harmful early experiences can result in a lot of anxiety and distressing feelings that make a child miserable. Each of the detrimental love styles are a particular response to inadequate love lessons and the resulting anxiety. As we discuss each imprint and the resulting love style, we will see how each style prefers to manage this core of anxiety in different ways.

The five love styles—avoider, pleaser, vacillator, controller, and victim—all grow out of a childhood reaction to anxiety prompted by a lack of comfort, affection, and emotional connection. Briefly, adults imprinted to avoid learned early on to minimize their feelings, be independent, and meet their own needs. Pleasers learned to be cautious and tried hard to be the good kids in order to avoid criticism and keep things peaceful. Vacillators found early on that connection was sometimes available but unpredictable, and these kids were often left waiting, so by the time attention was offered, they were too angry to receive it. Controllers and victims learned to cover their fears by either fighting back or detaching and complying. Each style is characterized by a particular way of coping with pain, which unfortunately abounds in too many family situations.

But the good news in all of this is that with a diagnosis of your love style, you will find a specific remedy. Remember, though, that only you can change you! We can help you recognize your unhealthy pattern and point out a road map for growth. But only as you engage with the growth goals in these pages and in the workbook will you begin to move toward a healthier, more mature destination and bring relief to your relationship.

Family Situations

Life is complex and difficult, and the many challenges we face can make us feel out of control. When families encounter many stresses and problems—loss of a job, divorce, illness, death, handicaps, disabilities—these circumstances can interrupt the parents' ability to help children develop secure imprints. Your family may have encountered one or more of these difficulties when you were young. (Chapter 3 of the corresponding workbook will help you discover the impact of your family's negative experiences.) Events in your family certainly contributed to your relational love style, and discovering just what that contribution produced is essential.

The Blame Game

In addition to family issues that can contribute to unhealthy relational patterns, each of us has a natural selfish tendency to blame others for our problems. To experience healthy, growing, reciprocal relationships, we first need to realize how pointing our fingers at our spouses sabotages our progress and runs counter to emotional health. If you recall, Jesus talked about looking inward not outward when it comes to our problems. In His famous Sermon on the Mount, He said, "First take the log out of your own eye, and then you will see clearly to take the speck out of your brother's eye" (Matthew 7:5). We must conquer that inherent desire to blame others and seek strength from our faith to do so.

Ignorance

Perhaps the greatest reason most of us miss out on closer connections is the painfully simple fact that we don't see our contributions to our marriage problems. Most of us are experts at ignoring, distancing, and distracting ourselves from the need to change when personal growth means facing the pain of our shortcomings and moving toward the uncomfortable terrain of change. Seeking out qualified help in the form of counselors, trusted friends, and truthful advisors is often a key to initiating growth. Even beyond that, finding an honest, objective point of view is important for all of us.

Married couples who just seem to know how to love each other did not magically happen. They came from families that taught them from the beginning specific dance steps for relating intimately and harmoniously. Either intuitively or consciously, these happy couples' parents knew the comfort circle and, by example, coached their children in the art of loving well.

Adults who have a secure foundation enter marriage with skills and experiences to draw from when they face relational challenges. Of course, these individuals aren't *perfect;* they're just *prepared.* Early and ongoing dance lessons like the ones they received make it worlds easier for them to move in unison with their mates. Yet, as we've seen, most of us were not so fortunate to have learned the dance steps of a secure relationship.

So now let's take a look at the five loves styles—or clumsy dance steps—that get us in trouble.

Part

2

⋈⋈⋈

Styles That Impair How We Love

Chapter 5

The Avoider Love Style

(Kay) first met Jack when his wife, Carol, said she'd leave him if he didn't come to marriage therapy. Jack agreed, mostly for the sake of their three young daughters, but he was not thrilled to be sitting in my office. I knew I would need to do some convincing. Carol's initial complaint was "Jack only wants me for sex, and he wants that plenty. He needs me to cook, clean, and take care of the girls, but that's about it."

So I turned to Jack and asked what he would like to change about his marriage. "Well, more sex would be nice," he said. "Overall, I'm pretty happy with the way things are. But for Carol, nothing I do for her is enough. I try, but she's never satisfied. That's why we're here."

I briefly explained the concept of imprints and my need to understand their childhood experiences. "I don't remember much," Jack said. "My mom and dad worked a lot and fought a lot. That's about it."

"You mentioned a divorce. Tell me about that."

"Well, I hated hearing my parents fighting. I used to go to my room, turn my music on loud, and wait it out." He grinned. "But I never thought it would be my mom who left. I guess I wasn't prepared for that." He kept smiling. "Life goes on. You get over it."

Jack's scant memories, his minimizing of feelings and details, and his smiling while he told about painful childhood events were all classic characteristics of an avoider imprint. I gently pressed for more specifics. "Tell me what you remember about the day she left."

Jack reflected a moment. "I guess it was a bad day." Silence.

"Tell me more."

"Like what?"

My guess was that Jack had never been asked to put details about his feelings to this story. It had lived silently inside him, and he was completely unaware that it was still influencing his life. "Tell me how old you were and how you realized she was really leaving," I coaxed.

Jack was quiet for several minutes. "How old are you in fifth grade? Ten, I guess. I remember coming home from school, and my aunt Laurel and my dad were there. My aunt told my brother and me that my mom had gone on a vacation—by herself—and would be back in a few weeks. I didn't think much of it. I thought it was kind of weird she didn't say good-bye, but my mom didn't talk all that much. She was sort of quiet and off in her own world. About a month later, she came home with a truck and started moving stuff out. Wow, I haven't thought about this in years," Jack said, his voice constricting. His body was tight, and his chest barely moved as he pushed the uncomfortable feelings down.

If I left it up to him, I knew Jack would be done with his story. "I know these questions are painful, Jack. In just a few minutes, I want to hear about Carol's memories. But what did you feel when your mom drove away?"

"Bad," he whispered.

I handed Jack a list of soul words. "I can't imagine how bad you felt, Jack. That was a horrible event, and you were only ten years old. Choose some words off this list so I can understand more about what you felt."

Jack reviewed the list. "Sad, scared, stunned, lonely. She never came back."

Carol's eyes glistened with tears. "Look at Carol's face," I said. Jack turned his eyes to Carol, and she reached out for his hand. Clearly surprised by her tears, Jack rubbed his eyes with his free hand, the uncomfortable surge of emotion forcing its way out.

"Let me make a guess," I offered. "I bet no one ever once asked you about your feelings that day or any time after she left."

"We never talked about it."

"Would it be accurate to say you survived or got over it by not thinking about it, not talking about it, and trying not to feel it?"

Jack nodded. "I got really into sports, and that became my life. I played almost every sport I could." Carol confirmed that he still did that. She could always tell when he was upset because he would spend more time at work or start projects around the house.

What was missing in their marriage was an emotional connection, and Jack couldn't understand what Carol wanted because he had never had that growing up. In his pain, no one had comforted or inquired about his feelings. Now, as an adult, he found it difficult to share details of his history, but the more he shared, the more the feelings began to push out. Although uncomfortable, Jack needed to learn not to minimize his feelings. He needed to remember how to need and learn how to accept comfort. Because sex was the only connection Jack deemed acceptable, he desired sex frequently, but Carol was not experiencing any kind of emotional connection with her husband. Over time Jack realized he needed someone to care about his feelings and experiences as well. As they connected on an emotional level, sex was more enjoyable for Carol. People who are not used to anyone responding to their feelings with compassion often don't even realize how this lack has influenced them.

For avoiders, learning to identify and deal with their feelings is like learning to play a new sport. It's awkward and challenging at first, but the more they do it, the more comfortable it gets. Because our feelings tell us what we need, it's imperative that we recognize and share those feelings. Although self-sufficiency is admirable, when it hides pain, it chokes the life out of relationships.

When people are imprinted to be hyperindependent, they have what we call an avoider love style. What do they avoid? Vulnerability, emotions, neediness, honest reflection that brings self-awareness—you name it. When avoiders were children, their parents were unable to tune in to their feelings, and as a result, their emotional life is underdeveloped. Receiving limited physical affection and emotional connection from their parents, they rid themselves of the anxiety of wanting but not having by restricting their feelings and limiting their need for others. It's no wonder that their answer to life is self-sufficiency. Also, if asked about their childhood experiences, these avoiders may say, "It was fine" or "My parents taught me a lot." When pressed for details, they have few specific memories.

When other people want emotional connection or affection, these avoider or autonomous adults may try to comply, but they ask nothing in return. And if their response is devoid of emotion, their actions don't seem to come from the heart. When mates become angry because they won't connect emotionally, they evade and minimize the conflict. Over the years, resentment builds in them since it seems that others always want something from them. They wonder, *Why can't others be more independent like I am?*

Unfortunately, this avoider love style is very common, and several kinds of home environments can cause this imprint.

THE HOME ENVIRONMENT

After some patient prodding of several avoiders, you might find some common characteristics of families who raise children to be hyperindependent like this. Though different children from the same family can come into adulthood with different imprints, avoiders are the ones who respond to lack of comfort and nurturing by disconnecting. Parents of avoiders often find a child's needs and emotions overwhelming and irritating, so they unwittingly teach their children not to "cause a scene," to ignore their feelings, and to downplay their needs. Faced with emotionally unavailable parents, children learn that independence pleases parents and begin looking for ways to prove how well they can take care of themselves just as their parents did.[1]

In such homes, the focus is on the physical tasks of life. Politeness and performance are highly valued. "Children should be seen and not heard" is the common if unspoken household rule. Recognition is given for achievements, and a strong work ethic stands in for deeper connection. Tragically, having fun and enjoying the wonder of childhood are foreign and threatening concepts to these parents. The child may enjoy being physically cared for, but very little bonding occurs. The predominant message is "You're fine! Grow up!"

WHAT'S IT LIKE TO BE THE KID?

Jack described his mother as quiet and locked in her own world. He had no memories of sitting on her lap or being offered affection. While his father was supportive of Jack's sports, he never noticed Jack's feelings. And the only touch Jack could recall was an occasional slap on the back after a good game.

Children raised like this type rarely, if ever, receive comfort when they are upset, especially as they get older. Babies may be indulged, but by the toddler and preschool years, the child's distress is likely to be met with resistance. As the child grows, he learns not to approach the parent for comfort or reassurance, instead isolating himself when emotions surface and trying unconsciously to master his feelings. Emotions become annoyances to get rid of rather than opportunities to develop closeness and experience comfort.

Children with an avoider imprint are shut down to their emotions and needs, often feeling a vague sense of emptiness. Powerless to make others respond to their confusing emotions, they frequently feel overwhelmed by wanting affection and not receiving any. These children learn early on to hide their needs under a convincing surface of independence, asking little from others and keeping their disappointment submerged. If they can capture a parent's attention by becoming proficient in a sport, activity, school, whatever, that's what they'll do.

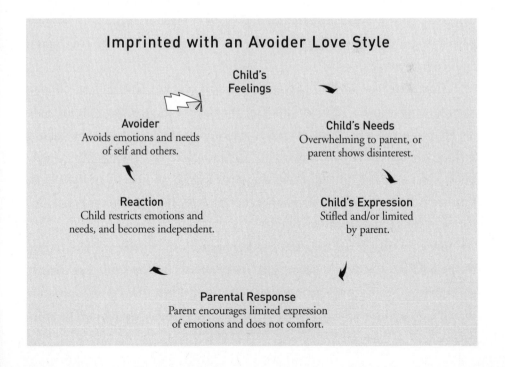

Imprinted with an Avoider Love Style

Child's Feelings

Avoider
Avoids emotions and needs
of self and others.

Child's Needs
Overwhelming to parent, or
parent shows disinterest.

Reaction
Child restricts emotions and
needs, and becomes independent.

Child's Expression
Stifled and/or limited
by parent.

Parental Response
Parent encourages limited expression
of emotions and does not comfort.

When adult avoiders ask their parents about their infancy and preschool years, they will often be described as good babies who were happy playing alone or entertaining themselves.[2] This observation helps explain why, in marriage, avoiders still seem so happy "playing alone." Before they marry, though, adolescent avoiders who are accustomed to a restricted range of emotions may become depressed and angry when stress levels increase, and they don't know how to reach out for help. They close off emotions and needs and try to stay busy, self-medicating with experiences—sex, drugs, and anything with a high danger quotient—that bring them temporary relief from the detachment. Pornography and masturbation can become obsessive for some teen boys, while girls will often go from boyfriend to boyfriend, their home life devoid of the relational pleasure, affection, and comfort they've told themselves they don't need.

WHAT ELSE MIGHT CAUSE AN AVOIDER LOVE STYLE?

Cynthia had a secure attachment with her mother. But when Cynthia was eight years old, her mother died in a car accident. Her father, overwhelmed and depressed, grew increasingly detached and rarely engaged with her after his long days at work. Her older siblings were left to baby-sit Cynthia, and they frequently ignored her completely.

Cynthia had no memory of being comforted or asked how she felt. No one even noticed when she began to withdraw. She came to therapy when she was feeling the need to get away from her own young children, only aware that they'd been making her increasingly uncomfortable. Cynthia had shut down her own emotions, and so she had difficulty tolerating their feelings and needs. Because Cynthia had to take care of herself after her mother died, she didn't know how to let her own children be dependent.

Any event that forces premature independence can imprint children to disengage and deaden their feelings. Still, trauma must be managed, and though children may not make a conscious vow to not need others, their survival requires that they go underground with their feelings when no nurturing support presents itself.

COMMON CHARACTERISTICS OF AVOIDERS

"I'm Just Not a Big 'Feeler'"

Individuals imprinted to avoid will experience a limited range of emotions. Most can no longer feel a desire for emotional connection and have no memory of longing to be close. This leaves them fairly even-tempered, although anger may surface when others push for connection. More introverted types passively withdraw, busying themselves with tasks in order to avoid relational demands. Chronic, low-grade depression is common but rarely addressed since it's such a familiar feeling. During a recent seminar, an avoider asked, "What if you just don't have feelings? Can't that just be your personality?" Imagine a baby who displayed no feelings. All children are born with the capacity to feel. The environment and unspoken rules about what is acceptable determine what happens to those feelings. Finally, hugs from avoiders may feel rigid and mechanical since their touch can be devoid of emotion. Prolonged eye contact is often avoided because it feels too intimate and uncomfortable.

"What's So Great About Comfort?"

People with avoider injuries never request comfort. The words just are not in their vocabulary. They isolate if they are upset, and since they have mastered the art of not feeling, it usually takes a great deal of stress before they experience much discomfort. Avoiders have learned to comfort themselves in nonrelational ways, through exercise, food, shopping, work, sports, gambling, alcohol, or drugs, to name a few. When someone they know is emotionally upset, avoiders expect that person to take care of the problem on his own because this is what they do.[3]

Besides, receiving comfort requires vulnerability, which is very difficult for people with an avoider imprint. Letting oneself be vulnerable is an important growth goal for them.

"I Don't Want to Talk About It"

Those of you in relationship with individuals who have an avoider love style have heard this phrase more times than you can count. Talking about anything, but especially emotionally charged topics, is a miserable experience for avoiders. After all, for the first eighteen years of their lives, there were few (if any) inquiries about their internal experiences and therefore no opportunities for self-disclosure. This struggle to open up is even a bigger problem for introverts, who because of their temperament already process their thoughts internally. Remember, avoiders have never learned soul words. When they are pressed to share, their momentary feelings of inadequacy are often subdued with a burst of irritation or anger.

When asked, "What are you feeling?" avoiders will look at you as though you are speaking another language. Disconnected from their emotions, they have little to no experience linking feelings to daily events. Those rare displays of emotion leave the avoider feeling weak and pathetic. The needs of others are overwhelming, and avoiders have a tendency to try to quickly stop any demonstrations of emotions.

Learning to feel and then talk about emotions was a big area of growth for Jack and Carol. As Jack began to open up to his blocked emotions, he felt a great deal of shame and embarrassment. Carol was good at reassuring him that she treasured his moments of vulnerability. In one session when Jack was tearful, Carol gently told him, "I feel like you are really letting me love you in the hurt places. Thank you for letting me inside your heart, Jack." He visibly relaxed when she spoke these words to him.

"Just Give Me Space"

Hyperindependents want to be in charge in order to keep others at a safe distance and to maintain control over their emotions. If pushed to be vulnerable, they are likely to respond with frustration and effectively push others away. Anger is the feeling most accessible to avoiders since it's not vulnerable, but rather powerful and tends to repel others. Since they spent much of their childhood being independent, they may find marriage constraining and entrapping without realizing why.

"I Am a Rock; I Am an Island"

Remember the line from that Paul Simon song "I Am a Rock"? "A rock feels no pain and an island never cries." This is the avoider's theme song. Having little to no experience of emotional connection, they don't even know they need it. And, since relationships have never brought them relief or comfort, it doesn't occur to them to ask for help. They'll figure things out on their own. When avoiders are asked what they need, a list of tasks is often the answer: "I need you to cook, play with the kids, and do the laundry." They don't say, "I need you not to need me," but that's what being with them feels like. Spouses of avoiders say they sometimes feel like they're purposefully being ignored. So, like Carol, spouses of avoiders need to realize their mate is not deliberately excluding them. They're simply acting out of their imprint. Once this is understood, the avoider reaction of withdrawing makes much more sense.

"I'll Take Care of It"

Avoiders have learned to make decisions on their own. As a result, it does not occur to them to include others in the decision-making process. They assess a situation, come to a conclusion, and resolve the problem without ever feeling the need to consult anyone. Those imprinted to be avoiders are doing what they were trained to do...take care of things independently. This conduct can leave the people around them feeling alienated and powerless. One wife lamented, "I don't ever feel like I have a partner in my marriage. We don't share ideas or make decisions together."

"I Get the Job Done"

For the autonomous adult, competence brings approval and neediness brings rejection. People with avoider imprints seek approval for the tasks they perform. Often quite accomplished at many things, they give by doing. A long to-do list keeps them feeling happy and competent while helping them avoid the emotional needs they find difficult to understand. Driven Type A personalities often have hyperindependent imprints and are at risk for becoming workaholics.

"At Least I Have the Dog"

Childhood pets may have met the avoider's need for touch and affection. And, as adults, they may lavish attention on an animal but have difficulty enjoying similar touch and affection with their spouse.

"At Least I Have This One Good Feeling"

As therapy progressed with Jack and Carol (whom we met earlier in this chapter), Jack revealed that he had been drawn to pornography as a young teen. This is common for boys raised in homes characterized by little physical affection and limited demonstrations of emotion. While avoider females may find sex uninspiring since they find it difficult to engage in a vulnerable way, men like Jack commonly describe teenage episodes with pornography and masturbation as the one good feeling in their lives.[4] As a teen, Jack had a big appetite for sexual release that compensated for the lack of relational pleasure at home. When he got married, Carol had difficulty keeping up, and she felt Jack wasn't present during their lovemaking.

As Jack and Carol strengthened their emotional bond, their sexual relationship became more satisfying. Carol found a deeper emotional connection, and Jack learned to make eye contact and talk to Carol when they made love. As Jack learned to receive from Carol in nonsexual ways, he found emotional relief in ways he never had previously, and that greatly reduced the tension between them. Jack's sex drive was still stronger than Carol's, but Jack continued to expand the ways he connected with Carol by learning to accept comfort from her.

"I Don't Cry"

Discarding emotions is a way of life for avoiders, but grief is at the bottom of the wastebasket. Since crying brought such misery, shame, and rejection during their early years, sad feelings are now practically inaccessible. I worked with a couple in therapy whose ten-year-old daughter was very ill with cancer. Her dad, Bill, had been imprinted to detach from emotions and neediness. As Brooke deteriorated, Bill was always stoic and reserved, with an edge of anger.[5] As his wife, Marie, sat on my couch crying and describing the latest treatments, Bill sat rigid and uncomfortable at the far end of the couch. I said to him, "I know it's very hard for you to put words to all this, Bill, but I would really like to know what this is like for you on the inside." He averted his eyes and was quiet. I tolerated the silence and hushed his wife as she started to answer for him. Several minutes passed.

"Bill, do you remember telling me about the time your dog died when you were eight years old? That dog was closer to you than any family member. You were heartbroken when she died. You told me how your dad and brothers made fun of your tears and teased you for weeks. That may be the last time you ever cried. No one was tender with your feelings of sadness. Now your daughter is suffering, and you cannot allow yourself to be sad."

Bill's jaw tightened in an effort to hold back his feelings. I got out of my chair, moved to face his averted eyes, and knelt before him. "What you are going through is awful, Bill. I know it's tearing you apart inside to watch your little girl suffer."

A huge sob racked his body. Bill gasped, closed his eyes, and tried to push the emotions away. "I'm sorry," he said. "I hate feeling weak."

I reassured him. "It's not weak to cry. God gave us tears to release the sadness. It's safe here. No one will make fun of you."

Tragically, Bill's daughter died six months after our session. He was devastated, but our work together allowed him much more freedom to grieve.

"Only Weak People Feel Scared or Sad"

Many times in our seminars the question arises, "Aren't men socialized not to cry or be afraid?" Sadly, yes. In many cultures, including ours, showing any emotion except anger is frequently viewed as unmanly. Ironically, although the goal of many Christian families in America is to become more like Jesus, the tendency is to suppress the natural expression of emotion. Jesus cried over Lazarus, shed tears over Jerusalem, and wailed in the Garden of Gethsemane. He also asked for companionship during this time of intense anguish. Despite His example, we tell our sons—directly and indirectly—that they shouldn't have or show emotions and don't need anyone when they are suffering.

No wonder the avoider love style is more common among men than women, but we have worked with many avoider women as well. During my first session with Jenny, she struggled to explain why she was seeking therapy. "Something isn't right. I have a great husband and two normal kids. I should be happy. But I feel like I'm on the outside looking in. Sort of going through the motions." Jenny shifted in her seat. "That sounds stupid. I don't even know why I came." She looked as if she wanted to get up and leave but was too polite to walk out.

"Actually, Jenny, what you're saying makes a lot of sense. Let me ask you a question that will seem a bit off subject. How easily do you cry? Do tears come freely, or do you seldom cry?"

Jenny looked relieved. "Well, let me think. I cried when each of our kids was born."

"Sort of happy tears, right? What about sad tears?"

Jenny searched a moment. "One time. When Heather was two, she had to be hospitalized. We found out she had spinal meningitis. I cried then."

"Who was with you?"

"My husband, Nathan. When the doctor told us, he hit the wall. I mean literally hit the wall. He startled me. He is never like that. As soon as the doctor left, I ran into the ladies room and cried."

"Quiet tears or loud tears?" I asked.

Jenny thought hard. "Quiet. There were two ladies in there, and I didn't want them to hear me."

"In the days that followed, did you cry again? And if so, did anyone ever comfort you?"

Jenny practically shouted. "Definitely not! I was mad after that. My mom came to the hospital, and as usual it became all about her. She was wringing her hands and walking around saying, 'Not my baby, Heather. Please don't let her die.' She made a big scene, insisting on seeing Heather and then throwing a fit when they told her no. I had to take her down to the cafeteria for a time-out. Nathan and I actually give her time-outs." Jenny laughed. "Mom doesn't really know it, of course."

"How about your girls? They are still preschool age. What do you do when they cry?"

"Oh, they are getting better about that. I tell them to go to their rooms and come out when they can find their smiles. It's easier for Heather than Lilly even though she's younger. Lilly is a little drama queen. She overreacts to everything."

"Okay," I said. "One last question. What are Nathan's biggest complaints about you?"

"Oh, that's easy. Too much anger and not enough affection." Jenny laughed. "I call him my puppy dog. But sometimes he feels more like a tick sucking me dry. But he's such a nice guy, I feel bad saying that."

"I'm going to make some guesses about what might be going on with you. It sounds like you have shut down your sad feelings. Maybe tears seem like a waste of time because you don't associate sadness with the need for comfort and relief. Anger causes a lot of tension in our bodies, and usually there is hurt of some kind underneath. If we don't allow ourselves to feel the hurt or cry, there is no release for that tension. You said you feel like you're on the outside looking in. People who have shut off their emotions describe that exact feeling. When life gets over-whelming, you isolate. Did you do that when you were a little girl?"

Jenny pondered the question. "I really don't remember crying much as a kid. I don't know."

"Well," I continued, "it seems there would not have been much room for your feelings when you were growing up. You had to focus on your mom's feelings, as you did in the hospital. Your mom could not offer you comfort when you were upset. Instead, you had to take her for a time-out and ignore your own feelings. Perhaps you learned to think of your mom's feelings as something negative and bothersome, like a burden you must manage on your own. I want you to think this week, Jenny, about how much of your childhood was spent managing your mother's emotions. Some specific memories might come to mind. Jot them down and share them next week."

When we believe emotions are something to get rid of—like the outbursts of an overreactive parent—we tend to discard our feelings. So it was no surprise when Jenny thought of her own child's feelings as negative, calling her a drama queen. Also, Nathan's complaints were classic responses to an avoider spouse. Most couples find that once the emotions under their spouse's anger can be acknowl-edged and explored, the avoider becomes far less angry.

GROWTH GOALS

If you relate to the avoider imprint, you might be thinking, *Darn it! I was sure my spouse was the problem!* Well, quit blaming your spouse, admit you're part of the problem, and take responsibility for your own contribution. And if you are married to an avoider, don't take his or her stoicism personally. "I'm fine" is a favorite phrase of avoiders, but when you avoiders think about it, you know you're not. You may have survived childhood by detaching from your feelings and needs, but now you've escaped and you have a challenge ahead. You're going to have to surrender to the process of change and be willing to recognize your injury instead of insisting that your childhood was just "normal kid stuff." The additional growth goals in the workbook will help you build intimacy in your marriage and help your spouse learn how to respond in healthy ways to your avoider tendencies and thereby encourage a more secure love style.

And it's time to get going! Now is the perfect time to discover some ways you can grow.

Chapter 6

The Pleaser Love Style

I f there were one word to describe Marshall, it would be *likable.* He won others with his contagious smile and witty sense of humor. His wife, Abby, remarked, "I'm probably the only one in the world who has a complaint. The kids adore him, and everyone at church and work love him. He's the nicest guy ever, but that's the problem. He's too nice. People at work take advantage of him, and I'm always the bad guy when it comes to disciplining the kids."

Marshall's eyes twinkled. "Men are like government bonds. They take sooo long to mature." I (Kay) laughed, and Abby rolled her eyes.

Marshall was serious and reserved when he and Abby came in for their third session. I commented on the change in his demeanor. He looked embarrassed and said to Abby, "You tell her."

Abby took Marshall's hand. "Well, I'm kind of in shock," she said. "Marshall made an appointment at the doctor's because he was having chest pains. He didn't tell me about it until today. They ran a bunch of tests, and his heart is fine. Dr. Donaldson says he's having panic attacks. He told me just before the session because the doctor wants him to discuss it with you. I don't even really know what panic attacks are," Abby explained.

"Tell me what you experience, Marshall," I inquired.

"Well, I remember these same feelings when I went away to college. My mom and dad had just divorced, and I was really worried about my mom. It was hard to leave for school. My sisters were all older and married by then, and they didn't realize how depressed and lonely Mom was."

Abby's eyes were big and round. "I never knew that," she said. "I was dating you then. You never told me about panic attacks."

"I didn't know that's what was happening. I just remember all of a sudden I would feel sweaty and like it was hard to breathe. My chest would get tight, my heart would pound, and I'd feel like I was going to lose control." Marshall shifted uncomfortably on the couch and looked out the window.

I filled the silence. "That must have been very scary. What do you think would have happened if you had lost control, Marshall?"

"Oh, I don't know. I always tried to get away from people so no one would see. It just went away after a while. I thought it was stress or something. It didn't happen again until Tim was born. I was driving home alone after I left Abby and Tim at the hospital, and it happened again."

Abby was shaking her head in disbelief. "You never told me that either." She looked as if she was seeing into some secret place inside Marshall that she never knew existed—and she was.

Marshall replied, "I didn't want to spoil the happiness. Besides, it's embarrassing. These episodes have happened on and off for the last ten years. It's worse lately. That's why I went to the doctor, and he tells me it's all in my head. Great!"

"It might be more accurate to say it's all in your body, Marshall. It's as if your body is talking for you since you don't share your feelings with anyone. A lot goes on inside you that Abby doesn't even know about. I think you try to ignore it too, and finally your body does the talking. If that tight chest and those sweaty hands could talk, what would they say?" I inquired.

Marshall changed the subject, as if I didn't really expect him to answer the question. "I made some progress this week in being the bad guy with the kids," he offered with a smile. I redirected him.

"Let's go back to the feelings in your body. I really want you to give a voice to that pounding heart and tight chest."

Marshall's smile faded. "I don't know. I guess my chest would say that I'm uptight. That it's too much. Everyone expects too much."

Marshall was struggling to get one more thought out. He started and stopped several times. "Take your time and find the words," I encouraged.

"Well, maybe it got worse again lately because Abby wanted to come to counseling." He turned to Abby. "I've been worrying that maybe you want a divorce and that we are coming here so you can tell me with a counselor present." Marshall looked miserable and rubbed his head as if he were trying to wake up from a bad dream. His chin started to quiver, and tears filled his eyes. "Great. Now I *am* going to lose it," he said.

Abby stroked his cheek, gently wiped his tears, and then wrapped her arms around him. "Oh baby, I never knew. You are really hurting, and I never knew. You always look fine. I want you to tell me every time this happens from now on, okay? Promise?" Marshall nodded in agreement.

Abby and I learned in later sessions that Marshall had taken on the responsibility of soothing his mother's fears and loneliness long before the divorce. Marshall's dad was distant, aloof, and rarely home. So Marshall's mom found her happiness in him, the baby of the family, and kept him close and dependent.

Marshall himself realized in a later session how overprotective his mother had been. "All the kids in the neighborhood hated to see her coming out the front door. She was such a mama bear. She scolded them plenty of times whenever I tattled on somebody. I was always right, and they were always wrong. Then she would say, 'Marshall, you don't have to play with those mean boys. Come inside and watch TV with me.'"

"What you are saying, Marshall, is that your mom fought your battles for you. She never taught you to stand up for yourself in a healthy way. Maybe that is why you find it difficult to stand up to your co-workers, your kids, and even Abby. I'm sure Abby will be thrilled when you improve your confrontation skills with her. She'll be so glad she brought you to therapy," I teased.

THE HOME ENVIRONMENT

So how does one arrive at adulthood with the imprint to perpetually please others? Some children experience a lot of anxiety growing up. It may be due to an overprotective parent who worries a lot and gives the message to the child, "Be careful. The world is scary, but you'll be okay if you are close to me." Angry or highly critical parents can also—and often unknowingly—create this imprint in their children, who then learn to be careful to avoid criticism or ire. A youngster adopts the role of the "good boy" or "good girl" in an attempt to gain approval or recognition and to reduce tension in the parent or the family by pleasing rather than causing problems. Some kids please in response to a parent's anxiety, while others are managing a parent's irritability. These children absorb a lot of tension and try to find relief for their own anxiety by making others happy. Being aware of and responsible for the feelings of others, the pleaser has no opportunity to contemplate or process the anxiety driving his or her own relational style.

In adult relationships, the underlying motivation for being in the helping role and focusing on the needs of others is to reduce one's own anxiety by keeping people close, content, and satisfied.[1] When those around pleasers are happy, they are happy too. If others are upset, pleasers are distressed as well. When others distance themselves, detach, or are angry, the result is space in the relationship. This space causes agitation and drives the pleaser into pursuit mode in an effort to close the gap. Conflict is often avoided, and anger—if felt—is expressed indirectly or not at all. After pleasers spend a number of years of chronic worry and overgiving, resentment often emerges.

Marshall's mom fit many of these characteristics of a parent who creates a pleaser love style in a child. Unhealthy fear and worry can be passed from generation to generation, and in some homes one parent's influence dominates the family. When that parent is driven by worry and fear, his or her anxiety will permeate the atmosphere of the home. Likewise, in overprotective homes, worrying parents often see danger around every corner. To reduce their own anxiety, these parents discourage the child from taking risks and shelter the child from stressful situations. Large amounts of control are exerted to keep the child from "getting hurt" emotionally or physically. The world is seen as a dangerous place, and the unspoken message is, "The world is scary but you will be okay as long as you stay close and let me protect you."[2]

These parents are often overwhelmed due to their excessive worrying. As the child enters the developmental stages of "exploration" (toddlerhood and adolescence), the stress level increases because the parents have difficulty letting go and relinquishing control. Fearful parents need control in order to minimize risk. In many respects, this dynamic becomes more about the parents' attempts to reduce their own anxiety by being in charge, rather than about their teaching the child to conquer his fears.

When the child has squabbles with other children, forgets to turn in homework, or gets in trouble at the neighbors', this parent readily steps in to rescue the child from unpleasant feelings or situations, not realizing the child is missing out on opportunities to learn how to "feel and deal." But parents have a hard time helping a child learn to manage her worries when they have not successfully completed this developmental task themselves.

In a subsequent session with Marshall and Abby, Marshall remembered being afraid at night when his dad was away on business trips. His mom told him there was nothing to be afraid of, yet she anxiously checked every door and window, closed each drape, carefully adjusted each one to cover any view into the house, and then turned on every light.

Common childhood fears about the dark, strangers, or scary dreams are met with, "There is nothing to be afraid of!" This message is at odds with the parent's constant worry, which the child feels on some level. Although children are told, "Don't be afraid," their fears are often indulged as they are taken to the parents' bed, escorted in the dark, picked up from friends' homes in the middle of the night, and not pushed to try new things.

Parents who worry excessively, however, rarely see themselves as fearful, but rather "concerned." Constant worry is the norm for these parents and therefore such a familiar experience that it is rarely recognized, much less addressed, as a problem. But this "concern" may promote a pattern of rescuing the child from upsetting experiences or feelings, because it is difficult for these parents to see their child in distress. They quickly step in to "help" when the child is frustrated or makes a mistake. Without realizing it, these parents send a harmful message to the child: "You can't do it by yourself; you need my help." And, over time, the child comes to believe it.

Furthermore, pampered children who are quickly rescued from distress are not able to develop resiliency and perseverance.[3] A child's displays of anger, sadness, or fear are quickly banished since the anxious parent takes this personally and feels inadequate. These moms and dads think that the child would be happy and satisfied if they were doing their job as parents correctly. One more thing. Since these parents find negative feelings overwhelming, they assume their child does as well.

Now you may be thinking that a child in this kind of environment receives too much comfort, but there is a big difference between comforting and rescuing. Remember that anxious parents are preoccupied with their own fears, so tuning in to the feelings of their child is next to impossible. Instead of helping the child accept, process, and manage negative feelings, these parents attempt to rescue the child from having to experience such feelings at all. Often weighed down with internal turmoil of their own, these parents find it difficult to draw out the child's feelings and offer relief. And because these children appear to be doing so well (they're busy pleasing), parents assume they are.

Pleasers also are created when an angry or critical parent dominates the scene, and a feeling of apprehension pervades the home. Children in such an environment must be careful since any behavior or decision will most likely be met with criticism. In such cases, some children keep trying to please and win the approval of the faultfinding parent. Others learn to step lightly to keep from setting off outbursts that frighten them.

What's It Like to Be the Kid?

Children raised by fearful, angry, or critical parents become fearful themselves. These are often sensitive kids who easily internalize the feelings of others. Distress produced by anxiety or anger causes them to adopt strategies that will relieve the parent. Children may take on the pleaser role to reduce tension and anxiety in adults and, ultimately, in themselves. These kids are anxious and upset when those around them are angry or worried. They find it hard to settle down until their parents are happy. Also, hugging and touching may be more for the parents' benefit as youngsters take care of their parents' need for soothing.[4]

Marshall commented in one session, "I used to feel guilty about going out with my friends in high school and leaving my mom home alone." He felt he had to pay more attention to his mother's feelings than his own. Consequently, Marshall struggled to separate from her and become his own person.

In overprotective homes, children may become fearful, clingy, and hypervigilant about possible danger. They sometimes develop separation anxiety at school, on overnight stays with friends or family, or when they are with baby-sitters. Since this anxiety is rarely soothed, these kids begin to develop a permanent and unremitting anxious core that begins to seem normal. These kids also learn to monitor their environment and attempt to fix problems as they arise. One client remembered cleaning the house when his mom got angry and agitated. "Look, Mom, you can be happy now. The house is being cleaned."

As we mentioned, being away from the house can be stressful for these kids. That's because they are unable to monitor the moods and atmosphere of the home environment when they are gone. Then returning home requires a reassessment of the prevailing mood so these young pleasers can adjust their behavior accordingly.

These kids train themselves to read and respond to the distress they perceive in others. So, as adults, they are set up to be in the pursuing role, seeking proximity with and taking care of others.

As these children grow, they may be embarrassed by their own fearfulness, especially if they're teased by peers or siblings. So they may make further attempts to push their anxiety out of awareness, but the core remains.

WHAT ELSE MIGHT CAUSE A PLEASER LOVE STYLE?

In addition to parenting styles, many other childhood experiences can cause children high anxiety. Separation from a parent for any reason such as illness, death, or divorce can result in high levels of distress for a child. Of course, the separation does not have to be physical to be damaging. Addictions, abuse, or violence in a home can cause a child enormous stress while the parent is present. Children in any of the above situations experience a form of abandonment. Addicted parents, for instance, are preoccupied with their addiction and not tuned in to the feelings, experiences, and needs of their child.

I've also worked with a number of clients who suffered through their school years with an undiagnosed learning disability. School was a nightmare of anxiety for them. Every day they were worried they might be asked to read aloud or do math on the chalkboard in front of the class. Their parents were frustrated by their grades but oblivious to their struggles and daily torment. These school experiences chipped away at their self-confidence, and they learned to take the pleaser role in order to draw others into relationship and keep them around. Generally, when no secure base offers children true relief from anxiety and they have no opportunity to learn to process and manage difficult events, an imprint to please may result.

TERI'S STORY

As she was growing up, Teri had a brother who created extreme fear and anxiety in her. Because she was so "good," her parents never realized the damage he was doing. So, although Teri's childhood experience was very different from Marshall's, it led to the same imprinted desire to keep everyone happy. And your childhood may have been very different from both Marshall's and Teri's, yet you may still strongly relate to the characteristics possessed by adults with this style. In fact, there are many ways to become an adult pleaser. We're simply looking at some of the more common ones. Let's hear Teri tell her story now.

Teri came to her first session visibly upset. She apologized profusely for being several minutes late and then asked me where to sit. When I invited her to sit anywhere, she had trouble deciding. "Is this okay, or is this your chair?"

"That's fine."

I gave her a few minutes to collect herself by reminding her what I had learned during our phone conversation. "You mentioned you were feeling very upset because of your work situation. You have a very difficult boss, Robert, and he is causing you a lot of stress."

"Yes," Teri said. "Last night, by the time I got home, I was a nervous wreck. Homework with the kids just about put me over the edge." Teri sighed heavily and nervously twisted the handle of her purse.

"Teri," I said, "I want to understand what you mean by 'over the edge.' If I were one of your kids in your home last night, what would I have seen?"

"Oh, you would have seen Mom as usual: superwoman in action. The kids don't really know how bad work is for me. I try to keep things happy at home, but my son Trevor is thirteen now, and he's really getting an attitude. He is hard for me to handle sometimes because he is getting a temper like his dad. I'm kind of scared of him. Trevor is better when his dad is home, but last night was Phil's night to play basketball with the guys."

"So what you're telling me, Teri, is that you are fairly good at hiding your stress from the kids," I reviewed.

Teri laughed. "I think you would have to be inside my body to see the stress. My stomach hurts all the time, and I get sort of nervous on Sunday night when I know the whole week is ahead of me."

"Does Phil know how you feel at work or on Sunday nights?" I inquired.

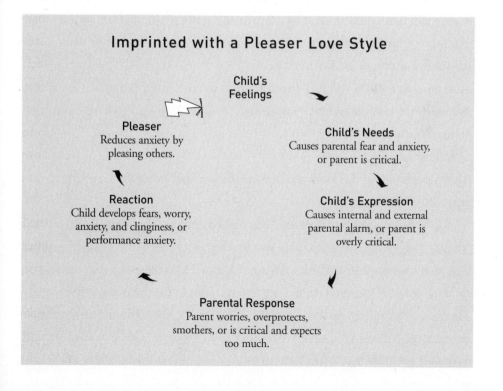

Imprinted with a Pleaser Love Style

Child's Feelings

Pleaser
Reduces anxiety by
pleasing others.

Child's Needs
Causes parental fear and anxiety,
or parent is critical.

Reaction
Child develops fears, worry,
anxiety, and clinginess, or
performance anxiety.

Child's Expression
Causes internal and external
parental alarm, or parent is
overly critical.

Parental Response
Parent worries, overprotects,
smothers, or is critical and expects
too much.

"Phil knows I don't really like Robert," Teri continued, "but I really can't complain because Phil and Robert are good friends. That's how I got the job, and we need the money. I would rather not have to work. I'm so busy with the kids and all. But Phil gets stressed over money, and two incomes help him relax."

"I see. So you're under a lot of stress, but your kids and husband are not all that aware that you are on the edge and feeling somewhat trapped in your job. Is that accurate?" I summarized.

"Yes. Wow, I'm sorry I'm rambling so much," Teri replied. "This is really about work, and I'm talking about my husband and kids."

"This is all helpful information," I reassured her. "Tell me more about your work."

"Well, Robert, my boss, seemed to like me at first. I've been working for him for about a year. I do all of his accounting, and his company is really growing, so it's taking more and more time. Sometimes I have to bring work home. About nine months ago, they landed a big contract, and that's when he started getting abrupt and unkind. Last week he came in and started yelling at me because there was not enough money for payroll tax. It cost the company a lot to win the big contract, so finances are tight."

I interrupted. "So Phil is stressed when money is tight, and Robert is also stressed when money is tight," I observed. "And you try hard to keep them from getting stressed."

"Well, yes, I guess I do."

"Tell me about the most recent time Robert's behavior was upsetting to you at work. What happened?"

"Oh, that would be yesterday," Teri replied, and another deep sigh made her shoulders sag into my couch. "He was looking for a letter that I had put on his desk that morning. I heard him talking to himself and throwing stuff around on his desk. It made me nervous, so I got up and went to the ladies room. Next thing I know, he's storming up and down the halls, yelling my name and asking where the letter is. I tried to tell him where I put it on his desk, but he wasn't listening. When he gets like that, I just have to wait until he cools down. He was a grump for the rest of the day. I even tried going downstairs and getting his favorite smoothie from the snack bar, but he didn't even say thank you."

"What you are saying is that you handle his bad moods by waiting him out and trying to change his mood through acts of kindness, like getting the smoothie. Do you ever feel angry at him, Teri?" I wondered.

Teri gave another hopeless sigh and closed her eyes. "Well, I hate to admit it, but, yes, lately I feel a little frustrated. Mostly he just makes me a nervous wreck. I try to be patient and kind, but he makes it really hard."

"All right, Teri. Let's try something. I'm not suggesting you do this at work. This is just something I want you to try in here with me. I would like you to imagine that I am Robert. You have just endured one of my verbal lashings, and you suddenly find yourself filled with courage to tell me (Robert) what you think and how I make you feel. There is no right or wrong way to do this. I just want you to be able to put words to your experience."

Teri's eyes widened ever so slightly and dropped to the floor. I knew she was uncomfortable about showing her feelings instead of hiding them. She glanced at me briefly and lowered her gaze again saying, "He makes me nervous."

"Teri, I know I am stretching you a bit here, but this is important. Imagine I am sitting in for Robert. Talk to me directly. Start with what you just said: 'Robert, you make me nervous.'"

Teri grabbed the pillow off my couch and held it tightly against her chest. I waited silently. Finally, she softly said, "Robert, you make me nervous."

"Good," I encouraged. "Keep going, Teri."

She continued in a meek voice, pausing long between sentences. "Why do you have to yell at me? Why can't you just be nice? I try hard to do a good job." Teri's eyes remained glued to the floor.

I urged Teri on. "Now tell me (as Robert) how your body feels when you're around me."

Teri complied, all the energy drained from her voice. "You make my stomach hurt, Robert. Sometimes you give me a headache."

"Great, Teri. You did a great job. Now I want you to get a mental picture of the family members in your home during your childhood years. Imagine your parents and siblings. Is there anyone you could say those exact same words to and they would fit?"

Teri was silent as she made the mental shift. Suddenly she grabbed a handful of tissues from the table and buried her face in them. "Oh," she whispered. "My older brother," she repeated several times through her tears. "He always hated me. He made me a nervous wreck too. I was scared to death when my parents left the house; he was so mean to me. It was the exact same stomachache I get with Robert. It's a feeling of dread." Teri struggled to compose herself. In a barely audible voice, Teri recounted several tragic memories of her brother's intimidation and the sadistic pleasure he felt in scaring her.

"I can see there is a lot of pain from your relationship with your brother. I think it is important for me to hear more about what happened between the two of you next week. Before we are out of time, though, I'd like to ask you to do one last thing. Take a moment to get a mental picture of your current family. Do the words you said to Robert fit anyone today?" I inquired.

Teri shifted into the present. "Sometimes Phil makes me feel nervous when he loses his temper. And Trevor is starting to make me feel that knot in my stomach. Wow, I never saw the connection before."

"I'm glad you can see it now, Teri. Your encounters with Robert and Phil cause a flood of feelings that you experienced first as a child before you ever met either of them. It is as though the past is flooding into the present in a feeling memory. That kind of memory can be rather overwhelming, because we tend to respond as we did when we were children. It seems you are sort of paralyzed in anxiety, and your body takes the brunt of it. You then try to hide your distress so you don't upset others. Does that sound accurate?"

"Yes, it does," Teri said.

"We will work on some ways you can better cope with these situations, ways that will make you feel more like an adult," I encouraged her.

We can see from Teri's story that a difficult relationship with a sibling may create an unhealthy imprint. In Teri's case, her brother's cruel treatment and sadistic teasing created a core of anxiety in her that greatly affected the adult Teri's relationships at home and at work.

COMMON CHARACTERISTICS OF PLEASERS

"I'm Not Worried; I'm Just Stressed"

Before we started meeting regularly, Marshall certainly would not have described himself as a fearful person. He was used to constant underlying levels of anxiety, and he kept these feelings submerged with his busy lifestyle. On those occasions when he experienced a round of panic attacks, he did not label them as anxiety but stress. Marshall later admitted that the responsibilities of the adult world were somewhat overwhelming to him, but he kept this truth well hidden, even from himself. Like many adults with this pleaser imprint, Marshall calmed himself by focusing on the needs of others and making them happy. Individuals who constantly try to avoid criticism also live with anxiety they don't always acknowledge. If you expect to be scrutinized for mistakes, you're going to be uneasy. Could it be that like Marshall you have endured a lifetime of anxiety without really naming it for what it is?

"I Just Want to Be with You"

Adults with an imprint to please may feel anxiety when a partner wants time alone or with friends.[5] Also, power struggles may develop with people who don't share the same level of apprehension over separation. Marshall and Abby, for instance, had numerous disagreements about time apart. Abby wanted to take weekend trips with her girlfriends. Marshall felt rejected and made Abby feel guilty for not wanting to be with him. Family vacations were also a source of disagreement. Abby wanted to take adventurous trips to exotic places without the kids. Marshall was hesitant to leave the kids at all, and he liked car trips closer to home. Marshall believed his desires were "right" and Abby's were "wrong" until he understood there was a lot of anxiety underneath his pleaser style. He realized he would have to learn to conquer his fears and tolerate time away from Abby and the kids. Abby was more willing to compromise when she realized the source of Marshall's anxiety.

"I'm Only Trying to Help"

Perpetual pleasers need someone to take care of. Since they calm their own anxiety by focusing on and caring for others, they can feel quite lost if no one is available. They depend on their caretaking role to take the focus off their own internal discomfort. While the avoider may prefer to be alone, pleasers actually feel lost and anxious when they're isolated. In fact, they may desire more connection than others want or need since quiet moments make them uneasy. Also, pleasers easily feel hurt and rejected when others don't accept their ministrations. Craving constant connection and fearing the loss or absence of their partner, pleasers can be very possessive and make others feel smothered.

"How Am I Doing?"

Pleasers may be dependent on the encouragement and support of others. If they were rescued and pampered as kids, these adults may feel incompetent and depend on others for reassurance and help. So, although Marshall was very successful in his sales job, he often complained to Abby that his boss gave him no feedback and didn't appreciate his good performance. Even when the sales numbers indicated a high level of success, Marshall craved the praise and reassurance of his boss. He had difficulty believing he was doing okay. A highly critical childhood environment may cause pleasers to develop unrealistic expectations for themselves, to question their abilities, or to expect that others will disapprove of them.

"Whatever You Decide"

Making decisions requires a level of self-reliance and self-confidence. Decision making becomes difficult when we are overly concerned about rejection or making others mad. That's why Marshall had difficulty making any decisions about his children without Abby's permission or reassurance. If left alone with the kids, he often called her to check on their requests. In fact, he tended to abdicate decision making in general to Abby. She handled the finances and managed the money. Anxiety causes every decision to be agonizing because of the possible dreadful outcomes. Fearing the rejection of others and the likelihood of mistakes, an overprotective parent can set pleasers up to feel inadequate to make decisions.[6]

"Don't Get Mad; I'm Only Trying to Be Nice"

During one session Marshall and Abby argued about Marshall's desire to give Abby a back rub in bed each night. Abby explained, "It's not about sex. I'm the one who usually initiates that. But sometimes I just don't want a back rub. My friends think I'm crazy for saying that. I know he is trying to do a nice thing for me, so usually I just let him. But the other night I told him no, and he was so hurt. Can't I just say no once in a while?"

I asked Abby to face Marshall on the couch and hold out her arms in an inviting gesture of connection. "Notice the feeling in your body, Marshall," I directed.

"My body feels relaxed," Marshall grinned.

I handed him the list of feeling words. "When Abby reaches out to you, how does it make you feel?"

Marshall picked words off the list. "Close, secure, safe, loving," he answered.

I then asked Abby to face Marshall again and this time extend her arm out toward his chest with her hand in a "stop" position. "Notice your body now," I requested again.

"Wow, my chest tightened up right away." Marshall continued, "I feel like Abby is mad at me. And I guess I do feel like you are mad at me, Abby, when you tell me not to rub your back."

I turned to Marshall. "So if Abby accepts your offer, you assume everything is okay between the two of you, and you can relax. If she refuses, you assume she is mad or unhappy with you in some way."

Marshall reflected, "So you are saying that the back rub is a way for me to see what mood she is in, so it's more for me than for her."

"Yes," I replied.

"That's why it bugs me," Abby exclaimed. "I never could understand why it just didn't feel right. Good grief, Marshall, it must drive you crazy to always be guessing if I'm mad or not. I'll tell you if I am, or you can ask me."

Marshall looked relieved. "That would be great. I think I take your emotional temperature a lot. Probably more than I even realize."

Fearful pleasers usually control in passive ways with one purpose in mind: to keep others close to them. When people around them detach emotionally or physically, the pleasers' apprehensions intensify. Much of their pursuing is self-focused even though they are "doing something for others." They may be unaware how much their need for continuous connection controls their own choices and decisions. These pleasers may believe they just want more out of relationships than others. But in reality they're trying to soothe the anxious core within.

"If Things Stay the Same, I Know What to Expect"

Perpetual pleasers take a cautious position in life; they avoid risk and prefer predictable patterns and habits. After Marshall, for example, turned down a job promotion, he explained to Abby that he felt overwhelmed by the new responsibilities of a different position.

Although Marshall was well qualified, change was stressful for him, and he preferred to stay in a place where he knew what to expect. As Marshall's experience illustrates, individuals struggling with fears about the unknown often don't realize their potential because the prospect of change causes them too much anxiety. Also, if a pleaser expects to be criticized, this expectation can cause them to be uneasy in new situations.

"Everybody Wants Too Much"

Disagreement and conflict can alienate people, so anger is often an underdeveloped emotion for pleasers. Over the years, however, their resentment builds as they minimize, ignore, and avoid expressing their frustrations. Saying no can indeed cause conflict and disapproval, so pleasers struggle with boundaries especially when they feel someone will be annoyed with them. As a result, time management can be a problem as their schedule becomes overcrowded and unmanageable in their attempts to make everyone happy. Marshall's panicky feelings and the pressure he felt about others "wanting too much" were greatly reduced as Marshall learned to say no and tolerate the displeasure of others.

"What Do I Want?"

Pleasers are good givers, but lousy receivers. They tend to ignore their own needs altogether by constantly focusing on others. When asked what they want or feel, pleasers often don't know. They also tend to have little awareness or compassion for the anxious suffering they endured as children. So they may readily feel grief for the sorrows of others but many times be unable to grieve for their own pain and losses. After all, when they were kids, no one asked them about their inner experiences. They do not have soul words because they did not learn to reflect and express their heart. As a result, pleasers are often unaware of their level of anxiety and the core of fear that governs their life.

"Aren't You Scared?"

Pleasers tend to be hyperalert about possible fearful responses from others, so they may overemphasize the need for protection. Having experienced a great deal of unresolved fear as kids, they unconsciously assume that those around them also have similar apprehension, so they may inappropriately intervene to protect their children. Since pleasers do not know what to do with their anxiety, it is difficult for them to help their children face their own fears and take risks.

GROWTH GOALS

If you do the dance of the pleaser, you'll want to know what Teri and Marshall did to create new imprints. Each of them committed themselves to the growth goals outlined in the workbook. So if this section has your name all over it, take time now to review the workbook and make the goals there your goals as well. If your spouse fits the description of the pleaser, the section in the workbook titled "Helping Pleasers" will enable you to relate better as he or she works toward a secure imprint.

Chapter 7

The Vacillator Love Style

Lea came to counseling confessing she was on the verge of an affair because she was so unhappy in her marriage. Six years into her marriage to Scott, she was attracted to Troy, one of the men she saw regularly at the gym. Scared about the intensity of her feelings for Troy, she admitted that she was flirting with the idea of an affair and that Troy was happy to oblige—that, in fact, he was pushing for it.

I (Kay) didn't have to do much prompting. Lea launched into the glory of Troy in contrast to the doldrums of her marriage. "Troy is so attentive and exciting. He has lots of interests, and he is always telling me how beautiful and smart I am. If my husband would pay half as much attention to me, I wouldn't be in this mess. I've been telling Scott for years how unhappy I am. He just doesn't care. All he wants to do is work and play golf, and I'm always waiting for him. He is a good dad, or I'd probably be gone by now. The girls adore him. He's just a lousy husband, and if I'm going to stay in my marriage, I have to get him to change." Continuing her list of complaints about Scott, Lea became more and more emphatic about her dissatisfaction.

Finally, I interrupted her. "I'm getting the picture, Lea. I want to understand how it was at first. You married Scott for some reason. What did you like about him when you were dating him?"

Lea didn't take a breath. "Oh, it was love at first sight. He is tall, blond, blue eyed. Gorgeous. Still is. If only good looks were enough, but he has hurt me over and over. How am I supposed to deal with all that?" Lea dove into the details of their latest fight. "If I get mad enough, he tries for a while, but it doesn't last."

I tried again to see if she could focus on anything good for more than a few seconds. "Lea, you were about to tell me what attracted you to Scott in the first place. You got sidetracked after you told me he was good looking. What else did you enjoy about Scott during your dating years?"

Lea paused for the first time. "Well, we met at a party. He was sort of quiet and shy, but he couldn't take his eyes off me. I introduced myself, and we talked all night. He wasn't able to get enough of me back then. He called me all the time, and we went everywhere together. He was calm and easy to be around. Never jealous like my previous boyfriend. He liked how energetic and outgoing I was. He called me his Energizer Bunny." Lea smiled for the first time.

"After six months we ran off to Las Vegas and got married. That just about killed my mom because she had been planning my wedding for years. She wanted to outshine all her friends and throw the biggest, best wedding all her Newport Beach friends had ever seen. I ruined all her big plans," Lea grinned, clearly enjoying the memory of spoiling her mom's expectations.

I decided to use Lea's comment to take a detour into her childhood. I wanted to test my suspicion that she might have been imprinted to be a vacillator. Her tendency to idealize and devalue, as well as her high degree of anger and reactivity, made me wonder if she had experienced only sporadic and unpredictable connection in her home growing up.

"Lea, tell me more about your mom."

"Do you have all day?" she laughed.

"Tell me your best and your worst memory," I guided her.

"Well, how can I pick one?" Lea began. "I guess the worst were all the times she got angry at my dad and threatened to leave. It would really scare me. One time she actually packed her suitcase. I was in the first grade, and I heard her yelling at my dad and telling him she was leaving. I was worried she would run out of money and not be able to get back home, so I put my piggy bank in her suitcase."

I was touched by this tender gesture. "That was a very sweet and sensitive thing for you to do, Lea. It sounds like you were a caring, perceptive little girl." Lea's eyes filled with tears. "And that scene would be very upsetting to a six-year-old. Did anyone realize how much it scared you?" I asked.

Lea was quiet. Finally she replied, "I guess not. I always knew when she was still mad at Dad, because she would ignore him and pay extra attention to me. She took me for ice cream or to a movie or shopping. Any excuse to get out of the house. I hated the look on my dad's face. He looked so sad and dejected when we would leave. When I got older, I started telling her I didn't want to go. Then she would blow up at me too."

"Do you remember any time you spent with your mom that was about your needs and not hers?" I asked.

"Once," Lea answered emphatically. "When I was ten, I was hospitalized after an accident on my bike. I had a bad concussion, and the doctor had to do surgery to relieve the pressure on my brain. My mom spent every night with me, and I especially remember her stroking my arm as she sat by my bed. That's the one time I felt she really cared about me. In a weird way, it's the best memory I have of my mom. I used to pretend I was sick after that, hoping she would do it again, but she never did. She was too busy at the country club."

Our time was up, and I needed to finish the session. "I'm going to do some wondering out loud, Lea, and I want you to think about this for next week. I wonder if your childhood left you with a deep need for consistent, predictable connection. When you first met Scott, it seemed you had found that. Unlike your mom, Scott is not volatile. You describe him as calm and easy to be around. When all the responsibilities of real life set in, though, and Scott is busy, I wonder if you feel ignored just as you did when you were a child and your mom was too busy. And just as you hoped your mom would come again and stroke your arm, I wonder if you are waiting for Scott to make you feel like you did when you were dating. In fact, I wonder how many of the feelings you have about Scott are old feelings just like the ones you had as a little girl. Think about it, and we will pick up here next week."

THE HOME ENVIRONMENT

Now consider why some people come into marriage doing the dance of the vacillator. First, it's important to understand that vacillators want connection. They idealize new relationships in hopes of satisfying their longing for love and attention. The "chase" is the most exciting phase of the relationship for them since intimacy is not yet realized but is just around the corner. New relationships hold the hope of a satisfying connection, and expectations are high. Dating is often intense and exciting. Sooner or later, though, reality sets in. Then, acutely sensitive to disappointments or possible rejection in relationships, vacillators' feelings get hurt when their high expectations are not met. And many respond with anger.

Now unsure and hesitant, they give mixed signals that reflect their inner confusion and conflict. They vacillate back and forth, first pushing others away and then wanting them to come back. "I do want you, but I'm mad because you aren't meeting my expectations; so I don't want you." This push-pull style of relating usually creates greater distance rather than the desired connection, and anger increases. The vacillator devalues the relationship and focuses on the hurts and disappointments, seeing little good or redeeming value.

Before we go any further, let's remember that parents usually do the best they can. All of us come into marriage and parenting with shortcomings. But, naturally, all of us want to feel we are doing our best as spouses and parents. To do our best, we have to take an honest look at what hinders us. Doing so isn't easy, but the rewards are worth it. So keep in mind that the goal isn't to find fault with our parents. The goal is to acknowledge the truth of our childhood so we have a road map for growth and change.

Basically, people imprinted to be vacillators commonly experience periods of abandonment growing up. At times their parents truly connect with them, but consistency is difficult. Mom or Dad suddenly disengage, becoming absorbed in their own emotions or interests, and thus are unavailable to their children. The children are left waiting, hoping for more attention—but how long will they have to wait? That is the question with no answer. Maybe a minute, maybe an hour, maybe a week or longer. Connection is experienced as inconsistent, unpredictable, and sporadic.[1] Out of sync with their child's needs, the availability of these parents is sometimes more dependent on their own mood and desires. Engaging in the parental role only when they are in the mood, they wind up giving their children a mixed message: "Come close… No, go away!"

The unspoken message received by a child but not understood is "Be available and need me when I feel like parenting, but survive on your own when I don't."

If the child does not comply, the parent may punish by emotionally withdrawing. Kids can tolerate a bad day now and then. But in the home we are talking about here, the parent's availability is almost always governed by the parent's disposition and whims.[2] I watched this dynamic play itself out at a birthday party for a five-year-old when a mother brought her daughter Megan to the celebration.

Megan was clingy and reluctant to participate. Talking with friends, her mom kept pushing Megan to go play in the bounce house with the other kids. After a few unsuccessful attempts, her mom was frustrated. She finally picked Megan up and pushed her through the small entrance into the bounce house. Megan clutched the netting and began to cry. Her mom walked away.

Megan slowly made her way out of the bounce house, walked over to her mom, and stood by her side whimpering. Her mom stopped talking and, picking her up, asked in a surprised tone, "What's wrong?" Megan began to kick, cry harder, and swing at her mom. She was too angry to receive the comfort she needed. Her mom casually put her down and continued her conversation. Megan melted into a heap on the grass, and her mom ignored her.

While I'm sure Megan and her mom have better moments, too many interactions like this will leave Megan with the idea that what matters most is what her mom wants. Megan is experiencing connection as unpredictable and often unavailable when she most needs it.

In this kind of family, a mother often prefers babies and young children who make her feel wanted, needed, and valuable. (If Mom didn't feel valuable and wanted during her own childhood, her own baby can fill this need.[3]) As the baby grows, develops a mind of his own, and no longer needs her in the same way he did earlier, this mom is likely to feel rejected and unwanted. Mothers like this tend to disengage more as children become older and assert their own personhood. Also, since a new baby keeps Mom's love tank full, the next youngest child may feel a profound withdrawal by Mom when a new sibling arrives.

Fathers with the imprint to vacillate, however, are more likely to engage when the child is older, but like the vacillating mom, his interest and moods will govern the contact. One ambivalent father I know wanted to take his teenage daughter to the car races every weekend. She was a sensitive, quiet girl who had absolutely no interest in cars. She disliked the loud noise of the races and was bored and restless. As with this example, a dad with the imprint to vacillate can be fun and engaging, but the activity will be about what he enjoys. His message is "Figure out what I want and do it. If you don't do it my way, I may withdraw from you." In other words, "Be what I need you to be."

WHAT'S IT LIKE TO BE THE KID?

"I'm Trying to Figure It Out"

Erratic interactions with parents leave children confused and hyperattuned to signs of connection and abandonment.[4] These kids become acutely sensitive to the emotional temperature of other people and learn to adjust their behavior accordingly. Being "other focused" like this, they grow up with poor self-reflection skills. Their own needs have rarely been the center of attention; the moods, needs, and behaviors of the parent dictated daily life. But these children have experienced enough connection to desire more, and they are frustrated by their futile efforts to receive attention when they need it. Preoccupied with reading the signals, they become discouraged and angry because they can't figure out how to get attention when they need it. Unable to achieve the connection they desire, they feel unwanted to some degree or another.

"I'm Too Mad to Want You"

In this kind of home, the child worries about the parents when they are absent, either physically or emotionally, but they feel anger when Mom and Dad return or try to reengage. A mother I talked to recently described this exact cycle.

"Shawn is two years old," she explained. "I went back to work last month because I missed my job. Being home all the time is suffocating. I have a really good baby-sitter, but it's so embarrassing when I pick Shawn up in the afternoon. I'm all excited to see him, and I think he'll come running to me, but it's just the opposite. He hides behind the couch and won't come out. I call him, but he won't come. He only comes when I tell him I'm leaving without him and start walking out the door. By then, he's screaming and having a tantrum. What's wrong with him?"

This interaction is classic vacillating style. Mom is self-focused and needs the accolades of the work environment. She has no clue that Shawn faces a tremendous adjustment being suddenly shuffled off to a baby-sitter. Mom wants Shawn to be excited to see her, which is about her need. Shawn's frustration and anger are his only way of communicating how mad he is at Mom for leaving him all day.

Focused on her own embarrassment and the desire to avoid a tantrum, Mom has no ability to assess Shawn's emotional needs. Poor Shawn, threatened with further abandonment if he does not comply, is too angry to receive the comfort he so desperately wants. His mom totally misses his signals and the fact that her son is attempting to communicate his feelings. Shawn will have to conform to get what he wants—his mom's acceptance—or stay angry and experience her rejection.

WHAT ELSE MIGHT CAUSE A VACILLATOR LOVE STYLE?

A parent with an imprint to vacillate may create the same imprint in her child, but that is not always the case. Any trauma during childhood years can produce a variety of unhealthy imprints. Circumstances may cause a parent's availability to be unpredictable. Divorce causes more irregular connection because of a parent's preoccupation with self and unavailability due to emotional distress. After the dust settles, a child may fill the empty spot left by the absent spouse. Again, this is about the parent's needs, not the child's. Also, due to visitation schedules or maybe guilt, some fathers spend more time with their children after a divorce than when the family was together. Other dads simply disappear.

Eventually Mom and Dad begin new relationships, and once again the parents become less available, now preoccupied and immersed in the dating process. Remarriage is another event that requires children to further share their parent, especially when stepchildren are involved. The children ride the roller coaster of each parent's sporadic availability, a ride that depends on where Mom and Dad are in the process of separation, divorce, dating, and remarriage. Many times the youngster's feelings are not addressed. In such cases, children may learn that connection is unpredictable and that the needs and moods of the parent dominate.

THE VACILLATOR BECOMES AN ADULT

"I Have a Right to Be Angry"

The main emotion of conflicted adults is anxiety submerged underneath a fair amount of anger. As they grew to adulthood, they were imprinted to believe that connection is unpredictable.[5] Often unaware that they are animated by their past experiences, they now erroneously assume that all significant others will eventually abandon them, and it will hurt just as deeply as it did in the past. Often, however, this thinking is not articulated on a conscious level. These thoughts are deeply embedded. *If I do get the relationship I want, it takes a lot of work—and it never lasts.* And they desperately want their connections to other people to last and to be predictable.

All of us have that deep need to find someone who can truly see our needs and stay engaged. Imprinted experiences of abandonment and withdrawal will,

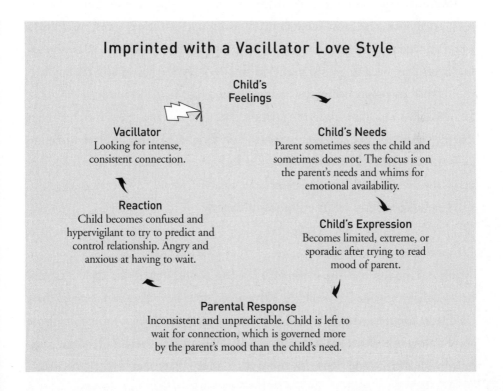

Imprinted with a Vacillator Love Style

Child's Feelings

Vacillator
Looking for intense, consistent connection.

Child's Needs
Parent sometimes sees the child and sometimes does not. The focus is on the parent's needs and whims for emotional availability.

Reaction
Child becomes confused and hypervigilant to try to predict and control relationship. Angry and anxious at having to wait.

Child's Expression
Becomes limited, extreme, or sporadic after trying to read mood of parent.

Parental Response
Inconsistent and unpredictable. Child is left to wait for connection, which is governed more by the parent's mood than the child's need.

however, produce an anxious core that keeps us alert for any hint of desertion or rejection.

As we've seen, avoiders minimize attachment needs, and pleasers resort to compulsive caregiving. Vacillators, however, are preoccupied with their distress and frustration and are therefore more prone to anger. Quick to feel neglected or unwanted, vacillators experience a building tension as their fruitless waiting and desperate wanting bring them close to familiar childhood pain. A burst of anger may provide temporary release of the tension so the underlying anxiety and shame remain unnoticed by them. As kids, vacillators learned to exaggerate their feelings in an attempt to be noticed and maintain contact.[6] They often continue this pattern in marriage as they resentfully withdraw and wait to be pursued after an angry outburst.

Vacillators are stuck in a state of protest about their unmet needs for connection. While vacillators' anger may be a healthy response to their unmet needs, their mates find themselves receiving the brunt of their rage. Also, because of their underlying sensitivity, vacillators have difficulty calming themselves down, and anger will dominate their interactions until they recognize their past hurts. We often tell vacillators they need to get sad, not mad, and to share the hurt under the anger.

As therapy progressed with Lea, she realized that new relationships made her feel energized and hopeful. During dating, the attention and extensive time spent together filled her deep need for consistent, predictable connection. Her attraction to Troy recaptured these feelings. But Lea had never considered what would happen if she divorced Scott and married Troy. Real life would have set in once again, and Lea was bound to feel the same familiar loss.

"It's Love at First Sight!"

When one person feels an instant captivating connection to another, it's often because that someone is a vacillator. Remember, vacillators have been trained from childhood to assess situations and be what others need. They have mastered the art of tuning in to those around them. Their ability to intuitively read others, combined with their strong desire for connection, make them magnetic connectors.

Vacillators can plunge into relationships with tremendous intensity and a strong desire for constant connection because any hint of separation and space does not feel good to them. Connection can sometimes take the form of intense sexual seduction and charm, which is often mistaken for intimacy. This idealized romance can blind both individuals to the red flags in each other. When problems arise, the hurt and betrayal the vacillator feels are extraordinary.

"You Are My Soul Mate"

Vacillators are on a quest for connection that lasts. Because of their charm, they are exciting and appealing. Romance is idealized as both people often feel they have met their soul mate. The intense feelings of dating become the expectation for the future, and the vacillator believes this intense love will continue.[7] Childhood wounds have left in these men and women a deep need to be truly seen and valued, and hope soars when they feel like genuine connection is finally a reality. But eventually the bubble bursts. When a partner does not provide the consistent intense connection hoped for, vacillators are easily hurt and, because of their predisposed sensitivities, have an uncanny ability to remember earlier infractions. Current disappointments are fueled by past hurts, and the vacillator is easily overcome by feelings of hopelessness and despair.

"I Want Out, Then I Want in It"

These lines from the popular country-western song, "Go Away," by Lorrie Morgan get this aspect of vacillators down perfectly. It could be their theme song. Vacillators feel anxious when away from their love interest but apprehensive during moments of connection. As much as they want intimacy, truly having it makes the possibility of getting hurt far more likely. Also, when they begin to feel close in a relationship, they don't trust it to last, and sometimes they sabotage the connection by pushing the other person away before that person can hurt them. Anger over past hurts can also spoil opportunities for closeness. So the message they communicate is the same they heard as a child: "Come here! No, go away!"

Lea began to realize she picked fights with Scott when he was really trying to please her. She liked his efforts, but she couldn't trust them to last. She anticipated his future failure and threw him a curve before he could hurt her. As she accepted her love style, though, Lea was able to lower her expectations and learn to enjoy the moment. Over time, her anger lessened.

I once worked with a couple who experienced a wonderful moment of connection when the husband let down his guard and held his wife as she cried. This was a tender encounter between a male avoider and a female vacillator as he exhibited the vulnerability she so desired. She studied his face and looked deeply into his eyes. I expected her to speak some affectionate words, but instead she said in a whiny voice, "Your hair is greasy. You need to wash it more." Needless to say, her comment ruined the moment. What a tragedy that her fear of trusting and then being hurt prevented her from accepting comfort when it was offered. On her deepest level she was afraid of allowing intimate connection because it required her to be vulnerable and take risks. "Connection never lasts" is the vacillator's mantra. It continues: "Love and attention mean that abandonment is just around the corner." Tortured by this fear of rejection, vacillators commonly sabotage their relationships.

"Why Don't You Want Me?"

In all relationships, problems develop after the honeymoon phase, yet disappointments are devastating for adult vacillators. Their high hopes set them up for big letdowns. When difficulties occur, vacillators feel overwhelming loss. "All good" turns to "all bad." Feeling special turns into feeling unwanted. As time goes on, anger surfaces with surprising intensity. Their old injuries fuel this high level of reactivity. Spouses may feel afraid and insecure, so they try to prevent the vacillator from becoming angry. This reactivity often intensifies, and others are repelled by—and want to avoid—the vacillator's anger and tension. This pulling away aggravates past themes of abandonment, causing vacillators to feel more strongly the threat of abandonment.

"You Hurt Me Too Much; It's Over"

Vacillators can feel betrayed by those they once idealized. They will often terminate a relationship because they view the other person as "all bad" for making them feel this way. Thus, vacillators frequently have a history of broken relationships. What they don't realize is that their own injuries from the past create in them this volatile emotional sensitivity and reactivity. Do you have a list of people you were once close to but who are no longer in your life? If so, carefully consider your part in this pattern.

"You Are the Problem. If You Would Change, I'd Be Happy"

Vacillators have learned to be so other-focused that they rarely contemplate their own brokenness. They tell themselves they just want more out of relationships than others want, and they see this as a positive attribute. Like pleasers, vacillators experience separation anxiety, but when they're disappointed, vacillators get angry whereas pleasers only try harder. Vacillators also want others to provide relief from their anxiety about possible abandonment, whereas the pleaser tries to find relief by keeping others happy. Vacillators have difficulty seeing their part in destructive patterns and more readily focus on the ways others hurt them. One client, for instance, finally realized that she had been acting out of her imprint when she was seeing her husband's actions as intentionally trying to hurt her. She went home from my office and told her husband she had unknowingly been expecting him to make up for all her childhood hurts. "I put an unfair burden on you," she told him. She didn't expect his response. "He hugged me and began to get all choked up," she told me. "He just kept saying 'thank you' over and over."

"Make Me Feel Special"

Another female client became friends with a woman who was a vacillator. What started as a great friendship progressed into a stormy, rocky relationship. They were on and off, up and down, pals and enemies. Hence the label *vacillator*. When she was contemplating a career change, my client consulted with me, her husband, and some other friends but made the mistake of neglecting to consult with her vacillator friend. Eventually that friend found out that she hadn't been consulted. She was furious and ended the relationship.

As that story illustrates, vacillators have a stronger than normal need to feel special. When someone is important to them, they desire an exclusive place in that person's life. They want to feel as though they have the greatest access to and privileges with the person, and they are deeply hurt if they see that time and attention directed elsewhere. They become threatened and jealous when they don't hold a central, exclusive position. When people in their life want to have a variety of friendships or interests, vacillators become agitated, feeling undesirable and unwanted. They may end a relationship rather than tolerate the agitation.[8]

"When the Vacillator Ain't Happy, Ain't Nobody Happy"

Country-western artist Tracy Byrd sings, "When Mama ain't happy, ain't nobody happy." Sadly, whether vacillators are mommas or papas, they characteristically dictate the emotional climate of the home, and everyone else adapts to their mood. When they decide to be happy, everyone breathes a sigh of relief and is happy too. When vacillators get over an angry outburst, they feel better and assume others do too. Furthermore, they often feel their anger was merited, and they don't see the negative impact it had on others. And family members are so relieved the episode is over that they—often unwittingly—ignore their own feelings, slap on the smile, and act as if the bomb that just went off never existed. Finally, a double standard often exists: the vacillator is allowed to express anger anytime, any way, but no one else ever can.

GROWTH GOALS

If you recognize yourself as a vacillator, that's huge—and the accompanying workbook is a must. (Of all the types, we find that vacillators have the most difficulty seeing their part in relational problems.) And if you are a vacillator, we are excited for you because understanding your love style and changing can mean dramatic progress toward achieving more of the deep connection and intimacy you have always desired. But first you need to recognize and take responsibility for your part. A good starting place is to be more direct about exactly what you want and need instead of believing, *If my spouse loved me, he would just know.* Learn to express the hurt instead of getting mad. Try to see both the good and bad in any person or situation instead of idealizing the situation and devaluing the other person.

Are you married to a vacillator? The workbook has some great ideas for how you can help your spouse along the journey of growth and healing. Learn from chapter 7 of the workbook what you can do to better support your spouse.

Chapter 8

The Chaotic (Controller and Victim) Love Styles

Just about any addiction you can name, Doug had battled. When I (Kay) counseled him, he was trying to save his third marriage. Recently arrested for punching his eleven-year-old stepson, Brian, Doug insisted, "The kid was asking for it." I didn't have to hear much about Doug's childhood to realize he grew up in a chaotic home. His history of addictions made sense in light of the pain he was trying to keep from his awareness.

Doug had become a Christian several years previously and, for the first time in his life, had experienced tender, gracious love from a small group of men in his church. They met regularly, caring for, encouraging, and accepting Doug. They also challenged him to grow. One of the men in the group referred him to me, and Doug cried as he told me how their faithful love was influencing his life.

I'm always encouraged by tears, especially from a man raised in a home like Doug's. He had a history of violent outbursts, and his tears were a sign that his childhood pain was leaking through a crack in his protective breastplate of anger.

But my first goal was not anger management. I've never seen an angry man get better by counting to ten. My first job was to dig out the child Doug from underneath the rubble of the past and stand him in front of the adult Doug until he could feel compassion and sympathy for the little guy. Until I could accomplish that, he would have no understanding or sympathy for Brian's feelings. As I considered this task, I was grateful for the love and caring from the men in his small group. They had opened a path for me to walk on.

As it turned out, the breakthrough took six months. Normally Doug recounted his tragic memories with laughter and sarcasm, but at this particular meeting he was very matter-of-fact as he described his earliest memory. He was five years old, and his dad was beating his mom. "It happened a lot. The old man took off when I was about seven or eight, or he probably would have killed her."

"Can you put yourself back in time and think about what a five-year-old little boy would feel watching that?" I inquired.

"I can't remember any feelings," Doug said in a flat, detached tone. "I can't believe I even remember that night. It was so long ago."

All of a sudden, I had an inspiration. "Doug, I want you to get up and go out into the waiting room of my office. A little boy is playing with his cars out there. I was just talking to him before you came in. He is about five or six. I want you to go get a drink of water from the cooler. Take a good look at him and talk to him for a second. Then come on back in my office."

Because the waiting room to my office is directly outside my door, I knew I would be able to hear this brief conversation, so I stayed in my seat. Doug looked surprised, but without a word, he got up and went to the cooler.

"Hey, nice cars," Doug said. I knew this little kid was talkative, and he did not disappoint me.

"They go fast. Watch this!" Sounds of motors and squealing wheels made Doug chuckle. "Wanna play? Here. You can have the orange car, but I want the green one 'cause it's the fastest."

Doug took a few seconds to push the cars around and suggested making a bridge out of the magazines. "I wish I could play longer, but I have to go talk to that lady in there," Doug said.

Doug returned to his chair and sat down. "How big is he?" I asked.

"Little," he replied.

"Did you ever ask your dad to play cars with you?" I continued.

"Never," he replied looking down at his knees.

"Doug," I said, "look at my eyes."

Doug looked up and made eye contact. I spoke directly to him, hoping to reach his heart. "That's how little you were when you watched your dad beat up your mom, Doug. You were just a little boy, small and defenseless. And you never felt relaxed or free enough to ask your dad to do anything with you. You were scared to death of him. How different would your life be if you could be that little boy out in the waiting room?"

"I never stopped to think how small you are at five," Doug said in a barely audible whisper. "That kid is so happy. He's cute." Doug broke eye contact. I asked him again to look at my eyes.

"Doug, can you imagine that little guy going home in a few minutes and watching his dad beat up his mom? How would he feel?"

"Like his whole world was coming apart." Doug began to cry.

"Yes," I said. "Your whole world did come apart when you were still so small. That is too much for a little boy to handle. He has been hiding down inside you for years, buried under a pile of anger."

As therapy progressed, Doug connected to more feelings of sadness and anxiety. Later, I was able to help him realize he created the same feelings of fear in his stepson, Brian, when he yelled and pushed him around. Remembering what it was like for him was a big motivator for changing his behavior toward Brian.

THE HOME ENVIRONMENT

The controller and the victim imprints are the result of serious problems in a child's home. People raised in chaotic environments learn that relationships are not safe and nurturing, but rather destructive and dangerous. Often their parents struggle with numerous addictions, deal with mental illnesses, or are absent altogether. For these kids, parents don't relieve stress, they create it, leaving the children with a huge dilemma. They need their parents in order to survive, but their parents are the source of danger, anxiety, and fear.[1]

Living in a chaotic home is like living in the path of a tornado. The chaos is unpredictable, and it hits with terrorizing fury. The eye of the storm offers moments of calm, but more intense devastation is just minutes away. Waiting is as distressing as the actual mayhem of the swirling wind. In these homes, pandemonium rules.

The extreme level of tension and stress produced by the physical, emotional, and verbal abuse causes extreme reactions in children. They cope with the constant terror in different ways, but often they move toward one of the two opposite extremes of aggression or passivity. Naturally strong kids learn to fight back, especially as they get older. Anger is power and preferable to humiliation, shame, fear, or grief. As these kids move into adulthood, experience has taught them to control others or be controlled. They have no other defense.[2]

Children who are more compliant and passive learn to detach from the situation and diminish their distressing feelings by becoming invisible. They work frantically to avoid conflict and to do what is expected.[3] They cannot overcome their fear in order to push back, so, as adults, they feel powerless to assert themselves and tend to marry controllers, who reinforce their belief that asserting oneself is dangerous and useless. The extreme mood swings produce a chaotic atmosphere that nevertheless grows familiar and therefore somewhat comfortable. But even moments of quiet are anxiety producing, since the kids learned long ago that any period of calm is just the lull before the storm.

Many times the stormy mistreatment in chaotic homes is passed from one generation to the next. Sadly, these parents were frequently abused themselves when they were growing up. They received little of value to pass on to their own children even though many of these folks desperately want to be good parents.

That desire is further foiled since relationships have never offered these folks much in the way of comfort or relief, so they are likely to numb their pain and quiet their struggles with one or more addictions to drugs, alcohol, sex, gambling, food, or pornography. These activities provide an escape and a distraction from the intense anxiety and pain held deep inside. Unfortunately a parent's preoccupation with these mood-altering activities renders him unavailable to his children, resulting in a repetitious cycle of abuse often passed from generation to generation.

There may be multiple marriages, divorces, and remarriages, but the structure of each tends to be a controller (victimizer) and a victim. One parent, the controller, controls with intimidation, fear, and/or violence. The partner is the underdog, helpless and passive in the face of ongoing abuse. Mental illnesses, such as major depression, postpartum depression, bipolar disorder, schizophrenia, and others, may contribute to the chaos.

Parents in chaotic homes have a high need to control and a low tolerance for noncompliance. And, since no one helped them learn to "feel and deal" and manage their feelings when they were kids, they also have a low threshold for stress and poor coping mechanisms as adults. Because these people's needs were never met when they were children, they are often children themselves living inside grown bodies. To survive childhood, they learned to cut off feelings of neediness or vulnerability. As a result, parenting is overwhelming, and the cries and demands of their own children give rise to feelings of agitation, frustration, and sometimes rage.

Furthermore, these parents do not have a well-developed internal system of self-reflection or self-restraint. For them, life is a series of reactions to the most recent event.[4] This lack of impulse control contributes to the likelihood of verbal, physical, or sexual abuse within the family. The presence of substance abuse, addictions, or mental illness adds to the chaos, resulting in a more bizarre and unpredictable environment for the child. These stressors can lead to extreme violence, sometimes resulting in homicide or suicide.

Marital discord is also pervasive in chaotic homes. Screaming, yelling, throwing things, and physical violence are how problems are addressed. Just as Doug did, children often witness violence between parents or the abuse of a sibling. One parent may disappear for periods of time and then return with no explanation. Divorce, live-ins, and remarriages all add to the confusion. Custody battles can be vicious and ugly, and children can become pawns in the parents' battle for revenge. If parents separate, siblings may be separated from one another, adding to each child's loss. If abuse is reported, children may be moved to a series of foster homes, adding to the instability of the child's world.

Unfortunately, chaotic homes are not as rare as we might hope. I was trying on clothes in a department-store dressing room recently. In the room next to me was a mother with her preschooler who appeared to be about three or four years old. He was whining and complaining that he was hungry and had to go to the bathroom. She began screaming at him to leave her alone. She told him to shut up and threatened him with a list of punishments if he did not comply. She ended her tirade with stinging words delivered in a disgusting tone: "I hate you, you little —— brat." The little boy yelled the words back at her with the same kind of terrifying anger. The exchange was heartbreaking. I tried to be sympathetic, gave her a business card, and said I'd like to help. She never called. And I couldn't help but wonder, if this was public behavior, what must have gone on at home behind closed doors.

WHAT'S IT LIKE TO BE THE KID?

In the chaotic home, connection is not just unavailable or sporadic. It's dangerous! While securely attached, mature parents can soothe and relieve their children's stress, chaotic parents are often the source of constant stress for their kids. In healthier homes, parents help when their children are anxious, but in chaotic families, the children become the target of many of their parents' negative emotions.

Infants respond to such an environment by avoiding eye contact, which is their only defense. Babies and toddlers become dazed and frozen almost as if they are trying to disappear.[5] Older children may run and hide or attempt to protect either younger siblings or the passive parent. To survive such an environment, children have to constantly adjust to the changing mood and behavior of their parents. While avoiders, pleasers, and vacillators are predictable parents, even in an unhealthy way, those moms and dads who have a chaotic love style leave children confused, disoriented, and unable to predict what will come next. Under such circumstances they can't learn a strategy for dealing with stress. Such a home environment presents "unsolvable paradoxes or overwhelming feelings without solutions."[6] Parents don't tolerate their children's expressions of sadness or anger because those emotions bring them too close to their own helplessness and the terror that remains unresolved.[7]

When They Can't Say It, They Play It

The effects of trauma are often observable in children's play—not everyday childhood play, but reenactments of traumatic events. What children have no words for, they often reenact in play. I have talked to women, for instance, who remember physically and sexually assaulting their dolls. I've spoken with men who confessed to torturing animals, never understanding the reason for this behavior. One woman described a play ritual she acted out with her brothers repeatedly. They pretended to be in a boat escaping from the parents, across the ocean, never to return.

Play is an attempt to get the trauma from the inside to the outside in a way that gives the child some control. I have observed children's abnormal play in my office that reveals knowledge beyond their years. One tool I provide is a sand tray and many small figures that can be used to create stories and scenes in the sand. During one session in my office, a young girl used those figures to enact a scene of group sex. As she created bizarre sex scenes, she became more and more anxious. Finally, in a frenzy, she buried the participants under every single toy on my shelves, a clear picture of her desire to bury these traumatic images in her head. She never uttered a word aloud; these were unspeakable things she had no words for. As a result of that session, I found out she had been exposed to pornography her dad had watched in her presence, and I understood more fully the story she was telling. The relief on her face at the end of that session was amazing.

An Impossible Task

During their preteen years in a chaotic home, most kids try not to rock the boat. They also become very adept at reading the signs of an approaching storm. These kids have to be constantly on the watch and alert to approaching danger. They also have to adapt to and live in this chaos. It is an impossible task. While some children become extremely compliant, others display their anger—away from their parents—by bullying other children, tormenting siblings, setting fires, or torturing animals. Their parents' behavior prompts overwhelming feelings, which the children are left to deal with on their own.

They're Here, But They're Far Away

When severe problems are ongoing, children become depressed or highly anxious. To survive the chaos of their life, imaginative children may learn to dissociate. (We all experience dissociation to some degree when we are absorbed in thought and unaware that we just passed our freeway exit.) As a response to abuse, children may cope by learning to "go someplace else" in their mind, entering a self-induced, hypnotic, trancelike state. Dissociation provides a way of escape so that the child is "not all there" during abusive episodes.

The act of forgetting is mastered over time since secrets must be guarded

under the threat of further abuse. Forgetting is made easier as the ability to dissociate improves. These God-given coping mechanisms can be so powerful that as
time goes on memories of the abuse can be forgotten and blocked from awareness
not long after the abuse occurs.[8]

Sybil's Not There

Taken a step further, when trauma is persistent, the child's personhood may frag-
ment into different pieces causing a condition known as dissociative identity disorder (formerly known as multiple personality disorder). The child uses the ability
to visualize and dissociate to create different people inside to cope with life's horrific events. Over time, the child's core self fragments into pieces. Different "parts"
emerge as needed, some of which endure the abuse and keep horrific events out of
the child's everyday awareness. This is an attempt to cope and spread the trauma
around so that day-to-day functioning is not completely impaired. These defenses
operate outside of awareness, though, so the child is not cognizant of these survival
strategies.

The movie *Sybil* offers an example of an adult who split into pieces. In this true
story, Sybil comes to her therapy appointments as completely different people who
have very dissimilar voices, mannerisms, and dress. This is an extreme example of
how some adults with this disorder (or defense) function; it's not the norm.

Clients with this disorder are often highly intelligent, and they do a masterful
job of hiding this inner chaos. It sometimes takes years for them to reveal how
extremely difficult and confusing life is for them. For many years of their lives, they
assumed other people had the same struggles and also felt confused, disoriented,
and overwhelmed. These clients are often unable to recognize the extent of their
injuries because their defenses developed slowly over many years, and they operate
automatically without awareness. Considering what they endured as kids, these
men and women have learned to compensate and function amazingly well.

Anxiety Is Their Constant Companion

Anxiety is the norm for kids who grow up in chaotic homes. It is omnipresent,
omnipotent, and all-consuming. Sleep disturbances, nightmares, and bedwetting

are all common. Learning difficulties may develop even if the child is very intelligent. Anxiety and the anticipation of going home can make focusing on schoolwork nearly impossible.

During adolescence, when the more strong-willed child becomes physically as big as the parents and able to match their strength, anger may erupt. The teen may take on the adult in the form of extremely violent altercations. Also, teenagers from chaotic homes are at jeopardy for substance abuse, sexual promiscuity, and high-risk behaviors, such as stealing or fighting, all of which provide an adrenaline rush that temporarily wards off depression. Finally, during these adolescent years, the tendency toward aggressiveness or passivity becomes more and more apparent. Eventually, kids from chaotic homes usually become intimidating controllers or passive victims, but sometimes use a combination of all the love styles.

WHAT ELSE MIGHT CAUSE A CHAOTIC LOVE STYLE?

Most chaotic love styles are a result of an environment created by injured parents, but abuse sometimes happens outside the home with devastating results. Case in point.

Raised by her grandmother after her mother abandoned her as an infant, Lilly was sexually abused by a neighbor for seven years. Only four years old when the abuse started, she was silenced by his threats to kill her grandmother if she told anyone. Lilly complied, and I was the first person to hear of her abuse.

Lilly had a few scant memories of abusive episodes when she began therapy, and she saw the abuse as irrelevant to her current problems. But she sought therapy after a string of relationships with abusive, controlling men, all of whom were selfish and exploited her sexually. At last Lilly began to see the connection between the past and her present relationships. Initially her grief was deeply buried, but over time her sadness emerged as she realized the profound effects of her abuse. Also, many of the men she dated had characteristics similar to her abuser, but her early experiences had taught her to ignore signs of danger and accept mistreatment. With time and hard work, Lilly learned to see red flags in relationships, assert herself, and set boundaries.

Another common problem in chaotic homes is sibling abuse because parental supervision is often seriously lacking. Older children may physically or sexually abuse younger children. Even in more intact homes, parents can be unaware of what occurs when children are left alone without someone in charge. Travis, for instance, suffered tremendously, and his parents had no idea. Travis was the favored child and a stellar athlete who absorbed what little attention his father had to give. His brother, Kent, was four years older and sullen, jealous, and angry. Mom worked as a real estate agent and was rarely home, especially on weekends.

When Travis was ten years old, Kent's anger erupted one day after school when no parent was home. Verbal bantering between the boys turned ugly. Kent beat Travis and then threatened to bash his head in with Travis's baseball bat. Kent became intoxicated with his newfound power, and the terrorizing became more vicious and regular. Kent's warning that he would smother Travis in his sleep if he told anyone was effective in keeping Travis quiet. It was four years before Travis could match his brother's strength, and the abuse stopped at that point. At twenty-four years old, Travis came to me for help because he was stressed by work, afraid of his boss, and suffering from anxiety and sleep disturbances.

THE CONTROLLER AND THE VICTIM BECOME ADULTS

What is life like after living in such homes growing up? Life can definitely get better, but it's a slow process, especially when the need for healing is not obvious. (Remember, when difficult circumstances are constant, they become the norm. If you live in a war zone long enough, you begin to forget the impact it is having on your mind, heart, and soul.) Sometimes when survivors of chaotic environments notice certain patterns repeating in their adulthood, it's a red flag that help is needed.

"Why Is Changing So Difficult?"

I regularly speak to groups of young (mostly Christian) mothers on this subject of how imprints influence the way we love. When I describe chaotic homes, I make a rather extreme statement, and so far it has never been refuted. "If you came from a chaotic home, you will struggle with anger and rage toward your own children. Even as a Christian. Praying can help, but it will not solve the problem entirely." In every group, tearful mothers come up to confirm my statement and share their struggles.

Why does that sentence strike such a chord? Many men and women from chaotic homes were afraid to express anger. When this is the case, anger gets buried and many times does not surface until chaotic adults marry and have their own children. The stresses of marriage and parenting often bring rage to the surface, and since they had no healthy childhood lessons on how to feel and deal, anger can feel overwhelming and unmanageable.

So why would a woman who was yelled at as a child rage at her own kids? Why would a woman abused as a child marry a violent man? Why does a teen, sexually abused as a child, get drawn into a life of prostitution? Why does a man, beaten regularly as a child by his own father, hook up with a woman who is verbally and physically abusive? Wouldn't it seem that as an adult one would be free to choose a better life? The injuries from these homes create deep wounds, and the resulting imprints are often more powerful than choices or desires. The challenges

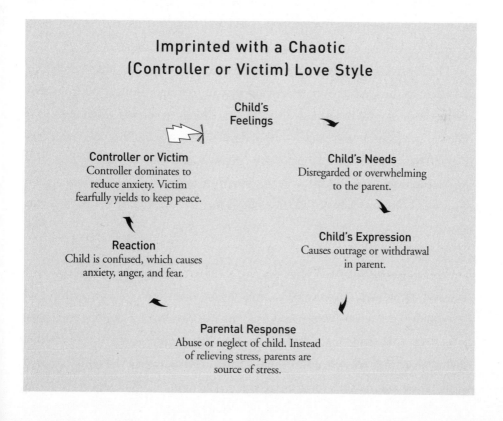

Imprinted with a Chaotic
(Controller or Victim) Love Style

Child's Feelings

Controller or Victim
Controller dominates to reduce anxiety. Victim fearfully yields to keep peace.

Child's Needs
Disregarded or overwhelming to the parent.

Reaction
Child is confused, which causes anxiety, anger, and fear.

Child's Expression
Causes outrage or withdrawal in parent.

Parental Response
Abuse or neglect of child. Instead of relieving stress, parents are source of stress.

of marriage are directly proportional to the depth of the childhood wounds. So be patient and give yourself time if this was your upbringing.

God has a tender heart toward these lost lambs. He often draws these wounded people into His family, and they are grateful for a loving Father who offers salvation. Certainly, salvation is a doorway into a new life where healing is possible, but the road is long, since there is a great deal of damage to work through. The church is full of adults who experienced chaotic homes. Sadly, even as believers, they tend to find one another and struggle with cycles of abuse in their own families.

"I Think I Was a Child Once; I Can't Remember"

I have not worked with a single person who came from a chaotic home who had any sympathy for the child he or she once was. Like Doug, whose story we just heard, these clients don't voluntarily talk about childhood events. When I ask them to do so, they minimize the experience with statements like "Everybody has problems" or "I survived." If I ask for specific memories, they have difficulty coming up with any. When they do remember sad and tragic events, they report those experiences with no emotion and often with laughter or a smile.

Detached from any feelings of pain or neediness, these wounded adults cannot relate to the tender, vulnerable child they once were. Also, cut off from their own feelings of grief or sadness, they find it difficult to tolerate those feelings in others. They have an unspoken—and understandable—belief that vulnerable feelings and shared needs expose one to pain, betrayal, and loss. Not having these feelings or expressing these needs protects them. And anger or depression and anxiety effectively keep their buried grief from surfacing.

"I Need Intensity"

The controller-victim style is often reactive and unpredictable, and for people with this style, high levels of stress are normal. Many times the only connection they experienced as children happened during intense moments of angry interchanges or inappropriate seduction. When things were calm and peaceful, these kids were often ignored, but they were apprehensive and nervous as they waited for the next battle. There was no such thing as relaxing in the moment. Who can relax during a tornado watch? The adrenaline rush produced by the body during intense, scary events can become addictive, and the addiction isn't resisted when the alternative is being left alone in anxious misery.

It's no wonder that with this background, chaotic adults can have a real need for intensity. Feeling agitated when things are peaceful, they may create chaos.[9] Provoking others into intense, angry, or seductive interchanges causes their adrenaline to flow, and life feels normal and familiar. Besides, aggravating or seducing or manipulating others gives chaotic adults control over the unpredictability of waiting. They call in the storm and get it over with—and this pattern operates without their conscious awareness.

As therapy progressed with Doug, he became aware how anxious he was when things were going well. "I'm always waiting for the rug to get pulled out from under me," he commented. Intensity was the norm for him. His first two marriages ended because of his temper. Then, like so many adults who have a chaotic love style, Doug was amazed how much better he could manage his anger after starting on medication. He was able to overcome his addiction to the marijuana he had used for years to calm his agitation. Many of our clients raised in chaotic homes respond extremely well to medication that helps to balance brain chemistry.[10]

The kind of intensity present in chaotic homes, the kind that unbalances brain chemistry, is a result of conflict. Kids growing up in that environment learn that when two people are fighting, they are connected. For some of these kids, this is the only kind of connection they have ever known. Once a client tried to bait me into fighting with her. When I wouldn't respond to any of her numerous attempts, she said in frustration, "I want you to fight with me!" She came from a family where criticism, fighting, and screaming were the norm. She wanted to feel a connection with me but was distrustful of kindness or tenderness, so she attempted to connect with me the only way she knew how.

"Why Is Marriage So Hard?"

If arguments always have a winner and a loser, where does one learn to compromise or negotiate? If chaotic adults were never asked how they felt, how can they access feelings and have words for them? If people have never experienced tenderness and nurturing, how can they know what they are missing? If relationships in the past have brought betrayal and abandonment, how can a person relax and trust?

These questions point to very real issues for people from chaotic childhoods, because value and respect are frequently unknown to them. Also, if their basic needs were neglected, they have no model for caring for themselves. It is easy to see how difficult their adult relationships are going to be if they enter marriage and parenting with negative imprints and no positive experiences of life's basic relational skills. Yet it's amazing how many people with this background tell us they're perplexed as to why marriage is so difficult. It had never occurred to them that they never acquired any skills growing up and that they will have to learn these as adults.

"Problems? What Problems?"

When trauma is the norm, extreme behaviors do not raise any concerns. But in dating or marital relationships, people from backgrounds that aren't chaotic may react with alarm at obvious signs of abuse while the chaotic couple is unperturbed. No alarms go off when things get out of hand. Old defenses kick in from long ago, and life goes on.

THE CONTROLLER BECOMES AN ADULT

Remember that the adult characteristics of every love style exist on a continuum from mild to extreme, and this is true for individuals with a chaotic love style. Males more often take the controller route, but females can also. In extreme cases, the controller will persistently exhibit the characteristics described in the next few paragraphs. Milder controllers may function quite well until they become stressed and these characteristics move to the foreground.

Deep wounds cause deep character problems, but of course, controllers have their own unique positive traits that vary from person to person. In the workbook, we emphasize the importance of identifying, appreciating, and encouraging specific positive qualities. These individuals received very little praise or admiration as kids, so they especially need it as adults.

Again, everyone has strengths and weaknesses, but we are focusing here on the problems a chaotic imprint causes when one's love style is control.

"It's Either Me or You"

Controllers need to be in charge because in their mind only one alternative exists: to be controlled. It's difficult for them to think otherwise if this is all they experienced growing up. Somebody wins, somebody loses, and there is no such thing as negotiation or compromise. Since controllers most often marry victims, it may not take much aggression, badgering, or harassment to keep their spouses in line. What was done to controllers as children, they now do to others. Their childhood wounds underlie this style, and being controlled by anyone or anything brings them all too close to the painful past, so it simply won't be tolerated. The problem is that controllers have little connection to those earlier painful experiences.

"I Don't Want You Out of My Sight"

Controllers are threatened when a spouse has other interests or relationships. They have never really felt wanted or cherished, so they are on guard, always expecting to be replaced or abandoned. To prevent this from happening, they may discourage or even forbid a spouse's contact with friends or relatives. This lowers their anxiety about potential loss. The spouse of the controller may face relentless questioning, being asked to account for every action and every minute of the day.

"Don't Question Me"

Controllers may be superficial and charming in order to get their way. They are frequently deceitful and manipulative in order to gain money, sex, or power. Lying can become pathological, and the controller may become full of rage if questioned.

"I Didn't Do Anything Wrong"

Controllers have difficulty feeling remorse and repentance, because they believe that others deserve what they get. Quick to blame others for their own actions, controllers are experts at rationalizing their behavior no matter what consequences they encounter. Controllers can, for instance, hurt loved ones, mistreat people, and steal without really feeling they have done anything wrong. Sometimes, after an episode of rage and violence, they make promises that it will not happen again in order to reengage the victim and regain control.

"How Could You Be So Stupid?"

The controller is highly critical of people and constantly belittles family members. Any noncompliance may be met with excessive punishment or increased measures of control. Withdrawing, threats of abandonment, beatings, and withholding money all serve to keep others in line.

"Anger Keeps Me Safe"

If one peels away their defenses, controllers have many flashes of insecurity and incompetence. How could it be otherwise? Void of early experiences of nurturing, support, and guidance, they are unprepared for the adult world. Anger keeps these insecure feelings from surfacing or becoming overwhelming. Many times in my office, when I observe an angry outburst, we stop and try to discover what triggered it. Often it begins with a flash of shame, unworthiness, guilt, or a feeling of incompetence. These were such painful and common childhood feelings that anger became and remains the controller's automatic and instant response, effectively blocking the pain.

"I Quit My Job; My Boss Is a Jerk"

Controllers have trouble with authority of any kind, so they impulsively quit jobs with no forethought as to the consequences. Or their unexplained absences from work and irresponsible behavior result in job loss and financial instability. These scenarios add stress to the marriage and family.

THE VICTIM BECOMES AN ADULT

"It's Not So Bad"

When one grows up in a chaotic home, survival depends on distorting reality, minimizing the insanity, and becoming used to living in intolerable circumstances.

Children have no other choice, so the skill of denial is well developed by the time they reach adulthood. And that skill helps explain why abuse is tolerated, excused, and rationalized—and why it continues.

"It's My Fault"

Victims are trapped in the belief that they are bad, flawed, defective, and unlovable. The controller readily gives out blame, and the victim readily accepts it. Internalizing the childhood message that the anger is their fault, victims truly believe they hold the power to make the controller behave more appropriately. If only they could "get it right," life would be better.

"Anything Is Better Than Being Alone"

The fear of being alone and unable to care for oneself or one's children keeps a victim dependent and trapped. Actual experiences of abandonment as a child may have been so painful that victims make frantic attempts to avoid getting close to that childhood wound. Often, therefore, they remain in unhealthy abusive relationships for long periods of time.

"It's Hopeless"

Being in the role of the victim is both humiliating and exhausting. Depression is practically a given, and suicidal urges may come and go. Self-destructive behaviors, such as anorexia and bulimia or self-mutilation, are common, as are addictive behaviors that help victims cope with the pain. Even when resources, such as money, shelter, or a caring person are available, victims often reject them, acting on feelings of worthlessness and hopelessness that are ingrained and pervasive.

"Numb Is Better"

Many victims live in a state of numbed detachment. No longer affected by the horrors in their lives, they go through the motions of life in a robotlike way, and the lifelessness in their eyes is observable. For them, feelings are mostly about pain, so it's better not to feel much of anything.

"I'll Be Good"

Complying with the demands of the controller, no matter how unreasonable, is the strategy by which victims try to ward off further abuse. When controllers make jealous inquiries as to their daily activities, victims will provide information, and when controllers make requests, victims will participate in dangerous, uncomfortable behaviors that often include sexual exploitation. Boundaries are nonexistent because any resistance will enrage the controller.

"The Secret Is Safe with Me"

What goes on behind closed doors is often well hidden from the public. The victim knows if the abuse is acknowledged or spoken about, retaliation will be swift, intense, and perhaps life threatening. So keeping up appearances is another exhausting job of the victim, but it's a job mastered long ago when childhood abuse was kept secret.

More than once, I have had the wives of church elders come for counseling and reveal the chaos that reigned in their homes. External appearances suggested the perfect, godly family. Behind closed doors, however, the family was ruled by a raging dictator. One former client had a father who was the pastor of a prosperous, growing, Bible-teaching church. Behind closed doors at home, though, he regularly sexually abused all three of his daughters. When they were teens, one of the girls—in desperation—told one of the church elders. The public act this family had put on for years was too good, and the elder decided her report couldn't be true. The elder secretly dismissed this young woman's brave action as a lie, and the abuse continued.

"I Don't Feel Well"

What cannot be spoken about will be carried around in the body, and the stress takes its toll, resulting in health problems. Headaches, gastric problems, fatigue, weight problems, high blood pressure, and so on, are common stress-induced ailments. When my clients are suffering from one, I often ask them to give a voice to the physical symptom: "If your ulcer could talk, what would it say?" The parallel to the feelings within the client is often remarkable, as the following example illustrates.

In my practice, I saw a female client who was living with an abusive and controlling man. His angry outbursts, verbal abuse, and sexual escapades outside the marriage were relentless. She spent several years in therapy, faced a great deal of pain, and grew tremendously, but she had difficulty taking the final step of leaving him.

She had constant stomach problems, which she complained about one day in a session. When I asked her to give her stomach a voice, she replied, "You will never get rid of me. I will always torment you and make you miserable." She gasped in recognition and decided to act on her biblical right to leave him (he had committed adultery). As soon as she was on her own, her stomach problems greatly decreased. Again, I am always amazed how closely physical aliments can reflect trauma.

"How Can I Protect the Kids When I'm Still One Myself?"

In a home where there is a controller and a victim, the victim functions like one of the children when the controller is present. I have known husbands who watched their wives abuse their children, and wives who have watched their husbands do the same. Denial, numbing, and fear of further angering the controller allow the abuse to continue. For victims to step in and act like adults is very difficult because no one helped them grow up in healthy ways.

"My Anger Has to Go Somewhere"

Many women and men seem to survive their chaotic backgrounds fairly well until they marry and have children. The stress of the long-term relationship and the demands of needy kids can push the internal chaos to the surface. When the controller is out of the home, for instance, the victim is left in charge. The victim's pent-up anger and humiliation can erupt toward the children, who may assert themselves more with the passive parent.

GROWTH GOALS

Although people from chaotic backgrounds have serious relational injuries, they rarely seek help. Financial difficulties, denial, and entrenched roles contribute to stubborn patterns of unhealthy independence and self-sufficiency that are difficult to acknowledge and break. The beginning of change may be prompted when the victim enters a shelter after years of domestic abuse or due to court-ordered therapy after the police or child protective services become involved with a family. Healing cannot take place in an unsafe environment, yet few chaotic individuals (if any) have ever experienced safety, acceptance, or grace. So their first steps of growth almost always take place outside the home, where controllers as well as victims can experience safety and support for the first time.

Remember Doug's story from the beginning of this chapter? His involvement in a men's group prompted the first healthy changes in his life. He is still in that group, and his family is noticing his growth. Initially, it was easier for him to experience love and acceptance from these men than from his own wife and family. Why? Because at home Doug was too controlled by his imprint to make much progress. He was very reactive in his relationships with his wife, kids, and stepkids. Facing daily problems and stresses within his family made it difficult for Doug to calm down long enough to experience any productive growth at home. Within his men's group, though, he was away from these stressors and able to respond positively to the men in his group. Eventually, as he experienced love and grace from these men, he softened, and his family could see the difference.

We hope some folks who have been hurt by chaotic homes when they were growing up will not only read this book but also take the time to do the exercises in the workbook. We have seen some marvelous examples of healing, but it takes time and hard work. But, when you think about it, that hard work beats the alternative of living your adult life in the prison of your past.

Chapter 9

Identifying Your Love Style

By now it's entirely possible you've been able to recognize your and your spouse's love styles. But if not, bear in mind that while recognizing your love styles is important, it's not necessary to nail down your definitive description immediately. Don't be alarmed if you don't strongly identify with any one particular style right away. Simply seeing how interactions between you and your spouse may be influenced by the different styles is an important starting point. Considering the different patterns you may have adopted and which styles your spouse sees in you is often an ongoing exercise.

As you work to identify your styles, it could be worthwhile to consider your parents' styles and those of stepparents or other influential people who helped raise you. Each influence likely played a role if you respond to close relationships in diverse ways. Reading about the combinations and core patterns in marriage may also help. You may also begin to see yourselves in the interactions that commonly occur as various imprints collide, or even as you read through the growth goals both here and in the workbook. If after doing all this you still relate to more than one style, start with the style that is predominant in your marriage. Look through the goals for that style and decide with your spouse which ones might be most helpful to work on in drawing you closer together.

Often, however, your husband's or wife's unhealthy love style may be much more obvious to you than your own. If you are struggling in your marriage, focusing on the behaviors of your spouse can make it difficult to see yourself objectively. You might ask your spouse what relational style best characterizes you.

Similarly, since identifying your imprint requires introspection, that identification may pose a problem if you've never stopped to reflect on your feelings and experiences growing up. Working through the first eight chapters of the workbook could help you think about how your childhood experiences shaped you.

Now, once you determine which love style characterizes you, you may not be able to connect to the type of family situation that produces that style. Ultimately, that's not so important. You don't have to understand the origin of your imprint to identify which style you resonate with. The goal is simply to find the starting point from which you can move on to begin the process of growth. As we said to a woman at a recent conference, "It doesn't matter why you're wearing the shoe; what matters is that it fits."

One more thing. We find that people from chaotic homes (discussed in chapter 8) often see themselves on nearly every page. (It's also not uncommon for people from chaotic backgrounds to initially feel confused as they read about the different imprints.) The chaotic imprint often produces a victim or a controller, but it can also result in an extremely vacillating style depending on the person's stage of life and current relationship. People from chaotic homes may also have erected a barrier of denial and developed the habit of minimizing the real trauma that occurred in their lives. Until there is a truthful picture about the past, your imprint may be difficult to assess.

What If You Have More Than One Style?

Many people have more than one style arising from several imprints in childhood. Some people may see themselves using one style in marriage and another at work or with friends. Marie, a pastor's wife, said, "I am a pleaser with my friends. I am definitely the giver and always playing the peacemaker and trying to make everyone happy. In my marriage I do a little of that, but I find myself acting more like an avoider with my husband. I think it might be because I never received much from my dad, so I'm uncomfortable being vulnerable or needing very much from my husband." Since her marriage is her most important relationship, I asked Marie to initially focus on her tendency to avoid.

Jerry had a different problem. Like Marie, he was an avoider in his marriage, but Jerry tended to be a vacillator in his work relationships, especially with women. He explained, "I gave up trying to be close to my wife after the kids were born. It was too much work. I have never had an affair, but I find myself feeling intensely attracted to several women at work. There is a passion that is missing in my marriage, and it's so easy to have deep talks with some of the women I meet in my sales job. I'm great at connecting, and I find myself planning my sales calls to coincide with the lunch hour so I have more time to talk. Eventually, I get scared and cool it because I don't want to wreck my marriage or hurt my kids, but it's hard to stop myself."

Jerry discovered that his intense attraction was not really about intimacy at all but about intensity. Flirting with danger made him feel excited in contrast to the boredom of his marriage. If he divorced his wife and married one of these women, real life would eventually set in, and he'd be on the hunt once again. We worked on Jerry's avoider tendencies with his wife, and that helped him develop a deeper, more vulnerable connection with her. As he began to grow, he realized that if he couldn't find intimacy in real life with his wife, he would struggle to find it with anyone else as well. He acknowledged that he liked the initial intensity with the women at work, but he saw that it was a counterfeit for deeper connection. If you see yourself as a blend of styles like Marie or Jerry, focus on the imprint that is most visible in your relationship with your spouse.

Some people, however, see themselves using a blend of several styles within their marriage. Lauren said, "I'm a blend of the avoider and the pleaser. I was a good kid growing up, and as an adult, I try hard to keep everyone happy. But I don't relate to the pleasers' pursuing when they are upset. I'm more likely to keep to myself if I think my husband is upset with me. I really relate to the avoider's tendency to isolate. When my sister died of breast cancer, I withdrew and distanced myself from my husband and friends. I never let anyone comfort me. It just never occurred to me that I needed comfort."

I asked Lauren what most hindered intimacy in her marriage, her tendency to please or to avoid. She thought for a few moments and said, "Probably avoid. I can see how I have difficulty being the receiver or asking for anything, especially if I'm feeling crummy. I don't always know what I feel." Lauren had found her starting place.

A final example is Sam's. Sam related to both the pleaser and the vacillator. His wife described him as very helpful and wanting to please at home and at work. She also noted that he was often overcommitted, because he was always helping somebody. Like the pleaser, Sam did not like being alone, but he wasn't fearful in that he loved adventure, travel, and new projects. It was easy for him to take risks in these areas. His vacillator traits showed up when he was tired and overextended. Unlike the pleaser and more like the vacillator, he got angry that others were not meeting his expectations, and he could see little good in his wife when he was upset and disappointed in her. He could not receive once he was angry, and he was impossible to console. At some point, though, he would be "over it" and back into the pleaser mode until the pattern repeated again. When I asked him which traits he considered most harmful to his marriage, he said, "I know I hurt my wife when I'm angry, because I say unkind things." I suggested he focus on the growth goals for the vacillator, especially the instruction about integrating good and bad.

Finally, bear in mind that each style exists on a continuum. You may act out your style at a moderate level in a particular relationship, but at a very high level in your other relationships. However, if you begin to recognize specific symptoms—behaviors and responses—of a particular style, focus on that chapter and pay special attention to any specific growth goals.

CAN YOU CHANGE STYLES?

We are often asked this question at seminars: "I was married to an avoider during my first marriage and I was a pleaser. I was always chasing my husband around trying to get him to pay attention to me, and I put up with a lot. Now I'm married to a pleaser, and I get more attention than I want. As a result, I act more like a vacillator. Can that be right?"

We may react differently when we are relating to people with different styles, especially in marriage. What's important is focusing on whatever dance you're doing in your current relationship, not comparing your behavior in one relationship to your behavior in another.

Since it's so important to understand the individual styles that create core patterns in marriage, let's take a few minutes to review the uniquenesses of each style before we move on to the combinations.

AVOIDERS

- I tend to be private and self-sufficient.
- I am usually "fine" and tend to resist connection and affection, and I am not very affectionate toward others.
- I have few emotions.
- Sometimes I comply simply to avoid arguments.
- I generally don't ask for any sort of emotional investment or commitment from people.
- I minimize and resist expressions of anger in others and myself, yet I do get angry when people try to get too close.
- I'm usually happiest when others are happy and don't want a lot from me.
- I'm a task-oriented high achiever.
- I prefer to do something for someone or give gifts rather than connect emotionally.
- I've felt resentment toward my spouse for wanting something more from me.
- I'm tired of hearing how distant I am.
- I don't really think about my own feelings and needs very often.

PLEASERS

- People knew me as "the good kid."
- I struggle with fear of rejection or criticism.
- Sometimes I seek deeper connection by working to meet others' needs.

- I have needs but they're not as big as most people's.
- At times I've had difficulty tolerating physical or emotional distance from my spouse.
- I prefer to deal with conflict by making up for it quickly and moving on.
- I can be very jealous, though I rarely show it.
- I have difficulty saying no and sometimes it makes me less than truthful.
- I generally don't feel angry, or if I do, I try to think about something else to get rid of it.
- Sometimes I resent giving more than I get and feel like a doormat.
- I don't often ask for help and feel uncomfortable when others try to give me assistance.

VACILLATORS

- I've always been especially sensitive.
- I desire deep, passionate connection with my spouse but never seem to get it.
- I've had a history of idealizing others early on in relationships.
- I easily feel disappointed, rejected, or unwanted.
- I sometimes become angry when my expectations are not met.
- I can feel betrayed, abandoned when others are not emotionally available.
- I experience internal conflict and a high level of emotional stress in relationships.
- My own conflicted responses sometimes confuse even me.
- Others have said they feel like they are walking on eggshells around me.
- I have difficulty accepting the weaknesses of others.
- I usually feel angry instead of sad over disappointment with others.
- I have difficulty being willing to reengage when anger blocks out other emotions.
- I tend to reflect more on how others have hurt me than on my own shortcomings.

CONTROLLERS

- Growing up, I experienced a great deal of intense anger and stress from a parent or parents.
- I'm used to chaos at home.
- I've learned to protect myself through aggression.
- I don't like to consider the alternative if I weren't so dominant.
- I tend not to think about the past and stay busy with the present.
- My spouse couldn't survive without me.
- Our relationship problems are usually my spouse's fault.
- I rarely feel any emotion except anger and sometimes guilt if my anger has gone too far.
- Things would go more smoothly if my spouse listened to me and did the things I ask.
- My spouse purposely makes me jealous.
- I get angry when others don't listen.
- I have few feelings about my childhood except I'm glad it's over because I wouldn't go back.

VICTIMS

- Growing up, I experienced a great deal of intense anger and stress from a parent or parents.
- I'm used to chaos at home.
- I've learned to protect myself through passivity.
- I don't like to consider the alternative if I weren't quiet and submissive.
- I don't often assert myself.
- Relationship problems are usually my own fault.
- I try very hard to keep my mate happy, but it doesn't always work.
- At times I'm honestly scared of my spouse.
- I'm resentful and angry but try not to focus on it.

- I feel trapped and hopeless most of the time.
- No one really knows me or what goes on in my marriage.
- My spouse is much nicer to friends than to me.

If you've been able to identify your love style from these statements, can you begin to imagine what happens when these love styles collide in a marriage? Each partner brings his or her individual imprint into the relationship. Those imprints eventually clash and become duets that damage. And, although every couple that comes to our workshops feels their problems are somehow unique, these duets have common themes. In fact, each of the various combinations of love styles will produce a very predictable core pattern or reactive dynamic which, when understood, can be changed. You will probably recognize the core pattern in your own marriage as you read the pages that follow.

These core patterns are like a dance that every husband and wife do as they try to relate to each other. Their dance steps were choreographed, learned, and imprinted long ago during their formative years. Although these adults may consider their childhood a distant memory, these imprints animate their feelings and reactions within their marriage. When a couple is unaware of these animating forces, their marriage is usually struggling, headed in a negative direction, and they feel helpless to change it. And as these couples contemplate the damage after a conflict, they usually feel very alone and isolated, imagining—wrongly—that the Smiths next door are somehow able to get along just fine.

Although there are many possible combinations, we are going to focus on the six damaging dances that we see most often. The duets are unpleasant, and the descriptions may prompt distressing emotions, but take heart. You'll find hope in the chapters ahead.

Part

3

⨝⨝⨝

Duets That Damage How We Love

Chapter 10

The Vacillator Marries the Avoider

J ulie called my (Milan's) office to make an appointment for herself and her husband, Brian, to begin marriage counseling. When I asked her to give me a brief overview of what was going on between them, she told me that I was the last resort. (I hate this kind of pressure.) She had been deeply wounded by her unavailable and uncommunicative husband.

She went on to say, "I've tried everything to get him to open up and want to be with me… He just shuts down again and again. I feel invisible around him. He just won't pay attention to me. We were madly in love when we were dating. We spent every day together, and he couldn't get enough of me. He was somewhat quiet, but I knew that our love would grow into something wonderful. He started his career, and I was tolerant, accommodating his busy schedule. He kept telling me he would have more time once his sales territory was built to a certain level, and I believed him. Sometimes I would get impatient with him, but he would snap at me, so I just stuffed my feelings because I was afraid to stress him further. I told myself that he was just under pressure and that as the stress subsided he would turn his attention to me, and it would be like when we were dating again."[1]

"Are there some good times?" I asked.

Julie continued. "Yes, it's wonderful when we go to Hawaii without the kids. He pays attention to me for a whole week, and it's like old times. I keep telling myself that soon things will be like this at home, too. Yet, even when we are on these trips, sometimes he just fades away on me, and when I ask him about it, he says he's thinking about work. That hurts. I mean, we're on vacation."

Julie had more to say. "It was somewhere between our first and second child that I began to get really angry with him. I concluded that life was really all about him and his work and that I was not important. I also gave up thinking he was going to change. What really infuriates me is he plays golf with his clients on Friday afternoons. If he has time to play golf, then he could be with me, but evidently he has chosen golf over me. I'm really hurt, and I consider this abusive. When he gets home, I remind him that he is late, and then I ask him 'So, when's it my turn?' He just gets angry and goes up to his study. Then I'm even angrier, so I follow him up to the room and we fight. Then the kids are crying, and the weekend is ruined.[2] So that's why I'm calling you! He needs another person to tell him how he is damaging me! Can you fix him?"

After setting an appointment, I thought my biggest challenge might not be "fixing" Brian but rather trying to convince Julie that she was also a part of the marital problem. I also had a hunch that Julie might be a vacillator. People with that imprint often don't recognize their own attachment injury. They are usually sensitive men and women who idealize relationship and romance and who are hurt when reality sets in. Lacking a level of introspection as to their culpability in the downward marital spiral, they become negatively fixated on those who hurt or disappoint them. Trying to help people like Julie see their role can be incredibly difficult because accumulated resentment and bitterness have built up by the time they walk into my office.

So what was really happening between Julie and Brian? Remember, for instance, Julie's idealization of marriage and romance evident in her initial refusal to see Brian's flaws and readiness to make excuses for him, all the while waiting for more attention. Julie herself was able to pinpoint the end of the idealization phase and identify when anger set in. I expected Julie to struggle to name any of Brian's positive traits, because the devaluing phase was now underway.

What Julie didn't yet realize was that Brian is most likely an avoider and that they have a core relational pattern typical of an avoider-vacillator combination.[3] In fact, unbeknownst to Julie, I was working with seven other avoider-vacillator couples.[4] In one of our recent workshops, roughly one third of the couples attending were dealing with this dynamic. The good news is that this common dynamic is predictable and repairable. (I don't like using Julie's word "fix." It reminds me of an animal getting spayed or neutered at the vet's office.)

After I saw Julie and Brian for several sessions, my suspicions were confirmed. I learned that Brian grew up in West Los Angeles, the last of three children whose arrival was a surprise to everyone. His father was a busy surgeon, and his mother had gone back to law school, passed the bar, and was in a busy family practice. There was a gap of eight years between Brian and the next sibling, so by the time Brian was in elementary school, his older siblings were busy in junior high and high school with sports and activities.

Brian's busy professional parents were engrossed in their jobs, and Brian was basically on his own. His parents came home late in the evenings, tired and emotionally distant after working their demanding jobs. They had high expectations for his performance at school and constantly nagged him about his grades. Brian learned to be self-sufficient: he would eat dinner alone and retreat to his room. Brian's parents saw him as easygoing and independent. As they praised his self-sufficiency, however, they unknowingly discouraged any healthy dependence. They didn't realize it, but their unstated message to Brian was, "Grow up and take care of yourself." Although Brian was lonely as a teenager, he valued his independence and had never given much thought to his relationship with his parents.

And Brian learned well to do exactly what his family of origin was telling him to do. He learned to keep his feelings inside and disavow any appearance of neediness. When Brian's girlfriend broke up with him during his senior year of high school, he was devastated. He isolated himself from others, poured himself into extra practice sessions for the golf team, and studied harder for his SAT exam. He didn't tell his parents anything until they happened to notice that she hadn't been around for several days, which in reality had been several weeks. Brian never shared his feelings or expected comfort. He had never learned soul words with which to share what was in his heart.

As Brian went through college, his avoider imprint grew more entrenched, so that by the time he graduated, he had unknowingly mastered the art of self-sufficiency and emotional detachment. But, like Julie, Brian was unaware of his relational dance or that he had difficulty connecting with others. During the end of his senior year of college, Brian met Julie at the gym. She was fun, outgoing, and quick to praise his positive qualities and laugh at his jokes. Brian loved the attention she lavished on him and wanted to be with her constantly. She made him feel so alive. For the first time in his life, someone was really paying attention to him.

Many times avoiders like Brian are initially attracted to vacillators, because it has been a long time since they have felt any level of connection, and vacillators are good at tuning in to others and making them feel noticed and important. For the avoider, this attention is water for a thirsty soul, and the first taste is intoxicating and satisfying. But what attracted Julie to Brian? A look into Julie's past will reveal the answer.

Julie came from a home with a lot of fighting and conflict rather than an emotionally distant home like Brian's. This frenzied atmosphere left Julie, a sensitive child, in a state of inner agitation and anxiousness. After I had several conversations with her in my office, Julie's history slowly began to unfold. Julie's mother was thrilled when she was born. She had especially wanted a little girl and was devoted and attentive to Julie. Her father had an affair, and the marriage ended when Julie was four years old. Julie's mom suffered through a serious depression after the breakup and was emotionally unavailable for much of the next year. Her mom remarried suddenly when Julie was seven, and the new marriage was a roller coaster with a lot of fighting. Julie recalled being scared of this new man in the house.

Julie's dad came to see her infrequently and sometimes forgot about the special times he promised to spend with her. When it was his week to be with her, per the joint-custody agreement, he sometimes forgot to pick up Julie after her long day at day care. Even when Julie was with her dad, she remembered how he fell asleep on the couch, and she would finish her homework and put herself to bed. (As an adult, Julie learned that her dad had a secret addiction to cocaine and sex. He was often gone to Las Vegas for the weekend.)

As Julie went through her teenage years, her mother divorced again. She soon began dating several men, and Julie was jealous, wanting her mother to herself. Her mother finally met Ted, a man whom she married when Julie was fourteen. Julie didn't like sharing her mom, especially since she got so little of her dad's attention. Angry, Julie often fought with her new stepdad, and that upset her mom. So, starved for consistent attention, Julie dated any boy who asked, compromising her values while telling herself that he really loved her. She hoped to keep these boys close by offering them sex because, after all, they really did love her...didn't they?

Julie knew she wanted a relationship that would last. Her dream was to have security and stability—and along came stable, successful Brian. He had worked all through college and by graduation had a reputation as a great businessman. He had proven himself to be a shooting star in a sales organization and was talked about as "the kid who could sell sand to Iran." At work, he was solid, professional, hard working, and very methodical about life and responsibilities. Julie was attracted to Brian's stability; she saw him as steady and consistent, a welcome relief from her shaky past. His handsome face and great physique were added bonuses. He was exactly what Julie had always wanted. After a few weeks of dating, she idolized him and knew he was the one. He was perfect! Or was he?

Remember, Brian was an avoider, imprinted to close off his emotions and retreat when he was uncomfortable. Julie, on the other hand, kept hoping for real connection, and she constantly looked for someone to pay attention to her. Believing that others had the power to make her feel wanted and valued, Julie focused on them. Having been abandoned as she grew up, she was intensely attuned to the attentiveness of others and the time they gave her. Julie keenly monitored closeness and distance in relationships, and distance meant betrayal and abandonment.

Looking at the Roots

Julie believed that all her happiness would be found in Brian. (This, by the way, is a weight that nobody can shoulder.) She idealized marriage and ignored from the start the fact that Brian really wasn't very engaging or self-disclosing. Julie mistook the initial intensity of their dating relationship as intimacy. Brian liked the attention and wanted to be with her, but he never showed any vulnerable feelings because he didn't know how to. Now, as they sat in my office, Brian was no different from when Julie had married him. What had changed was her perception of him.

In the early years of their marriage, Julie stuffed her desire for closeness because

Brian would snap at her when she made him uncomfortable. She coped by using subtle forms of denial and clinging to her hopes for an idealized future. One day, though, Julie realized that the gap between fantasy and reality would always exist, and the lonely feelings of abandonment she had felt many times as a child and adolescent—feelings which she had thought were a thing of the past—swelled up within her. Brian was not only hurting her by his avoidance, but his persistent lack of attention was triggering old feelings of abandonment from the past. Julie's anger at Brian was definitely turbocharged.

Brian, on the other hand, had no idea what she wanted out of "being together." He wanted and needed very little emotional connection, and he could not understand what all the fuss was about. Julie's praise and attention—which he'd loved—had turned into complaints and anger, and at this point, he would rather be alone. The pressure and intensity of her emotions caused him to retreat further. Brian felt overwhelmed by Julie's neediness. After a conflict, Julie would withdraw and sulk for days. Attempts to assuage her anger were often met with statements that he would have to pay back or earn his way out of the hole he was in. Soon Brian also became angry, but he expressed his anger quietly. He simply found excuses to stay away from the house longer.

The Core Pattern: The Vacillator and the Avoider

The avoider and the vacillator handle their childhood hurts in opposite ways. The avoider gives up the desire for connection and becomes self-sufficient, but vacillators make connection their primary goal. They believe something good—something that will make life wonderful—is just around the corner. After the avoider has been married to the vacillator for a while, the vacillator pursues the independent spouse in an effort to get his or her attention. Avoiders then feel overwhelmed and anxious, so they disengage and retreat. This retreat agitates the vacillators, and their anger intensifies as they feel rebuffed and abandoned. Their displays of anger and disappointment make avoiders retreat further. Over time, the chase scene picks up speed as well as intensity and leads this couple on a perilous, roller-coaster journey.[5] But there is a way off, and we'll get to that in a minute. First, let's look at another couple dealing with this vacillator-avoider dynamic.

ELIZABETH AND JOE

Elizabeth and Joe first met at church in the career singles group. When mutual friends invited them to double date, they enjoyed the evening and discovered they had many mutual interests, such as roller blading, jogging, and bike riding. They dated for one year, and Joe began talking about marriage. Elizabeth wanted to finish her marketing degree, and having gone through a difficult divorce, she wasn't as anxious to get married. But when Joe surprised her with a ring, she set her fears aside, and they became officially engaged.

Wanting this marriage to succeed, Elizabeth read book after book, attempting to learn all she needed to know. And Joe was so excited about the wedding day that he could hardly contain himself. He secretly had a larger diamond set into the middle of Elizabeth's ring. During the ceremony, her eyes almost popped out as he put the new ring on her finger. Later he watched proudly as her bridal party ogled over it.

Elizabeth and Joe had taken dance lessons, and their bride-and-groom dance was a smooth swing version of "Moondance" by Van Morrison. They were a sensation and got a standing ovation, which thrilled Joe to no end. Later, though, he was surprised to feel a twinge of anxiety when he found himself alone for a few minutes, on the sidelines, watching his new bride dance with all the girls in her bridal party. She was having so much fun…without him. Soon it was time to cut the cake, so he brushed off the unpleasant feelings and had fun exchanging bites (smears) of cake. He promptly forgot about the incident. After all, an exciting night of romance and closeness awaited him.

The next day Joe whisked Elizabeth off to an incredibly exotic island in the South Pacific for a two-week honeymoon. The thoughts of uninterrupted romance and constant connection made his heart beat faster. On the third day, though, Joe and Elizabeth had a fight that agitated them both, and for Joe, the trip was ruined. Here's what happened.

Joe had already been irritated, feeling ignored because Elizabeth had been reading by the pool for much of the afternoon. When she asked him to go for a run down the beach and he didn't want to, she went by herself. He sat there, alone by the pool, with the same loneliness and irritation he had felt at the wedding reception; he was on the sidelines, left out, again.

When Elizabeth returned forty-five minutes later, she was baffled that Joe was so withdrawn, had his eyes closed, and was answering her with one-word responses and grunts. Assuming he was tired and trying to rest, she picked up her book and started to read again. Evidently, this was all he could take, and she was shocked when he picked up his towel in a huff and walked up to their room where he pouted and sulked.

After a couple of days, things settled down, and the rest of the honeymoon was fairly uneventful. But a small seed of distrust had been implanted into their hearts and minds. Joe's attitude toward Elizabeth had cooled slightly by the end of the trip, and Elizabeth's stomach had begun to hurt some of the time, which she soothed by reading and running.

When they came into my office two years later, the pattern had escalated. Joe was always angry and irritated at Elizabeth for not meeting his expectations, and she was scared, angry, and contemplating divorce. Her recent fact-finding trip to the lawyer, which Joe had found out about, had pushed him over the edge, and he was furious.

"Why can't I get closer to her?" he wanted to know. "And why won't she have sex with me as often as I want? Why won't she pursue me with the same intensity I pursued her?"

And Elizabeth had her own questions: "Why can't he give me space and room to breathe? Why can't I ever say no to sex and not have him pout for the next two days? I can't get him off my back. He overwhelms me, and I feel like I'm getting an ulcer."

LOOKING AT THE ROOTS

After listening to their story, I thought to myself, "Vacillator and avoider combo!" So I said, "Let me take a guess. Somewhere in your childhood, Elizabeth, you learned to live in a somewhat independent way. Odds are that no one ever asked you much about the things inside your head and heart, and you adapted by mastering your studies and achieving your goals. I bet your parents were proud of your accomplishments and appreciated your self-sufficiency. Perhaps you spent a lot of time alone. But when your family was together, I'm guessing that feelings were minimized and emotions were rarely shown."

Looking at Joe I said, "And it sounds like you experienced some abandonment in your childhood, and you couldn't count on anyone being there for you. Perhaps someone would pay attention, but then that person would disappear, leaving you unhappy and wondering when he or she would come back."

They stared at me and then turned to each other and said, "Did you call him and talk with him before we came in? What did you tell him?" Shaking their heads, they looked at me and said, "How do you know?"

I smiled and asked for more details about what growing up had been like for both of them. In the next half hour, I learned that Joe's dad was an alcoholic, and his mom had divorced him when Joe was two years old. He grew up spending a lot of time in day care longing for the headlights of his mom's car to appear in the parking lot. Often he was one of the last kids out the door. She was a dedicated, hard-working mom who loved him deeply, yet as a single mom, she had many responsibilities.

Joe's dad would promise a weekend visit but often wouldn't show up. His mom tried to be positive, but after Joe watched at the door for several hours, she would say, "I guess he's not coming. Maybe he's busy at work so we'll try to give him a call later." Many years later his dad missed his college graduation.

Joe's longing for people to notice and care for him had become paramount in his hierarchy of needs and desires. He had, however, never considered that he wanted Elizabeth to make up for the empty, lonely parts of his childhood. And those many childhood experiences of waiting for others to be available for him were triggered when he felt left out in his marriage. When Elizabeth understood some of Joe's painful childhood experiences, she had more empathy for him, and as Joe was able to express his sadness, he better understood himself. He began to realize, for instance, that Elizabeth's run on the beach or dance with the girls was not abandonment because, unlike his father, she would faithfully return. Her departure wasn't fatal or final. Now, though, it would take some time for his deeply embedded emotional patterns to catch up with what he understood in his head.

During that session I also learned that Elizabeth's dad was a very busy minister—and an avoider. He spent long days and nights ministering to the world and preaching about God's love and compassion, but at home he was feeding his family emotional leftovers. While the Bible truths flowed, the memory verses were learned, and the songs were sung, no one ever stopped to ask, "How do you feel today, Elizabeth?" Rather, life at home was about chores, checklists, and orderliness.

When Elizabeth was hurting or disappointed, her well-meaning parents would quote verses telling her, "In this world you will have trouble. But take heart! I have overcome the world" (John 16:33, NIV). Although this is a wonderful verse and a glorious truth that can carry us through tough times, what Elizabeth needed at that moment was for someone to hold her and share her pain, just as Jesus did when He met Mary and Martha after their brother Lazarus's death. Coming alongside Mary and Martha after their brother's death, "Jesus wept" (John 11:35, NIV). Elizabeth needed to be listened to and hugged; she needed comfort from her mom and dad.

So Elizabeth learned to stuff her feelings and to keep herself busy when she felt twinges of emotions. At times when she was overwhelmed, like after her divorce, she cried softly in her room so no one would hear. She was still playing by the childhood rule, "Look good and have your act together, or else what will people think?" Her avoidance of emotional connections had contributed to the failure of her first marriage, and now it was causing problems in the second. Yet, after understanding the absence of nurturing comfort in her childhood home, Joe had more compassion for her struggles to connect with him. Seeing her make efforts to share more of her feelings with him also encouraged him.

WANT TO DANCE?

Avoiders who have learned to go through life never being too excited or too dejected may experience strong feelings when they encounter a vacillator who is good at sparking intense, passionate connections. The avoider feels energized, noticed, understood, even adored, a feeling not experienced in the childhood home.

A vacillator is often attracted to the consistency, strength, and predictability of an avoider and enjoys being able to make that person respond. The vacillator has found in an avoider the consistent, responsive parent who was missing during the growing-up years. Also, an avoider's stability and predictability soothe the vacillator's anxiety over the unexpected twists and turns that naturally result from their unpredictable style in relationships.

STUMBLING STEPS

When these two imprints collide, avoiders constantly feel in trouble for disappointing their spouse. And the passionate connection and intense good feelings of the early relationship are replaced by the vacillator's passionate anger, hurt, and the disappointment that comes as "real life" sets in. So avoiders retreat and take care of themselves just as they have always done.

At the same time that avoiders are learning to deal with their feelings, vacillators are devastated when the passionate connection is lost. They feel angry, betrayed, and abandoned as they discover the avoider's inability to connect. Initially willing to work hard to get the avoider to respond and engage, vacillators become increasingly angry when they see that the avoider is incapable of providing the consistent, passionate connection they desire. Unlike the pleaser, though, vacillators voice their anger, further driving the avoider into retreat mode.

WHAT EACH PERSON FEELS

The Avoider
- It's like I'm walking on eggshells in my marriage.
- I get anxious that an inevitable blowup is coming.
- No matter how hard I try, I never do enough.
- Relationships are too hard; so why even try to make them work?
- Sometimes I look for excuses to get away.

- I never know what to expect.
- My spouse's reactivity annoys me.
- My spouse makes a big deal over little things.
- My spouse doesn't even appreciate my efforts when I do try to engage.

The Vacillator

- My spouse just hurts me over and over again.
- I feel empty and lonely. Where's the passion?
- My spouse's only efforts are too little, too late.
- My spouse doesn't want to be with me, especially when I'm upset.
- My spouse doesn't seem to need me.
- I tell my spouse what I need, but nothing happens.
- Given my situation, I have a right to be angry.
- I thought my spouse loved me at one time, but now I'm not sure.

Does this dance sound like the core pattern of your marriage? If you have already been working on your individual imprints, chapter 10 of the workbook will help you begin to work through the dynamics of the vacillator-avoider combination.

Chapter 11

The Pleaser Marries the Vacillator

Peter and Shannon met in an English class during their senior year of college. They were both attracted to Shakespeare's brilliant blend of tragedy, romance, and comedy, and each was eager to attend anything Shakespearean—from the Old Globe Theatre in San Diego's Balboa Park to the Ashland festival in Oregon. They greeted each other with "My lady" and "My lord" and kept track of each other with "Where art thou?" and "Whither thou goest, my love?" as well as "Pray tell, thee, how is thy soul?" Shannon couldn't imagine a more wonderful companion.

Soon inseparable, Peter and Shannon fell deeply in love and became engaged at the end of their senior year. Their formal Christmas wedding was elegant, and the Renaissance-flavored reception came complete with a horse-drawn carriage. Surely the enchantment would continue as they lived happily ever after. Neither would ever have imagined that the mundane nature of normal life would chippeth away at their rapturous love and bringeth it down to a common and boorish level and even causeth it to stinketh.

Two years into their marriage, they were both missing the enchanted life and decided to attend one of our weekend seminars. When Shannon and Peter volunteered to work with us in front of the group, we all learned more about them. During the lunch break we got to better understand their dynamic.

Shannon was finding herself increasingly irritated by Peter's diminishing ability to make her feel wanted and valuable. The anxiety that prompted in Peter caused him to scurry around seeking ways to appease her and assuage her anger. Shannon actually got sick to her stomach when Peter's pleaser tendencies reminded her of her henpecked dad. It was harder for her to see that her angry demeanor was like her mom.

Peter, in turn, was horrified by Shannon's sharp tones and outbursts of anger, all of which reminded him of the harsh and critical home from which he had escaped. As Peter's panic intensified, he felt as if he were in an inescapable hell. Looking back at their dating, he thought, *Didn't I find the perfect match? What happened?*

LOOKING AT THE ROOTS

All families have their unwritten rules as, for instance, parents teach by example how feelings and emotions should be handled. Think about how your family handled feelings, such as happiness, anger, frustration, sadness, and fear, when you were a child. Did both parents express all these emotions? What about the other family members? In many homes, the man of the house can speak freely, and all other members have to hold their tongue. But maybe your mom ruled the roost. What did that teach you? As you grew up, were you taught to accept and tolerate double standards? Did some people get to play by their own rules? And—the big question—which family rules, presuppositions, and convictions have you unconsciously carried into your adult world and into your marriage?

Double standards were a part of Shannon's experience. Her mom completely dominated the family and played by her own rules. A quiet and compliant man, her dad seemed to be the "nicest" dad in the world, but he was actually very disengaged. He worked hard in his accounting career and, after many dedicated years, became the corporate controller. Although extremely competent in financial matters, Shannon's dad dutifully handed his paycheck over to his wife and let her run the finances. Where there is money, there is control. For as long as Shannon could remember, her mom controlled everyone and everything. Her mom had an explosive temper and raged when things didn't go her way. Her dad reacted by scurrying around the house trying to make his wife happy and always falling short. Also, firmly in command of the household, Shannon's mom could say anything she wanted, but whenever her dad spoke angrily, her furious mom said, "How dare you speak to me that way!"

Shannon developed a keen awareness of closeness and distance in relationships. She learned to read the currents of her mom's emotions and stayed constantly alert for changes in her mother's moods. Shannon was very aware of anything that might set off her mother's anger and tried hard to prevent it, especially since her mom often completely ignored her after an angry outburst. But then suddenly, for no apparent reason, the mood would shift, and Shannon again had an attentive mom. Shannon looked for the warm soft times to approach her mom, but just like her dad, Shannon found herself always on edge, always fearing a sudden change in her mother's unpredictable moods.

As she matured into an adult, Shannon naturally took her hypervigilant tendencies into her adult relationships where she was starved for connection and acutely attentive toward any sign of positive attention from others. When she began dating, she was delighted by the boys' attention. When she was seventeen, Shannon became pregnant, and after delivering several stern lectures, her mom arranged an abortion.

Not fully comprehending her tendency to trust people too quickly, Shannon moved on to college, majoring in sorority and fraternity life with a minor in education. Although she had never connected the dots, all of her relationships were very similar. At first she idealized her roommates and boyfriends, and she very quickly entrusted her heart to them, only to be somehow disappointed later. This disillusionment marked the beginning of the end of every relationship. By the end of her junior year, Shannon had left a long trail of relational debris behind her.

Peter's experience was different. As a child, he felt that his mom and dad had very high expectations of him. Peter recalled his mom having an impatient, high-pitched tone of voice that required him to snap to attention. For as long as he could remember, he tried hard to live up to his parents' expectations; he wanted to make them proud and happy. In spite of his efforts, he rarely got any positive reinforcement, so he felt they were never satisfied.

When Peter left his childhood home, he tended to react internally to certain behaviors, words, and tones of voice. He had also formed a key core belief: "It's hard to please others, but I'm willing to try hard because I'm happy when they're happy." Also, Peter was so accustomed to feeling uptight that he truly didn't realize that he rarely felt calm. In fact, he had never even labeled his inner experience as anxiety until he looked at our soul words list of feelings (see page 291).

Now imagine what happened when Shannon's voice was impatient and shrill. Peter's body had responded with anxiety to that tone of voice many times as he was growing up. His stomach would ache and his chest would get tight—and it didn't take much for Shannon's voice to trigger that same old response. His response, however, was often exaggerated and disproportionate to the situation. Realizing that, he would find himself feeling apprehensive and eager to make Shannon happy.

After lunch that day, as we prompted them to share marriage and childhood experiences in front of the group, their damaging duet of pleaser and vacillator became obvious. Both Peter and Shannon benefited from recognizing how their pasts had created their core patterns. Peter learned that his imprint to please kept him dancing to keep Shannon happy. He also saw that he was programmed to over-react to Shannon's complaints, to easily feel hopeless and overwhelmed. Shannon learned she was a vacillator whose anger and disappointment characterized all her relationships. She learned to identify the hurt under her anger and talk about that to Peter rather than scold him. New understanding helped them embrace the hurts and losses they each brought into the marriage. They were excited about gaining new tools they could use so that their core patterns had less control over them.

THE CORE PATTERN: THE PLEASER AND THE VACILLATOR

When they meet, vacillators romantically idealize the giving, attentive nature of a pleaser and readily believe they have found their soul mate. Internally, pleasers are quite delighted, thinking that they have made their partner happy. Over time, however, the vacillator's unrealistic expectations are somehow shattered by disappointment. Disillusioned, the vacillator gradually becomes angry and demanding. Pleasers react with fear that causes them to try harder and harder to make their spouse happy. They try to please by doing things around the house, fixing or repairing, surprising with gifts or lavishing indulgences upon their angry partner. With so much focus on the other person, they lose a part of themselves in the process. After years of living out this pattern, the pleaser is walking on eggshells—

and resents it. The vacillator remains chronically unhappy, sensing that the connection is based on fear and duty, not passion. Although this pattern is similar to the vacillator and avoider dance, here the pleaser tries harder, whereas an avoider retreats. Let's look at another couple that has been doing this dance.

MICHAEL AND SANDY

When Sandy and Michael arrived in my (Milan's) office, their nervous laughs and smiles revealed that they were both feeling quite uneasy. After thanking them for coming, I asked if we could pray together and ask for God's help. Then I explained that this initial interview would help me assess what was going on between them and to see if I could help. I reassured them that we all—myself included—struggle in our relationships. Then I asked them to tell me a bit about their situation.

Sandy began, "We've been married twenty-four years, and we have three children who are twenty-three, twenty, and seventeen."

That was as far as she got. Michael abruptly began to talk in an agitated manner. Sandy's whole body tensed as she glared at Michael and then looked away. "Sandy announced she's leaving me. At first I was shocked; now I feel mad. You have to talk her into staying in the marriage. She has no biblical reason to leave. I've never cheated on her or anything like that. I've even put up with her hurting me over and over, and now she says she is the one who is leaving. She doesn't really listen to what I want or need even though I make it very clear. I think that she doesn't respond just to irritate me! I feel unloved, but you don't end a marriage. It's just not right."

"Give me an example of how she doesn't listen, so I can understand."

"That's easy," said Michael. "She is always on the phone. She has time for all her girlfriends. She can talk to them for hours. I've asked her over and over to talk to them when I'm at work. How hard is that? They still call in the evening, and Sandy won't tell them to call another time. I want my time with her, but she gives it away to everyone else. She has to hear about everyone's problems. All I want is time for us. It wrecks the evening when she ignores me. If she really loved me, she would listen."

I asked Sandy how she felt about Michael's comments. "I could throw the phone out the window, and Michael would find something else to complain about. I get a knot in my stomach every morning as soon as I get out of the shower to go downstairs. It's better after he goes to work, but as soon as the garage door goes up at night, my stomach feels sick again. I've tried to make him happy for years, and sometimes I get it right. But I usually get it wrong. Sometimes he tells me what he wants, but most of the time I'm supposed to read his mind, figure out what he wants, and just do it. And I can't do anything without it being a statement to Michael about love and loyalty.

"But back to the phone. To me, if someone needs to talk on the phone, it's no big deal. It bothers Michael because he doesn't have any friends. Last night my daughter called and was crying over a problem with her roommate. Michael was annoyed when I got off the phone, but he didn't bother to ask who I'd been talking to. And with Michael, everything is a stinking litmus test of affection. I'm done and I want out."

Clearly, she was completely worn out after trying to please him for over two decades. But she was on a cathartic roll and went on to say that they were fine for the first six months of their marriage. Then suddenly Michael began to tell her about all the things she was doing that irritated him. Time after time she tried to please him, and she found herself becoming increasingly more nervous.

When they had children, she would finally get them down for the night and crawl into bed only to find a jealous Michael who was angry that she hadn't gotten there more quickly. "You're married to me, Sandy. Not the kids!"

Sandy would freeze up in fear and be quiet. After a scolding from Michael, she offered some weak apology, and he would turn, give her a hug, and want to have sex. Many a night she found herself having sex with Michael, but wishing she were somewhere else where she could simply rest from it all.

After they shared one or two other scenes from their marriage and I heard subsequent rebuttals, Sandy announced again that she was calling it quits and leaving Michael. "The kids are grown, and I can't stand the pressure any longer. At work I'm around men who treat me respectfully, and it's refreshing."

I looked at her and thought to myself, *The pleaser has run out of energy and turned bitter.* That commonly happens when this dance goes on for years. I knew I had little hope of changing her mind. "Well," I said, "as long as you're here, maybe I can help you understand why you've been stuck in this pattern for so long."

Each of them was willing to talk about their childhood experiences, so we continued.

LOOKING AT THE ROOTS

Michael was the last of three children born into a blue-collar family that had just come to America, and when his father, Joe, learned he'd had a son, he bought a round for everyone at the steel mill. Michael's mom, Sophie, was sweet and kind and didn't oppose Joe very often. The family did whatever Dad told them, and Joe pushed the kids to perform well in school. The early years of school were easy for Michael academically, but difficult socially. The kids teased him about his clothes and funny accent, and Michael learned to get tough and fight back. Later, Michael worked hard in high school, always hoping for a nod of approval from Dad. Depending on Dad's mood, sometimes he found favor, but other times his dad ignored him completely.

"You never knew what was going to set him off," Michael explained. "When I was ten, my dad made me sleep in the park all night, because I didn't appreciate how hard he worked to give me a home. I said something about us being poor, and he blew up, grabbed me by the collar, walked me down to the park, and told me if my home wasn't good enough, I could sleep in the park. He pushed me down on the grass and said, 'Don't come home until morning.'"

"What happened?" asked Sandy, wide-eyed. "Did your mom come get you?"

Michael looked down. "If she had, my dad would have made her sleep in the park too. I was scared to death, but I hid in some bushes for a while and then crept into our backyard and stayed there until morning. I think my dad felt guilty, because the next night he was nicer than usual. I think he even gave me a hug."

The shocked look on Sandy's face told me she had never visited Michael's past with him.

"Michael," I said, "that reminds me of what Sandy said earlier; that she feels like her every action is a litmus test of love and loyalty. It sounds like you might understand that feeling. I wonder how many other innocent comments you made as a child were a litmus test to your dad of your love and affection. Also, you never knew if you were going to do things right or wrong with your dad, just like Sandy doesn't know if she is going to please you or make you mad." Michael quietly pondered my words. "It's important for you to remember those feelings, Michael. Otherwise you won't understand how you make Sandy feel," I added.

Michael went on to say that Joe wanted to be sure that Michael, as the only male, would end up being a successful boss in their new country. So after high school, at the insistence of his dad, Michael left home and studied economics at the university.

Michael was excited to finally get out of the house, and he enjoyed being out from under his dad's unpredictable moods. Yet Michael found himself preoccupied with other people's perceptions of him, and he often felt angry when his friends didn't appreciate or value him. Sometimes his ill feelings were over something as simple as not being noticed. He was really hurt one evening when several friends spontaneously made a midnight run to a fast-food restaurant and didn't ask him to come along. Eventually, people around him began to feel as though they were walking on eggshells.

Having come from a small farming community in the heartland of America, Sandy had led a very different life. Her mom and dad were soybean farmers and very devoted to their family and church. Their days started early, they worked until sunset six days a week, and all the kids (Sandy was one of the younger ones) had their own chores around the farm.

When Sandy was about five, one of her older brother's jobs was to take care of her several afternoons a week. Her brother was loud and wild and constantly agitating shy Sandy with his noises and sounds. Sometimes they would play King and Slave, and he would make her do his chores. When he was bored, he would tease her and chase her around with baby animals or scary toys. When she cried, he finally stopped tormenting her and told her not to be a baby. He promised to be nice if she gently scratched his back, and she was glad to oblige.

"Were you afraid of him?" I asked.

"Probably, a little. Well, maybe more than a little."

"Sandy, you were talking earlier about the knot in your stomach when the garage door opens at night. Did being around your brother cause a similar feeling, the same knot?"

Sandy nodded, her eyes welling with tears. "I've been playing King and Slave my whole life," she said quietly. "And I'm done," she added firmly.

At a very early age Sandy had learned about anxiety and having to hold in her fears. She was embarrassed to tell me that she wet the bed until she was almost ten years old. Her mom loved her and could always count on her to pick up around the house and go the extra mile for the family, yet she was clueless as to why Sandy was always complaining about her stomach hurting.

Michael was a vacillator who saw Sandy's every action as good or bad, right or wrong, loving or unloving, without much middle ground. If Sandy got something wrong, it was proof she didn't love or care about him. The thought of being unloved made Michael anxious, a vulnerable feeling that he quickly covered with anger. Just as Michael had been expected to prove his love for his father by figuring out what Joe wanted and complying, he expected Sandy to do the same for him. After all, isn't that how you love?

Sandy's sensitive and compliant nature made her an easy target for Michael. She was imprinted early on to anxiously please people. Her only rest was in doing everything right. To her, averting conflict was showing love.

WANT TO DANCE?

Pleasers have been trying to make others happy long before they meet their future mate. And, initially, they find the vacillator delighted by their efforts to please. The vacillator responds in ways that make the pleaser feel successful, and the pleaser's anxiety fades. The vacillator's response also feels great to pleasers because growing up, they usually didn't have much success making everyone happy.

Vacillators have often grown up with a parent who is difficult to predict and please. So, initially, a pleaser is just about the nicest person the vacillator has ever met. In this dance, vacillators keep waiting for the angry outburst, and when it doesn't come, they're hooked. They have found a consistently nice person, and they are thrilled.

STUMBLING STEPS

As the imprints collide, pleasers find they cannot keep up with the idealized expectations of the vacillator. As they make mistakes and sense the vacillator's irritation, their anxiety returns, and they become concerned about avoiding conflict. So they try harder to please the vacillator, wanting to again know that person's pleasure and praise.

Vacillators, however, are disillusioned when the relationship's initial passion begins to wane. They want someone to understand them and want them, not just please them. The pleaser's anxious scurrying around makes them feel placated rather than known and valued. This isn't what they expected, and over time the pleaser's efforts become annoying. Vacillators become more agitated and upset, and they don't understand that pleasers just don't know how to connect in a reciprocal way, because they don't know how to receive. Growing up, pleasers also did not learn soul words, and no one was asking about their hearts, so they cannot connect that way either.

So, continuing the dance, pleasers try to fix any negative emotions by doing nice things that will make their spouse happy. Moving toward the difficult feelings of others (or even their own) makes pleasers anxious, because they don't know what to do. Vacillators don't understand this, so they feel more and more unloved, more and more disillusioned and angry.

Yet pleasers keep trying. After all, they have been pleasing their whole lives. But, over time, their resentment begins to build. Since they rarely express anger openly, though, it may be expressed in passive ways, such as by subtly spending less time at home with their spouses, working more, volunteering for activities with the children, or developing hobbies, which help them maintain a safe distance from their mates ("Guess what? I'm training for a triathlon"). These pleasers also feel as if they are walking on eggshells, and while their efforts may make the vacillator happy for a while, life won't be peaceful for long. If the pattern continues long enough, the pleasers' resentment may build to the point that they avoid or even leave their spouses. If the couple remains in this pattern for years, their marriage is often filled with bitterness and resentment.

What Each Person Feels

The Pleaser

- I feel as though I am walking on eggshells in my marriage.
- I get anxious thinking about the blowup that I know is coming.
- No matter how hard I try, I can never do enough.
- I never know what to expect. The relationship can be really good, and then suddenly it's very bad.
- I can't understand why little things make my spouse so reactive and mad.
- Other people appreciate me much more than my spouse does.
- If I left the marriage, my spouse would see just how good he or she has it.

The Vacillator

- My spouse just hurts me over and over again.
- I feel empty and lonely. Where's the passion?
- I don't respect my spouse, and it annoys me when he or she does things to try to please me that I don't even care about.
- Everybody thinks I'm married to the greatest person, but those folks don't know how it is to live with him or her.
- I tell my spouse what I need, but nothing happens.
- Yes, I'm angry. Anyone would be angry in my situation.

If you identify with this core pattern, you need to know it's one of the most common we see. Growth will depend on working on the healing goals for your own love style that are outlined in the workbook. Begin today to take small steps to change this core pattern.

Chapter 12

The Controller Marries the Victim

Carlie asked to see me (Milan). After eighteen years of marriage and almost two decades of intimidation and rage from Bill, she had grown up enough inside to set a boundary and confront Bill: "I'm out of here! The kids are old enough to handle this, and I can't take it anymore." Bill was caught off guard, and at first he tried to intimidate and bully her into staying. But when he saw a resolve in Carlie that was firmer than he had ever seen before, he became scared and, for the first time in his life, began to cry.

The prospect of losing Carlie was too much for Bill, and he begged for another chance. She looked at him with contempt and couldn't imagine that his tears represented true change. He had been sorry before, especially when he had pushed her around or left bruises on her arms from grabbing her. But Carlie couldn't stop seeing Bill's brokenhearted face in her mind. She began to question her decision and called for an appointment to talk. She was wondering if, in fact, this time Bill might truly want to change.

Of course, I began by asking Carlie what her childhood home was like. "It was pretty normal," she replied.

When I asked her to expand her answer and probed a bit, I discovered that her definition of normal was a dad who had been in prison as a drug dealer and moving several times with her mother and sister. After the prison term was up and the family was reunited, Carlie's dad drifted from job to job and did not handle life very well. The combination of a prison record and being a high-school dropout relegated him to low-paying jobs that he hated and complained about daily.

Carlie explained, "When I needed anything, like a prom dress for my senior dance, my dad had a hissy fit. I'd try to just tell my mom and not let my dad know, and she was good about keeping secrets. My mom sewed my dress and told me I would be the belle of the ball. On the night of the dance, my mom drove me to a friend's house. It was Friday night, and that meant my dad was going to down a couple of six-packs of beer. Who knows what would have happened if he had seen me in that dress?"

Carlie continued her story. "Bill and I had been dating since our junior year of high school. My dad didn't know about that either. Anyway, Bill took me to the prom, and he bought me a beautiful corsage. That was the first time anyone had ever given me flowers. I still have it in a special box at home. Bill was nicer to me back then. In fact, he stuck up for me at the dance when someone made fun of my handmade dress. Bill grabbed him by the throat and demanded an apology." Carlie laughed at the memory. "That guy was so shocked. It was nice to have someone defend me for a change. He made me feel protected and loved."

Carlie's story made me sad, and I decided to tell her. "Carlie, as you were telling me this story, I couldn't help but think about my own daughters and how much I enjoyed seeing them all dressed up for prom. It was like a first glimpse as to how they might look at their weddings someday. I'm sad that you didn't have a dad who could enjoy that moment before the prom. How nice it would have been for you to have a father who was excited for you and told you how beautiful you looked. Instead, you had to keep lots of secrets just to stay safe."

Carlie just stared at me. "I can't imagine having that kind of dad," she said. "And I never had a wedding dress, because I didn't want my dad walking me down the aisle. Bill and I eloped and got married in Las Vegas. I think I was wearing blue jeans."

"Tell me a bit about Bill's upbringing," I continued. "If I understand a bit about each of your histories, I can better understand why you get stuck in your marriage."

"Well," Carlie continued, "Bill's dad was never in jail, but I remember his parents fighting a lot, especially if they started drinking, which was almost every night. His family lived in this little duplex, and he had to share a room with his two older brothers. He and his brothers use to beat up on each other, and it would scare me to death. I never liked to be at his house, because people were always fighting."

"What was Bill's mom like?" I asked.

"His real mom left the boys when Bill was six. She ran off with some guy because she couldn't take it anymore. I never met her, and Bill won't talk about her even though I've asked him a few times. Gloria is his stepmom. Well, actually, his second stepmom. She and Bill never got along. She's still around, but I think it's a pretty ugly marriage. They really hate each other. It's even worse than our marriage."

"Carlie, tell me when your marriage changed. You said that, at first, Bill was loving and protective. What happened?"

Carlie was quiet. "We started fighting more after we got married. I took a job as a waitress, and he accused me of flirting with all the guys. He questioned me about the people I talked to and what they said. He was jealous of any little thing. If I got a good tip, that meant I was too nice. There was no reasoning with him.

"It wasn't a problem for long, though, because I got pregnant after six months. Then I was home. Now he is suspicious of the neighbors. It's always somebody— and that's the cause of most of our fights. His suspicions, and money. We never have enough, and I'm supposed to run the house on a shoestring, but Bill always has money in his pocket to go have a bunch of drinks with his buddies at the pool hall. He even had a little fling with some girl he met there. He finally admitted it after she kept calling our home, but he blamed me for not giving him enough sex. I guess there is some truth to that. I hate having sex with him."

"Has Bill ever pushed you or hit you?" I asked.

"After he's been drinking with the guys, he really picks on me. A few times a year, it gets violent. He's sorry the next morning—if he can remember anything about it. Over the years I've really started to hate him, but until the kids got older, I was stuck. After this last bout, I realized I don't have to take this anymore. I'm in a women's Bible study at church, and one of my friends said I could move in with her until I'm on my feet. I told Bill, and I actually thought he wouldn't care. I'm surprised how broken up he is over the whole thing; I thought he would be glad. He says he wants to change, but I've heard that before, so I don't trust it. What do you think?" Carlie asked.

LOOKING AT THE ROOTS

"Well, Carlie, the dynamic in your marriage is more common than you might think. Both of you come from homes with a lot of problems. Neither of you ever had an opportunity to observe a healthy relationship where a husband and wife respectfully settle their differences. Also, as you were growing up, each of you became accustomed to lots of stress, anxiety, and secrets, plus anger that was fueled by too much alcohol. Stress and chaos are common and normal for you both.

"At first Bill was only angry with other people, not you," I continued. "His jealousy came into full bloom after you married, and so did his anger."

"But I don't see why," Carlie interrupted me. "I have never given him any real reason to be jealous. I'm loyal to a fault."

"I think it probably has to do with Bill's mom leaving him when he was six years old," I explained to Carlie. "When someone that important walks out of your life, it leaves a deep wound of insecurity and distrust. The fact that he won't talk about it tells me it's a painful place in his heart, and he doesn't want to revisit those feelings. Since his mom didn't stay, you might not either, so Bill is controlling to prevent you from leaving. If you did leave, it would make him feel the loss of someone very important once again."

Carlie closed her eyes. "I never thought of it like that," she said. "Now I feel guilty for wanting to leave."

"Let's look at it another way, Carlie. You might be doing Bill a big favor if you left him. Your announcement definitely brought some of his feelings to the surface, although he probably doesn't see the connection between how devastated he feels now and his mother leaving so many years ago. And Bill will probably be jealous, angry, and controlling until he sees some of these connections between past and present and realizes just how sad and hurt he is from those painful events in his childhood. I'm not recommending a divorce at this point, because Bill has never been as motivated to get better as he might be now if you move out rather than file for divorce. If he really wants you back, he will have to get the help he needs to make some deep changes. A legal separation would protect you physically and financially, but I encourage you to take some time before making the divorce final.

Give Bill time to put actions behind his words. You will know, over time, if he is going to truly change. And if you are out of the house and physically safe, you'll have time to both work on your own issues and see if Bill can stick to his promises."

"Am I being selfish for wanting to leave?" Carlie asked.

"I wouldn't call it selfish, Carlie. Your mom taught you by her example to put up with a lot of anger in a marriage and to survive by keeping secrets. She herself didn't have healthy boundaries, so she couldn't teach you how to stand up for yourself. The fact that you have put up with double standards and episodes of physical violence for years tells me you have a hard time imagining that you deserve better treatment. You are finally willing to take a stand, which is a healthy change for you. You need to continue on that road of growth. Also, if you quickly divorce Bill and move right into dating, you are likely to repeat the pattern again. Let's schedule a session with both of you so we can discuss some of these ideas with Bill."

THE CORE PATTERN: THE CONTROLLER AND THE VICTIM

Unwittingly, as a result of attachment injuries sustained during their chaotic childhoods, Carlie and Bill had each taken a role in their marriage that was known and familiar to them. They had grown up watching a one-up-one-down relationship between spouses and replicated it in their relationship. Changing is difficult due to the two parties' high levels of reactivity and deep levels of hurt. Although one person usually dominates and the other is victimized, occasionally the fight for control is fierce, resulting in even higher levels of chaos, violence, and confusion.[1]

LESLIE AND PAUL

Paul wondered if he should call the police. Leslie was out of control, and the baby was now awake and screaming hysterically. Miraculously their three-year-old son was still asleep. He could hear Leslie in the bedroom ripping his clothes out of the closet, cursing, and yelling at him to get a suitcase because she was kicking him out. His stomach was in knots, and he could feel his insides shaking. He was in a no-win situation, and whatever he did now, he would pay for later.[2]

Paul had called the police once before, and Leslie threatened to take a hammer to his new car if he didn't send them away once they got to the house. Paul believed she would be more than happy to wreck his new car. During their first year of marriage, when he accused her of drinking too much while she was pregnant, she had smashed his guitar to bits. "If it weren't for the kids, I'd be gone," he muttered. He felt confused and helpless, and he hated to admit it, but he was truly afraid of her. Leslie's temper was bad enough when she was sober, but after she drank three or four glasses of wine, he could count on a fight.

Paul heard her coming down the hall toward the kitchen where he was standing. She had a handful of clothes in one hand and his cell phone in the other. She heaved the phone at him and screamed, "Take your junk and get out!"

He stood frozen, paralyzed. He didn't want to leave the kids alone with her. When he didn't move, she lunged for him and caught his cheek with her fingernails. Suddenly there was a loud rap on the front door. "Police! Open up!"

Leslie looked at Paul with pure hatred and staggered back toward the bedroom. Paul opened the door.

"Had a call from one of your neighbors, and it sounds like there's a problem," said one of the officers. Paul was trembling, and he collapsed on the couch, buried his face in his hands, and began to weep. It was then he realized he was bleeding. He felt humiliated, pathetic, and worn out. He wished at that moment he could disappear forever. They came to me (Kay) after the courts ordered them into individual and couples therapy as well as Alcoholics Anonymous and Al-Anon.

LOOKING AT THE ROOTS

I explained to Leslie and Paul that I was going to spend the first session getting to know Leslie. "This week you will be the observing guest," I told Paul. "Next week it will be just the opposite. I will get to know you, Paul, and Leslie will be the observing guest." Both looked relieved that there would be no opportunity to fight.

After hearing the tragedy of Leslie's early years, I could see why she struggled with rage and used alcohol to deaden her pain. And it was no surprise that, when we talked about her childhood, Leslie reported facts in a detached way, as though she were describing a horror movie she had watched with someone other than herself as the main character.

"I never knew my dad. I really don't think my mom even knew who my dad was. She had a different man in the house every couple of days. I'm sure she got paid for the first guy that ever came into my room at night. I was little then, maybe eight or nine. At first I really didn't know what he wanted. After that night, I decided I would rather die than go through that again, so I fought like a wild animal the next time she sent someone into my room. I really didn't care if he killed me. In fact, I think I was sort of hoping he would. I remember giving the guy a bloody nose, and I bit his hand so hard when he tried to cover my mouth that he screamed like a girl." Leslie laughed.

Paul looked horrified. I said to Leslie, "You might want to take a look at Paul's face. His response is what the little girl in the bedroom would have wanted to see."

Leslie looked at Paul. The pained look on his face was more valuable than words.

"What happened next?" I asked.

"I guess he figured having me wasn't worth the fight, and I heard him arguing with my mom after he left my room. He probably wanted his money back. My sister got the worst of it after that. Mom never tried to send any of those creeps into my room again."

Leslie had been telling me this story with little eye contact as she looked back and forth between her feet and the toys on my shelf. She glanced up, and I saw a flash of bewilderment and confusion cross her face when she saw tears in my eyes. She quickly looked away and carefully avoided my eyes, looking instead around the room at every detail in my office. "Why do you have all these toys?" she asked, trying to change the subject.

"Toys are the language of children," I answered. "I find that adults still have that language inside if they will let themselves find it. Why don't you go over to the shelf and pick one thing that reminds you of your mom when you were little and one thing that might represent you as a child."

Leslie eagerly got up and studied all the miniature figures on my shelves. Paul watched with interest. After picking two items, she came back and sat down. "This is my mom," she said. She held up a winter tree, brown dry sticks on a slim trunk. "This is me." She held up a black bull with red eyes, head down, and ready to charge. I could see I was going to enjoy Leslie's ability to use symbols to express the truth of her childhood.

"Very creative," I said. We sat in silence for a few minutes. "Would it be safe to say, Leslie, that anger helped you survive your childhood?"

Leslie answered, "I guess so. I sure don't let anybody mess with me or take advantage of me."

I replied, "That's about the only thing your childhood taught you about relationships. Your mom and the men she had around messed with you and took advantage of you. You had to turn into a bull to keep from getting completely run over. Pretty brave move for a little girl." I wanted Paul to understand that Leslie's anger was her only protection as a child. She had no idea how to leave it behind now that she was an adult. I continued, "Leslie, tell me about the tree. Pretend you are the tree and your mother at the same time. Start with the words, 'I am dry and brown.'"

Leslie twirled the trunk between her fingers. She was silent for a while. Finally she began, the words slowly trickling out. "I am dry and brown. I have nothing to give—no leaves, no shade, no fruit." Leslie's voice dropped to a whisper. "I'll always be this way. It will never be spring or summer. Get used to it." The first drop of truth rolled down Leslie's cheek, and she wiped it away with the back of her hand. "I can't believe I'm crying," she said. "I never cry."

"Of course not," I said. "Who would be there to hold you and wipe your tears? Bulls can't afford to cry, but you don't have to be a bull here in my office. And I'm hoping we can find the Leslie who existed before she had to become a bull."

The following week it was Paul's turn. He began by describing his loneliness as a child. "My dad was in the military, and we moved every two years, sometimes sooner. I'm the youngest, with one older sister. I've always been shy, and I hate being in strange places with people I don't know. School was a nightmare for me. I never had friends, and there was always some bully who made my life miserable. My mom always said it would be better the next time we moved, but it actually got worse. By junior high, the girls were making fun of me too, and I think if it weren't for my dog, I might have checked out."

"You mean ended your life?" I asked. Paul was silent and I waited. Finally he said, "I just wanted to disappear. Dad had guns in the house, and I knew where they were. I got one out a few times when no one was home, but like my dad said, I was a sissy, a mama's boy, and I could never bring myself to do it."

"Your dad's a jerk," Leslie interjected. "I've always wanted to…" I held my hand toward Leslie, signaling her to stop.

"You are the observing guest, Leslie, remember?" She followed my lead and was quiet. I turned back to Paul and asked, "Tell me more about your dad."

Paul continued, "I was a big disappointment to him. At first he was glad to have a boy, but I was too quiet and sensitive, and he was always trying to toughen me up."

"Can you give me an example, Paul?"

"Oh, you know, he was always making threats, most of which he carried out, like, if you don't stop crying now, I'll give you something to cry about. One time I kept crying because I accidentally lost my baseball mitt and was late for a game. He kept yelling at me to shut up and stop, and I didn't. He spanked me with his belt until I could take it like a man and not cry. After that, I took his threats seriously. Saturdays and Sundays were bad because he would start drinking at noon down at the Officers Club."

Paul began to scratch his arms nervously. He dropped his head into his hands and rubbed his eyes as though he was trying to erase a picture from his mind. I could tell he was becoming more and more agitated. I quietly said, "Did you remember something, Paul?"

He nodded his head, still covering his face with his hands. "Take your time," I urged. "I can tell it's very disturbing." I sat quietly until Paul could speak of the anguish inside of him. Leslie leaned forward and waited, anxiously biting her nails.

In a burst of emotion, Paul yelled, "I hate him! I hate him! He made me shoot my dog!" and then he wept uncontrollably. Through the sobs, he kept saying, "I had to! I had to—or he was going to tie her to a tree and do it with my baseball bat." A wave of nausea passed through me. Leslie's face was ashen. She got out of her seat, sat next to Paul, and cradled him in her arms. We sat quietly and let Paul finally release the agony in his heart.

I found out in the third session that Leslie was going to make my job easier than I had anticipated. "Last week was an eye opener," she began. "I never really realized what I put Paul through when I drink too much and get so mad. I was a wreck all week, because I could see that I'm like his dad. It just about killed me because I can't stand that man. I've been sober all week, and I'm working on my first step in AA with my sponsor, and that has helped."

"It sounds like there is a very sensitive, determined young woman speaking to me right now," I commented.

Leslie smiled and said, "Yeah, the bull's been put in the pen."

"Well," I continued, "I think we can tame that bull as you learn to bring to me and to Paul all the sadness and pain underlying that anger. Until now, alcohol has been your relief, because you could not imagine relief coming from a person."

"That's true," Leslie said. "I noticed this week that I'm pretty anxious without my bottle of booze." Leslie laughed. "Was that a Freudian slip, that I said *bottle*? It made me think of a baby bottle. I used to sneak one of my sister's bottles into bed at night and drink it under the covers… I haven't thought of that in years."

"Sounds like you were trying hard to be a good mommy to yourself," I said. "You and Paul both endured a lot of trauma growing up, with no one to protect or help you. You dealt with the chaos in opposite ways. While you got mad, Leslie, and decided to control others with your anger, Paul tried to stay out of everyone's way and defuse the bombs. Either relational style takes a lot of energy to maintain. And neither of you had an example of how to communicate or play by a fair set of rules, so you will have to learn that with me. I'm encouraged by how quickly you catch on. Leslie, your ability to comfort Paul last week was wonderful. I'd like to know how that felt for each of you."

"I've never seen Paul that broken up," said Leslie. "My heart ached for him, and at the same time, I wanted to go scream at his dad for doing that to him. And usually I'm not very affectionate, but for some reason it was easy for me to comfort him."

I turned to Paul, "How about you?"

Paul began, "I was surprised when I realized Leslie was beside me. When I felt her put her arms around me, it actually made my cry harder. It was comforting to have her next to me like that." Paul's voice trembled. "I've never felt that before in my entire life."

WANT TO DANCE?

Initial attraction between controllers-victims has some interesting distinctives. As young adults, controllers are starved for affection, attention, and praise. They fall hard and fast because if it isn't intense, it isn't love. Controllers have an uncanny ability to pick individuals who don't threaten their need for control. Because they were never able to entirely possess their parents, it feels wonderful to possess their lover and have that person all to themselves.

Victims, too, are starved for affection, attention, and praise. Intensity is mistaken for intimacy, and for a while, control is mistaken for protection. Many times victims have never felt protection of any kind, so being exclusively possessed by the controller can make them feel special and loved.

STUMBLING STEPS

Over time the controllers' insecurities about losing their spouse increase. To lower their anxiety, controllers exert more power. After all, controllers believe that, to get their needs met, they have to violate, exploit, and control others. They believe they must take what they want or have nothing. Any feelings of weakness or vulnerability are loaded with humiliation and shame and therefore quickly buried by anger.

Victims submit to the controller believing they will otherwise be left alone with no one to meet their needs. Accustomed to high anxiety, victims accept mistreatment, not fully recognizing the seriousness of the abuse.[3]

WHAT EACH PERSON FEELS

The Controller
- If my spouse would listen to me, I wouldn't get so angry.
- My spouse does things behind my back, and it drives me crazy.

- I feel angry when my spouse ignores me.
- My spouse does things that make me jealous.
- I lose my temper a lot, especially at home, but my spouse or kids deserve it.
- My spouse ignores me when I ask him or her to do things a certain way.

The Victim

- I have to keep my mate from knowing certain things because he or she would be angry.
- My spouse complains no matter how hard I try.
- I am afraid of making my spouse angry. Sometimes I pick a fight just to get it over with.
- My spouse mistreats me, but I stay because it would be worse to be alone.
- I get nervous when things are calm because I know it won't last. I'm always waiting for my spouse to get angry or critical.
- I apologize to my spouse just to get him or her off my back.
- I feel tense when my spouse is home and more relaxed when he or she is gone.
- I feel humiliated when my spouse calls me names and puts me down.

Do you see your marriage here? If you suffered like this as a child, take courage. Change is possible, if you seek it. Chapters 8 and 12 of the workbook will give you a good start.

Chapter 13

The Avoider Marries the Pleaser

Sharon was returning from a weekend with her girlfriends, and Don was anxiously anticipating her arrival. The kids were in their pj's, scrubbed and in bed, and dinner was in the oven. Don was ready; the table was set, the candles were lighted, and the wine was chilled.

During the car ride home, Sharon reflected on the weekend as her two friends chatted in the front seat. *They could talk forever,* she thought. Her friends had talked half the night about the problems in their marriages, and Sharon was shocked by how open they were. They teased her, saying she was married to Mr. Wonderful and that's why she didn't have much to say. In truth, Sharon wasn't comfortable revealing such personal information. The shopping trips had been enjoyable, but talking half the night was not her idea of fun. But when she suggested going to bed at midnight, they laughed at her, so she stayed up, mostly listening to the conversation between her friends.

Sharon arrived home just as Don was picking up the last of the toys scattered around the family room. As her two friends helped her bring in her belongings from the car, they teased, "Wow, dinner is ready and the house is clean. Let's stay here. How about it, Don? Can you set two more places at the table? Maybe if we stay until midnight, our husbands will have the kids fed and in bed."

Don smiled and, shifting nervously from foot to foot, looked at Sharon. Did she want him to extend an invitation? Sharon sighed. "Relax, Don. They're just kidding." She knew that look on Don's face. He wanted her all to himself, and he was worried it wasn't going to happen.

Her friends headed for the door saying, "Really, Sharon, you are so lucky. Don is so nice." Sharon's back was to Don, and she rolled her eyes. She was tired of hearing how nice Don was. It was true. He *was* nice—and why did it bug her so much?

I wish I could go back to Palm Springs for two weeks, all by myself, Sharon thought. *My weekend with the girls was fun, but I'm dead tired. A candlelight dinner means Don expects sex, and knowing Don, I bet the candles upstairs are already lighted too. And since I had my weekend with the girls, he is going to expect extra time and attention this week.*

Sharon thought back to their phone conversation while she was away. Don had suggested that Sharon skip her quilting class on Wednesday night so they could spend the evening together. She found herself getting more irritated. *I don't want to give that up. It's the only two hours during the whole week that no one expects anything from me.* Her thoughts were interrupted as Don handed her a glass of wine. "Have a seat," he said. "I'll serve dinner."

"Here's to you being home," Don said as he lifted his glass toward Sharon. "I really missed you." Sharon smiled and halfheartedly lifted her glass. She had missed him back when they were dating. She could remember that. Especially the summer he worked as a camp counselor at Hume Lake. He was gone for eight weeks, and she couldn't wait for him to get back. *Why don't I ever feel that way any more?* she thought.

"What's wrong?" Don asked. "You seem like you are a million miles away. I thought you would be in a really good mood tonight after being away all weekend."

Sharon could see disappointment creeping across his face. She wasn't in the mood for the same old argument, and that was often the line that pulled them into their familiar fight.

"Nothing. I'm fine. Just tired," Sharon said, avoiding Don's eyes. She knew he was staring her down, trying to take her emotional temperature.

"Well," he continued, "something is up. You didn't even kiss or hug me when you walked through the door. A little affection would be nice after you have been gone all weekend. I've worked really hard to make it nice for you, and now you don't even seem that happy to be home. I don't get it."

Sharon sighed. She was losing her appetite. Don continued. "What's the sigh for? Am I wrong? Am I asking too much?"

Sharon forced another smile. "Thanks for cooking dinner. I really do appreciate it. I didn't even realize I didn't give you a hug. And it's no big deal, but I was expecting to see the kids before they went to bed. I think I got a little distracted looking for them. Let's just enjoy dinner."

Don was quiet, his face clouded with rejection. They ate in uncomfortable silence. Sharon anticipated the next turn in this predictable road they continually traveled down. If she stayed quiet, he would begin to give her more examples of how she fell short in making him feel important and loved. She would defend herself until she was annoyed enough that he backed down. Then she would have to endure his quiet sulking. If she ignored his sulking long enough, he would eventually start being extra nice to make her happy and try to close the gap between them. All would go well until the next disappointment.

Sharon decided to try to steer them in another direction. "Hey, Margie said her family is going to rent a houseboat on Lake Shasta this summer. She asked if we wanted to join them. It wouldn't be that expensive if we split the cost between three families. I think the Farrell family wants to go too. The reservations have to be in by next week, so I told Margie we'd talk and I'd call her next week. Doesn't that sound fun?"

"Yeah, sure," said Don. "That would be great if we don't even want to see each other. I already told you that I want my mom to keep the kids so we can go spend some time alone together. If we go to Lake Shasta, you'll just talk to the girls, and I'll be stuck with Tom and Sean. Tom's a nice guy, but Sean's the king of sarcastic humor. I can't believe you want to do that."

"Fine, Don. Just forget it. But if your mom baby-sits, you can take the week off after we get home and get the kids back in line. They are always little terrors after she has them for a week. By the way, why do you always have to take everything as some sign that I don't want to be with you? I just got home, and I already feel smothered. Now I have a headache. I'm going to bed."

"Don't get mad," said Don. "If it means that much to you, we can go to Lake Shasta. I didn't mean to make you mad. I just want to be with you, that's all. I just heard your friends say they wished their husbands were as thoughtful as I am.

Most women would love it if their husbands paid more attention to them and wanted to be with them more."

Sharon pushed her chair out from the table and went upstairs. She never really had a good answer for that line because she knew it was true. Her friends were jealous. She crawled into bed trying to find the part of her that was supposed to want Don more. She was tired of trying to explain why being affectionate was hard for her. She was tired of hearing about Don's feelings of rejection. She was tired of this same fight that went nowhere. Don's voice interrupted her thoughts.

"Here, honey. I know you like a glass of water by your bed. Give me a kiss good night." Sharon sat up and kissed him, even though the gesture was devoid of any feelings. She was relieved he wasn't going to pout. The glass of water was a peace offering meant to erase the uneasy feelings they had just encountered. Her kiss sealed the unspoken agreement to forget the whole thing by morning.

LOOKING AT THE ROOTS

Let's take a look at the roots of Don and Sharon's core patterns. First, Sharon is experiencing struggles common to people with an imprint to avoid. She holds a lot inside as she questions the emotions and feelings that are bubbling up within. She is confused by her reactions to Don and notices that she feels somewhat uneasy during conversations with the girls. Let's look back at Sharon's upbringing.

The second of three girls, Sharon was raised in the suburbs of Denver, Colorado. In one of our first conversations, she described her mom to me. "My mom has had more than her fair share of problems," Sharon said, "and she is truly amazing. My oldest sister, Suzanne, was born with severe autism. I came along when she was two, and I think Suzanne wore my mom out. Mom says Suzanne cried nonstop for the first year of her life, and by the time she was eighteen months old, it was pretty obvious she was in her own world. She went to years of therapy. I remember being in the car a lot, going to all her therapy appointments. My mom did everything humanly possible to help my sister. My dad wasn't that involved because he owned his own business and had to work long hours.

"My younger sister, Marie, came along fourteen months after me, and she is still, to this day, the strongest willed person imaginable. When we were kids and Marie didn't get her way, she could throw a tantrum that the neighbors four houses down the block could hear. One time Mom took Marie and me to a department store, and someone called the police because they thought Marie was being kidnapped. She was screaming at the top of her lungs, 'Help, help! Don't take me away!' as my mom was dragging her out of the store. It was so embarrassing. In fact, both my sisters embarrassed me, and I never had friends over because of them. Marie was even worse as a teenager. She still gives my parents a run for their money, and she is twenty-five! But she was just diagnosed as bipolar, and she's doing better on the medicine they prescribed for her. It's a good thing I was an easy kid, or I think my mom would have gone over the edge."

I (Kay) pictured Sharon sandwiched between these two kids who both required so much of her mother. I commented, "Your mom does sound amazing, Sharon. She had a lot to deal with, and you're right, she did have more than her fair share of problems. Have you ever considered how all that stress affected you?"

Sharon sat quietly, reflecting on my question. "I don't remember much. I guess I learned to persevere when things are hard. And my mom is a great example of handling whatever life deals to you. I think I learned to be self-sufficient and take care of myself. That's one of the things Don really admired when we first started dating. I met Don just after I returned home from traveling by myself for three months in Europe. He was so impressed when I showed him all my pictures. He kept saying that he couldn't believe I traveled by myself. I didn't think it was such a big deal."

"I'm wondering something, Sharon. Am I correct in assuming that you tried hard to be extra good so your mom didn't have more on her plate? Is part of being good being self-sufficient?"

"Well, I never thought of it like that," said Sharon. "Maybe so. I do remember watching Mom go into her bedroom and shut the door. I'd stand outside her door and hear her crying. I was afraid she was going to fall apart. I guess I never asked for her time or attention because I felt there wasn't any to give.

"As I think about it, that's what made me fall in love with Don." Sharon reached over and put her hand on Don's knee. Patting his leg she said, "He gave me so much time and attention. I had never felt that special. Why does it irritate me now? It's so confusing."

"That's a great question, Sharon. I think I'll have a good answer for you after we listen to Don's story. So, Don, why don't you tell me your best and worst memories about your relationship with each parent."

"I'll start with my mom since I have a lot of good memories about her. I'm an only child, so I got a lot of attention from my mom. In fact, I wished I had a brother or sister to take the focus off of me once in a while. My best memories about my mom are about how she was always there for me. I came home from school to fresh-baked cookies, and she was involved in everything I did—Boy Scouts, Little League, soccer, room mom at school, the whole bit."

"She's still involved, and you still are the focus," Sharon chimed in. "She comes over all the time without calling first. I've told Don it drives me crazy, but he won't talk to her about it. I think…"

Don interrupted, "Sharon, if you lived with my dad, you would want to get away too. You know what a grouch he can be. My mom just wants to get out of the house. Can you blame her?"

I noted this problem for a later session and redirected Don. "Tell me about your dad, Don."

"Well, the good memory about Dad is that he went to work so we had some peace. The bad memory is, he came home at night," Don laughed. "The man could hardly ever smile. He was always picking on my mom or me. I'd do my homework in the dining room and call my mom to come help me when he started in on her. He never realized I didn't need the help, even though he knew I was a straight-A student. Sometimes when my dad was a real jerk, my mom got quiet and sort of down. I could usually cheer her up by helping her around the house or taking her a bowl of ice cream."

This was all I needed to know about Don's dad. "Is there anything you would have liked to change about your mom?" I asked.

Don didn't hesitate. "Yes, she was a little overprotective. She wouldn't let me play catcher in Little League because she didn't want someone swinging a bat that close to my head. Soccer wasn't too much of a problem for her, but football was out of the question. That really bugged me, because with my height and weight and athletic ability, I think I would have been really good. I even took a big risk when I was a freshman in high school and told my dad I wanted to play football. I'll never forget his response. He looked at me with disgust and said, 'So you want to be a dumb jock, huh? Forget it. It's a waste of time and money.' That was the end of the discussion."

I was ready to connect some dots. "Sharon and Don, after hearing some of the things you fight about and listening to some of your family histories, I'd like to help you understand what's happening between the two of you. Sharon, I think your early experiences imprinted you to be an avoider. Let me explain. Your mom had only so much to give, and she used it all up on your sisters. She needed you to be a good child, as you said. Unfortunately, you didn't really get to depend on her as much as you needed to. So I have a question for you. Sharon, do you remember, when you were growing up, did anyone ever inquire about what was in your heart and soul or about what it was like living with two difficult siblings?"

"No, I've never even thought about it," Sharon replied.

"That's my point. And it doesn't occur to you now, as a married woman, to look at what is inside you or to share that with Don. When something bothers you, you solve the problem the best you can and then move on, just as you did as a child. Also, I'm sure you have never considered the things you had to give up to keep the family functioning. You protected your mom from falling apart by not needing much of anything. Do you feel like you really need Don now?"

Sharon looked at the floor and in a barely audible voice replied, "No, not really." I could see Sharon's embarrassment in admitting this.

I commented, "It's not your fault, Sharon. When you were growing up, you never learned how to let yourself really need another person or share what was in your heart, so you don't know how to do so now." I glanced over at Don and noticed tears in his eyes.

"Tell me about your tears, Don."

He cleared his throat and in a choked voice said, "I never thought about any of this. I feel sad for her."

"Don, I'd like you to tell that to Sharon directly. Sharon, please look into Don's eyes." Sharon lifted her eyes and met Don's gaze. When she saw his tears, her eyes welled up. Don said, "I feel sad that you never got to depend on your mom. I can see now why it's hard for you to let yourself need me." He pulled Sharon into his arms, and I was quiet while they shared this tender moment.

As they settled back into the couch, again facing me, I said, "Don, I think your imprint is to please. Your experience was the opposite of Sharon's in some ways and similar in others. While Sharon had very little of her mom, you had your mom's constant attention. So to you, love means someone is always there, close by, ready to give you time and attention. Even during your high-school years, your mom was making decisions for you and didn't give you much practice in soaring on your own wings. You keep trying to recreate that feeling with Sharon. You feel good, like things are as they should be, if you have lots of Sharon's time and attention."

"That's true," said Don. "I guess I was trained to expect that."

I continued, "Don, let me ask you the same question I asked Sharon. When you were growing up, did anyone ever ask about the anxiety you felt living with a critical father?"

Don thought about my question. "No. Mom and I really never talked about it. I guess maybe I was nervous around him. I've never really thought about it. We really never talked about feelings."

"It sounds like you don't have much experience sharing your heart either. Also, like Sharon, you protected your mom. You rescued her from your dad's presence and offered your help around the house to cheer her up after your dad dumped on her. So now, when Sharon is taking care of herself and being self-sufficient, I think you feel she is withdrawn and unavailable. And you do today what you did as a child. You scurry around trying to please her so she will be available and attentive. It would be helpful for you to begin to pay attention to the level of anxiety you feel when Sharon is unavailable. I bet it's very similar to what you felt as a child when your mom was quiet, depressed, and unavailable.

"Finally, Sharon, I think you are annoyed by Don's pleasing tendencies because they have more to do with reducing his anxiety than meeting your expressed needs. This will improve when Don meets a need you can feel, like when he hugged you earlier."

"That did feel very different," Sharon said.

THE CORE PATTERN: THE AVOIDER AND THE PLEASER

When they meet, pleasers give avoiders more focused time and attention than these avoiders often received as children. An avoider responds with appreciation to a pleaser's demonstrations of support and caring.

Pleasers often had a volatile, critical, or fearful parent when they were growing up, so initially they enjoy the even-keeled manner of the avoider. Over time, though, as avoiders maintain their self-sufficient style, the pleaser begins to feel rejected and ignored. Space and distance in relationships cause pleasers to feel anxious and insecure, so they try harder to please, hoping to secure more time and attention from the avoider.

At that point, avoiders begin to feel smothered and annoyed by the neediness of their spouse, so they retreat. As the avoider detaches, the anxieties and fears of the pleaser increase, so the chase intensifies. Round and round they go, and the circle continues, causing stress and arguments.

HENRY AND JOLLIE

"Did you hear what I just said?" Jollie asked Henry. They were sitting at the dinner table, and Henry was staring out the window as Jollie recounted her day.

"Uh-huh. I'm listening," Henry replied.

"Then what did I say?" Jollie questioned.

Henry sighed. "You were telling me about your day."

"Exactly what was I telling you, Henry?"

Now Henry was getting irritated. "I don't know, Jollie. You go on and on with so many details. Who could remember everything you say? I've told you that I'm tired when I come home from the office. I just need some peace and quiet. Is that too much to ask?" Henry's voice was rising. "I'm going to go work on my bike in the garage. Leave me alone for a while, okay?"

As Henry left the table, Jollie got in the last comment. "Why do I even want to be with you? You act like being with me is some big chore." Henry ignored her and went into the garage.

Jollie's mind raced as she cleaned up the dishes. *Why doesn't he help me with the dishes?* she wondered. *Henry has been more distant than usual. Maybe he's having an affair. I don't think Henry would do that, but I don't know. Maybe he's just got his eye on somebody else. It just doesn't seem like he's attracted to me anymore. All my friends talk about how much their husbands want to have sex. I'd like to have that problem for a change. Henry always waits for me to initiate. It sure would be nice if it were his idea once in a while. He used to be more interested when we were first married. I wonder what happened. Maybe he is having an affair. Oh, I'm driving myself crazy trying to figure this out. Maybe I'll take a bowl of Henry's favorite ice cream out to the garage and sit with him. Maybe he will talk to me if he's working on his bike. He's always happy when he's working on that stupid bike. Maybe I should turn myself into a bike, and then he'd be all over me.* Jollie wasn't laughing.

Jollie put two bowls of chocolate mint ice cream on a tray and pushed open the door to the garage. "Your favorite ice cream," she announced. "Special delivery."

"Thanks," Henry said as he took his bowl and set it on the ground next to him. Jollie sat on the stool by the workbench and ate quietly. "Now what do you want, Jollie?" Henry asked.

"Nothing; I don't want anything. I'm just eating my ice cream out here with you. I'll be quiet."

Henry sighed. He was tired of trying to explain himself. "Jollie, don't take this personally. I just need some space, okay?"

Now Jollie was hurt to the core. Why did she always set herself up for this? "What!" she said. "I can't even eat my ice cream out here?"

Henry wasn't sure whether he should just give up or insist on some time for himself. "Why don't you go read your new book; the one we bought for you the other day," he suggested.

"I can read when you're not here, Henry. I haven't seen you all day, and I want to be together."

Henry was exasperated. "How many times do I have to say it? Jollie, I want my space!"

Jollie left her ice cream on the workbench and walked out of the garage without a word. She crawled into bed and cried quietly. She knew Henry wouldn't come looking for her. *Maybe this is the beginning of the end,* she thought.

Jollie told Henry the next evening that she had made an appointment with me. "Something is wrong with our marriage, Henry. So I made an appointment with a counselor for Wednesday. I know it's your day off, and I thought maybe you could come with me."

Henry rolled his eyes. "You always have to make a big deal about nothing, Jollie. I think our marriage is fine. You're the one who's always complaining. Not me. You go to a counselor if you want, but I'm not going. I have nothing to say."

LOOKING AT THE ROOTS

As Jollie shared her story, it didn't take me (Kay) long to see that she was dealing with the core pattern that is common when pleasers and avoiders marry. Jollie was the baby of the family, the last of three children, with two older brothers. Her mom delivered a premature baby—the daughter she had always wanted—prior to Jollie's birth. The baby only lived for two weeks. Jollie's mom was devastated by the loss, and then she became very anxious when she discovered she was pregnant again. She rarely left the house for the nine months she was pregnant, fearing she would catch some virus and lose this baby as well. She was relieved and delighted when Jollie was born a healthy, full-term baby.

"I never thought of it until now," Jollie said. "But that is probably why she was so overprotective. She wouldn't let me out of her sight, and she was always worrying about me getting sick or kidnapped. Mom wouldn't let me play in the front yard or go down the block by myself because there might be strangers around. She sort of freaked me out, so I'd get my friends to come play in the backyard by bribing them with the candy jar. We always had a great stash of junk food, so I was never lacking for friends to play with."

"So some of your mom's fear rubbed off on you?" I asked.

"Probably so. I'm definitely a worrier. I guess that's where I learned it."

"Were you worried about other things when you were growing up?" I asked.

"I was really afraid my parents would get a divorce," Jollie explained. "They never fought in front of us, but I sensed a lot of tension in their relationship. My dad adored me. I think he was really happy to have a girl after I was actually born. He grew up with a bunch of brothers, and he told my mom before I was born that he didn't know what to do with a girl. As it turned out, he adored me, and I'm still the apple of his eye. But I don't really think he liked my mom all that much. They are still married, but they sort of live separate lives. Dad goes hunting a lot and has a boat down at the harbor. Mom does a lot of volunteer work at the church."

Now I was ready to hear about Henry. "Jollie, tell me what you know about Henry's growing up years."

Jollie answered, "He doesn't tell me much, but I know he was an only child. His parents died in a car accident two years after we were married. When I ask him what it was like for him growing up, he always says, 'I don't remember much. It was fine.' Personally, if I had grown up in his house, I would have been bored stiff. When we were first married, I used to insist that we go over to his parents' house for a visit. They lived five miles from us, but Henry never wanted much to do with them. It was awkward because they were so quiet, and I'd end up doing all the talking. His mom and dad would just sit there and wait for someone to start the conversation. It was weird. No one could get a word in edgewise at my house growing up. When my family sat down to dinner, we were always talking over each other. Henry said his house was quiet, and no one hardly ever talked at dinner. Can you imagine? I'd be bored stiff."

I went back to Jollie's comment about the car accident. If Henry is an avoider (my hunch), he probably didn't have a long-lasting emotional reaction to their deaths. "Jollie, tell me more about the car accident when Henry's parents died."

"It was so sad. They were driving home from the grocery store in the middle of the day, and a drunk driver hit them head-on. Can you believe it? The guy was wasted, and it wasn't even noon. Henry got the call at work, and I just fell apart when he called me. I can't imagine losing my mom or my dad. I'll be a basket case when that happens. Henry had to calm me down, but he was amazingly stoic. He had to take care of all the details since he is the only child, and it was a lot of work, going through their belongings, selling the house, and all. At first I think he was too busy to really let it sink in. I kept waiting for him to fall apart, but he never did. Whenever I asked him about it, he always said, 'I'm fine. I don't really think about it much.' Is that normal?"

"Well, Jollie, if Henry didn't have much of an emotional connection with his parents and he never looked to them for help or support, maybe there isn't much for him to miss. You only miss people when they are gone if they have met some important need in your life. From what you tell me, his parents could hardly have even a superficial conversation. Do you think they ever got to know you very well?"

Jollie was quiet, contemplating my question. "Now that I think about it, they didn't know me at all. I can't remember their ever asking me one question."

"That's my point," I said. "Maybe they really didn't know Henry either."

"You're probably right," said Jollie. "How sad."

I continued. "You two have a relational pattern that is more common than you might think. Henry was influenced by his early experiences not to need much from relationships. Let's call him an avoider, because he avoids being too needy or too emotional. He probably became quite self-sufficient, and he held back any emotions because his parents would have had difficulty knowing how to respond. I bet he was stable and confident when you met him, but not very self-disclosing."

"That's true, but he wanted to be with me a lot more when we were dating. Now he doesn't. I don't get it."

"Jollie," I explained, "I'm sure that, at first, Henry loved all the attention you gave him. Can you imagine how good that would feel after growing up in such a quiet house with his parents? But avoiders like Henry often struggle once they marry because they are used to being independent. Marriage is about needing and being needed. He's a rookie at those things. He truly doesn't know what you are looking for with all this 'Let's be together' talk. Growing up, Henry never experienced enough togetherness to know what he's missing or what you're wanting."

"I get it!" exclaimed Jollie. "This really helps. I've been feeling so rejected. It feels like Henry just doesn't love me, but you're saying he didn't get enough connection from his mom or dad to be a good giver or receiver."

"Exactly," I confirmed. "Henry would probably be struggling with this no matter who he married."

"Now let's think about how your upbringing influenced you, Jollie. Can you see how you had to take care of your mom's fear and relieve her anxiety by staying nearby? She taught you that distance or separation put you in some kind of danger. Can you remember being anxious when you were away from your mom?"

"Absolutely," said Jollie. "I used to scream my head off if a baby-sitter came over. And more than once Mom came and picked me up from a friend's house when I tried to spend the night. My brothers used to tease me about being a scaredy-cat."

"I'm not surprised," I said. "You adopted a caretaking, pleasing role to keep your mom happy. Accommodating her wishes and staying close relieved anxiety for both of you. Your home influenced you to be a pleaser, Jollie. What I mean is that you try to make others happy so they will stay close by. For example, taking Henry the bowl of ice cream gave you a reason to be near him. When Henry wants space, which is normal for him, it goes against your childhood training to stay close, which is normal for you. You are a pleaser and he is an avoider. On the surface it looks like you want more from the relationship than Henry does. While that may be partly true, your pleasing is more about relieving your anxiety than anything else."

Jollie was quietly digesting all this. "At least I'm close to my mom," Jollie said. "That's more than Henry got."

"That's true," I replied. "You learned something about depending on another person, Jollie, but staying nearby and relieving her fears also kept you from learning to take risks and venture out. I wonder how your mom handled some of your deeper fears. Did you ever tell her that you worried about them divorcing?"

"I remember trying to talk to my mom about that one time. She just laughed at me and told me not to worry my silly little head about it."

"Did that help?" I asked.

"No," replied Jollie. "For years I lay in bed at night worrying about it."

"So, Jollie, is it accurate to say that you didn't have anyone you could depend on to help you with your deepest fears?"

Jollie reflected, "I never thought about it like that. I guess I'm not close to my mom in that way. Come to think of it, neither Henry nor I learned how to deal with our inner feelings as children, so no wonder we struggle so much in our marriage. But how can we change as a couple if Henry won't come in?"

"Let's take a few more weeks to continue talking together. And today, when you get home, write down everything you remember about our session. Try to think of other memories from the past or scenes from the present that show your role as a pleaser or Henry's style as an avoider. When you can describe your core pattern to me and I feel like you really understand it, then I'll send you home to talk to Henry about it. We'll see what happens from there. Even if Henry won't come in or listen to what you are learning, he will notice changes in you. And I think you'll be surprised by how different your marriage can be if you just work on your part. So let's take this one week at a time."

WANT TO DANCE?

Initially, avoiders see pleasers as sweet, caring, and attentive. The pleasers' considerate, thoughtful, acts make avoiders feel noticed and special. This feels great because they didn't get a lot of personal attention growing up. Also, since avoiders are used to taking care of themselves, the pleasers' acts of kindness are pleasant and enjoyable.

Pleasers like the consistency, strength, confidence, and even temperament of avoiders. Furthermore, avoiders are easy to please because they don't expect much out of a relationship. So pleasers feel successful. They often had to work much harder to get recognition when they were growing up. Also, if a pleaser had a critical or volatile parent, this relationship with an avoider feels like a breeze because the avoider doesn't get upset very easily.

STUMBLING STEPS

Over time, however, the pleaser begins to feel rejected by the avoider's independent, self-sufficient relational style. The avoider's tendencies to disengage and detach make the pleaser feel anxious about the relationship; the pleaser wonders what is wrong. Pleasers also wonder why avoiders don't need them as much as they used to. And when pleasers feel cut off, they pursue in an effort to close the gap and lower their anxiety.

Avoiders become annoyed when a pleaser interprets their need for space as personal rejection. This conclusion is baffling to avoiders who have always been independent and self-sufficient. They begin to see the pleaser as smothering and too needy. They distance and continue to be self-sufficient as they have always been.

An avoider's irritation increases a pleaser's anxiety. Wondering why their spouse isn't happier and doesn't want to be closer, pleasers increase their efforts to get closer. Then they begin to resent the fact that they give more in the relationship. This extra effort irritates avoiders because they weren't asking for anything in the first place.

And the dance continues.

WHAT EACH PERSON FEELS

The Avoider

- My spouse thinks something is wrong if I want some space or time alone.
- I feel smothered by how much my spouse wants.
- I wish my spouse had his or her own interests and didn't lean on me so much.
- My spouse gives me things and does things for me that I don't want or need.
- Sometimes my spouse is too nice, and it feels fake.

- I feel as if my spouse is always taking my emotional temperature in indirect ways.
- My spouse makes me feel guilty if I want time away.

The Pleaser

- I feel rejected and anxious when my spouse does not want to be with me.
- I fear that my anger will push my spouse further away, so I try to keep things peaceful and pleasant.
- I try to read my spouse's mood and feelings and adjust so he or she will want to be with me.
- I sometimes feel resentful because I give a lot more to the marriage than my spouse gives, but I usually don't voice my anger.
- It feels as if my spouse doesn't need me very much.
- I am always closing the gap or saying I'm sorry after I sense tension in the relationship.

Does this dance resemble what goes on in your marriage? If so, you have lots of company. But know that other couples have broken this core pattern by doing the exercises in the workbook (chapter 13 especially). Take a few minutes to read through those exercises now and then take that first step toward change.

Chapter 14

Other Challenging Combinations

By now, you've seen many of the challenging dances that result when relational imprints collide. We've looked at the most common combinations we see, but what if you happen to recognize a different core pattern in your interaction as a couple? Though the following combinations are less common, they can be every bit as challenging as the ones we've already discussed.

THE AVOIDER-AVOIDER DANCE

Pleasant talk and shared interests cause two avoiders to enjoy spending time together. Since both individuals are independent and self-sufficient, they may be satisfied with less contact than most dating couples find satisfactory. Long-distance relationships are also more acceptable to this combination, and usually the level of emotional connection between this pair is somewhat superficial because it is familiar and comfortable. Also, since neither partner is comfortable with emotional displays, this relationship is often even-keeled; the couple experiences few ups and downs. Not surprisingly, feelings are rarely the topic of conversations, but intellectual discussions about subjects of mutual interest may be quite deep. If both people are introverts, each will value and maintain space, solitude, and privacy.

As long as they don't encounter major stressors, this couple can coast through life with minimal conflict. Each person tends to deal with problems independently, minimizing and ignoring irritations that arise. Over time, inner resentments may build, but the partners are committed to avoiding confrontation so problems are rarely addressed or resolved. If this couple remains childless, projects, hobbies, or travel are enjoyable diversions that take the focus off underlying problems or unspoken resentment.

If two avoiders do have children, the stresses of parenting may press them to communicate more, but parenting concerns will be the focus of their conversations. Since mastery of life's challenges is important to avoiders, the demands of parenting will be taken seriously and divert attention away from the marriage relationship. Then, when the kids leave home, two strangers are left looking at each other.

For this couple, the marriage dance will get difficult when they face a crisis that makes it hard for one or both of them to maintain the composure to which each is accustomed. Lisa and Jerry are a good example of what can happen when stress takes the lid off locked-up feelings. Their first fifteen years of married life were uneventful, but everything changed when Lisa was diagnosed with breast cancer. Jerry had only known Lisa as cool, calm, and collected, and Lisa had always prided herself on her logical approach to life. Lisa's composure lasted through the first round of chemo, and then her emotional walls began to crumble. She wanted sympathy and comfort from Jerry, and he was lost. Jerry kept telling Lisa not to get emotional, that everything would be okay, and Lisa resented Jerry's simplistic approach. The illness pushed both Lisa and Jerry way out of their comfort zones, and they were suddenly stepping all over each other's toes. Navigating new life challenges may require the couple to learn how to handle emotions and address problems more openly.

Common Beliefs of Avoider-Avoider Pairs

- In our marriage, both of us are independent and self-reliant.
- I like the fact that my spouse is logical and analytical.
- We like to be together, but we don't show a lot of affection.
- We rarely fight because we solve problems on our own.
- Both of us enjoy time alone.
- Privacy is important to both of us.
- In our marriage, nothing gets us too bothered or upset.
- Rarely does either of us openly show our emotions.

Since avoider-avoider couples don't often address problems, they rarely seek counseling unless they find themselves in the middle of a crisis. And since most couples do face major challenges some time in their married life, it is wise to work on the growth goals for this relational style if you relate to this duo. (We have found that our biggest challenge in working with this combination is getting them to sit down and have a face-to-face conversation about their relationship, including their feelings.)

THE VACILLATOR-VACILLATOR, CONTROLLER-VACILLATOR, CONTROLLER-CONTROLLER DANCES

In all three of these combinations, two people who both need control are marrying each other. The resulting core patterns are similar, so we will talk about all three combinations together.

When a couple like this meets, there is often an immediate strong and passionate connection. The chemistry seems to be just right, and the intense good feelings are a welcome relief from the pain of the past. The relationship is all good as long as the idealization phase lasts. Then it goes downhill with the same intensity.

Being in one of these three combos is like being on a wild roller-coaster ride that never ends. Intense fights followed by passionate reunions characterize the constant battle for control. Usually there is a history of deep hurts, abandonment, and chaos in the childhood homes of each partner, and the deeper their hurts, the wilder the ride. Experiences from the past sit like a pool of gasoline inside each person. A current conflict that brings up old, buried feelings sparks the fuse and ignites the gasoline. Each partner's feelings are intense as the past floods into the present, and nothing positive happens when feelings are off the charts. Often unaware of the connection between the current conflict and past hurts, the two partners begin to blame and hate each other, each believing that the other is the cause of all their misery.

When the controller marries the victim, someone relinquishes control. But these three combos are often more volatile because both people have been imprinted to need control. Vacillators, whose childhood relationships were often unpredictable, like to have control in order to keep their partners consistently focused on them. They do not want any possibility of abandonment. Likewise, controllers want to have power over others because they were dealt with so harshly and unfairly as kids. To be controlled is to suffer—that was the childhood experience of the controller. In addition, both controllers and vacillators tend to bounce back and forth between extremes of good or bad, all or nothing, idealizing or undervaluing, possessive or indifferent, and so forth. At any given moment, this couple feels really good or really bad; they know little middle ground.

So just getting two of these people to sit through a counseling session without a major blowup is a challenge. I (Kay) once watched two vacillators battling it out in my office and getting nowhere fast. I said, "Is this how it usually goes for you two?" They ignored me. I waited awhile longer and asked, "Do you two want to pay me a hundred dollars to watch you fight for the rest of the hour?" Still they ignored me. Then I told them, "I see the pattern. Now let's try something different." Their battle continued. Finally I stood up, plopped myself down between them, held my hands up, and yelled, "STOP!" That worked.

Common Beliefs of These Pairs
- When we first met, we never imagined our marriage would be this rocky.
- I love my spouse, but at the same time I hate him or her.
- We have big fights, but when we make up, it feels great.
- We have many ups and downs in our relationship.
- Our feelings are very intense when we fight.
- We both end up yelling and screaming when we fight.
- We try not to fight in front of the kids, but it happens anyway.
- Both of us are strong-willed, and neither of us likes to give in.
- My spouse never listens; he or she just wants me to hear his or her point of view.

If you recognize your marriage in the descriptions above, it will be necessary for you and your spouse to really work on the growth goals for your style suggested in the workbook. When both partners do some changing and growing, the intensity of their core pattern begins to quiet down. Understanding your triggers, which we'll discuss in chapter 16, is also extremely important to changing this dynamic.

DO SECURE PEOPLE MARRY INSECURE PEOPLE?

When it comes to marriage, anything is possible, but we do see strong trends as we work with couples. First of all, people have a way of finding partners who have similar levels of pain in their backgrounds. While their childhood homes may have been very different, they usually suffered in similar ways that are not always apparent at first glance. For example, Milan and I came from very different backgrounds. His family was overly engaged, and mine was more disengaged. Growing up, we defended ourselves from pain differently. He tried to please, and I detached and took care of myself. What we had in common was that we were both lonely, wishing for someone to search our hearts and know us deeply.

Many times during initial meetings with couples, one person will announce, "I came from a great family, but my spouse had a messed-up family." In my mind I'm thinking, "We will see." Many times, as we review the histories, the facts tell a different story. One couple I worked with, Marsha and Mark, started therapy with this belief that one person's family was fine and the other's was not. Marsha's family did have obvious problems, and the source of her anxiety was readily apparent. Mark's family was in many ways much more functional.

What we discovered, however, was that Mark had secretly worried for years that his parents would divorce, and he carefully monitored their relationship for any sign of distress. During the night his imagination went wild, and he played out many possible scenarios if a divorce were to happen. He thought about the agony of choosing whom he would live with and how much he would miss being together. Then his thinking got more catastrophic after he watched a story on the evening news about some children whose parents had died in a tragic car accident. Mark added that possibility to his nighttime imaginations. Anxiety was his constant companion for years, and no one ever suspected anything was remotely wrong. But the anxiety levels Mark experienced growing up were very similar to the level of anxiety his wife, Marsha, experienced in her childhood home. A brief note about their relationship: in their marriage, Mark was a pleaser, still monitoring for signs of disaster, and Marsha was an avoider who managed her anxiety with exercise that bordered on excessive.

Breaking Your Core Pattern

Milan: Living in a negative core pattern is like having one person dance to salsa music while the partner is moving to a three-beat waltz. The goal of healing is to create a new core pattern so both are dancing to the same tune. If positive changes are going to happen, though, a mental shift must first take place in which the two individuals see things differently.

In the movie *A Beautiful Mind,* Russell Crowe brilliantly plays the part of Dr. John Nash, a genius mathematics professor at Princeton University. As the movie begins, Dr. Nash—together with the audience—is unaware that he has a mental illness. Over time we learn that schizophrenia is animating his thoughts and bizarre behaviors. Ignoring the pleas of his wife, doctor, and associates, he continues to listen to and believe the voices of the three imaginary people within his mind, who he believes are real. One of the three voices he listens to is that of a little girl.

At a dramatic moment in the movie, Dr. Nash's marriage is in shambles, and his wife is hurriedly driving their baby away in the car. John Nash jumps out in front of the car, forcing his wife to stop. As he stands in front of it with his hands on the hood, he shouts to his wife, "The little girl isn't real! She's not real… She never grows up… She can't be real!" At that moment Dr. Nash experienced a mental shift, and with that shift, he saw life differently and chose to live in a different manner. For the rest of his life, he chose to recognize the source of those voices and refused to let them control his life.

Toward the end of the story, an associate asks an aged and healthier Dr. Nash, "Are they (the three people) still there?" John Nash looks over to his right side, and the three people are walking next to him with their gazes firmly fixed on him. John looks back at his associate and says, "Yes, but I don't talk with them anymore." And, at the end of the movie, after he is awarded a Nobel Peace Prize, Dr. Nash is helping his wife put on her overcoat. She says, "Are they here?" Again, John Nash looks over to his right, and the three persons are across the lobby staring at him. But he turns back, warmly smiles at his wife, looks sweetly into her eyes, and says, "Yes, they are, but let's you and I go out to dinner and enjoy our evening." Dr. Nash had broken a core pattern, and it changed how he loved.

THERE IS HOPE!

Just like Dr. Nash, you must personally decide to make changes in your wounded love style. God wishes for all of us to grow up in our broken parts so that we more resemble His character and attributes. This means that we must each come to a place of managing our own injuries and subsequent reactive responses. Kay often says, "Insight is easy, but change is hard." She is right, because deep transformation happens only with hard work and persistence over time. Our hope is that God offers us a way out of our negative core patterns by showing us a path through the profitable pain of growth.

God says that trials will make us "perfect and complete" (see James 1:1–4). Have you ever thought of your marriage as a trial that God wants to use to change both your characters? As hard as it may be to imagine, Kay has been one of the most challenging trials in my life. Yet God has used her to be my greatest source of personal growth. I look back and see that I became stronger and more complete in my emotional and spiritual life because of daily workouts in the marriage gymnasium—which I now affectionately refer to as "Kayzercise."

We are all in this together—most people are dealing with the same core patterns. If Kay and I can do it, so can you. Some of the treatment we recommend is in the workbook, and you will benefit if you take the time to go through the exercises we have provided. Part 4 of this book will also give you some specific guidelines to follow.

We hope and pray that once you understand your core pattern, as well as your individual part of your marriage dance, you will begin to experience a mental shift and feel inspired to choose a new path. We hope this book is already changing how you love as you focus on loving in a new way that is healthier and more secure. In the next part of this book, you will find some practical ways to help that happen.

Part

4

Changing How
We Love

Chapter 15

The Comfort Circle

Now that we've seen how imprints collide to create unhealthy and even destructive core patterns, we need to see how to escape those old dances. We have already challenged you to develop a new awareness of your own impaired love style, take charge of it, and work toward becoming a secure connector. You'll find many more specific solutions and growth goals in the workbook, but by now you should have a pretty good idea of what your marriage dance looks like, and you know some adjustments are necessary if you want to do a new and healthier dance together. You will need to learn how to take steps around the comfort circle. Remember the comfort question in chapter 2: can you recall being comforted as a child after a time of emotional distress? If you're like many people, you have little or no memory of comfort and did not feel deeply known and valued by your parents when you were growing up. So we want to make sure you develop the ability to bring comfort and relief to each other in your marriage. The steps around the comfort circle are designed to help you do just that. Learning to become vulnerable, share your feelings, speak truthfully, listen deeply, and bring relief to your mate will revolutionize how you love.

But I (Milan) will bet some of you are like me. When I face something new and challenging, I often feel overwhelmed. Sometimes it's so hard to get started. Even here, faced with the high stakes of staying locked in the old patterns of our relationship and continuing to step on each other's toes, I can still remember my initial resistance to giving the comfort circle a try. Though now I can see how foolish I was to fear the decision that's brought me more happiness in life than any other I've made, I had no such assurance then. All I knew was that I didn't want my marriage to stay the same.

Before we get started with this comfort circle, let me ask you a question. Do you think you could run a marathon? That's a 26.2-mile run without stopping. Most people would probably say, "No way!" Yet, barring any major medical problem, you actually could run a marathon. How? Well, by training, of course. Initially, the training is slow and gradual. You may begin by simply walking one mile on the first day of the program. Within a few weeks you'd be jogging one mile. Within a couple of months, you could enter your first 5K fun run. Gradually, as you followed the training schedule, your distances would increase, and within a few more months, you'd be ready to run your first marathon. And you'd never have known you could do it if you hadn't tried.

Learning these new dance steps is a lot like training for a marathon. For some of you husbands, though, dance lessons are probably the last thing you want to be doing on your Saturday evenings. But let me ask you: Have you ever imagined the thrill on the other side of all that work? What exhilaration is waiting after the time and effort you'd be putting in? Many men and women will never know, but that's their choice. This choice is yours too. You *can* do this. Believe me. We could share story after story of people who have discovered the importance of emotion and the joy of expressing it in a healthy, reciprocal, accepting relationship. As you work on changing your imprint, you will begin to break the destructive core pattern that has plagued your marriage. You'll learn to trust the principles and to chart your progress. You will begin to notice positive changes in the patterns you have unconsciously danced for so many years. Remember, a caterpillar doesn't turn into a butterfly in a day, and neither will your marriage be transformed overnight. But as you gradually begin to see results, you'll be dancing smoothly together just as Kay and I have learned to do.

All we're asking you to do is try some new steps that will help you love better and become vulnerable in sharing your feelings, speaking truthfully and deeply listening and comforting each other. As simple as that idea is, many people are absolutely terrified by it. The thought of embracing their emotions is worse than a thousand deaths. While women sometimes find it an easier concept to consider, that's not always the case. Enough ugly history, and anyone would resist. And then there's the stereotype that one witty woman described: "Men are like mascara. They usually run at the first sign of emotion." Besides not necessarily wanting to embrace their emotions, men also have to deal with the social stigma against men expressing emotion and experiencing intimacy. Also, as a rule, men usually have less experience identifying and sharing emotions, and what they learned about the subject from their families was not pleasant or helpful.

All right, you might be saying, *so I've got problems. Who doesn't? I don't really need to fundamentally change how I engage with my spouse, do I?*

Let me tell you about Al and Tamara's experience, and you decide. Tamara had been trying to change their dance for years. She had asked Al to talk more; she wanted them to share their feelings and get to know each other on a deeper level. She had wanted to have more fun together, take dancing lessons, go to museums and art galleries, and start attending musical and cultural events at their local music center and theater. An avowed avoider, though, Al was resistant and continued to distance himself from Tamara until one day she announced she was leaving him because she had fallen in love with another man. Tamara happened to meet him at a local coffee shop that was close to the freeway that each of them took to work. Gradually, they saw more and more of each other until it became a daily event of talking, listening, sharing feelings, and comforting each other. Within a few months, this person who engaged in the comfort circle with her had captured Tamara's heart, and she ended up walking away from a fifteen-year marriage with Al.

Al was very hurt, angry, and disappointed by his wife's abandonment, and in his mind, she was the guilty one. While Tamara shouldn't have ended their marriage, neither should Al have ignored her pleas for connection and stubbornly allowed the gap between them to widen.

But here's the ironic part. After losing Tamara, Al eventually met another woman. He had no idea he was falling in love with a woman who was so much like his former wife. Al ended up taking dance lessons with her, buying season tickets to the local theater, and attending cheerleading and dance events his new girlfriend was directing. He did for his new girlfriend exactly what Tamara had asked him to do for years.

Additionally, Al and Tamara's divorce had lasting consequences and aftereffects that extended into their next marriages. For years, they had sticky legal battles, custody issues, visitation schedules, alimony payments, properties to sell, and step-children to get to know. It was all very costly and time consuming. So, I ask, why not forgo the mess, learn a new dance, and fall in love again with the one you already know so well? Life is full of critical choices that result in either future blessings or far-reaching consequences. You can work at your relationship now or pay the price of neglect later. Either way, it's going to cost you time and effort. Again, you can stay locked in your old pattern or try something new. Why not try some new dance steps?

As you take the steps outlined in the chapters that follow, the new behaviors will allow you to start on a healthier path and reap the blessings for your efforts.

"BUT MY WIFE BOUGHT THE BOOK!"

If your wife handed this book to you and said, "Here, read this," I apologize. Believe me, brother, I feel your pain. If the guys at work ever heard you were learning how to be a better comforter and nurturer, they'd laugh you out of the lunchroom. So I'll let you in on a little secret: don't tell them. Spare yourself their ignorant ridicule and keep the day-to-day work with your wife between the two of you. Be tough on the job and tender at home. There's nothing wrong with having a public life and a private life. Eventually, they'll see the fruit of your efforts down the road, and you will have a story of your own to tell.

We would like to suggest that it will be worth every bit of time you put into your marriage. Now is the time to begin. When you're older and the kids are gone, what will you have then? You will only have each other. So, as I say to couples, "Why not make the second half better than the first?"

There are some great rewards to learning this new dance. Consider some of the reports from men who have given the new steps a try:

- "I drive home from work without anxiety!"
- "Our sex life is incredible!"
- "When I walk in the door, I'm greeted with a smile and a hug."

- "The sex is amazing!"
- "We have no secrets anymore. We feel so much freer with each other."
- "Our sex life has never been better!"
- "I'm accepted and free to say what I think!"

You may say, "That all sounds good, but I'm no professional." Actually, Kay and I are very much like you. We began our marriage journey before we were counseling couples. We have our weaknesses and fears just like anyone. All of us married folks really are on the same road, subject to the same relational problems and difficulties everyone else faces. Kay and I have just learned some new dance steps. We have not forgotten how hard marriage was at times, but we also know how incredibly rewarding our effort has been. We persevered because we knew God wanted us to. So, men, be courageous and take the lead. We're not asking you to do anything we haven't seen countless people come through. And, by the way, learning this new comfort circle really does improve the sex.

THE NEW STEPS

The task before you now involves you and your spouse learning the steps to a new dance, the bonding dance. We are going to spend some time talking about the four critical steps every couple must learn in order to break out of familiar old cycles and embrace the essential techniques of the bonding dance.

In chapter 4, we talked about how trust and respect are established in the relationship between parents and babies who successfully go around the comfort circle. Except for the baby talk (unless you are into baby talk), the process is the same for a married couple wanting to form a strong, secure bond with each other. We have to learn the same steps plus a few extra ones. But—again—the rewards are worth it. Think about how, when you are upset and your spouse is aware of it and able to offer you comfort and relief, the trust in your relationship deepens. The more times this happens, the stronger your bond becomes.

Now, back to the comfort question. Were you able to remember receiving comfort as a child when you were distressed? For many of us the answer was no, but what if you and your spouse learned to give comfort to each other now, as adults?

Many of us did not feel deeply known or understood as children or teenagers. But if our mates have tools to explore the deep recesses of our hearts and will tenderly hold our pain, our love for them will grow deeper. And what if our mates could see our shameful secrets and our inadequacies and still love us? We would cherish that gift of grace. Our marriages would be different. If a couple follows the format of this comfort circle, over time it will yield the fruit of comfort, trust, and respect. That kind of deep, meaningful bond is the secret to a happy marriage. And as it becomes your new dance, you will find yourselves relaxing, enjoying each other more, and experiencing relief as your bond deepens.

THE STEPS AROUND THE COMFORT CIRCLE

Here are the simple steps around the comfort circle. Please see the detailed diagram on the following page.

1. *Seek Awareness.* Partners discover their feelings, underlying needs, and triggers.
2. *Engage.* Partners decide to bring their new awareness into the relationship.
3. *Explore.* The speaker shares while the listener clarifies by asking further questions. The listener responds with understanding, validates the speaker's feelings, and offers to meet the needs of the speaker after asking the question, "What do you need?"
4. *Resolve.* Resolution brings relief. The speaker offers some closure, which may involve negotiation, problem solving, compromising, owning, confessing, and forgiving. Sometimes it involves comfort and nurture. The speaker's needs are met or deferred until an agreed-upon time.

BONDING BY NUMBERS

That sounds like bonding by numbers. Are you kidding? Nope! Actually, Kay and I do this day after day with each other. As Kay and I work on our own individual hurtful imprints, we take trips around the comfort circle at the same time. The

The Comfort Circle

1. Seek Awareness
of feelings and underlying needs.

4. Resolve
needs verbally and with touch,
seeking how and when needs
may be met in the future.

2. Engage
with feelings and
acknowledge needs openly.

3. Explore
the speaker's thoughts and feelings—
listening, validating, and concluding
with, "What do you need?"

Note: Completing the circle should bring relief—an increase in trust and feelings of connectedness. If hurtful action or inaction is experienced at any point in the circle, you should begin again.

---

steps around the circle might look simple, but their effects are profound. In fact, you'll probably find that getting around this circle is a bit more challenging than it looks at first glance. But we think it's vitally important the steps be simple and easily understood since many of us start out so afraid of true intimacy. Many people we see in our offices cannot get past point number one because much of the time they do not know what they feel. They have not learned to say to themselves, *Self, what are you feeling right now?*

With practice and repetition, trial and error, any couple can learn to do this dance. Trust us, it works! When I have new couples in my office, I tell them I have one major goal for them, and that is to learn to get around this circle. My job is simply to help them figure out where they're stuck and help them get back on track.

I'm the type of person who needs numbers to follow. Most folks find it helpful to follow a sequence or a numbered order as they start to do something new. Recently, for instance, a friend was trying to teach us the salsa. While I prefer the kind that goes with chips, he was telling us to follow the numbers that he was counting out loud. I was finding that the salsa is different from the cha-cha and the waltz, and for some reason I was messing up and couldn't follow. Eventually, as the teacher kept counting, I caught on and did an awkward version of the salsa. Just about the time I was really getting my groove on—*Nice move, Rico Suave!*— I stepped on Kay's foot and bumped into the poor guy behind me who was as lost as I was. Suddenly, the Rico fantasy was gone and I had come back to my senses realizing this was going to take awhile.

When you watch professional dancers, cheerleaders, or other performers practice, you will often hear the coach or choreographer counting aloud or clapping hands to set the cadence for the athlete. By the time of the performance, though, you will no longer hear the numbers shouted aloud, for they are implanted in the performer's mind and body. The athlete is still moving by the numbers, yet the steps are now so automatic that one movement simply flows into the next. The same thing happens in the comfort circle. If you follow the numbers long enough, you will become proficient and automatic in your responses; you'll understand exactly how to navigate any emotional encounter.

Tim and Clair's first attempt around the circle was something I'll never forget.

When Tim walked into my office, I noticed right away the classic military haircut they call high and tight. He was a tough customer and obviously calculated in his approach to life, which I suspect is exactly the kind of person the government wants flying a thirty-five-million-dollar plane. He looked at me with obvious contempt, not completely unreasonable since, at the time, I was sporting a mullet. I'd have explained my theory of compensatory lengthening—that is, as my hair begins to recede from the front, I let it grow longer in the back—but I could see he wasn't interested.

Not surprisingly, Tim's wife had made the appointment, so I began by assuring Tim that I would hold his visit in strict confidence and that only those whom he chose to tell would know of our meetings. I suspected he'd keep our meetings a closely guarded secret. After talking with the two of them for a while, I deduced that Tim was flying in the absolutely wrong direction in his marriage, and, according to Clair, all of his relational approaches were crash landings. Life was not a joy ride for either of them, and after three years of marriage and a one-year-old toddler, Clair was ready to push the eject button.

SEEK AWARENESS

I began the trip around the circle by saying, "Tim, tell me your perspective on the problems in your marriage."

This first step simply involves developing an awareness of our emotions. Yet for many people, this step is incredibly difficult. It is amazing how many people cannot identify their feelings. But, then again, when we were growing up, most of us never had someone older and wiser invite us to share our true feelings.

After several minutes, Tim said, "Clair is so emotional and always crying. She cries when I'm home, when I'm out on maneuvers, and when I'm out on six-month deployments."

I asked Tim to tell me what he feels when Clair cries. He looked at me rather defiantly and said, "I get mad at her and tell her to shut up. Crying doesn't change anything."

I asked Tim to consider what feeling might be underneath his anger. After a prolonged silence, he turned to me with a deer-in-the-headlights look and said, "I have no idea!"

No surprise there. I handed him our soul words list of feelings. "Take your time and pick any of the words that seem to best fit," I said, noting the set in his jaw.

He sighed and slowly worked his way down the page. After a while, he blinked, and his head nodded slightly as he shifted in his seat and sighed again. "It looks like you've found a word," I said.

Tim reluctantly looked up. "I guess underneath my anger I'm a little agitated and scared."

Clair looked at him, and her jaw dropped. "Scared? You're never scared! You're a fighter pilot, for Pete's sake!"

I quickly stepped in, gave Miss Helpful a quick time-out sign with my hands, and thanked Tim for his honesty. He needed some encouragement to become aware of his feelings, and a large reason for his discomfort was obviously Clair, who could have—had I let her—easily sealed off the mineshaft of emotions that Tim had just opened. Nonetheless, the first step of awareness was taken, and we moved on to the second.

ENGAGE

The goal of the second step is to bring the newly discovered feelings, thoughts, and reactions out from the hidden recesses of our souls and into the open light of relationship. Negative or painful feelings do not diminish when we hold them in the dark recesses of our minds. In fact, nothing can change until we take a risk and speak truthfully about what is inside us. As the Bible says, "The truth will make you free" (John 8:32). But at first truth telling can be quite distressing, especially if we learned growing up to be indirect, evasive, or artificial.

I told Tim that his feelings of anger and fear about Clair's crying were not going to get better unless he was willing to engage with Clair and allow her to explore his emotions with him. He was resistant at first because I am certain he could not imagine feeling differently about wanting her tears to stop, for they made him very uncomfortable.

"Tim," I said, "do you remember the movie *Top Gun*?" Tim nodded slowly. "Remember the scene where Maverick first goes up with his new navigator after Goose has died and they're up in the clouds fighting off the Russian MiGs?" Tim stared, daring me to go on. "A brush with one of the enemy planes nearly sends Maverick into another tailspin, and he has a sudden flashback to when Goose was killed. All of his fragile emotions are triggered, and he begins to turn the jet around and disengage. Eventually, he collects his emotions, puts his fear in check, and reengages, but he had to gather some emotional resolve.

"Tim, I think we're all a bit like Maverick. Hurtful encounters from our past cause us to shy away from sharing our emotions and listening to our spouse's feelings. Yet, in order to succeed in relationships, we must get past the triggers and engage. If we pull out of every dogfight, we will lose the battle for sure. Would you be willing to engage for a few minutes in an honest talk with Clair if I get in the cockpit and help you navigate?"

Reluctantly, Tim said, "I guess so."

"Great," I said, "but while I'm in the cockpit, don't call me Goose. Just Milan is fine." He gave a faint smile, and we moved to the third step.

EXPLORE

I explained that, for the next few minutes, Tim would be the speaker and Clair would be the listener. As they sat on the couch in my office, I asked Tim to turn and face Clair, and I gave Clair an opening question to get the ball rolling. "Clair, ask Tim to tell you again about the emotions he experiences when you cry."

Before she could begin, Tim looked at me and said, "Why do I have to say it again? I already said it."

I answered, "Tim, it's important for you to say your feelings directly to Clair while you are looking into her eyes." The subsequent results were encouraging. As their eyes met, both Clair and Tim welled up with tears, and he said, "I'm afraid deep inside when you cry. Your emotions scare me. I just want them to stop. I feel horrible inside when I see you cry. So I get mad at you to try to get you to stop."

At that moment, his vulnerability, honesty, and transparency began to soften her heart. Her countenance changed, and she started to look at him with love. I asked him to tell me what he saw on her face. "Some empathy and compassion."

"Tim, how does it make you feel to see her softened demeanor?"

"Surprised," Tim replied. "She has built up so much anger and resentment toward me over the last year. I haven't seen that look in her eyes in a long time."

It never ceases to amaze me how differently our conversations go when we are clear in our communication and we risk being honest and vulnerable.

At this point, I looked at Clair, the listener, and instructed her to go into a phase of extended listening, which is the second part of step three. At this point, the goal is to do just the opposite of what comes naturally—not listening and internally planning a rebuttal. In this example, extended listening meant that Clair would ask thoughtful questions, reflect back what she hears to check for accuracy, and then, in her own words, acknowledge Tim's emotions. I encouraged Clair to find out more about what Tim had just shared by asking any questions she wanted. She hesitated for a few moments and looked back at me, bewildered. "Close your eyes, take a deep breath, and just find out more about what Tim just said."

As a pleaser who had become angry over time, she struggled with what to say and how to say it so that it would be most palatable. "I don't know what to ask."

I reassured her that she was in good company and that all of us are so used to planning our response while another person is talking that it never occurs to us to ask questions. "Look at Tim and ask him why he felt scared when you cried and if he ever felt that way as a child."

Although Clair already knew that Tim had grown up in a military family, he went on to tell her that his dad was a "man's man" and not very available emotionally. "Fear was never in my dad's vocabulary, and he often laughed at me when I would become emotional. He would hug me sometimes, but if I ever started to cry, he told me that I needed to be a man and take care of Mom."

I prompted Clair to another question, which I pointed to on the list of listener questions (see pages 256–58). "Were there other times you were scared?" she asked.

Tim replied, "Yes, even worse was when Dad was on maneuvers or deployed overseas. Mom would cry a lot, and I used to lie in bed at night worrying."

At this point Clair was getting the hang of her role, so I encouraged her to come up with her own question. "Tim, that must have been horrible. I never knew that," she said as she reached over and touched his shoulder. She was beginning to see young Tim. "When your dad said to take care of your mom and she was crying, what did you think you were supposed to do?"

Great question! Tim was quiet for almost a minute. Clair started to say something, and I stopped her. "Just wait a bit longer," I said.

Finally, softly, Tim said, "I just remember being afraid that something was dreadfully wrong, and I just wanted it all to stop. I didn't know what I was supposed to do. It just killed me to hear Mom cry like that. Now I realize she was probably wondering if Dad was going to come home, or if she would end up a widow raising us all by herself. I was scared of that also. My best friend's dad didn't come home. I knew it could happen to me, but we never talked about it. I guess I worried a lot as a kid, now that I think about it. But no one ever knew."

Clair was clearly surprised by the depth of Tim's sharing. All this—and more—was inside Tim, but no one had ever asked him a single question about his emotional state as a child.

For many people, the essential point to learn about good communication is to accept silence and become comfortable with waiting. And Clair was learning.

Clarify and Validate

A part of finding out more is to clarify what you have heard and validate the experience so that the person feels seen and known. Here, the goal is to expand the listener's understanding of the speaker's feelings as the listener uses, among other things, reflective statements. Remember that the goal of the listener is not to fix, solve, debate, or defend. It is to enter into the mind-set and experience of the speaker in order to see things through that person's eyes. At this point, listeners clarify what they have heard and check to make sure they correctly understand what was said. After that, the goal is to validate the position of the speaker and try to determine that person's needs.

"Use a reflective statement," I suggested. "This will be a real Clair-ification."

She glanced at me as if I were nuts, took a breath, and wiped her eyes. "Tim, it is so sad that you had to suffer alone all those years. You had no one to help you with your fears. I don't blame you for being afraid. I'd be afraid too. I feel sad for you." As she was speaking, she again reached out and touched his arm. As she did, Tim's tears spilled over, and he began to cry. Seeing Tim's emotions, Clair began to cry.

I motioned to her to put her arm around Tim, hug him, and wait for as long as it took him to calm down. After a few minutes, they both looked at me with questions on their faces. Like two kids who reel in their first fish and wonder what to do with it, they had never been here before and had no idea what to do next.

Wanting to give them an emotional recess, I took a teaching moment to explain that Tim's response was classic for the avoider love style. Never having any opportunity to share his feelings, he had been imprinted to detach and take care of himself. Tim had not known what to do with emotions as a child, and now that he was an adult, he simply froze in fear when tears came from Clair. The response that eased his discomfort was to yell at her to shut up and then to retreat and cool down from his anger. Tim had developed a defensive pattern that was harming his marriage.

I also explained that the goal was not to stop Clair's emotions but to teach Tim to grow in his ability to contain—to put his physical and emotional arms around—his own feelings as well as Clair's emotions and reactions. I wanted Tim to learn to go beyond merely tolerating Clair's feelings and teach him how to help and comfort her when she was sad. Without ever having experienced comfort for his own distress, it was no wonder he was unable to deal with her tears.

The last part in this clarification-and-validation step was for Clair to ask Tim the all-important comfort question, "What do you need?" So she asked him, "Honey, what do you need from me right now?"

RESOLVE

Resolution brings relief. Tim thought for a few moments and then said to Clair, "When you're crying, it would be helpful for you to tell me what you are crying about and for you to reassure me that everything will be okay." His requests of

Clair spoke loudly to me of his internal anxiety. It was as though his soul was crying from long ago, "Just tell me what is going on and what to do, so I can relax."

When Clair agreed to his request, it was as if she had given him a million dollars. "I will try very hard to let you know what I'm thinking and feeling, Tim. I won't be perfect, and it may even take me a few minutes for me to figure out what to say. Maybe we can switch roles. You could be the listener and help me figure it out."

The look on Tim's face reflected a profound change from the beginning of the session. He went from rigid and tight to relaxed and smiling. He still had tears in his eyes, but he was able to say, "Thanks, and I'll try to be a good listener too."

Perhaps for the very first time in their marriage, Tim and Clair had experienced true relief.

And I had experienced success! Tim and Clair had connected in a guided conversation. You might ask, "How do you know they were really successful?" And I would explain that I asked them two diagnostic questions that I use frequently in my office. The first is, On a scale from one to ten, what is your level of anxiety right now? They both said, "Low!" When I asked for a number, Tim said, "Three," and Clair said, "Two." Then I asked what their anxiety level had been at the beginning of our session, and Clair said, "A full-blown ten!" Tim smiled and said, "Forty thousand feet." When anxiety levels are low, trust is always higher.

The second question I ask to determine success is, On a scale from one to ten, how close to each other do you feel right this very minute? Tim said, "Eight to nine!" and Clair said, "Roger, that's a niner"—which got a smile out of Tim.

When connection is high and anxiety is low, couples are beginning to bond. And even though I have a recessive math gene, I am going to do the unthinkable and actually write out a formula of sorts:

Low Anxiety + High Closeness = Trust and Bonding

As they left my office, Clair gave me a hug, and I gave my best civilian salute to Captain Tim. He smiled and said, "Get a haircut. Mullets are out!" We all laughed and guess what? I left work that day and got a haircut.

"Three...Two...One...Liftoff!"

When the space shuttle blasts off at Cape Canaveral, the engines roar into a furious rage, but very little seems to happen at first. Then, slowly but surely, the rocket begins to move and gain momentum. After a few minutes, all the fuel in the huge external tanks that was used to overcome gravity is gone, and the shuttle jettisons those tanks. Within a few minutes, the orbiter is two hundred miles high and traveling fast. At that point, it takes very little fuel for the shuttle to maneuver in space. Small puffs of spray from tiny jets at the hands of a talented pilot can make the shuttle turn in any direction. In the hands of these professionals, flight looks so effortless, yet much energy was required initially. So were thousands of practice repetitions conducted in earthbound simulators, so that when it really mattered, the pilots were able to perform with ease.

While we cannot control the way we were raised, we can control how we choose to live the rest of our lives. Remember, many of our parents did the best they knew how to do. Odds are they were not able to parent at a level higher than what they themselves had experienced. By God's grace and mercy, though, He has provided a way for us to learn, grow up, and escape the gravitational field of our injured imprints. Just like the shuttle launch, changing our relational directions takes a lot of energy at first, and it can seem like nothing is happening. That's why, in my office, I regularly hear from rookie relational pilots, "This is so hard. It ought to be easier!" "Yes, it is hard," I say, "but keep practicing. Soon it will feel so much easier. And in time you will use your new relational skills to perform marital maneuvers that will astound your spouse and even yourself."

Reaching Escape Velocity

In chapters 1–14, we took an in-depth look at how and why we struggle so much in our relationships. We saw that we have broken and ineffective love styles that we learned as children, styles that do not serve us well in our adult relationships. In addition, we also have selfish natures that want to go in directions other than what's good for us. Even when we are well meaning and our hearts want to do the right thing, our minds can battle with our inner spirits. Lastly, we live in a broken world of distorted perspectives. If we buy in to the brokenness, we end up loving the wrong things, climbing ladders only to find that they are leaning against the wrong wall, accumulating stuff that does not satisfy, and finding our hearts still yearning for something that's missing. The gravitational forces of injurious imprints, our selfish, blaming attitudes, and the lures of the world—all these contribute to disappointments and failures within marriage.

But God is in the business of redeeming what is broken and helping us find our way toward a satisfying marriage relationship. The next chapters will help you and your mate escape the gravitational fields that hold you back and find deeper levels of fulfillment and contentment with each other.

"But You Haven't Met My Spouse!"

"He will never change his selfish ways!"

"She has been nasty and controlling for thirty years, and I can't imagine her ever being different."

These and many other similar comments are common in our relationship counseling. Most people are skeptical about true character change because, sadly, they rarely see people around them actually changing. And very, very few of us have ever been privileged to hear a parent, friend, sibling, or close associate come up and say to us, "I've really thought about how injurious my behavior has been to you. I'm working on this, and I hope you can forgive me and trust me more as I demonstrate my growth."

According to God's design, though, our growth as individuals is to be consistent and obvious. The apostle Paul charged us to "take pains with these things; be absorbed in them, so that your progress will be evident to all" (1 Timothy 4:15). Each of us is to model growth in such a way that others can see character development, improvements in attitude, and healthier personal and professional relationships. When others can observe the tender buds of new growth in us, it is like springtime. The gray of winter turning into the colors of spring brings joy to all who watch the transformation.

So, for the moment, forget about your spouse and what he or she is or is not doing. Focus on yourself. Bring some springtime into your marriage by acknowledging your areas of deficiency and committing yourself to the process of change.

BUT WHAT IF YOUR SPOUSE WON'T COOPERATE?

Kay and I have been consistently amazed by how dramatically a marriage can change even if just one person begins to work on growth goals. As one person changes in a relationship, the mate has to begin relating to a new and different person. This often breaks a longstanding stalemate. I can think of two recent examples.

One of my clients identified herself as a pleaser. She began working against her pleasing tendencies by being more honest, standing up (in a respectful way) to her husband, and learning to tolerate the uncomfortable feelings of conflict. Her husband was very agitated every time she spoke the truth, and initially he was surprised and annoyed. But she kept growing, and eventually he admitted that he had a lot more respect for her. It was the beginning of some wonderful changes in their marriage, all because of her willingness to engage in the process of change and to be uncomfortable along the way.

Another woman I worked with recently came alone because her husband absolutely refused to come with her. I taught her the skill of extended listening. She took this new skill into her marriage, and her husband's response was shocking to her. She told me, "I didn't realize it until recently, but for our entire married life I've never really known how to listen to my husband. He is opening up to me in ways he never has before, and I'm getting better at learning to ask questions to find out more about his thoughts and feelings." We are to grow up in all aspects of our inner lives, and as we do, the dynamics in our marriages begin to change.

So how do we begin the process of bonding with our spouses? Let's take a closer look at the first step of the comfort circle.

Chapter 16

Seek Awareness

A wareness—the act of attending to our souls—is essential every day of our lives. When we get into our cars, we better be aware of the needle on the dashboard that signals how much fuel is in the tank. Otherwise we may not reach our destination. If we don't watch the flashing light on the dashboard that warns of internal problems, we'll find ourselves in need of a tow truck.

Marriages are similar, although we often aren't as attentive to our relationships as we are to our cars. So, if you'll pardon the mixed metaphor, I (Milan) would like to suggest that, in our marriages, we can't effectively dance this healthy comfort circle with our partners unless we're getting regular fill-ups that energize and rejuvenate our souls.

Remember the idea that we have to learn how to fill our emotional tanks? As a matter of fact, each of us has two tanks inside, tanks we need to be aware of and pay close attention to, so we can repair what's wrong and prevent a breakdown. One of these tanks needs fuel—a regular fill-up with words and responses from others that invigorate and uplift, that encourage, enliven, soothe, and strengthen us. Praise, appreciation, compliments, admiration, approval, respect, attention, thoughtfulness, concern, and interest in us are fuel for our souls. The second internal tank is full of pressure that needs to be released on a regular basis. This tank fills up with stress, unexpressed feelings, and unresolved issues. The more the pressure builds, the more extremely we act out our imprints. The avoider withdraws, the pleaser pleases, the vacillator gets angry and hopeless, the controller intimidates, and the victim scurries to appease. But when we know how to fill the fuel tank and empty the stress tank, relief is the result. And the comfort circle is our ticket to finding fuel and releasing pressure in constructive ways.

Sometimes, when a person's pressure tank has been filling for years, it first starts to empty when he or she comes in for therapy. As people learn to reflect and become aware of their feelings, we commonly hear them say that they feel so relieved just to talk about what's inside. Many times they've never told anyone about their issues before. Shame and fear are powerful forces that cause each of us to hold the pressure inside. It is such a relief to get the built-up emotions out, yet the vulnerability required can be so frightening. Opening up about feelings that we have blocked for years can be intensely unsettling.

I recall one client who looked at me with huge, frightened eyes and said, "When I let myself feel my emotions, my anxiety increases. It's so overwhelming. I feel scared, and then I feel out of control—and I just want them to stop!" She'd held it all inside for so many years that her pressure tank was about ready to burst.

I told her a story that I'll tell you now. A year and a half ago, Kay and I were invited to go to France and Germany, where we'd never been before, with some friends. At a restaurant in Paris, I asked the waiter for bottled water. He said, "Wiz gas or wizout gas?" I asked him to repeat himself, and he said it again: "Wiz gas or wizout gas?" Nervous, I looked to my friends for help. "Wiz gas?" I asked. They laughed and explained that he was asking if I wanted mineral water with bubbles or regular, still water without bubbles.

I told my client that our internal pressure tank is like a bottle of bubbling mineral water. When the lid is on tightly, you can't see any bubbles, but when the lid comes off, you hear a burst of air, and bubbles seem to come from nowhere—and they just keep coming. I told her that she was "wiz gas" and that, as she kept allowing herself to feel and talk about her soul, the pressure would eventually escape, and the emotions wouldn't be so scary anymore. She was like a bottle of bubbly mineral water, but her soul needed to become like peaceful, still water.

Kay: Maybe you'd describe yourself or your spouse as "wiz gas." Since life can be stressful, most of us are pretty gassy. But we humans are designed to function best when emotional pressures are allowed to escape. If our emotions are blocked, we need to get rid of the blockage and let our marriages do what they were designed to do. This often requires becoming aware—sometimes for the first time—of our two tanks.

Milan and I have begun playfully using the waiter's phrases to help us communicate how we're doing. On any particular day, I may say to Milan, "I am 'wizout' gas," letting him know I could use some encouragement. Or perhaps he's aware that his pressure tank is filling, and he'll say, "I'm 'wiz gas.'" We've found it a simple way to indicate how our tanks are doing, but we're also careful to indicate whether the building pressure or the lack of fuel is a result of something the other person did. If I've done something to hurt or irritate Milan, he lets me know he's feeling pressure and it's about me. It's our playful way of saying we need to take a trip around the circle to relieve some pressure and get refueled. The whole process starts with our being aware of our signals in the midst of life's busyness.

So how are your two tanks? Ideally, your gas tank will be full and your pressure tank will be empty. That's when life feels good. But are you even aware when your emotional fuel tank is "wizout gas"? Do you know when your pressure tank is "wiz gas"? Could your spouse help relieve that internal pressure by listening?

Before we can clearly communicate our internal states, though, we need to learn some self-reflective skills. Many people feel emotions but never take the time to identify them, let alone talk about them with someone else. So one of the best things we can do for ourselves—and our marriage—is to take some quiet moments to contemplate what is inside that's prompting our feelings and reactions. We need to connect with ourselves before we can help our spouses know and understand us. Psalm 51:6 says, "[God] desire[s] truth in the innermost being," but such awareness comes only from taking the time to ponder the thoughts and feelings that give rise to our behaviors and responses. If we remain unaware, we live in denial, inattentive to the very things that our hearts are trying to tell us.

If you're struggling to get a handle on what you're feeling, take a minute right now to think about some of the emotions you have had as you've read this book. What stories did you identify with? Which statements by people reminded you of yourself? What were some of your feelings as you read through those stories? Turn to the soul words list of feelings (page 291) and consider for a moment whether you've felt sad, anxious, fearful, hopeful, angry, happy, or something else. You may have felt a mixture of different emotions. Write your feelings down or say them aloud to give yourself a chance to verbalize some of your emotions.

Milan: During our seminars, we notice people feeling many emotions, especially when a volunteer couple tells their story and goes around the different steps of the comfort circle in front of the audience. Kay and I will coach and encourage the couple through each step, and it usually takes about an hour to complete the process. In one of our recent workshops, the couple's discussion was absolutely riveting as both individuals became extremely vulnerable and honest. I looked out at the audience and saw many women—and men!—with tears in their eyes and sitting spellbound on the edge of their seats. This segment is commonly the most incredible event of the seminar, and we marvel at how openly couples share their souls.

After this particular demonstration was over, we asked for questions or comments from the audience. Several people commented about the couple's increased awareness, that each of them gained new insights as they made efforts to listen deeply to each other. One conferee said, "It was like watching a scary movie. I wanted to turn away, but I couldn't!" It's true: at times a couple's story is a scary thing to see. After all, we are hearing them talk about some powerful emotions! Don't let that discourage you, though. With practice, you'll find that there isn't an emotion that doesn't settle down once we know how to process and manage it.

IS YOUR AWARENESS METER BROKEN?

When difficult emotions come up, we may find ourselves retreating from their true significance. Troubled and agitated by their intensity, we just want to make the feelings go away. It's hard to think about our pain. So we might eat, shop, exercise, seek out addictions of various kinds, and—above all—*stay busy.* The net result is poor self-reflection skills; we lack the ability to come up with any real sense of our feelings, let alone why we are behaving in certain ways. And, of course, this lack of awareness limits our ability to communicate in our marriage.

God created us to have emotions, not get rid of them. Ignoring our feelings can literally make us sick. I (Kay) have seen a number of people in my office who came to counseling for various reasons. While hearing their stories, I discovered they suffered from chronic illnesses. Many times these clients routinely ignored their feelings. As they became aware of their emotions and learned to process them, they were surprised to see their health improve. Suppressed feelings are the cause of more illness than anyone realizes. Holding emotions inside without ever releasing them is hard on the body.

Some of us, however, grew up in homes where positive thinking was the rule. There is nothing wrong with positive thinking unless it means we can't deal with our negative feelings. Perhaps you grew up with "Look on the bright side," "Ignore it and it will go away," or even "Rejoice always." These simple answers do little to help our souls, because some feelings linger and even intensify long after the cause has passed. As you may have found, emotions won't just go away.

Whatever the reason we find ourselves emotionally underdeveloped as adults, we owe it to ourselves and to our spouses to become more familiar with these most human of responses. Avoiders especially learned to tune out and not pay attention to potentially distressing emotions. Pleasers and vacillators were too preoccupied to figure out their own feelings, and controllers and victims have been too locked within their damaged responses to recognize the true source of their anxiety. Almost everyone concludes at some point that thinking about feelings is of little value and only leads to more pain, so why go there?

Recently Milan was talking to a friend (a pleaser) who was questioning why he felt so disinterested in his job and was struggling to focus on his daily tasks and long-term goals. As they talked, Milan reviewed the many losses and difficulties his friend had faced during the last year and said, "I think you are depressed and out of energy." Up to this point, our friend hadn't considered that his fuel tank might be empty and his pressure tank full, but when he took time to talk and reflect, he began to see the link between his emotional state over the past year and his current lethargy. He called later that week to thank Milan for the conversation and the exciting results of his newfound awareness.

Like Milan's friend, many people aren't even aware that their emotion-awareness meter is broken. Having never developed self-reflective skills, they can't see the rewards of peering inside and taking a look at what's there. If you break a bone, you get it wrapped in a plaster cast to protect it from further injury. But the muscle atrophies, so when the cast is removed, the muscle is weak and of little use at first. Until you build up your underdeveloped emotions and poor self-reflective skills, you're going to have trouble recognizing the condition of your tanks, not to mention your spouse's tanks.

One more point about being aware of our emotions. When we say we're stressed, what exactly do we mean? Aren't we saying that we have a bunch of feelings that have piled up and we're overwhelmed by them? Become aware of your feelings and take the first step to relieving that stress. Your body will thank you.

BUILDING UP AWARENESS MUSCLES

When we were growing up, Milan and I were not taught the skill of exercising our emotion-awareness muscles. And as we mentioned earlier, we spent our first years as parents raising our kids the same way. Our youngest child, Kelly, was a baby, and the older three were in late elementary school and junior high school before we realized that we needed to spend time getting to know our feelings. We sat the older kids down and explained that we were going to try to learn together how to become more aware of our feelings. We began to use words from the soul words list in our conversations. When a subject came up or someone had a problem, we looked for two or three words that fit the emotions prompted by the experience, and we learned to link our feelings to our daily lives. The kids fought it at times—"I don't want to *say* my feelings. I don't *care*!" But over time they discovered what we discovered in our marriage: you don't realize all you're feeling until you work to get it out.

The results we noticed after trying this for a while were nothing short of dramatic. There was a marked improvement in everyone's moods after these talks, and we all began to grow familiar with the wonderful experience of relief. Kelly, our youngest, had the benefit of being young enough not to remember a time before our family did this, and to this day we are amazed by her ability to manage her feelings and process what she's going through. Her self-reflective skills and ability to express her thoughts and feelings leave the rest of us envious and wanting to work harder at overcoming our early training.

Talking

Have you ever asked people how they feel and have them answer the question without telling you a feeling at all? I asked a woman at church, "How do you feel about your husband's new job?" She said, "I feel like he's overqualified." That's an interesting fact, but I'm still guessing at what she really feels about his new position. She could be mad he took the job or thrilled because he'll have an easier time coming home early. I know what she *thought,* but I still didn't know what she *felt.* Using soul words is a good way to develop a greater awareness of your inner experiences so that you can answer "How do you feel?" questions. And once you begin the awareness process, you will be amazed at how thoughts, feelings, and reactions become clearer to you. You will also notice when you ask someone to share a feeling and that person gives you a fact.

And you may be a lot like that. You may tend to talk just about the facts of the day and rarely share any feelings. If so, you as well as your spouse might be helped by having a "feelings talk." Put the soul words list on the table and, for starters, choose a subject that isn't about the two of you. You might talk about work, friends, relatives, church, hobbies, dreams, memories, inspirations, passions, vacations, movies, holidays, health, books, aspirations…anything that isn't likely to cause an argument or disagreement. As you share about this topic, make sure to include words from the list.

As you practice discussing your feelings, start paying more attention to your two tanks. Ask each other how you're doing, and share what you might need to get refueled. Do you need some praise, appreciation, compliments, admiration, approval, attention, romance, or time alone? Don't blame; simply tell how you might be rejuvenated. And if your pressure tank is full, do your best to share what's in the tank. How does it make you feel? Later you'll be ready to take the next steps toward resolution and relief.

Writing

Bringing our feelings and emotions into the open and talking with someone safe about them is how we start the healing process. For many, however, to just start talking may be too big of a step. We encourage these people to start writing their feelings and thoughts in a journal. Many of the exercises within the workbook will ask you to write and contemplate your own soul before you talk aloud about your inner self. Writing is another way to get feelings from the inside to the outside where you can sort them. Kay and I began to journal our thoughts and feelings as a part of our Bible studies and prayer lives. Over time, I began to write more about my pastoral position, leadership challenges, children, marriage, and relational conflicts. Then one day something happened that shocked me and changed my life forever.

I did something that I had never done before. I sat down with a cup of coffee and read through two years of my journal entries. By the time I reached the end of the last page, it hit me like a ton of bricks. I said to myself, "I am a fearful person!" I had never thought of myself that way before. I was shocked, but the evidence in my journals was conclusive. I noticed a pattern in my writing that I had never seen previously: I had written the majority of my journal entries when I was anxious. Apparently when I was feeling good about things, I hardly ever sat down to write in my journal. I was stunned. It was clear. I was a fearful guy.

Being an athlete, church-planting pastor, dad, and husband, I had never thought of myself as weak. After all, wouldn't a fearful person be a weakling? At the time—a few years ago, before I was a grandpa—I was a "macho" guy, in the best shape of my life, doing triathlons, and able to leap tall buildings in a single bound. *Milan, fearful?* I couldn't stand the idea. So I stuffed that miserable thought, ran five miles, ate a huge dinner, and then downed a pack of graham crackers and drank a quart of milk. That took care of those feelings!

Something was happening within me, however, that was disconcerting, yet at the same time it brought relief. Almost involuntarily I was beginning to connect the dots between my new awareness of my fearfulness and memories from the past. I remembered not wanting to stay overnight at my grandmother's house. I remembered not wanting to stay at the YMCA summer day camp and crying because I wanted to be picked up by my mom.

I also remembered the trauma, when I was seven years old, of being in the same room with my grandfather the moment he died. It was a Friday afternoon.

I was watching *The Mickey Mouse Club,* and he was in a chair directly behind me. He asked me his last question: "Is that a slingshot you have with you, Mike?" (I grew up being called Mike.) "Yeah, it is, Pa!"

Moments later, I heard funny sounds, got scared, and ran to the kitchen and told my mom. Everyone was frantically running around, and I remember being horrified as I watched the doctor from down the street push a four-inch cardiac needle through Grandpa's chest to try to revive him. I remember the ambulance driver putting him on a gurney and wheeling him out. It was my first taste of death, up close and personal.

My parents were as loving and comforting as they could be while they dealt with their own grief, but looking back, I'm sure it was a critical moment that greatly contributed to my tendencies to worry. As a child, I was anxious, obsessed about dying, and preoccupied with the possibility of traumatic events occurring in my life. I wasn't a free kid inside. My stomach was upset all the time, and when I was eight or nine, a surgeon took out my appendix, thinking that it was the culprit of my stomach woes. No one ever asked me what I was afraid of. Instead I was told, "Don't be afraid. Everything is fine." That statement just didn't fit with what I had witnessed in the living room.

As I processed my journals and my memories, I realized that I felt the same feelings in my stomach as an adult that I had felt as a kid. Anytime something was wrong in my marriage or in the church, I felt sick inside. I wanted to put my head down, just as I had done years earlier on the picnic bench at the YMCA, and have someone come and pick me up. This insight explained so much—why I was so diplomatic, why I took so long to make my point in a conversation (don't ever want to offend the listener!), and why I chased after Kay when I thought something was wrong. I also understood why I smiled all the time (Smilin' Milan was my nickname). My fearfulness was a clear identifier that I was a pleaser. If everyone else was happy, I felt relieved, and I could relax for a few minutes and be happy too.

My new awareness was a significant catalyst for growth. As I shared these memories (and others) with Kay, I let her know me more deeply. Seeing the compassion in her eyes helped me feel like I could be a man and still be real about how my early experiences had influenced my entire life. Kay kept reassuring me that I was not weak, but that I was injured and that she felt it was brave of me to own my fear and face it. She even thanked me for letting her be a partner in helping me overcome it. We prayed together that God would help me heal from these habitual tendencies toward feeling overwhelmed, and God is slowly answering that prayer. It is a relief to no longer hide and run from those feelings. For the men reading this, I hope you will risk being vulnerable and find the relief that comes with letting down your guard. And for the wives reading, keep in mind that this kind of sharing may be the bravest thing your husband ever does.

Perhaps you also have journals you can read through to gain awareness about yourself. Some of you may dislike writing and think journaling sounds like a real chore. You might be more willing to just jot down notes the way Tim and Clair learned to do. Tim, who commutes daily to the military base, keeps a small leather-bound notebook in his briefcase. On his drive home, he takes a few moments to reflect back on his day, and when he comes to a stoplight, he scribbles down whatever is on his mind—and he thinks about his feelings too. Clair put a copy of the soul words list on the refrigerator (just as we had done for many years), and she looks at the list, thinks about her busy day with their one-year-old, and writes down a few quick notes about her thoughts and emotions.

Tim and Clair have since grown immensely in their ability to connect and bond with each other because their "quick notes" give them a lot to talk about every day when Tim comes home. They are beginning to do something rare among couples. That is, they are paying attention to their souls instead of dismissing or stuffing their uncomfortable feelings. When Tim and Clair individually write down their soul words, they are increasing their internal awareness, which they then bring into their relationship.

Reflecting

Of course the first step toward better awareness is being quiet and listening to the things your body and soul are telling you. So take some time alone with the soul words list and intentionally ask yourself, "How am I doing?" Being quiet and alone is often the best way to connect the dots of your past and understand the links to the present. (If you find this difficult, the workbook has numerous questions throughout to help you with this.)

Kay and I also learned more about ourselves by talking to our parents, our siblings, and some distant family members who remembered us as kids. We gained insight by looking at yearbooks, scouring family photo albums, and watching old family videos together. And we learned a great deal from watching how our families relate in the present. As we were discovering aspects of each other we hadn't understood before, we shared our feelings with each other, listened when the other felt angry, and comforted when we hit pockets of grief. Feelings are stirred all the time, and every time we don't reflect on what we're feeling, we miss an opportunity to grow closer to our spouse.

"What If I'm Just Not an Emotional Person?"

Of course, it's not socially acceptable for men to display their feelings, especially in the corporate world. It's as though a set of rules is posted on office walls or in a locker room somewhere: "Acceptable emotions from men are to be really angry, to be chipper, or to sulk. Whiny boys and crybabies will be excommunicated and sent to our competitors' offices." And God help you if you should get your feelings hurt. You won't last long if you try to buck the system. So, as I (Milan) said before, go ahead and follow the "man rules" at work, but don't try to carry these cultural norms into your marriage.

Also, Christians, remember that Jesus was a man's man, a courageous rule-breaker when it came to being congruous with His emotions. He openly displayed exactly what He felt, whether it was anger, sadness, loneliness, joy, or apprehension. He even cried manly, bloody tears. What was on the inside always matched what was showing on the outside. Jesus's awareness of His feelings was unequalled.

While it's true that a higher percentage of females, and even those females with analytical temperaments, can more easily identify their feelings, those people predisposed not to have this natural awareness benefit immensely as they try to develop this sensitivity. In the book *Please Understand Me,* David Keirsey and Marilyn Bates make the following observation (F stands for "feeling" and T for "thinker":

People with the F preference may have an advantage over those with the T preference for developing the less-desired preference. Formal schooling addresses the T areas far more than the F. Thus, those with a natural preference for F also tend to develop their T, while those with a natural preference for T do not have an equal opportunity to develop their F side, which may remain relatively primitive.[1]

Granted, some people's personalities are more objective, logical, and analytical, giving them the ability to make good decisions quickly. While a thinker's preference for logic is natural and will remain, that person's mate can better understand what's needed and assess the condition of the two tanks if the thinker uses the soul words list. I, for example, test as a strong thinker, yet I have developed my ability to identify, understand, and manage my own emotions as well as the emotions of others.

Remember, awareness is important because if we don't know what we feel, we won't know what we need. Like the lights on the dashboard of a car, our emotions tell us when it's time to pay attention to the engine. If we aren't paying attention to the dashboard, we aren't going to know what in our souls needs attention.

BECOMING AWARE OF YOUR TRIGGERS

Now let's turn our attention to those feelings that indicate a deeper problem. We call these feelings *triggers*. When we are flooded with negative feelings during an argument or encounter with our spouse and we notice the conversation going downhill fast, it's usually because someone has hit on a trigger (something unresolved from the past) and the result is strong anxiety, anger, frustration, or perhaps withdrawal. Swamped by some familiar unpleasant feeling we can't deny, we become more defensive and irritated with our spouse.[2] The sudden flood of feelings inside is often accompanied by a racing heart and spike in blood pressure. Whether or not our reaction is visible, the fact is that we are overwhelmed and cannot listen or think clearly. Clearly, we need to learn about how triggers work and what to do when something inside us is triggered.

And we're not talking about Roy Rogers's horse, Trigger, who's now on display in Branson, Missouri. Instead of a trusty steed, we're talking about old rusty deeds—people's words and actions that hurt us very deeply. These events may have been instances of acute injury, or they could have been long, drawn-out patterns of hurt and abuse. But, like a rusty nail, each event punctured deeply, and sometimes that old wound has remained unhealed for decades.

Remember how Tim experienced such strong feelings when Clair cried? He quickly became agitated and lashed out. He had been triggered. We define a trigger as a strong reactive feeling about something that is happening in the present, a feeling turbocharged by a hurt in the past. In Tim's case, his anxiety over hearing his mother cry when he was younger was triggered by Clair's crying. When Clair cried, all of Tim's pain from the past with his mom came flooding into the present, and poor Clair got caught in the washout. Tim's extreme response was disproportionate to Clair's behavior, but until they came into my office, they had no clue what was going on. Once they understood the dynamic—once Tim gained awareness—he knew why his feelings were so intense. Then, with help, Tim brought his high levels of reactivity into check instead of continuing to unleash them on Clair.

When some people—like Tim—hit triggers, it's obvious. For others, the emotional reaction all happens inside, but the surge of feeling causes some sort of withdrawal or immediate separation from their environment. When I (Milan) was working with Kim and John, for instance, John was quiet; he rarely showed any emotion. But whenever his wife's voice got whiny and high-pitched, I noticed that he would clench his jaw, tighten his shoulders, and look out the window. I wondered if a trigger was being tripped. I handed him the soul words list and said, "Pick a word that describes how you feel when your wife uses that tone of voice."

John looked down the list and said, "Agitated, beaten down, exhausted, and apathetic."

"On a scale of one to ten, how strong are those feelings?"

"Ten," he answered without hesitation. Kim was stunned by John's intense feelings, hidden just under the surface. John's body language was the only indicator that a lot was going on inside him.

The way to identify a trigger in someone else is to look for a situation in which you thought you were lighting a small firecracker and got two tons of dynamite instead. Boom! You have an opportunity to see what you did to trigger that explosion.

PINPOINTING YOUR TRIGGERS

Literally anything can be a trigger. It can be a tone of voice, attitude, behavior, opinion, or even the sincere emotions of your spouse. How can you become aware of what triggers in you emotional responses that are rooted in the past? First, notice your (over)reaction, and, second, look at what prompted it. Also take the time to follow my next suggestion.

When you notice yourself feeling intense reactions to something or someone (even if others don't notice), take a deep breath, settle down, and ask yourself three questions: (1) When have I felt this in the past? (2) Who was I with? and (3) What soul words describe this intense reaction? Sometimes it also helps to think of who it is in your past you'd like to respond to. Using these diagnostic questions will help raise your awareness level, and you'll probably find a link between what you're feeling in the present and a similar feeling you had in the past.

Back to John and Kim. After John identified his intense feelings, I asked Kim to take the listener role and ask him the three questions above. She found out that John's older sister ran the house with her whining and complaining, refusing to stop until she got her way. When John told us the words he wanted to say to his sister, he put his hands over his ears and yelled, "Shut up, shut up, shut up! You are not the queen of the universe, and I'm sick of you getting your way!" John was beaten down, exhausted, and worn out by his sister's constant whining, so it didn't take much for Kim's tone of voice to send John over the edge. He'd check out and stop hearing anything Kim said.

Now let's be clear: We're absolutely *not* suggesting that John should have said these exact words to his sister. We just want you to see that becoming aware requires reflecting. Often, stopping to ask, "What words fit with my strong feelings?" helps us look back at our past to see if those feelings were going on long before our situation with our spouse.

When we are able to identify our triggers and then share our insights with our spouse, some wonderful things can happen. Your spouse will understand you more deeply and may be more careful to not touch an old wound. In addition, your spouse can become your confidant and consoler as you share hurts from the past. Awareness brings a new realization that your emotional reaction isn't only about the person who just irritated you, but rather about an old rusty injury that's still sensitive and painful.

Remember that anything can be a trigger. Too many people, for instance, don't see their negative feelings about the holidays linked to unpleasant events of the past. Circumstances, events, dates, or seasons can also set us off. This year, for example, Kay found herself agitated during the month of October because her mom had passed away during October the previous year.

By identifying your triggers as Kay did, you can begin to take responsibility for your reactivity in your relationship. After all, when we have a surge of negative emotion, it's common to try to deflect the blame onto others, specifically our spouse. And our spouse may hit dangerously close to an old wound or unpleasant experience from our past. But we don't often recognize that someone in our past deserves the real blame for making us feel what we're feeling. Discovering what your spouse's current behaviors, attitudes, expectations, or tones of voice remind you of will help you learn why you overreact, and realizing that connection can help defuse the flood of feelings and considerably scale down the present conflict. Your poor spouse doesn't deserve to get a supercharged response because of your past. Directing those negative feelings where they belong is often key to reducing the intensity of our reactions.

"WHAT HAPPENS IF I START TO FEEL BUT MY SPOUSE DOESN'T?"

I recognized before Milan did that my past was influencing the present and that I needed to uncover some buried feelings. As I journaled and talked about memories with a therapist, I began to cry more, and occasionally I even let myself get a little mad. At that time anger was showing up regularly in my dreams, but I couldn't feel it much when I was awake. At first Milan thought this was a passing phase that I would soon snap out of. Uncomfortable, he regularly asked if I was "just about over the hump." As an avoider, I was just discovering that one reason why I was always so even-keeled was because I didn't allow myself to feel anything. My moods were getting more unpredictable, which of course made Milan more and more anxious. (Sounds fun, doesn't it?)

I felt a lot of pressure from Milan to get it over with, so one day when he asked his regular question, I finally got mad and said, "You are asking me not to feel, and I've done that my whole life. I've lived many years with my feelings buried inside, and I'm not going to do that anymore. I'm going to take as long as I need even though it makes you uncomfortable."

Being a good pleaser, Milan didn't argue with me—he just left the room. That very day, he had an interesting encounter on a drive up to Long Beach.

Milan: As I took off on the eighty-mile drive to Long Beach and back, I was upset. Kay's comments had agitated me, and I had already been anxious about this "awareness phase" Kay was in. So I kept reacting to her moods, and it was frustrating both of us. I remember driving and just praying, "God, what's going on? What am I not seeing? Help me, please!"

I kept driving, and after a little while, I experienced something profound. A new insight caused a mental shift in my thinking. For the first time ever, I saw Kay, the little girl, clearly in my mind. I saw a sensitive, quiet, shy, deeply contemplative little girl feeling alone and misunderstood. I remembered some of the memories she'd shared with me, and suddenly I could picture her childhood.

I also recalled that, in the Myers-Briggs temperament test, Kay was an INFP, the most sensitive, idealistic, insightful, and conflicted of all the types.[3] It dawned on me that Kay didn't become that way as an adult, but that she had been that way since she was a little girl. From that point on, I saw her differently. I had a sudden swelling of compassion and empathy for her that I'd never experienced before. The Lord had answered my prayer in a completely unexpected way: I believe that He helped me see her as He saw her.

When I got home, I went into our room and told Kay that I could see the hurt little girl inside her. I shared that, although I was afraid of the pain because I didn't know what to do, I would try to love her no matter what happened or how uncomfortable it would make me. I said that she could take as long as she needed to heal and that I would try to help and not hinder the process. I remember her staring at me. And then she cried.

Kay: When Milan shared those words with me, I felt more loved and cherished than I ever had in my entire life. He held true to his commitment, and he learned over time to hold and comfort me when I hurt. Allowing him to hold me was very uncomfortable at first, because I had always isolated myself when I was in pain. To begin sharing was awkward, but it became easier. And the sharing deepened my awareness of my own soul in so many ways.

"What If My New Awareness Makes Me Angry at a Parent or Relative?"

Unless you had a perfect upbringing, it's hard not to feel sad or angry with your parents, relatives, or in-laws. In fact, as you may have already found out, an honest look at your past can often bring up some unsettling feelings and realizations. To share those emotions with members of your extended family, especially when you are initially working through them, is usually counterproductive. Your immediate goal is to process those feelings in order to reach a place of acceptance and resolve, not to cause division in your family. So focus on building the bond with your spouse and use the negative emotions constructively in your relationship with him or her.

After you come to the point of resolution and relief with your spouse, you may become aware of ways to improve your relationship with your parents by sharing with them your perception of your childhood experiences. At that point, a discussion with them might indeed be productive. Before you do so, though, ask yourself, "Can I handle any response I might get?" Remember, the goal isn't to place blame, but if your parents are open and willing to talk about their own upbringing, you may discover some truths that increase your compassion for and understanding of them.

"What If My Feelings Overwhelm My Spouse or Me?"

Many times people say, "If I let myself start crying, I'll never stop." Actually, a crying spell usually lasts from ten minutes to an hour at the most. Then your body will rest. And people who rarely cry are often amazed by how much better they feel afterward.

Recently I was talking to a young man who hadn't cried in years. When the dam finally broke, he was a bit scared by the intensity. "Did you feel better afterward?" I asked.

"Yes," he said. "I felt lighter and happier than I have in a long time. I've been really depressed." It's not uncommon for people's depression and anxiety to lift after a good cry.

If you feel overwhelmed by your feelings, it's a good idea to turn to your spouse for support. But your spouse can't be your only resource. If you do feel overwhelmed by the struggle in your past, seek out some good professional therapy. People who can't manage anger, for example, may have unresolved grief. Excessive anger can also be a sign of chemical imbalances or brain injuries. A medical evaluation can be helpful if you suspect one of these issues.

Also, remember that things do get easier with practice. We have to know about our feelings before we can learn to manage them, and that process always takes time.

Helpful Ideas As You Seek Awareness in Yourself and Others

Pleaser: Anger is an underdeveloped emotion for the pleaser. But if you're a pleaser, you won't be very motivated to set boundaries and say no unless you develop an awareness of your anger and learn to express it appropriately. As a child, you were focused on the feelings of others, so you will probably identify the emotions and moods of others more easily than you identify your own. Learn to become aware of how much you let the moods of others dictate what you feel and how you behave. You will find it easier to be aware of your spouse's two tanks than your own. Work on acknowledging and communicating the condition of your two tanks.

Vacillator: You may find it easier to be mad than sad. So when you are mad, stop and ask yourself, "What is the hurt under the anger?" Share your hurt feelings straightforwardly, not with irritation, anger, or disgust in your voice. Try to identify what triggers your emotional overreactions and what from your history is fueling those overreactions. Share your insights with your spouse. Of all the styles, you are probably the most aware of your two tanks. Because of your disappointments, though, you may forget that your spouse has two tanks also. Even though you feel hurt, angry, and frustrated, remember, *it's not all about you.* There's another person in this marriage partnership. Make sure that you equally divide your time so that you focus on filling your spouse's fuel tank by going around the comfort circle and meeting his or her needs. Often, spouses of vacillators have not been refueled by their vacillator mate for a long time. Finally, ask about your spouse's pressure tank and show interest in the stress he or she is experiencing.

Avoider: Finding words to match your internal discomforts may be a first for you. The soul words list is an indispensable tool. It isn't enough to just notice your feelings. You have to learn to say them aloud, so practice! Admitting that you have needs feels very vulnerable and uncomfortable. After all, if you are even aware of your two tanks, you attempt to manage them all by yourself, and you probably have not experienced enough help in your lifetime to know how good it might feel. Also, take the risky step of trying to share your feelings. Your spouse will love you for trying.

Controller: Due to the high levels of agitation and anger you've experienced, you've probably never thought about sadness. Look at the soul words list, and every day try to find at least one word that is about something other than rage or anger. You probably entered adulthood with an empty fuel tank and a pressure tank that is so full of stress it is always ready to blow. Work on recognizing that your level of anger and reactivity is related to childhood pain. Nothing will change until you make this connection and get help to work through the pain. Good intentions are not enough. It is too difficult to relate successfully or calmly with anyone when your pressure tank is causing constant explosions.

Victim: Spend some time thinking quietly about what you feel. You've been so preoccupied with running away that you may have trouble giving your feelings much thought. And often the only feelings someone in self-preservation mode knows are depression and anxiety. Look at the soul words list and see what might be going on inside. You may have had few people put anything positive in your fuel tank when you were growing up, and now that tank may have little room for anything good, because it's been filled with denigration, criticism, and condemnation instead. You may need to seek out some people who see your worth and value and can help you expose the lies you've been told about who you are. Also, numb feelings can lift when you find someone safe to listen to what's inside. That is your first priority. (For help knowing what to look for in a safe person, see pages 236–37.)

Chapter 17

Engage

L ike every married couple, Milan and I have stories from when we first started
dating and began getting to know each other. During those days, it was easy
to engage and connect as we anticipated spending time together and delighted in
each other's company. There were few problems to solve, and we had not yet discovered the pressures of living together. But as with all marriages, life began to
throw us its difficulties and stresses, and engaging with each other became more
challenging. The idea of engagement is making a mutual decision to connect,
sometimes as the giver and sometimes as the receiver. Again, it sounds so simple,
but it's not easy.

Around our twelfth year of marriage, we decided it would be fun to have one
more child and actually plan for the addition rather than being surprised as we
were with the first three. Given our history, we were amazed that we didn't con-
ceive right away. After months of trying, we joyfully announced we were expecting our fourth child. Around this time Milan had been a pastor at the same church
for about nine years. Our church was going through some tough times, and I considered the pregnancy one of God's blessings during a difficult season.

When I was almost four months into the pregnancy, I went for a routine
check-up, and my doctor couldn't hear a heartbeat. Our baby was dead. I was
stunned. My doctor explained I was too far along for a D&C, and he scheduled a
delivery for the following morning. I drove home like a zombie and told the family the news. After the procedure I kept to myself for days. Remember that my
imprint was to isolate, and it didn't occur to me to ask for company or help. I had

to battle things out on my own. I was mad at God, depressed, and struggling to function in my normal routine as a wife and mother. After a few days I realized I was falling apart, so I called Milan at work and told him, "I'm a basket case. I'm going away for a few days by myself to pull myself together."

"Where?" he asked.

"I don't know. Maybe San Diego." I could tell he was confused and didn't know what to say. I just wanted to get off the phone and go.

I got a hotel room in San Diego and began crying, journaling, and crying some more. And I was perfectly comfortable being alone. That's the way I wanted it because it was all I'd ever known. At that time in our marriage, Milan had never seen me come unglued. He had no idea how to help me, so each of us was on our own in a crisis bigger than any we'd ever faced before. I had no idea how to reach out, and he had no idea how to reach in.

A couple years later we went to a seminar called "Changes That Heal" with John Townsend and Henry Cloud. It was there I heard them say, "People who aren't bonded isolate when they are in pain." Immediately, I was flooded with memories of San Diego; I was smacked with the reality of my situation. We weren't as bonded together as we had thought, for I realized that a truly bonded person would bring their pain *into* relationship rather than isolate in pain. Up to that point, I felt I'd made a good decision to leave and be alone after I lost the baby. Yet at that seminar, Milan and I experienced a shift in our thinking, and we committed ourselves toward improving our bonding with each other.

Even now, as I sit here writing this, that experience seems like another lifetime. I can hardly believe that was me who ran away to San Diego. But not once in the first fifteen years of our marriage did I ever allow Milan to hold me as I cried. Now I have learned how to engage, how to be a giver and a receiver, and though at first I found it awkward and just plain frightening to be so vulnerable, now I can't count the number of times I've been held while I cried. Milan and I just needed to learn how to engage.

My mom gave me a poem a few years back thinking we might use it in one of our seminars. I think it speaks to this problem we married couples have with engaging.

The Wall

Their wedding picture mocked them from the other table,
these two whose minds no longer touched each other.

They lived with such a heavy barricade between them
that neither battering ram of words
nor artilleries of touch could break it down.

Somewhere, between the oldest child's first tooth
and the youngest daughter's graduation,
they lost each other.

Throughout the years each slowly unraveled
that tangled ball of string called self,
and as they tugged at stubborn knots,
each hid his searching from the other.

Sometimes she cried at night and begged
the whispering darkness to tell her who she was.
He lay beside her, snoring like a hibernating bear,
unaware of her winter.

Once, after they had made love,
he wanted to tell her how afraid he was of dying,
but fearful to show his naked soul,
he spoke instead of the beauty of her body.

She took a course on modern art,
trying to find herself in colors splashed upon a canvas,
complaining to the other women about men
who are insensitive.

He climbed into a tomb called "The Office,"
wrapped his mind in a shroud of paper figures,
and buried himself in customers.

Slowly, the wall between them rose,
cemented by the mortar of indifference.

One day, reaching out to each other,
they found a barrier they could not penetrate,
and recoiling from the coldness of the stone,
each retreated from the stranger on the other side.

For when love dies, it is not in a moment of angry battle,
not when fiery bodies lose their heat.
It lies panting, exhausted
expiring at the bottom of a wall it could not scale.

—Author Unknown

Are you like this couple? Are you unaware of each other's winters? Have you been on the verge of speaking a deep truth but fell silent, afraid to show your spouse your naked soul? Along the way, if couples decide not to engage, the walls get higher until two strangers stand on opposite sides. There is no real giving or receiving, no true health or vitality, none of the life-giving reciprocity that comes with engaging each other. The problem is each of us has entered marriage imprinted with patterns that interfere with giving and receiving.

THE WALLS CREATED BY YOUR IMPRINTS

Some couples reading this may need a wrecking ball to break down the wall between them. If you're one of those, instead of aiming that ball at each other, you need to aim it at the wall that is keeping you both from giving and receiving.

As I've told you, my imprint to avoid created a wall of self-sufficiency. I isolated when I was hurting. Avoiders like me have to work at taking down the wall that keeps us from receiving. It will take some courage to share your struggles and ask for help, but I can assure you it's worth the effort. Until you allow yourself to receive, you won't know the experience of being comforted. And once you experience comfort, giving to others becomes easier because you understand the relief you're offering.

Pleasers create a wall that prevents reciprocity because, like avoiders, they're also terrible receivers. Pleasers have spent their lives learning to be good givers (yet their motivation is often more about reducing their own anxiety than meeting the needs of their spouses). As we were writing this book, my pleaser husband was agitated after reading one of my stories about him. He was surprised by how much it affected him and asked me to pray for him. I suggested we do more than that and that he come sit and tell me about his feelings. We had a great time of talking, and though it didn't occur to either one of us how much our emotions would be provoked by writing this book, engaging with each other while in emotional distress helped us get through the writing process.

Definitely different from the pleasers and avoiders, vacillators engage as both the giver and the receiver as long as the relationship is meeting their idealistic standards. But when the inevitable disappointments happen, walls of anger, fear of abandonment, and general irritation can go up, depending on the vacillator's mood. Once ambivalence sets in, vacillators become conflicted about the wall. Expecting more disappointment, they both want and don't want to receive, and they secretly wish their spouses were aware of their dilemma and would scale the wall. Until vacillators learn to accept their disappointments and strive to give to and receive from their spouses as they originally did, they won't be able to accept the good of the relationship along with the bad.

Then we come to the controllers. They don't receive; they take. They may give if they've pushed their spouse to the breaking point, but they cannot sustain it for long. And victims give no matter how they are treated, and they expect little in return. Sadly, the defenses required to survive childhood make finding reciprocity as adults extremely challenging. Victims need specific, objective help from a qualified counselor to overcome the deep hurts of the past before they can learn to engage.

As you can see, if we are going to engage in a reciprocal way as both a giver and a receiver in marriage, we have to take responsibility for our struggles to do so. Yet when hurts and resentments have remained unresolved for years, we may find ourselves living with an enemy.

ENGAGING WITH THE ENEMY

By the time people come to our offices, they're often in enemy territory, peeking over the top of the wall to take potshots at each other. Battles only end with a truce and a peace plan. That is the starting point. It takes one person to initiate a truce, so if you find yourself here, sit down with your mate and tell him or her that you are tired of living in a war zone. Draw a line in the sand and come up with a peace plan. Your spouse may look at you with skepticism, but go ahead and ask for one specific, observable thing you can do that will make you a safer person. Then do it. Also, apologize for all you have done to contribute to the wall. No matter how your spouse responds, you will know you did the right thing by accepting responsibility.

You may say, "I no longer feel any love for my spouse. How can I 'love' him or her and not be fake or hypocritical?" That's a great question. Some people do not deserve our love due to the way they have treated us. But Jesus went so far as to say, "Love your enemies" (Matthew 5:44, NIV). I read this verse to a client once, and she tried to dodge the point. "My husband isn't my enemy. I just hate him!" she said. I started laughing, and eventually she did too.

Victims, we're not suggesting that you remain in a relationship where you are in physical danger. If that's the case, you need to get out. The kind of love Jesus is commanding in Matthew 5:44 is agape love. God can ask us to extend this kind of love to our enemies because it does not involve warm feelings per se, but kind and benevolent actions. Agape love requires a nonretaliatory mind-set that leaves retribution to God. Instead of returning evil for evil and insult for insult, we are to extend a blessing. Simply stated, when the warm feelings run out, we act according to agape love. This does not mean we can't say no and have healthy personal boundaries. Agape love means we keep engaging as the giver even if we receive little in return.

Taking Down the Wall

Whatever has created the wall in your marriage, we believe that no wall is impenetrable. But how do you take down the wall? What can you do in order to engage with your spouse in a productive way? Let's consider some ways to remove those bricks.

Get to Know Your Spouse

Milan tells people he has been married to three different women...because he's been married to three different versions of me. I've been married to at least four versions of him. And if we hadn't kept up with the changes, we would no longer know each other. Life changes us. Kids change us. Health changes us. Our jobs change. Our friends change. Growing older changes us. We need time to talk and get to know our spouses again and again as we navigate the different stages of life.

How well do you know your spouse at the present moment? Do you know his dreams and aspirations? Do you know what she considers her finest accomplishments? How about his deepest fears? What would she most like to change about her current circumstances? What most soothes him? What is her happiest memory with you?

As well as I know Milan after thirty-seven years, I heard a childhood memory the other day I had never heard before. I'm also often surprised by the interesting facts tucked inside his head that I've never heard until some random conversation. And when we recently became grandparents, he had to get used to the idea of sleeping with a grandma, which was another adjustment. Up until that time, he had never considered that an attractive idea. Our grandson Reece calls me Nana, and having grown accustomed to the concept of being sexually attracted to me as a grandma, Milan now calls me Hottie Nana. We've spent these years keeping current with each other as new roles and life stages have developed. Take the time to sit down with your mate and find out who he or she is. Ask questions like those in the preceding paragraph if you're not sure where to start.

Have Fun

Are you in one of those stressful seasons when most encounters with your spouse involve a problem or complaint? If so, there is only one way out: go have some fun! Plan time together where the only goal is to have fun, and agree not to discuss problems or anything serious. Decide together that, for that one day, topics of conversation be limited to appreciations, compliments, good memories, and anything positive from the day. One couple took a trip to Disneyland without their kids and didn't tell them where they were going. The following week they found themselves sitting closer together on the couch and laughing about the details of their secret rendezvous. They decided to buy season passes and make an effort to go together once a month. They found some playfulness, and their marriage was better for it.

Become a Safer Person

How do you know if someone is safe? And what makes a person unsafe? To answer those questions, think of a pyramid divided into three levels. The bottom level represents your acquaintances, the middle section contains your friends, and the smallest level at the top is reserved for safe people. All people, including your spouse, enter at the bottom and, over time, earn their way to the top.

We know someone is safe when that person is careful with our feelings and guards our confidentiality. Over time, safe people demonstrate that they can tolerate differences between themselves and others and be both the giver and receiver in a relationship. Safe people are willing to be honest and let us know when we have hurt them. And we see that someone is safe when we can say no and that person respects our boundaries without getting mad or pushy. All these characteristics and experiences build trust.

So where is your spouse on your pyramid? And where would your spouse place you? What would have to happen for you to move your spouse up to a higher level? For many couples their mate is not in the top of the pyramid. Maybe, for instance, you admitted your spouse into your safe place for a time, but then some hurt or betrayal caused you to push him or her down a level.

Have a discussion with your spouse about the pyramid. Share one thing each of you could do that would increase the level of trust and safety. Make sure your request is specific and achievable instead of something vague, like "I want you to treat me better" or "I want you to make me the most important person in your life." Instead make your request something concrete: "I need you to give me one hour a week to listen to my feelings" or "Every day I need to hear one thing you appreciate about me." Building trust takes time, but if both of you are seeking to move to the top of your spouse's pyramid by fostering his or her trust, this is the best goal that you can set, one that will be worth the effort and time you invest.

Be Honest

During the first fifteen years of our marriage, some of the bricks in the wall between Milan and me were the result of our hiding and dishonesty. In fact, one of the reasons Milan and I couldn't engage after we lost the baby was that we hadn't ever been able to be deeply honest with each other. We were both used to concealing painful feelings, and when my emotions got too big to hide, we were on shaky ground. We literally did not know how to be honest about our feelings. After I realized that stuffing my feelings and hiding my pain were symptoms of an impaired love style, I had a new option. I could choose to keep hiding, or I could choose to understand my feelings, put words to them, and ask for comfort. Growth meant I had to first be honest with myself about what was inside me and then allow Milan to see my neediness.

Sometimes I was dishonest because I wanted to avoid conflict. I rationalized by telling myself that my honesty would hurt Milan's feelings. I finally admitted that my dishonesty was hurting the relationship and that nothing was going to improve until I was able to speak the truth. I made a decision to start being more truthful. It was a choice—and I'd been right. My honesty did hurt Milan's feelings. It took us a while to work through this change, and it was a hard and uncomfortable learning curve for both of us. But looking back, we can see that the new attempt to live more honestly was the beginning of some wonderful changes in our relationship.

Milan also had a problem with honesty, a problem typical of pleasers. He tended to edge around the truth because it made him anxious to have anyone angry or upset with him. He found it risky to tell the truth or to say no because I might get mad and distance myself. He'd always rather avoid conflict. I remember one of the first times he set a limit with a relative. He told that person the truth and took the risk of making an enemy. Rather than being angry, though, that person was absolutely furious! Milan was so upset. Exactly what he had feared would happen had come true. This was a big opportunity for Milan and me to learn that rejection can be endured, that it's not deadly.

Now some people won't relate to Milan's and my experience at all. Many people have no problem telling the truth no matter what. The problem is, there may also be little consideration to how that truth is delivered. Maybe you have a spouse who regularly tosses brutal bombs of honesty over the wall at you, and you're feeling wounded. Delivering hurtful opinions and calling it honesty only adds bricks to the wall. We've heard vacillators and controllers speak the truth in ways that would make anyone want to plug both ears. Maybe your mate has heard the "truth" so many times that he or she could write a book about it. You might try a new approach of engaging. Try some confession. When you tell the truth about yourself, it's disarming. When we are willing to confess our weaknesses and shortcomings and admit our own faults and deficiencies, loads of bricks fall off the wall. When is the last time you confessed one of your shortcomings to your spouse?

Some of the bricks on our wall came off when I told Milan I understood what he meant when it felt like I was distancing from him. I said, "I've realized that part of my damaged imprint resulted in this tendency to detach and go off into my own world. And though sharing my heart is hard and scary for me, I'm going to try. Can you tell me when you see me distancing?" He was more than willing to help, and he quickly had something to share about my lack of eye contact when I was trying to hide. I wasn't even aware of it. If I gave myself some quiet time and sat down with my journal, I found he was right almost every time he talked to me about a distancing behavior. Then I could share with him what I had discovered.

Share Your Secrets

I'm amazed by the number of people who are willing to engage in therapy, pay me an hourly fee, and then lie to me. It might look as if we are getting somewhere for a while, but the bottom falls out sooner or later. When the secrets begin to peel off, sometimes years later, we are back to square one. Secrets not only affect counseling, but they will slowly destroy a marriage. It takes a lot of energy to keep things hidden, and eventually the lying increases to cover the growing trail of deceit. When we lie, we definitely build up the wall.

Confessing a secret or a lie might be one of the hardest things you ever do. It could cost you your marriage, but it isn't much of a marriage when you have to pretend. Many times I have seen the life and vitality come back to a relationship after a secret has come out. I'm not saying it's a smooth, easy road, but revealing secrets often puts a spark of hope into a dying relationship. Suddenly there is a possibility of true change. A secret can be revealed in one of two ways: it can either be caught (your spouse finds out) or confessed. Obviously, the second is more likely to build trust, and the first will destroy it. Choose not to truly engage with your spouse, and you'll keep your secrets. But doing so will eventually destroy you.

Is there a secret you need to confess? Pray about it and ask God to give you the courage to be honest.

Be a Learner

Do you believe your spouse has something to teach you? Can you listen and take his or her advice? When we know our contributions are valued, we are more likely to want to engage with a person. When we allow our mates to influence us, we are saying, "Your opinion counts. You have good ideas. Your perspective is enlightening." Again, the key to success here is reciprocity. If one person dominates the relationship, what's the point of trying to engage? The decision is already made and a discussion is useless.

So are you a learner? When is the last time your mate changed your mind? When is the last time you praised him or her for a great idea? How defensive are you when your spouse disagrees with you? What strengths does your mate bring to a discussion that you don't have? Have you mentioned lately to your spouse that you appreciate those strengths?

Be Vulnerable

Vulnerability is risky. It means we have to set aside our pride, drop our defenses, and admit what we lack. Vulnerability is apparent when we confess our short-comings and failings and when we offer heartfelt apologies. Being vulnerable is the most humble kind of engagement, and it can repair deep wounds as well as minor abrasions in our marriages. None of us is perfect, and vulnerability is about accepting that fact and embracing our humanness.

Part of vulnerability is confession. If you've wronged someone, apologizing is necessary. Have your parents ever apologized for mistakes they made raising you? How would you feel if they did? Our parents are the ones who teach us how to be open or defensive about our mistakes. If you never heard an apology from a parent, you may have more difficulty learning to be vulnerable enough to apologize.

Besides blocking apologies, pride also keeps us from expressing remorse, and our marriages will suffer for it. Again, like genuine apologies, our openness about our heartfelt regrets for our words and actions takes down walls. I have witnessed it many times. If a spouse refuses to apologize or express remorse for appalling actions and behaviors, more bricks are added to the wall.

When is the last time you engaged your spouse and expressed your regrets, confessed bad attitudes, or apologized for hurtful words or actions?

"WHAT IF I'VE TRIED BEING VULNERABLE AND MY MATE USES WHAT I SHARE AGAINST ME?"

This comment routinely comes up in our offices and seminars. First, let us say that talk is cheap, and your spouse may know it and, yes, use it against you. If you share your weaknesses or apologize but do nothing to change, you're basically saying, "I wasn't really serious; you're stuck with me the way I am." That's not what we mean by "owning" weaknesses. Vulnerable engagement isn't just about revealing our struggles; it's about changing, so our mates can see growth and transformation. I'll never forget the day Milan came to me and admitted his newfound awareness that he was a fearful person. He didn't stop there. He set some growth goals, he asked for God's help, and he made efforts to overcome his fear. He is still making efforts, and I love and respect his willingness to grow. It's one of his greatest gifts to me.

Second, how we handle our mates' vulnerable revelations determines how likely they are to share again. When our mates disclose something personal, we need to handle it tenderly and cherish it as a gift from the soul. If we use it as a weapon or make sarcastic jokes about it, we have proven ourselves unsafe.

CAREFULLY CHOOSING YOUR WORDS

Every time we open our mouths to bring up a problem, we have a brick in our hands. We will either add it to the wall or put it on the scrap pile. The choice is ours. Our attitudes and tones of voice, for instance, have a lot to do with how the conversation will go. Blurting out what bothers us is a recipe for disaster. The best thing we can do when sarcastic, critical words come out of our mouths is to apologize.

The most difficult conversations we have in marriage are about problems with our mates. When you need to address a problem, think about your words, and be sensitive about your timing. You can share a problem or complaint and still be positive. For example, "I'm sick of your never coming home on time" can be made positive by saying, "I appreciate how hard you work to provide for the family, which is why I work hard to make a nice dinner. I need to talk to you about your work schedule so I don't end up feeling so frustrated when dinner is ready and you're not here to share it with us." The rule of thumb is to always confront problems tenderly.

Here's an overview of how people with different imprints struggle with engaging:

Avoider: Even though others want to engage more than you do, you need to make an effort to engage with your spouse. And not just for your spouse, but for you. Your growth goal is to share a feeling or make a request of your own. Take a deep breath and tell your spouse that you have something to say. If necessary, explain that it's hard for you to ask for help. Ask your mate to listen and be patient with you.

Vacillator: You will probably want to engage more than your spouse does, and you may tend to focus on releasing the pressure in your stress tank way too often. Your spouse may be more receptive to hearing your feelings if you also engage just to have fun and agree not to focus so much on the problems in your relationship. Also, if your spouse has things to share, try to engage by really listening and not debating every point.

Pleaser: The first thing you need to do is to address your fears about rejection. Then, when you engage, learn to be direct, use fewer words, and make an effort to stop being so careful. Don't be mean; just be straightforward. You tend to dance around the topics, all the while taking people's emotional temperature. But you need to just tell the person what you want to say.

Controller: Anger is in your way. You must express the hurt and fear under you fury and learn to receive comfort rather than exploding and blaming. For productive conversation to happen, you need to learn how to get past the anger (and that will probably require outside help). Since engagement was fearful for you growing up, ask your spouse to sit quietly with you and try to relax in his or her presence. Any engagement that's not intense is progress. Also, your gas tank needs filling, and you need to fill your spouse's. So make efforts to start with expressing positive things before you attempt to address problems.

Victim: Through the years, people have engaged with you in disrespectful ways, and you have accepted their mistreatment. So now, most important, you need a safe place to both recover as well as *uncover* who you are, what you feel, and what it is you want. If your marriage is a war zone, a recovery group or a shelter may be in order. If your spouse is abusive, do not attempt to engage; safety is your first priority. Finding a safe haven will require outside help, so please seek it out.

Finally, engagement is a decision that says, "I'm willing to learn to be both a giver and a receiver in my marriage." It's a decision to connect through vulnerability. The workbook has further ideas as well as tips about how the different imprints can approach this step.

Chapter 18

Explore

Regina and Ken were arguing about the division of household chores, and Ken was getting more irritated by the moment.

"I work all day, and you stay home with the kids. I get home, and you expect me to take over your job and watch the kids, and I want five minutes…"

Regina interrupted, "You work all day—and I don't? I can't believe you said that. Maybe you should stay home one day and try my job. You wouldn't last five minutes with a screaming baby and a two-year-old who's into everything. All I want is…"

Ken began to talk over her. "Come on, Regina. You have coffee with the neighbors, take your little trips to the mall, and buy stuff you don't need. I'll take your job any day."

Regina began to cry. "You don't appreciate anything I do. No one is giving me a thank you. You never support me, Ken. All you can think about when you get home is your stupid bike."

"Hey! I haven't been on my bike for a week! And I baby-sat the kids last night so you could go off with your…"

"*Baby-sat?*" Regina shouted. "They are your kids, Ken! You don't baby-sit your own kids."

As I (Kay) listened to this, I thought of a Ping-Pong game—back and forth, back and forth, until someone is out. But so many couples are far too familiar with conversations like Ken and Regina's. Throw any topic between the paddles, and the result is the same. No one is listening. It's all about who can come up with the best defense. Both Regina and Ken assumed they already understood their mate's point of view without listening. While they probably knew on the surface, neither had taken the time to discover what else might be going on underneath. "A fool finds no pleasure in understanding but delights in airing his own opinions," says Proverbs 18:2 (NIV). Ouch! That ancient statement kind of says it all, don't you think?

So how about a quick lesson in communicating? A great conversation has several essential components, among them, sharing thoughts and feelings, extended listening, and clarification of the other's experience. In the last chapter, we talked about making a choice to engage with our spouse in an honest, vulnerable way and about taking turns as the giver and receiver. Once we make a decision to engage, though, we have to know how to communicate our feelings and thoughts in an effective way. After all, good communication is essential to being able to move your spouse up into the top level of the pyramid reserved for safe people.

One of the greatest gifts you can give your spouse is to learn to be a great listener. In fact, as we work with couples in our offices, it's amazing what happens when couples learn how to really listen. That's why we're going to discuss the art of extended listening to help you build new levels of trust with your mate. By learning to ask good questions (an aspect of extended listening), you can draw out the feelings and thoughts from deep within your mate and reach an intimacy you didn't think possible. This richer intimacy comes with understanding your spouse better. And your spouse won't be able to help but fall more in love with you when you put down the accusatory finger and take the time to hear all that's in his or her heart. It will literally change how the two of you love each other.

So keep in mind that, when you listen, it is important for you to clarify and recap what you have heard and then attempt to validate the speaker's feelings. After all, hearing what you have spoken presented back to you in a thoughtful and clear way confirms that the listener has really heard your heart and understands your feelings. (On the other hand, speakers may discover that a listener misunderstood what they were trying to say, and that's important to know.) It is a satisfying and rewarding experience to feel heard and understood, and it's easy to be drawn to those who invest time in us and care to truly know us.

Remember how I (Milan) asked Clair to turn on the couch, face Tim, and ask him to repeat the emotion that he felt when she cried? He looked at me and said, "Why do I have to say it again? I already said it." I told Tim it was important for him to look Clair in the eyes, take ownership, and confess the fearful emotions inside him. This is a very hard thing for many of us to do. I, too, had to grow up in this area of speaking, listening, and validating. I discovered that my childhood feelings of shame and embarrassment that came when I make mistakes were keeping me from growing.

And I know I'm not the only one. Many times when we are working with couples in our offices, they are embarrassed or hesitant when they don't know how to communicate effectively. We often ask, "When you were growing up, did someone model good communication?" "Did someone take the time to listen and ask good questions in order to understand you?" "Did you ever hear an adult express anger appropriately, watch a fair fight, or see problems resolved in front of you?" More often than not, the answer to all these questions is no. You can't expect to know how to communicate well in your marriage if no one ever taught you how.

And good communication is a learned skill; it is not inborn. For many people, this fact is a new idea. So give each other room to make an effort and stumble around a bit. Expect to be tongue-tied at first because we are asking you to really think about your words rather than just react. Like any new skill, learning to be an effective communicator (and that includes listening) just takes practice before you feel comfortable with this new skill.

IT'S NOT WHAT YOU SAY...

Have you seen the beer commercials on television that warn people to "drink responsibly"? The same rule applies to our tongues. We all need to learn to speak responsibly! But whether we're the speaker or the listener, there are guidelines to follow so we don't cause damage or serious injury to another person.

After all, just as drunk drivers have the power of life and death in their hands, "the tongue has the power of life and death" (Proverbs 18:21, NIV). That's a lot of power. Have you ever considered that your tongue really can be just like a drunk driver swerving all over and forcing people to jump out of the way? Do we realize how much our words enliven or destroy those around us? Many people in my office tell me that they have never heard the words "I love you" from their mother or father. And I have seen many men and women cry with joy as they report how an older parent finally spoke these life-giving words.

We are told, "Speak truth each one of you with his neighbor, for we are members of one another" (Ephesians 4:25). But *how* we speak the truth is also important. "Sweetness of speech increases persuasiveness," and "The heart of the wise instructs his mouth and adds persuasiveness to his lips" (Proverbs 16:21, 23). No one makes us talk a certain way. We alone are responsible for the words as well as the tone of voice that come from our mouth.

Where Do You Start?

In a good conversation, giving and receiving equates to listening and speaking. So, to begin a conversation, first decide who will be the listener and who will be the speaker. Listeners are going to give their full attention to their spouse, listening and asking questions, clarifying and recapping until they are sure they fully understand what is being said. If you have done a good job as the listener, you will see the topic from the speaker's perspective and be able to articulate that person's feelings and beliefs, whether or not you agree. The speakers are clearly the receivers, receiving from their spouse the gift of being fully heard. The speaker's job is to clearly communicate feelings and thoughts about one topic, being careful to speak in a manner that does not raise the defensives of the listener.

Remember Ken and Regina whose conversation was going nowhere fast? I (Kay) explained to them how to change their game of Ping-Pong. "Let's slow down the pace and try something new. Ken, you are going to be the listener, and Regina, you are going to be the speaker. Ken, when Regina says something to you, she's serving the ball to your side of the table. Instead of slamming it right back at her, you are going to put your paddle down, pick up the ball, and examine it. Hold it, look at it, and then find out more about it. After she tells you more about what she just said, clarify and recap until she agrees that you understand. Every time she answers one of your questions, she's serving you another ball. Do the same thing each time. Find out more and recap. For the next ten minutes, it's all about her. Don't share your views, argue, defend, or roll your eyes. Just say what you hear and then find out more. After ten minutes, we will reverse roles, and Regina will listen to you."

Of course, these tips—and the following—can also work for you and your spouse.

GOALS FOR THE SPEAKER

Pick One Topic and Be Direct

I turned to Regina and said, "Let's say you and Ken are at home, and you want to talk about something that is bothering you. Here are a few things I want you to keep in mind." And I shared with her the following ideas.

A good way to get started is to be very clear and direct about the topic. Say, for example, "I want to talk about the finances" or "I want to share some feelings about how we discipline the kids." Share your concern and ask your mate for a good time to talk about the topic.

Many people communicate indirectly by merely dropping hints or making subtle suggestions. Don't hint. Be direct and speak forthrightly. When you tell your spouse what you want to talk about, try to prepare him or her and give time to think about it. Be considerate of emotional energy levels and capacities to listen. Agree upon a time, but then check your spouse's readiness to listen. If you agree to talk at a later time, make sure you follow through and initiate the conversation. Don't wait for your spouse to bring up the topic.

It will be easier for your spouse to listen if you talk about yourself, your experiences, and your feelings. Use "I" statements instead of "you" statements so you don't sound accusatory and prompt defensiveness. Say, for example, "I am feeling sad that I didn't get to spend any time with you" works better than "You are always busy and never make time for me."

"All right, Regina," I said, "let's give it a try. Tell Ken what you would like to talk about."

Regina was silent for a moment as she carefully chose her words. "Ken, I would like to talk about what I need when you come home from work. Is now a good time?"

"How about next year?" Ken teased. Ken's smile faded, and he turned to me and said, "Why would I want to say yes to that question? I'm just going to get blasted."

"Let's see if you feel that way by the end of the session," I said and turned back to Regina. "Okay, add one more thing to your request. If you want to talk about something that is likely to raise Ken's defenses, start and end with a positive affirmation. For example, I might say to my husband, 'I love and appreciate many things that you do, but I want to talk about how it affects me when you don't pick up after yourself. I love you, and I don't like to feel irritated at you. When could we discuss this?' Try one more time, Regina."

Regina cleared her throat. "Ken, I really appreciate how hard you work, and I'm very grateful I get to stay at home with the kids. I'm having a hard time, though, since the baby has been born, and it would help me if we could talk about what I need when you come home from work. I don't want to blast you. I just want you to understand and see if we can work something out. When would be a good time to talk?"

"Wow, Regina, great job!" I said. "How was that for you, Ken?"

"Better," he admitted.

"Now we're ready for the talk." I handed Regina the soul words list, and I gave Ken a list of possible questions he could ask as the listener. I got out my whiteboard and, in large letters, wrote "Topic: Regina's feelings and needs when Ken comes home."

"There is a reason I'm writing our topic down," I explained. "We want to make sure we stay on track. Like in corporate sales meetings, no matter what the discussion is, everyone needs an occasional reminder of the original question. Too many couples begin a conversation on one topic and go all over the map." I took a moment to let this concept sink in and then turned to Regina, "As the speaker, Regina, you begin. Turn to Ken and talk to him about the topic you picked."

Regina faced her husband. "Ken, I'm happy to see you when you first get home, but then I don't like it when you want to hop right on your bike and leave again. I've been counting the minutes and watching the clock, waiting for you to come through the door. I need your help." Regina stopped and looked at her husband.

"She just served into your court, Ken. Pick up the ball and find out more. Focus on finding out about her feelings."

Ken looked at me. "I know her feelings. She's mad, and she wants me not to ride my bike and help her."

"Don't assume you know all there is to know. Try this"—I pointed to a question on the sheet Ken was holding—"and let's see if you learn something new."

"How does it make you feel when I do that?" Ken asked.

Regina scanned the list of words. "It makes me feel overwhelmed, grouchy, and panicky." Ken looked to me for help.

"Find out more about the feeling you know the least about," I said.

Ken turned back to Regina, "I don't understand the panicky feeling. Tell me more about that."

Regina was quiet, contemplating her feeling. After several minutes she said, "I feel like I'm going to crack up if I have the kids by myself for another forty-five minutes. I love the kids, but I didn't think it would be this hard having two. I think I'm sort of panicky and scared about how mad I feel when they both cry at the same time. I want to be a good mom, and sometimes I'm not. I guess I could add guilty to the list."

"Recap and find out more," I urged Ken.

"So, Regina, you are saying that having two kids is hard. Sometimes you get mad, and that makes you feel out of control and scares you. I told you we shouldn't have had them so close together."

Regina shot back, "You're the one who didn't want to use birth control!"

"Wait a minute," I said. "We're back to Ping-Pong. Regina, instead of shooting a retort back to Ken when he makes that kind of statement, stop and tell him how his words affect you. For example, 'Ken, that comment makes me want to give up sharing my heart with you.'"

"I'm sorry," Ken said. "I'd rather hit the ball than hold it. Let's keep going." Ken repeated his recap.

I asked, "Ken, can you understand how Regina might feel after being home all day with two young children?"

"Yes," he said. "They make me feel stressed sometimes, too, but not to that degree."

"You don't have to share the exact experience to validate your wife's feelings," I said. "Simply telling Regina that her feelings make sense helps her feel understood. You just gave an excellent recap of what Regina said. Now you need to validate her feelings."

"Regina, I can understand how you could feel at the end of your rope by the time I get home." Ken looked to me. "Now I will feel guilty whenever I go ride my bike."

"So, Ken, if you offer understanding, it feels like Regina wins but you lose?"

"Exactly," he replied. "Good recap."

I laughed. "When you hang a win-lose scoreboard over a conversation, it pretty much kills your ability to listen effectively. Try to see this another way. It's not about winning or losing; it's about understanding the deeper feelings and thoughts underlying the issue. I think you'll both be more open to negotiating a compromise once you have heard each other's hearts. You might be surprised what will happen if you take the scoreboard down. Let's get back to the conversation. Ken, you gave a recap and validated Regina's feelings. Now find out more."

Ken looked over his list of questions. "Is your current panicky feeling an old or familiar feeling that you have felt at times in the past?"

Regina was quiet again. "I really don't think so. I don't remember feeling this way when I was younger."

"Now what?" Ken asked.

"It was a good question, Ken," I said. "She might have found a connection, but you don't know until you ask. Pick another question."

Ken scanned the list again. "What are your hopes, Regina?"

"My hopes are that you could see how much I need you right now. I don't think it will always be this hard, but I guess I hope you would want to be with the kids and not just see them as a chore."

Without looking at the sheet or at me, Ken asked, "How does it make you feel when I act like it's a chore?"

"It makes me sad," Regina replied. "I guess part of the panicky feeling is that I don't want your relationship with the girls to be like the one I had with my dad. And I'm scared it will turn out the same."

Ken was clearly surprised. "So you feel like I see the kids as a chore and I don't enjoy them, just as your dad didn't enjoy you."

Hearing her fear spoken aloud, Regina's eyes became damp. After a few moments she said, "I'm probably mad at my dad for that, and maybe I'm partly taking that out on you."

Ken put his arm around her, and I smiled.

What Do You Do with Anger?

After you've tried a speaker-listener exercise, reflect on the pace of the conversation. The first thing you'll notice is how calm and slow it is compared to the breakneck speed of the typical Ping-Pong game.

The pace almost picked up for Regina and Ken when anger started to interfere with their conversation. Usually listeners become angry when something is said they don't agree with or they feel is inaccurate. When that happens, stop the conversation for a moment and make a note about what it is you want to say as the speaker. But then listen.

If you feel too angry to listen, say that and take a deep breath. Pause for a few moments and work at uncovering the feelings under your anger. Is there any hurt or sadness underneath? Take a time-out, if necessary. But do not use time-outs as a way to escape and avoid; use them to look for something constructive to share. If you're really steamed or think you've found a trigger, you might say, "I'm getting angry, and I need to call a time-out so I can cool down. Let's get back together in a few minutes." Likewise, if you sense your spouse growing angry, suggest a quick break and let him or her work through that feeling. Don't accuse or blame, but do commit to keep going.

Sometimes if the speakers changed something about their delivery, that would make it easier for listeners to listen. If that's the case for you as the listener, ask the speaker to make the change. One man I worked with, for instance, was very triggered by raised voices. His wife wasn't yelling, but her tone of voice was determined and passionate. He'd listened to his parents' frequent bouts of screaming, and when his wife raised her voice, he shut down. He learned to say, "Could you speak more softly? It will help me keep listening." At first his wife felt it was unfair that she couldn't just "be herself," but when she saw how much better he was able to listen when she was quieter, she was willing to change.

THE LISTENER

It takes growth and practice to be an effective speaker and an effective listener. But, overall, the listener role is more challenging and takes a bit more practice to master. Asking good questions about what we hear someone say is definitely a learned skill.

And we can learn an important lesson from James 1:19, which says, "But everyone must be quick to hear, slow to speak and slow to anger." What transformations would happen in our lives if we took this charge to heart? "Quick to hear" means "I listen before I respond." After all, the goal of listening is to find out what is going on underneath the surface, and the quest often yields new insights for speaker as well as listener. So, as the listener, make it your ambition to get as much information as you can in order to understand another's perspective. Don't miss the word *heart* here either. Letting the speaker's words affect your heart can make all the difference in your connection.

Someone wisely said that God made us with two ears and one mouth, so we should listen twice as much as we speak. As Stephen R. Covey wrote in *The Seven Habits of Highly Effective People*, "Seek first to understand, then to be understood." This wise statement helped impress upon me the need for slowing ourselves down so that we can be really good listeners. Wise advice. Over and over I have to learn to ask and recap, ask and recap, and the lessons I've learned in my own life I teach to every couple in my office.

Not long ago during my kung fu workout, my teacher Russ made us hold a stance called a "full horse" for several minutes. My feet were spread from a semi-squat position, and my back was straight. The exercise improves strength, flexibility, and stability. "A little longer and a little lower," Russ kept saying. After a few minutes I was thinking, *You've got to be kidding. I can't possibly stay in this pose any longer.* But having practiced the full horse weekly, I found I had developed endurance, and after a while I could hold the pose much longer and even begin to relax in it.

Extended listening is like kung fu. As a dedicated listener, you might be thinking, "Are you kidding? I'm supposed to be quiet and not say anything after what she just said?" Yes, stay in that pose and be a listener for ten to twenty minutes before you reverse roles. Think of yourself as Larry King or Barbara Walters. They ask a lot of questions because they're focused on finding out as much as they can about the person to whom they are talking. Show a similar intense interest as you listen to your spouse and remember that your payoff is a closer connection with him or her.

I'm not asking you to do anything I haven't done myself. I remember well how awkward this was for me to learn, especially when strong emotions were involved. I will never forget one of the first times I tried the listener role with Kay. It was a Saturday afternoon, and I asked the kids to give us some time alone. I said, "Mom and I are going into the bedroom to talk, and if there is a true emergency, you may knock on the door." I'm sure our thirteen-year-old had his own ideas about why we were going in there, but our time together turned out to be extraordinary and intimate. It was one of the first times Kay was vulnerable and let me see her—and be with her—when she was really distressed.

I could tell Kay was distraught, and I knew she was processing some feelings about her past. I took her hand and said, "We need to talk; I can tell you are really upset." So we sat in the middle of the bed together and prayed briefly for wisdom. I said, "What hurts the most inside? You can say anything you want, and I'll listen and try to understand." What happened next was as incredible as it was nerve-racking. Kay sat there for at least ten minutes without saying a single word. An introvert who processes thoughts and feelings internally, Kay was reviewing things, going over them with deep sighs, and staring out the window.

My biggest challenge was to keep my mouth shut and allow the silence to continue indefinitely. Man, it was oppressive. When she finally did speak, it startled me. She then began a catharsis that covered years, places, people, and events. When she shared about events or situations, I asked her to tell me more. If she talked about a person, I said, "Pretend I am that person and say to me what you would like to say to him or her." Man, it was hard, and it was disconcerting. I had never seen that much emotion come from Kay. I felt as if I were caring for a child with the flu as I dodged projectiles and tried to comfort her as she thrashed and kicked.

My emotions were all over the map. I felt strength, concern, terror, sympathy, lack of control, compassion—and all the while I was repeating inside, "Help me, Lord!" Eventually, after ten hours of this—okay, just kidding; actually it was only about an hour—Kay let me hold her, and she cried in my arms. I laid her down on the bed, and soon she fell asleep. I got up and walked out of the room as if I just endured a full-on, massive assault by twelve assailants. But I also felt closer to her than I ever had. I felt I had seen her soul.

The kids looked at me and asked, "Is Mom okay?" Reassuring them that she was, I explained that we'd had a great talk and that she was feeling much better but now needed to sleep. After attending to the kids for a while, I caught my reflection in a mirror.

We did it! I thought. *Something sacred and holy just took place. Our souls were just knit more closely together.*

This was the first of hundreds of similar conversations (we've lost count) that have taken place over the last nineteen years. Not all of them were this emotional, and when it was about a problem between us, that kind of conversation had its own learning curve. But I never felt defensive during that first talk because it wasn't about me at all. But since that conversation we've covered many topics, starting as novices without a clue about what to do. Over time, though, we progressed to greater levels, and finally we earned our black belts in extended listening.

But now let's consider the speaker's responsibilities. Contemplate these ancient words of wisdom: "Pleasant words are a honeycomb, sweet to the soul and healing to the bones" (Proverbs 16:24, NIV). When we speak, we need to choose words that are diplomatic and kind. If we choose harsh and mean-spirited words, we will kill a conversation and put another stack of bricks in the wall between our spouses and us. But on a positive note, your choice of words and mine can actually bring about healing in another's soul!

The Bible also says, "He who restrains his words has knowledge, and he who has a cool spirit is a man of understanding" (Proverbs 17:27). To keep listening, we have to restrain our tendencies to defend ourselves and debate issues. We cannot be listening and planning our rebuttal at the same time. One of my favorite proverbs—because it inspires me to be a great listener—is, "A plan in the heart of a man is like deep water, but a man of understanding draws it out" (Proverbs 20:5). My goal is to draw out the deep waters of another human's soul.

Are you game?

If so—and I hope so—here's another tip. Being aware of your nonverbal responses and your body language also helps you become a great listener. We've all experienced responses and behaviors that turn us off to deep conversation. Rolling eyes, sighs, groans, refusing to make eye contact, or defensive staring can all ruin an otherwise good talk.

The most important thing a listener can do is show genuine, personal interest in what the person is saying. And that may mean letting yourself be interrupted. Kay and I, for instance, have become excellent slackers as we've learned to stop projects, let brushes and paint rollers dry, and leave bushes half-trimmed, lawns partially mowed, and cars half-washed in order to show our interest in a family member who needed to talk. At times we set boundaries and asked people to wait a while, but if emotions are present, they're our cue that it's time to listen.

One last thing. If your spouse happens to be a part of the estimated 25 percent[1] of the population that is introverted, he or she has probably spent most of life not feeling fully understood. The reason is, introverts commonly process thoughts internally before they speak. So if you ask them, "What is the twenty-third letter of the alphabet?" they will ponder for a moment and then say, "W." Extroverts, however, will just start talking: "Let's see, a, b, c—did you see my new shoes?—d, e, f, g, h, i—I like your shoes too—j, k…" And eventually they'll get to it. Introverts get cut off in conversations because extroverts naturally dominate. So here is some advice to you extroverts: ask one question, sit back, shut up, and wait.

Seriously. I have waited multiple minutes for introverts to respond to questions. It's worth the wait, and they love you for it.

VALIDATION

I walked into my doctor's office the other day, and the receptionist greeted me with a smile. "How are you? Do you need validation today?"

"Thanks, I'm good," I said. "My wife and I had a good talk this morning."

"I meant the parking, sir," she said.

The fact is, we all need validation. As we saw in Ken and Regina's conversation, many people have difficulty giving thoughtful validation to their spouses' emotions and experiences. Telling someone we understand his or her feelings doesn't necessarily mean we agree with that person's thoughts or point of view. Validating our spouses' emotions simply means letting them know that their feelings make sense to us and that we've viewed the situation from their perspectives. Whether or not we agree with their points of view, we can still say something like, "Wow! That must have been a very difficult experience for you to go through." Statements like this can set the stage for deep trust.

The key to validation is an attitude of acceptance. Over the years, Kay and I have learned to accept that we are two different people and that we aren't always going to agree with each other. Over time, we also grew to accept each other's unique experiences, feelings, and perspectives instead of making everything a matter of right or wrong, good or bad, correct or incorrect. What a person is feeling is what a person is feeling, no matter how I view the situation. To accept the reality that the feelings are there whether I like them or not is to validate that person's experience. This acceptance is a sign of the maturity that separates the amateur listeners from the professionals.

LISTENER QUESTIONS

Often, as couples are first learning to be good listeners, they get stuck. Whatever the topic being discussed, I (Kay) encourage them to always ask about feelings even if they think they know each other's emotions already. The following list of questions may be useful to refer to when you get stuck in a conversation. They may feel mechanical at first, but they really do work.

- "Tell me more. I want to understand."
- "What can I do to make it safe for you to open up to me?"
- "Please pick three feeling words off the soul words list so I will understand your emotions about this topic."
- "How long have you been feeling this way?"
- "Are you feeling anything in addition to the emotion you just shared?"
- "At what other times have you felt this way?"
- "When did you feel this as a child?"
- "What are your hopes?"
- "What are your expectations?"
- "What are your desires?"
- "On a scale of one to ten, how strong is your feeling?"
- "I can tell you are really upset. Do you think you are feeling triggered in some way?"
- "If you could share the same feeling you have right now with someone else in the present or the past, who would it be? What would you say to that person?"
- "Does your current feeling remind you of an old or familiar feeling that you perhaps felt when you were growing up?"
- "What does your body feel like right now? What part of your body feels the strongest sensation? If that part of your body could speak, what would it say?"
- "What do you need?" (closing question)

Recapping Statements
- "What you are saying is…"
- "Stop for a minute and let me summarize…"
- "So you are feeling…because…"
- "From your point of view, you think…and feel…"

Validation Statements

- "I understand how you could feel that way."
- "From your perspective, your feelings make sense."
- "I would probably feel the same way if I were in your situation."
- "I see your tears, and I see how much this upsets you."
- "I see how angry you feel and how upset this makes you."
- "It makes sense to me that you would feel…"

Conversation Starters

- "Pick a word from the soul words list that fits with an event in your day and tell me about it."
- "Tell me about the best thing in your day and the worst thing in your day."
- "Choose an area in your life—work, relationships, church, friends, hobbies, and so on—and then pick a few feeling words that describe your current experiences and feelings about that area."
- "Pick a feeling and tell me about a childhood experience when you felt that emotion."
- "Choose the feeling you felt most during your day and tell me about it."

These five conversation starters are good topics for practicing the art of conversation. They give you the opportunity to talk about things that aren't current problems between you and your spouse. Those problem areas are the most difficult topics for conversation and the most likely to raise defenses, so instead start with topics that are more neutral and learn to stay in the listener role for an extended time. As your skills improve, you'll be establishing a good foundation for tackling the more sensitive subjects.

GOALS FOR EACH IMPRINT AS LISTENERS AND SPEAKERS

Here are a few facts about each imprint to keep in mind as you sharpen your conversational skills:

Pleaser: As the listener, you may get very uncomfortable when your spouse expresses anger, and you may apologize or you may try to cut off the conversation to avoid further confrontation. You probably often smile without realizing it in order to minimize the discomfort you feel. So you need to learn to tolerate another person's anger and keep listening. When it's your turn to share difficult feelings (especially anger), you will beat around the bush, take too long to get to the point, and struggle to be truthful. You will want to minimize your emotions and make them sound too pretty. Be bold!

Avoider: As a listener, you will ask few questions and may even say with your words or body language, "Are you done yet?" You need to work on helping your spouse feel that you really want to hear what he or she has to say. Be patient with yourself as you learn to ask questions. You could look at this as a new task to master, which, if you recall from chapter 5, is a characteristic of an avoider. Then, as speaker, you will not want to talk at all, or you'll hope to have minimal conversations, and you'll struggle to identify your feelings. You will resist initiating a talk and agonize about how to do it correctly. You'll be tentative if you encounter turbulence and will clam up. A word of encouragement to all you avoiders: you have to experience connection before you can value it. Also, you might be surprised to learn all that is inside you when you give your spouse an opportunity to listen.

Vacillator: When you listen, you may become impatient and tend to interrupt if the speaker is saying something you don't feel is accurate. Also, since you tend to see things as right or wrong, you may struggle to keep listening when you don't agree. Remember that each person's perspective is unique. Try to keep listening and allow your spouse to see things from another perspective. Be careful to ask questions that promote understanding rather than entrapping the speaker in order to prove your point. Now, when it comes to speaking, vacillators are often skilled verbally and want to be understood. So, when you are speaking, you may tend to talk too much and overwhelm your spouse with details and examples, believing that he or she won't understand you unless you give all this information. Try to be brief and concise (limit yourself to five or six sentences) and then give your spouse time to recap. And try to be patient if you sense that your spouse is struggling to ask good questions or understand your point of view.

Controller: You get so uncomfortable with any emotion that you will tend to lash out in anger to stop the noise and nonsense. You have to learn to control your anger before it is possible to have a good conversation. So try to remember what it was like for you when you were a child and no one ever listened to you. It does not feel good. When it's your turn to talk, you'll struggle to speak kindly to the listener. Used to intimidation tactics, you'll need to prepare yourself to speak in quiet tones and to share their hurt and pain underneath your bravado. Again, you'll have to learn to control your anger before this kind of speaking is possible for you.

Victim: You will listen fearfully and try to remember all the details so that you don't get in trouble with a misstep. You may have to learn to listen in a safe place (often outside the home) so you can think without being afraid. It is difficult to listen when you are full of fear or being berated. When it's time to switch roles, you will simply need to speak up and say something even though it will be hard for you to trust that anyone could want to hear your heart. Also, you cannot open up in an unsafe environment. So, before you can express an idea contrary to your spouse's point of view, your spouse has to make it safe for you by managing his or her anger.

Chapter 19

Resolve

(Milan) remember one couple who came for counseling in which the husband said, "I don't try to meet my wife's needs because I have less than a fifty-fifty chance of doing it right. Those are lousy odds!"

"What if I could give you a new way of meeting her needs that will give you a very high chance of success every time?" I said.

"That'd be more valuable than the fountain of youth!" he said, looking at me as if I were going to hand him the Holy Grail.

"Just ask her," I said.

He blinked. "That's it?"

I nodded. A small smile appeared on his wife's face as she began to nod as well.

After giving our spouses the gifts of extended listening, clarification, and validation, we are finally ready to ask, "What do you need?" A wide variety of responses can come when you ask this question because we all need something different to help us feel better. By the way, most of the time, guessing what our spouses need means trying to impose on them what *we* would like. No wonder those efforts fail. Identifying the best choice for resolution of the feelings is the way to relief and comfort, and the person feeling the emotions can tell you what that best choice is.

Sadly, however, most conversations will never arrive at this point. Instead, they will get lost in an emotional black hole or get stuck at the base of the wall that stands between husband and wife. But after thorough speaking, careful listening, and heartfelt validating, practice asking what your spouse needs. It takes all the guesswork and stress out of trying to come up with something on your own, and it eliminates having to read your spouse's mind. When a spouse clearly defines and communicates his or her needs, the listener enjoys very high odds for successfully meeting the needs. And that's what you call a win-win situation.

So what are some mutually satisfying resolutions? Here are some of the things we've discovered.

LISTEN AND HEAR

Sometimes your thorough listening, clarification, and validation are all that your spouse needs. And that could be expressed with a statement like "You know, I don't think I need anything right now. I just feel better having gotten that off my chest." That is what I said to Kay one evening in Paris. We had decided to walk from the Orsay Museum to the Eiffel Tower, which was farther than we would ever walk in our own hometown. It didn't look far on the little map, but it was probably four miles or so, and by the time we got close, we were exhausted, tired, and hungry. As we sat down in a little café a few blocks from the tower, something in our conversation reminded me of a painful moment from when I was growing up. While I can't remember the details, I'm sure that I was probably triggered by something to do with travel or separation anxiety. After all, Paris is a long, long way from home.

As I shared the memory with Kay, dinner was getting cold. She was holding my hand, and the waiter looked at us apprehensively from time to time. I had tears streaming down my face as I recounted the difficult memory that I hadn't thought of in years. Her loving gaze, thoughtful questions, and empathetic tones gave me tremendous comfort. So when she said, "What do you need?" I told her that her listening and caring were enough. As I had brought my thoughts and feelings out in the open, the connection with Kay filled up my emotional tank and relieved some pressure that had suddenly popped up. It was amazing how much relief I felt within a very short period. After dinner we had a wonderful time riding up to the top of the tower and seeing the spectacular view, the whole city of Paris lighted up and shining. My soul was shining just as brightly.

It's amazing and wonderful that just listening can be enough. A spouse who knows you well can drain the pressure out of your tank just by taking the time to look into your eyes and hear what's in your heart. It was so surprising how much better I felt after Kay listened, and other couples have reported the same thing. The knowledge that we're known—knowledge that comes when someone practices extended listening with us—brings swift relief to our souls.

OWN AND CONFESS

At times, one of you will need to hear an apology from the other. You might say, "I need you to admit, own, or confess your part in the problem. I am not the whole reason for our problem. Can you take your share of responsibility for this terrible core pattern we are in and stop blaming me?" Jim said words like this to his wife after she had listened to him patiently for over twenty minutes. Let me share their story.

Jim was an avoider, and Sherri was a vacillator. When they entered my office, the bull's-eye was on Jim, and he struggled with constantly feeling inadequate. "If he really loved me, he would just know what to do," Sherri insisted. Jim, however, had not spent a lifetime watching others and memorizing their cues as Sherri had done. Jim avoided emotions and was generally clueless about anticipating and meeting Sherri's needs. He needed clear instructions that Sherri just didn't want to give him. "If you have to spell it out and ask for it, then it's not love," she said (a typical response from a vacillator).

After several weeks and some good listening time on her part, Sherri was finally able to see Jim's point. At the end of the conversation, she said, "I can see how I've expected you to know what to do for me. My imprint has made me focus on you, and I've made you my adversary. But I see now why it's hard for you to anticipate my needs."

When Jim heard this, his jaw dropped and he sat there quiet for a few moments. Sherri had owned her part in their unhealthy dance.

FORGIVE AND REASSURE

Jim was more courageous than I expected. "I really appreciate what you just said, Sherri, because your anger has hurt me. I think it would help to hear an apology."

Sherri took a deep breath and looked at me for guidance. I said, "Just add it on to what you've told him already."

She looked at Jim and said, "My behavior has been unfair, and I know I have hurt you. I am truly sorry and ask for your forgiveness." Jim's face softened, reflecting the relief he felt.

Many of us have asked for apologies in the past and gotten the one-word response: "Sorry!" What Sherri did here, though, was offer a heartfelt statement that was seeking true forgiveness. If Sherri had just said, "Sorry," she would not have helped the relationship at all. Only after really listening to Jim could Sherri construct a genuine apology, and then she chose to do so. Her request for forgiveness had depth, humility, and sincerity.

What apology—or other statement—do you need to hear from your spouse? And what apology or other statement does your spouse need to hear from you? "I need to hear from you that things will be okay." "Please tell me that you will work on your anger." "I need to hear that you still really love me." "I need to know if you are still committed to the relationship." No matter what our love styles, all of us need reassurance. Our anxieties and fears can too easily become a downward spiral of worry that begins to circle around the drain of bad endings. We imagine the worst, and we can ruminate for days over a single word or phrase from our spouses.

At one point in my work with Sherri and Jim, he said, "I guess I'm anxious because I just never know when she is going to file for divorce."

Sherri whipped her head toward him. "What are you talking about?"

They locked eyes, and Jim was clearly flustered. "What you said a few weeks ago!"

"What did I say?"

"That you were out of here!"

Sherri looked at him and said, "You're kidding! I was hormonal, the kids were late for school, I was supposed to be room mom for the day, and you were on your way to the airport for the second time in two weeks! I didn't mean that!"

Poor Jim just stared.

"You've really been thinking about this for the last month?" she asked.

He nodded.

Obviously, Sherri wasn't completely at fault here, but during a moment of frustration, any of us can easily create insecurity in our spouses by something we say or do. Sometimes we need to explain ourselves, do some backtracking, and reassure our spouses of our love and commitment. Jim had spent a week thinking catastrophically and playing out all the different scenarios in his mind. He was miserable, and Sherri had absolutely no idea how her comment had affected him.

As it turned out, Jim had been deeply triggered by her comment because his mother left his dad when he was a child. Sherri's "one little comment" in a moment of legitimate frustration threw Jim into a tailspin that he could not pull out of by himself. He needed to talk and share his fears. He needed serious reassurance! Again, Sherri rose to the occasion. She cried genuine tears of pain for him, took his hand, and looked him in the eye as she said, "For better and for worse, I am yours and you are mine." It was an inspiring moment to see—right before my eyes—Sherri learning how to love.

AGREE AND DISAGREE

"I still don't agree, but I know we understand and accept each other." An essential component of acceptance is to not just allow differences to exist, but rather to celebrate and even encourage them. God created each of us different as male, female, extrovert, introvert, sensitive, tough, and the list goes on. We have different needs and abilities as thinkers, emoters, and relaters. Sometimes resolution means that we agree to be different from each other; we agree to take a break from our attempts to make others behave like we do.

One of the biggest struggles couples have is their differing levels of sexual desire. Zach, for instance, was a fit and handsome client who was crushed because his wife didn't desire him as much as he did her. He had hounded her to become more sexually aggressive, trying different tactics for years. I asked his wife, Emily, "How do you feel about Zach's complaints?"

Her answer was typical: "They make me feel like something is wrong with me, like I'm a failure. I never measure up, and that makes me want sex even less."

I explained to Zach that perhaps he'd bought into the popular culture's representation of women and that what he was looking for was a guy in a girl's body. "She only exists in Hollywood, Zach," I said. "She's a mythological being with the body and mind of a woman, but the sexual appetite of a male."

Emily started giggling, but Zach was still confused. "Zach, the sexual spouse you desire isn't real. Your wife is different from you, and like many women, she doesn't think about sex all day or sit around imagining you in your underwear. Will you accept her the way she is and agree to disagree rather than expect her to be like you?"

"How do I do that?" he asked.

"You must see her as God does, as unique with tastes, likes, and preferences that differ from yours." I already knew from talking to Emily that she needed the usual slow buildup of ten to fifteen minutes of foreplay for her desire to match Zach's. "Quit pressuring Emily to begin with the same level of passion you feel. Praise her for her ability to respond to you and find out what kind of touch and experiences will help her mood match yours. *Then* enjoy the fireworks."

Once Zach was on the right path in the passion department, it was time to discuss another important component of healthy resolution.

NEGOTIATE AND COMPROMISE

Compromise addresses the problem of imbalance within the relationship. Zach and Emily would need to learn to compromise, to find some middle ground, and that meant negotiating from both sides. Once Emily realized there was nothing wrong with her taking a while to become aroused, she found it easier to initiate sex, and she began to enjoy her ability to respond. If she was tired or on the fence, a little effort could help her accept Zach's initiation.

Other times, Emily needed the freedom to say no without Zach pouting or withdrawing. If she was upset, Zach needed to table his desire and take time to go around the comfort circle and see what was going on inside his wife. For most men, doing this involves a mental shift; they need to remember women are not like men. Some of the angriest women I have encountered have husbands who disregard their desires and emotions. So, for Zach, compromise meant postponing sex and talking for as long as was necessary to get Emily's feelings resolved. Most of the time, this would mean no sex that evening, and Zach simply needed to accept that and be willing to put his wife's needs before his own.

DIVERSION AND DISTRACTION

"Let's go out, have fun, and forget it all for a while!" Often our stresses are consuming, and we cannot easily shake off the emotions or get them out of our minds. Sometimes Kay and I will look at each other after getting around the comfort circle, and in response to "What do you need?" one of us will say, "Let's get out of Dodge and do something that will get our minds off this problem." We will go to the beach, shopping, or surfing; we'll go to the movies, walk in a shopping mall, or take a day trip to LA, San Diego, or Disneyland. (A *little* retail therapy never hurt anyone.)

Time out for a brief word study. The word *muse* is not used often anymore, but it means "to consider, think, contemplate, or mull over in one's mind." *Amuse,* then, literally means "without musing, thinking, or pondering." At times we need to escape from internal contemplation, and amusement offers a total distraction from the heavy things that plague our hearts and minds. Yes, Kay and I shamelessly admit that we occasionally look for diversions so we can escape it all.

Now please take note of the word *occasionally.* For some people, diversion is their only solution, or it is the first response to relational challenges. Healthy diversion, however, is a choice made at the end of the comfort circle, not in place of it. Being balanced means we can use all of the resolution possibilities, not just favor one.

CELEBRATE AND ENJOY

One of the joys of life is to take into the comfort circle the euphoric emotions from a wonderful experience you shared. After Kay and I conduct a daylong workshop or retreat, for instance, we are always exhausted and out of energy. So we frequently find a quiet restaurant and sit and blankly stare into nothingness for a little while.

Eventually, one of us starts talking about the day, and each of us processes how we feel about the effectiveness of our teaching both individually and together. We listen to each other's feelings and thoughts as we take turns processing our way around the comfort circle. We are not afraid to take the time to acknowledge and work through the difficulties that we each experienced during the day. Eventually, we integrate these frustrations with the good things that happened, and we end up celebrating the day together with funny stories, praise of each other's work, and thanks to God for his blessings. Many times we have clicked our beverage glasses together, made a toast to each other, and said, "Way to go, partner!"

So keep your eyes open for occasions to celebrate. When Kay received the letter from the Board of Behavioral Sciences that she had successfully passed her oral exams as a marriage and family therapist, I arrived home before she did, saw the letter, and rejoiced that all her hard work had paid off. I got on the phone and called our closest friends and family, and when Kay got home from the office, she read the good news for herself and understood why we were having a party. We celebrated, she cried, we thanked the Lord, and everyone in the room told Kay why they appreciated her. We all shared in Kay's massive sense of relief and enjoyed sharing her happiness and joy. That fun evening stands out in both of our minds as a memorable bonding and connecting experience.

When was the last time you celebrated something with your spouse?

SUPPORT AND ENCOURAGE

Recently, a couple in my office was going around the comfort circle. When they got to the question "What do you need?" he answered, "I need you to just support and encourage me while I go through this tough season of life."

Max was in the "sandwich phase" of life with his dependent children and wife on one side and, on the other, an aging parent who was causing him a lot of stress and grief. Max's two siblings were thousands of miles away, and the caregiving burden was falling on him because he lived just a few miles from his mom. Max and his wife, Cindy, had watched as his mom steadily declined in her capacity to care for herself. She was losing track of her medications, forgetting to bathe, and had recently taken a nasty fall. Max knew he had to take action.

Max's mom continued to resist him as he looked at various retirement facilities that had assisted-living options. She would argue and make him feel guilty for not honoring her wishes to stay alone in her house. Max struggled with guilt and was deeply conflicted about doing what he knew was in his mom's best interest. He made the final decision when his mom was in a skilled nursing facility recovering from her fall on the bathroom floor. When she asked him, "When am I going home, Max?" he said to her, "Mom, in a week you are moving to your new home upstairs in the assisted-living section of this new retirement facility." She was angry, she felt betrayed, and she argued bitterly with him. Heaping guilt upon Max, she was unkind to him as she was suffering her loss of independence.

As Max was learning painful truths about aging, he was also learning about being a pleaser. The deep conflict in his soul began to come out as he recounted the story to Cindy and me. "I just need your support, Cindy. This is one of the hardest things I have ever had to do."

Cindy simply put her arms around Max and let him feel his emotions. After a few minutes she said, "How else can I support you?"

Over the next few minutes, they outlined specific ways she and the kids could help Max.

"And you can have as many hugs and neck rubs as you want," Cindy said. Max left my office that day feeling relieved and supported.

ANALYZE AND SOLVE

"Would you help me figure out how to solve this recurring problem?" This is how men think, and usually their first priority is to fix it, stop it, repair it, overhaul it, improve it, tune it, turbocharge it, return it, or just turn it off. (Hey, it works for me!) But in our journey toward intimacy, we males have to learn that these approaches do not work well with emotions—neither hers nor ours. Yes, there is a time for fixing it, but we men too often tend to minimize emotions. Many of us need to learn to ask an important question at the beginning of a conversation: "Do you want me just to listen, or do you want me to problem solve?" We need to develop the skills to do both.

Sometimes our spouses will just want to vent their emotions, but sometimes our spouses will need a solution. My dad was an engineer who knew about solutions. I was used to seeing a clean pad of paper and a sharp #2 pencil present for many of our discussions. I remember being worried about finances one time, and he provided comfort and reassurance as he methodically worked through the numbers with me. Sometimes our spouses need such concrete solutions. They need help balancing the checkbook, making a plan for retirement, paying bills, dividing the household labor, adjusting our parenting with the kids, or finding out why the engine light is on in the car. So at times, our spouses' relief may come from solving problems.

SPACE AND SEPARATENESS

"I need some space." At any given time, these words can strike fear in the hearts of people who have injured love styles. Sometimes they can even be fighting words: "What do you mean, you need space?" Some people struggle with departure anxiety when a loved one needs time alone or with friends. Only the avoider thinks, *Take all the space you want.* Avoiders have no problem with space, but they struggle with connecting. Often the pleaser, vacillator, and controller are uncomfortable with time apart, and they may manipulate to keep their spouses close. And people with abandonment in their background may be triggered by separation. The need for constant connection will make this spouse feel smothered, while too much separateness feels lonely and isolating.

A healthy relationship, however, does need to breathe. Just as you need both inhaling and exhaling, couples function best when—according to God's design—we are able to enjoy both bonding (inhaling) and being separate (exhaling). The healthiest marriages are those that are in a rhythmic routine of bonding and being separate, and each spouse is comfortable with both. Partners need a sense of security in order to view separation as something to be encouraged, valued, and promoted. The more secure their attachment to each other, the easier it is for spouses to allow each other space within the relationship—space to breathe and the freedom to be different—without it triggering fear and anxiety. In fact, allowing and encouraging our spouses to move away for short periods often brings them back more refreshed than if they had stayed in constant contact. And let me clarify: I'm not talking here about retreating because you don't know how to connect. That's what Kay did when she went away to process the loss of our baby. If you are an avoider, you need to work on connection.

While it is always important to bring our emotions into relationship with our spouses, sometimes when we are dealing with strong emotions, such as grief, sadness, and anger, time alone can be beneficial for thinking, praying, processing, and gaining some emotional equilibrium within our own souls. When Jesus heard that John the Baptist had died, for example, "He withdrew from there in a boat to a secluded place by Himself" (Matthew 14:13). Sad news, difficult emotions, and especially pain inflicted by our spouses may require some time alone for the purpose of recovery and grieving. Separateness for several hours or a day may be a very important step in the process of healing and forgiveness. Being introspective and calming our own reactions and triggers can relieve relational stress. After some time alone, we can come back with a calmer spirit to work things out.

Finally, an important aspect of separation is being able to say no at times. We can't possibly comply with every request our spouses make. We are not always emotionally prepared to respond, and we may need some time to think or to get used to an idea. Highly anxious or controlling people may make unhealthy requests. A fearful wife, for instance, might say, "I need you to be home every night before dark." A compulsive cleaner might say, "I need the kitchen spotless and the house vacuumed before we go to bed." A controlling person may say, "I need you to do things my way." Deep-seated phobias can cause people to make strange requests. Internal distress may cause some spouses to make demands to settle their own anxiety. Without compliance, these spouses may feel unloved and irritated. But, truthfully, it's unloving to comply with unhealthy requests. If you're in that kind of situation, the most loving thing you as a spouse can do is insist that your mate get professional help. We routinely see lives transformed with individual therapy and a season of proper medication to calm the anxiety.

TOUCH AND NURTURE

"Would you please hold me and comfort me while I cry?"

I'm not exactly sure when I first held Kay in my arms cradled like a child, and I'm not sure when I first put my head in her lap. All I recall is that we gradually learned how important touch is to deeper connections. Over time, physical touch has helped us become each other's safest source of comfort. When I'm distressed, Kay is my go-to person, and I am hers. And that's how it should be.

In chapter 2, we explained how recognizing our imprint starts with a question about comfort. For many of us who were unable to remember receiving emotional comfort when we were children, marriage is our chance to get what we've missed. When a couple goes around the comfort circle after making an emotional connection, physical nurture can be the grand finish. Touch communicates "I see, know, and value the real you inside, and I love you."

But many factors will keep you from being able to give and receive nurture as a couple. Some people, for instance, are unconvinced that they need nurturing comfort, because they never experienced it when they were children. Others handle distress by doing what Kay did after she lost the baby: isolate themselves and deal with the pain on their own. To these people, physical nurturing and being comforted for their "silly emotions" seem unnecessary. Yet if they were to dig deeper, they'd probably find that they feel threatened and afraid to face their emotions, and being touched and comforted may feel too risky. But as we age, we experience more and greater losses, and we will suffer alone unnecessarily if we don't know how to ask for and receive nurture and comfort from each other.

So, to help people learn the value of touch and its ability to encourage vulnerability, we've developed a deceptively simple but powerful technique we call holding time. During a holding time, the listener sits upright on a couch or love seat and literally cradles the speaker in his or her arms. With practice, these holding times become more comfortable, and soon couples find this position—chest to chest and eye to eye—the ultimate kind of nurture. But if you never experienced being comforted while you were growing up, a holding time with your mate will probably feel downright awkward at first. Yet, in our offices, we routinely see couples who try this position find deeper connection and greater relief. We often ask couples how the position feels, and we've heard everything imaginable: "Amazing! I'm never getting up," "Kinda weird, but I like it," "Uncomfortable and embarrassing." Yet when couples stick with it, their initial discomfort passes, and they tell us that holding time deepens their bond with each other.

Now for some specifics. When you practice holding times, it's important that you don't try to fix each other's emotions. Also, don't let busyness or stress get in the way. Just let the emotions that come simply be what they are. Get rid of the external clock that's trying to control the internal world. If you're a man and you have a strong aversion to physical nurturing and emotions (yours and anyone else's), face your fear and don't try to stifle emotions. You're not going to die from crying, and you aren't going to scare the kids. And when you're the listener, all you need to do is hold your spouse and say, "It's okay to feel whatever is inside; I'll be here with you."

Remember, too, that it takes time to engage emotions because they're unpredictable and can't be scheduled or anticipated. We must slow down our hectic lives and be willing to stop or delay activities when strong emotions arise within our souls. I know that many of you will find this idea hard to accept, but sometimes we need to let other activities wait, sit down, and engage with emotions—our emotions or the emotions of someone we love. Impatience and unwillingness to let go of your agenda will rob you of the intimacy you have always wanted.

Also, men, if you're afraid of looking weak in front of your woman, realize that your emotions could in fact become your most attractive trait. You think all those actors with their hearts on their sleeves and tears in their eyes don't make her heart flutter? What is the average woman's response to these men on the silver screen? I rest my case. If you offer to comfort your wife and hold her—without any sexual strings attached—you will be a hero of proportions you've never imagined. Let me tell you one more story that illustrates the power of these holding times.

A few years back Kay and I were speaking at a marriage retreat in the San Diego area. We'd both been upset all weekend because we had learned the week before that our college-age daughter was being stalked. She worked in a large department store, and this man would appear and watch her. Every attempt to protect her had failed, and we were scared and angry.

Now a little background. At the close of our seminars, we always model the comfort circle—complete with a holding time. Beforehand, we decide which of us will be the speaker and which the listener , but we don't talk about what the topic will be so that our conversation will be spontaneous and realistic. It is a high-risk maneuver, like trapeze artists who, trusting they will be caught, let go of the bar in midair—and we, like those high-flying circus stars, perform in front of hundreds of spectators.

This time Kay was playing the speaker role, and I was the listener. We were onstage sitting together on a couch, and I had her cradled in my arms as she lay across my lap. I asked what she wanted to talk about, and she said, "Amy and the stalker." A gasp went up from the crowd, and I briefly filled them in on the details. For the next thirty minutes, I held Kay as she shared her fears, how totally unable she was to protect Amy, and how utterly helpless she felt. The audience was absolutely silent, and as Kay and I talked, cried, and prayed together, we forgot that anyone else was in the room. At the end of the session, Kay sat up, and as we looked around, many people were crying. The silence was still hovering over the room. *This was good* was all I could think. Kay and I had experienced sacred intimacy—and the audience had seen what happens when two hearts truly connect.

At the end of the seminar, it took us ages to get away because so many people wanted to thank us. People kept saying how amazed they were, and they wanted to learn to connect like that in their marriages. Yet others were extremely agitated, like one man who told us he felt panicky and claustrophobic and had to get up and stand by the door. Eventually, Amy's stalker uneventfully disappeared from our lives, but over the next few months and years, many people from that seminar told us they had never forgotten the weekend and that they had been inspired to take their connection with their spouses to deeper levels. We were thrilled to learn that, as a result of our sharing, other couples had pushed through their initial discomfort and found a deeper intimacy.

The goal of touch and nurture, then, is to comfort your spouse when he or she is hurting. I want Kay to know in every possible way that I am with her in her pain, and touch says that in ways words cannot. Besides, if you want to dance, you have to touch, and—metaphorically speaking—to be involved in the bonding dance, your goal must be to validate the inner experiences through empathy and touch.

Now let's get specific about touch. On a progressive scale, holding hands would be on the light end of the spectrum, and at the other end would be a holding session. This position makes sharing your heart more feasible and, we have found, feelings more accessible. If either of you is uncomfortable, though, don't be afraid to tell your spouse and adjust to a more comfortable position—but keep holding.

For example, if Kay is holding me, I stretch out on the couch and lie on my back with my head in her lap. When we're in this position, Kay and I are no longer alone in our pain. When Kay holds me, I feel something words simply can't express. She offers me a place of peace, rest, comfort, solace, utter acceptance, and deep love. It is a place of absolute comfort, a place of sacredness, because God is always a part of the experience as the holder prays for the other person and asks God to perform the deep work in our souls that only He can do. Undoubtedly, this is one of the most intimate forms of resolution possible.

Early on in our learning curve, though, when Kay would first let me hold her, she always kept her eyes closed. One day I said to her, "Can you look me in the eyes?" It took a few minutes before she opened one eye and peeked at me for a few seconds. Doing so threatened her (as it does me) because there is shame within each of us that can be exposed by vulnerability. Eventually, after many holding sessions, we got to the point where we could look into each other's eyes for an extended period of time. In a recent holding session, Kay looked up at me, smiled, and said, "You look blurry!" I said, "So do you. We're over fifty, you know, and we need our bifocals to see up close!" We laughed, and that was the end of that particular session. When Kay starts making jokes, I know her tanks must be in good shape.

So how in the world do you start to make holding sessions a regular part of your married life? First, you must be willing. Willingness is the most important ingredient to being a good comforter, and when you're open, you will learn as you go. So tell your spouse that you are willing to try until holding sessions feel more natural. Also, we have each learned by experimenting to ask for what feels good, and sometimes we want different things. Sometimes Kay wants me to hold her tightly. Sometimes she wants to look in my eyes and just observe. Sometimes she will stroke my head. Other times we simply want to be quiet together. The hardest thing about learning to do this kind of holding was pushing through the awkwardness of trying something new and different. It feels vulnerable to be held and allow yourself to need in this way. I held Kay quite a few times before I was brave enough to let her hold me. So try holding for short periods of time at first and just talk about the experience and how it feels. What's important is to be courageous enough to be vulnerable and learn. The important thing is to have your spouse by your side, touching you so you are not alone.

Of course, you won't have a holding time with every trip around the comfort circle, but touch is important even if you are just sitting and talking. After all, when your spouse is hurting, it's not hard to simply reach out and hold a hand, put your hand on his knee or shoulder, stroke her hair in sympathy, pat him on the back, sit closely side by side, or put your arm around her. Again, your goal is to start showing that you care with some simple expression of touch.

Also, we must learn to get used to our own feelings, to accept the emotions of others, and to tolerate their tears. Some men feel so helpless when they see people crying that they don't know what to do. Emotions can be frightening because they are truthful displays of the inner soul. But don't worry. Crying will eventually stop and your spouse will usually settle down. So try to reassure your mate with "It's okay. You can cry here with me" or "Take your time. We're not in a hurry." Soon you will be more comfortable with tears.

Patiently taking the time to go around the comfort circle and listening for an extended period definitely lets your spouse know you care. You can cement that message by touching your spouse. That touch lets him or her know physically of your love and comfort. It also creates a profound bond that's unique and special.

At first, though, Milan and I had to just get used to emotions—our own as well as each other's. In an earlier chapter, Milan told you how he was afraid of my pain (so was I!), but we kept trying. We have come to recognize the subtle indications that the other person needs some touch or holding time. I stop making eye contact and withdraw. Milan loses his sense of humor and gets edgy. We have different ways of showing that our pressure tanks are getting full, and talking or touch always releases the pressure. Finally, as holding time gets less awkward and you begin to notice how much better you feel afterward, you won't need to be convinced to keep it up.

SEX AND INTIMACY

If you're a guy, you are probably asking, "What about the sex?" If you're a woman, you may be thinking this whole book has been about sex.

Seriously, couples who enter our offices often say, "We fight about sex all the time," "How can we improve our sexual relationship?" and "If I get close to him, he always wants to have sex." Actually, it is interesting how little time I (Milan) actually spend talking with couples about sex. Why? Because emotional connection naturally brings unparalleled sexual connection.

Before we get to some specifics, did you know that most men are really looking for closeness, intimacy, romance, and security as much as women are? The problem is that sex is how we've been conditioned by our society to think that we will find it. Yet trying to tune your marriage by starting in bed is like trying to tune an orchestra backward. A lone note from an oboe provides the pitch for the delicate strings. Then the oboe prompts the woodwinds, the heavier brass, and ultimately the heaviest percussion pieces like the timpani. Imagine trying to tune the orchestra starting with the timpani. It just wouldn't work. Those drums don't give a clear enough tone. Sadly, though, many people try to tune their relationship by starting in the sexual arena. But the most intense sexual experiences cannot tune the delicate strings of the heart. It's only when the heartstrings are tuned by clear emotional connection that love can create symphonies in the bedroom.

So let me say to the men, if you would like the sexual battles in your marriage to diminish, you need to prove yourself worthy by learning the comfort circle. (Trust me, it works.) We men also need to do some self-examination and readjust our expectations. Romance and connection don't always mean hot and heavy. Paul wrote, "Stop depriving one another [sexually], except by agreement for a time, that you may devote yourselves to prayer, and come together again so that Satan will not tempt you because of your lack of self-control" (1 Corinthians 7:5). Men, when was the last time you told your wife that you wanted to—in obedience to this verse—abstain from sex for a period of time and devote yourselves to prayer for your marriage? Consider taking this step, and you could find yourself becoming more balanced. Also consider trying holding times. You could be quite surprised by the relief you find as your wife holds you and listens to your heart.

Now, women, a brief word for you. I know that many of you resent that your husband holds you during sex but not for comfort and nurture. I don't blame you for being irritated at this glaring inconsistency. As a result, many of you have stopped having sex with your husbands, or else it is infrequent. The problem is that most of the physical contact we have in marriage comes from our sexual relationship, and for many men, sex is the closest thing to comfort they have ever known. Furthermore, sexual deprivation can make your husband angry, edgy, and set him up to struggle with purity and faithfulness. The lack of sex will drive a wedge into your relationship that will cause you to drift apart. Regular sexual contact is very important and necessary to keep your husband close to you. So have mercy. If sex is infrequent, talk about why, close that chapter of your marriage, and start over. And who should go first? Should he talk with you first so you can enjoy sex, or could regular sex cause him to want to be closer to you? Again, it needs to work both ways.

TAKE CARE OF YOURSELF

We all need relief for our internal stresses and hurts, and our goal in the comfort circle is to bring all of ourselves into relationship so we can find the comfort we need. Although developing this skill is important, I want to take a moment to talk about the need for self-soothing and seeking relief individually. Your spouse cannot do it all for you. You still are responsible for managing your own body, mind, and soul.

On an airplane flight to New York, I was upset and hurting. I had wrestled for months through a painful season of personal growth. When the preview of the movie came on, it didn't appeal to me, so I declined the headphones and decided to sleep.

My agitation made it difficult for me to rest. I could see the screen in front of me where the silent (for me) movie was going on. Bruce Willis was playing a corporate hothead—an angry controller, it seemed to me. A kid soon showed up. He was Bruce's character as a little boy. Somehow, Bruce was seeing the child version of himself.

Eventually, the man begins to engage with the little boy as he becomes more aware of him. The man accompanies the child through such experiences as his parents fighting and the loneliness and isolation he felt when kids on the playground bullied him. I found myself riveted to the silent screen as the anguished adult bent down to hug and hold the little boy. All three of us had tears streaming down our faces as the man acknowledged his painful past and grieved the loss. Bruce's grief and reconnection with his past brought him incredible resolution and relief. His acceptance and tenderness toward the little boy left him a changed man, kinder toward himself and others, and able to leave his anger in the past where it belonged.

I, too, was changed when I stepped off that plane. I felt relief because I'd acknowledged and felt my own childhood pain. I had allowed myself to feel what was inside and, as a result, felt far less anxious than I had before. Someday I may rent that movie *The Kid* and listen to the words, but even without the dialogue, it remains one of the most powerful movies I have ever seen.

That airplane movie was an unexpected time of self-soothing, but we also need to be intentional. We need to learn to slow down, make time for ourselves, and take our distress before God and ask Him to quiet our souls. We can also process our thoughts and feelings alone through reading, journaling, drawing, or painting. Maybe a good workout, some yard work, or just tinkering in the garage. Sometimes I will just sit alone and quiet my mind. We all need to learn the skill of self-soothing; it is unfair to expect our spouses to do it all.

Keep in mind, however, that there are good ways and bad ways to self-soothe. Addictive behaviors can easily pop up as temptations when we seek out unhealthy ways of finding relief. All of these addictions—sex, pornography, shopping, busyness, alcohol, pot, eating, exercising, computer games—meet legitimate needs for relief, but they are distractions from the real relief we were meant to find in relationships with our spouses, our friends, and God.

And real relief can help you learn new and healthy ways of connecting with people. You cannot change your history, but you can create a new imprint of intimacy that more closely resembles secure attachment. For adults, a more secure style of attachment is a conscious choice that can feel like growing up all over again. But once you get past the basic training and learn the ropes, you will start to feel the benefits of being able to bond more deeply with people. All this kind of transformation takes is a teachable heart and a willing spirit.

Finally, one of the more important characteristics of deep comfort is that we can depend on it to be available to us again. After all, bold love isn't afraid to ask, "How is that pain in there coming along?" When that someone who loves us listens to us, validates our feelings, and comforts us by meeting our needs, we want to spend more time with that person. The result is healthy intimacy and connection. Then, as we finish this dance of the comfort circle, we find our spirits refreshed, and we begin to experience oneness in our marriage that is truly extraordinary.

GROWTH GOALS FOR EACH LOVE STYLE

Most couples have never done a holding time, so finding the place to start can be a challenge. If there is a lot of unresolved anger in your marriage, trying a holding time will be especially challenging, as it means you will have to momentarily lay aside your resentment. We suggest that, initially, you stay away from sharing current conflicts during holding and talk about childhood memories instead. The universal goal for holding time is to become comfortable asking for and offering holding, and using eye contact.

Avoiders: Trying a holding time as the giver or receiver will be an important but difficult step for you. Since you were a child, you've learned not to want or ask for this kind of connection, and you will feel self-conscious with this level of intimacy. Being held and comforted will be a new experience, and you will need a lot of encouragement and reassurance. In our work with some avoiders, holding time is a key to recovery of blocked feelings, so it's critical you be willing to give it a try.

Pleasers: You will most likely enjoy holding your spouse, as you are a good giver. Yet, initially you may be uncomfortable with your spouse expressing grief. Keep in mind that the freedom to feel and express difficult emotions brings relief and makes more room for good feelings. If you are married to a pleaser, remember the pleaser's difficulty with receiving; you will likely need to pursue the pleaser with reassurance that you want to hold him or her. Since pleasers rarely focus on their own feelings and needs, being held can give them an opportunity to reflect and share what is in their hearts.

Vacillators: You will likely love the idea of holding times but may be surprised to find them hard to accept—because they require that you lay aside some past resentment. You may initially feel upset at having had to wait so long to feel this type of intimacy. When your mate holds you, try to enjoy this time of closeness without reviewing past hurts. When you hold your mate, keep focused on his or her needs and show by example how to be a great nurturer.

Controllers: Since controllers do their best to avoid vulnerability of any kind, allowing yourself to be held will be a big step. Let your spouse hold you, and ask yourself how different your life would've been if someone had done this for you when you were a child. There is a pile of grief under all your anger, and this is the best way to let it surface.

Victims: We realize there has to be some evidence that your spouse is growing before you will be safe enough to allow him or her to hold you. Take your time and make sure you feel you are out of harm's way before you try this.

Chapter 20

Seeing into Your Spouse's Soul

Y ou didn't need to read this book to discover that marriage is challenging. But now that you understand how you and your spouse were imprinted by experiences in your early years and how those imprints affect your marriage, you have some tools for getting to know your spouse's heart in profound ways you never dreamed possible. As you learn to listen and engage more fully with each other, you'll be entering into all the life experiences of your spouse—the good and the bad, the beautiful and the ugly, the inspiring and the routine, the admirable and the mediocre, the happiness and the pain. Remember, deepening in your bond means embracing the whole person.

While we cherish and love our spouses for their strengths and the good things they bring to our lives, we are wounded by their failures and weaknesses, and in those times we'd most like them to simply get their acts together! But we turn a corner when we identify with the pain, the suffering, and the struggles our mates have encountered along life's journey—and then work to love them in the places they are damaged. Mike Mason states this eloquently in his book *The Mystery of Marriage* when he writes the following:

> Love consists in seeing into the very center of the twistedness and sin and
> self-love that are in the heart of another person, and yet not being repelled:
> holding onto the grace by which we ourselves are loved and finding in it
> the strength to descend with another into their darkest place. If we love
> other people for their saintliness, then we do not love at all. Love is wasted
> on saints. It is meant for the sinner.[1]

SINGING IN THE MINOR KEYS

It's easy for me to feel worthy of Milan's love when I share a new insight, support a career change, or cook a great meal. I'm offering something good, and he loves me. But I do not always act in loving ways to Milan, and as an avoider, I have hurt him with my detaching, my distancing, and my periods of depression. I don't feel worthy of being loved when I'm struggling with those weaknesses.

One of the hardest things I've had to learn as an adult is, first, to know what I feel and then to understand what my feelings are telling me I need so that I can communicate those needs. Sometimes what I have to share is simple and light-hearted, but other times I have to risk letting Milan see my deepest disappointments, failures, and inadequacies. But he has already entered my darkest places. He has taken the time to understand the origins of my imprint, and he still consistently encourages and loves me.

Allowing—or, even harder, asking—Milan to hold me when I'm sad was hugely uncomfortable for me at first, but over time being able to do so has become profoundly life changing. When we first married, I had absolutely no idea how adept I was at blocking my feelings. But I began to realize that my turning inward and becoming depressed was not always in response to anything specific, but was simply part of the way I had learned to respond to emotion. I also discovered that my depression often lifted when Milan held me and I cried, even though at times I wasn't sure what the tears were about. I learned to accept both the tears and the not having a "good reason" to cry, in part because Milan was willing to get down in the pit with me and help me dig out. As he put his own arms around my pain, his love became the most profound and healing experience I've known, and he lavishes it on my pain and inadequacies.

I remember one of the first times I asked Milan to hold and nurture me. It was a Saturday, and I was driving home from lunch with a friend. Thinking our get-together was going to be a lighthearted time, I was not prepared for the struggle and pain she shared with me. After a week of counseling clients, I found my fuel tank close to empty. I silently asked God for grace, He allowed me to offer her support and insight, but I left for home feeling exhausted. Why is so much of life about pain? I remember thinking, *I need to be held. I need to cry.* But old recordings started playing: *I'm fine. I'll just take a nap. Milan's probably busy. It's no big deal.*

I struggled to push those unhealthy thoughts aside as I walked into the house and found Milan. "I need a nurture time," I said. "I need you to hold me." He did, and I cried. It's such a vivid memory because, after the tears stopped, it was one of the first times I, feeling very vulnerable, was able to look deeply into Milan's eyes and take in the love I saw there. His eyes reached down into my soul, and I knew I was so deeply loved. It was like seeing into the eyes of God. I'll never forget it, and I cry every time I think of it.

Since then, I've heard these same words from other people who have pushed past the embarrassment of needing nurture and comfort. I had one client tell me recently, "When you have seen into someone's soul, you know it."

Just as my imprint to avoid caused pain in our marriage, so did Milan's anxiety. I felt it before either of us could identify it or name it, and it annoyed me. It felt like he was constantly hovering over me and taking my emotional temperature to see if I was happy. And if I wasn't, he wasn't either. It didn't leave me much room to be myself.

When Milan first confessed to me that he was a fearful person, I didn't say, "Well, duh!" I'd like to say the reason was because I'm so sensitive and spiritual. The truth is, I was a little surprised. He had done such a good job masking his fear, and I had no idea how pervasive it was. Yet as he shared childhood memories, I started to understand more clearly. And on a trip to Fiji I saw the true depth of the injury.

Some years ago, Milan and I traveled to Fiji on a corporate rewards trip with twelve other couples. The first week had many scheduled activities, and it was fun, but busy. The second week I reserved a room for just the two of us at a small bed-and-breakfast on an island called Taveuni. When our single-engine plane landed at the "airport"—which consisted of a dirt runway and a wooden shack—I thought, *Okay, this is my dreamland.* It was a beautiful island, quiet and tranquil. Milan was subdued compared to his usual extroverted self, and he looked a little pale. I asked, "Are you okay?" He said that he was feeling triggered and anxious about the isolation and that childhood memories were surfacing.

Milan shared some of those memories and the feelings behind them, all the while reassuring me that he would be okay. But by the next morning, his skin looked gray, and the dark circles under his eyes told me he was suffering miserably. I realized that the little boy part of Milan was taking over, and my heart went out to him. I held him and said, "Let's go back to the big island and stay at the hotel we just came from. It's familiar, and I think you can relax better there. He told me in a raspy voice, "I feel so embarrassed and ashamed that I can't get a hold of myself."

It was my turn to love Milan when he felt most unworthy and undeserving. But my heart was so full of compassion, and it was so easy to love him in his vulnerable place. He holds that memory as one of his most profound experiences of love. We went back to the big island and had a wonderful week. He kept thanking me for loving him, and to this day I don't think he understands how easy it was for me. I had never seen him so vulnerable, and I could feel how much he needed me. Our previous efforts of learning to hold and comfort one another gave me the skills I needed to meet Milan at his point of deepest need.

Your imprint most likely leads to some dark places in your heart and soul. It produces thoughts, behaviors, and attitudes that are not lovely. And whatever your spouse's imprint, you have undoubtedly felt its impact on your marriage. I can't encourage you enough to make the choice to love your spouse in those places that are most unworthy of love. At the same time, be honest and let your spouse see the things you would rather hide. When the two of you do this, love has a chance to do its deep work of healing and restoration. You will find yourself making beautiful music together even in the minor keys.

You might be wondering if my depression and Milan's anxiety have vanished since we started working on our imprints. The answer is no. Those things will never be completely gone this side of heaven, but they are far better. And our core pattern is a thing of the past. During stressful periods, our tendencies to avoid and please still pop up, but the difference now is that we understand just how far back those propensities go. We also have tools to help and show compassion for each other.

What If Your Spouse Doesn't Want to Cooperate?

Milan and I know how fortunate we are that each of us has been willing to grow and change. But some of you are married to spouses who stubbornly resist looking at their part in the marriage dance.

So what can you do to get your spouse to try this with you? We'd recommend several things. First, spark some curiosity by sharing what you're learning about yourself. It's enticing to hear a spouse say, "I'm learning from this book why I've struggled to love you in certain ways, and one of my first goals to change this is going to be [fill in the blank]." Share a growth goal from this book or the workbook to which you will commit. Then show your spouse that this book can make a difference in how you love by proving it with your actions.

Second, be curious about your spouse's childhood and pray for his or her willingness to share memories with you. Ask to look at some old photographs of the growing-up years and ask questions about the pictures. Here is your chance to practice being the listener and find out more about your mate. Offer compassion and share your feelings about any painful memories, even if your spouse discounts the significance of those events.

If your husband or wife really doesn't want to get involved, don't let that keep you from making progress in the area of personal healing and growth. And keep in mind that marriage is the voluntary joining of two individuals who choose to walk through life together. Because they are separate individuals, they will have different levels of interest and desire when it comes to change and growth. So you may simply need to sing solo for a while, and that's okay. After all, if you've heard the Master Conductor tap the music stand to get your attention, you need to heed His call. It's time to retune. Now is the moment to listen to the oboe and begin to pay personal attention to your own imprint. You can learn your original melody and retune it even if your spouse isn't paying attention. You can invite your husband or wife to join you, but you can't force the issue.

Sometimes we need to leave our spouses in God's hands and focus on learning a new song by ourselves. It's important not to let ourselves be distracted by blame and an unforgiving attitude. Focusing too much on the one who hurt or disappointed us can distract us from our own efforts to change and grow. Besides, God tells us that we are to fully meditate upon His massive and magnificent act of forgiveness so that we will have the grace to forgive others (see Matthew 18:21–35). The greatest definition of forgiveness I've ever heard is letting another person off the hook so that you can go free.

Persevering Through the Rough Spots

At a worship service recently, we heard the leader keep saying, "God wants you to leave here a changed man and a changed woman." The most that can change in one hour is an attitude or a mind-set. If you go home and make a true effort to change, that attitude and mind-set will be tested and challenged, and you may want to give up after a few hours. Genuine growth always happens over time, and the effort requires perseverance especially when the path gets bumpy and rough.

Small aircraft have to watch out for bumpy and rough weather. When an approaching weather system is intensifying to hurricane status, small aircraft simply do not fly. Rather, they stay on the ground with wings tied down to bolts on the Tarmac. The major airlines may continue to fly the bigger jets, but they change their flight paths and cancel certain flights to avoid the worst weather.

The US National Weather Service, on the other hand, does something quite different. Brave men and women from the United States Air Force climb into a C-130 Hercules, strap themselves in, and fly right into the heart of the storm. They have to be in the middle of the squall before they can gather information and find out certain things about the storm: "How big are you?" "Where are you going?" "How fast are you spinning?" "How agitated are you?"

Now, I (Milan) have been fairly candid about my journey out of anxiety. Do you think I would want to be on that plane? You are correct: no way. While I love to fly on commercial airliners that steer clear of turbulence, I'm no hurricane chaser. Yet Kay and I have actually learned to be hurricane chasers in our marriage. We have flown into the heart of each other's storms. Of course, we were a little nervous at first, and it was nerve-racking during the flight. Sometimes during especially turbulent times, we were looking for the air-sickness bags and para-chutes. But after hundreds of such trips, we've become a bit like those crazy, storm-chasing pilots. Now we know what to expect, how to fly the plane in turbulence, and what to do to gather the information necessary to both keep us safe and set-tle the storms inside our souls. Learning these skills took time *and* the willingness to keep flying into the storms.

So expect some turbulence but keep in mind that navigating them will get eas-ier. After a while, as your competence grows, you'll begin to relax in the process of growth. Just like awareness is the first step in the comfort circle, it is also the first step of growth. Like a big *X* on a map indicating your location, your awareness tells you, "You are here." You'll become more aware of your own growth and know that all is well.

A couple came into my office recently and said, "We were right in the middle of our core pattern, and we stopped, looked at each other, and said, 'We're doing it. Let's get the comfort circle out and try to go around it.' We made it to point three on the circle and had a great talk, but we couldn't get through resolution."

"That's growth," I told them. "You stopped when you recognized your loca-tion and you tried to change course. Keep it up, and you'll get further around the circle each time."

CHANGING HOW YOU LOVE

Our goal in sharing so much of our journey with you is to help the love in your marriage flourish and grow as you gain wisdom and insight about changing how you love. As you gain insight about your imprint and the way it influences your relationship, this new knowledge will give you a starting point for going around the comfort circle with your mate, and that path will give you the opportunity to take turns being the giver and the receiver. Soon you will discover what we have: the relief that comes from resolution, deep understanding, and comfort.

Also, remember that if you get stuck, essential help can be found in the *How We Love* companion workbook. Specific growth goals for each imprint and for the core pattern combinations, as well as insights and ideas about how to support your mate, will help make your efforts more productive as you work on developing a more secure relational style. If you remain stuck and cannot move toward growth as a couple, don't continue to suffer unduly. Rather, be bold, act quickly, and find a competent counselor that can help you start moving toward change.

As Milan and I finished this manuscript, we sat down and prayed for you and all the other couples who will read this book. After working with people for over twenty-five years, we know that you likely entered the gateway of marriage with deep wounds from your early years that make your relationship with your spouse especially challenging. But perhaps you were fortunate enough to learn from your family of origin some skills for forming close, healthy bonds with your spouse. Whatever your story, this is our prayer for you as well as for ourselves:

> Lord, we ask for each person who has taken the time to read this book, and for ourselves as well, that you would grant us the courage to continue to grow. Give us each wisdom and insight to love our mates more deeply and with more compassion as we become aware of their wounds. Help us persevere through the storms we bring into each other's lives. Grant us the ability to love as you love, with a willingness to bear each other's sin and shame. As you left the glory of heaven and entered into a broken world, give us the courage to enter into the broken places in our spouses and love them in their darkest places. Grant us the profound experience of seeing into each other's souls. Encourage us along the way when we are tired and weary and want to give up. Show us glimpses of the redemptive power of love and teach us to sing a new song as we change *how we love*. Amen.
>
> With love,
> Milan and Kay

SOUL WORDS

HAPPY, cheerful, delighted, elated, encouraged, glad, gratified, joyful, lighthearted, overjoyed, pleased, relieved, satisfied, thrilled, secure

LOVING, affectionate, cozy, passionate, romantic, sexy, warm, tender, responsive, thankful, appreciative, refreshed, pleased

HIGH ENERGY, energetic, enthusiastic, excited, playful, rejuvenated, talkative, pumped, motivated, driven, determined, obsessed

AMAZED, stunned, surprised, shocked, jolted

ANXIOUS, uneasy, embarrassed, frustrated, nauseated, ashamed, nervous, restless, worried, stressed

CONFIDENT, positive, secure, self-assured, assertive

PEACEFUL, at ease, calm, comforted, cool, relaxed, serene

AFRAID, scared, anxious, apprehensive, boxed in, burdened, confused, distressed, fearful, frightened, guarded, hard pressed, overwhelmed, panicky, paralyzed, tense, terrified, worried, insecure

TRAUMATIZED, shocked, disturbed, injured, damaged

ANGRY, annoyed, controlled, manipulated, furious, grouchy, grumpy, irritated, provoked, frustrated

LOW ENERGY, beaten down, exhausted, tired, weak, listless, depressed, detached, withdrawn, indifferent, apathetic

ALONE, avoidant, lonely, abandoned, deserted, forlorn, isolated, cut off, detached

SAD, unhappy, crushed, dejected, depressed, desperate, despondent, grieved, heartbroken, heavy, weepy

BETRAYED, deceived, fooled, duped, tricked

CONFUSED, baffled, perplexed, mystified, bewildered

ASHAMED, guilty, mortified, humiliated, embarrassed, exposed

For Further Study: Attachment Theory

The central concepts of attachment theory come from a multitude of researchers. Some of the most important figures giving rise to the concepts in this book are, among many others, John Bowlby, Mary Ainsworth, Mary Main, Selma Frailberg, Alan Shore, Daniel Siegel, Robert Karen, Jude Cassidy, and Phillip R. Shaver (see "Notes and Bibliography" for further credits). Ainsworth discovered and described patterns of attachment by watching toddlers interact with their mothers during episodes of separation and reunion. She observed the differences and categorized the children's responses to their mothers as secure or insecure. Insecure responses were further divided into two groups, children with avoidant responses and children with ambivalent responses.

Ainsworth observed that secure toddlers were distressed when their moms left and readily approached them for comfort upon reunion. Secure kids were successfully soothed and happily returned to their play. Avoidant toddlers were also upset when Mom left but ignored their mothers and did not seek comfort when she returned having learned early on that mom was not a reliable source for providing relief. Ambivalent children protested loudly when Mom left and approached her for comfort upon reunion but vacillated between wanting comfort and being to angry to receive it.[1] Ainsworth's student Mary Main discovered a fourth category she labeled "disorganized" that described the effects of abuse, loss, or trauma on attachment. These children had no predictable response to Mom's leaving or return, displaying both avoidant and ambivalent responses, but in extremely disorganized and unpredictable ways.[2]

As a result of the Adult Berkeley Attachment Interview, Main and her colleagues demonstrated that the groupings of love styles can be observed in an adult's overall "state of mind with respect to attachment."[3] Hazan, Shaver, and Bradshaw

(1988) agreed. Feeney summarizes their findings: "In these papers, Hazan and Shaver argued that romantic love can be conceptualized as an attachment process. That is, relationships between spouses and between unmarried but committed lovers are affectional bonds that involve complex socioemotional processes. They further argued that variations in early social experience produce relatively lasting differences in relationship styles, and that the three major love styles described in the infant literature ('secure,' 'avoidant,' and 'ambivalent') are manifested in romantic love."[4]

Research shows that relationship styles learned early on establish belief systems about relationships that shape our expectations, beliefs, and behaviors in all future relationships. In this book we call this belief system an imprint. While most of the research utilizes the four-group approach—secure (sometimes called "autonomous"), avoidant (sometimes called "dismissing"), ambivalent (sometimes called "preoccupied"), and disorganized (sometimes called "unresolved" or "chaotic")— some researchers add one more category, describing a "fearful" attachment style. Judith Feeney summarizes research supporting the four-group model (five groups including "secure") and concludes, "Given these findings, researchers have increasingly adopted the four-group model of adult attachment. This model is consistent with infant research suggesting the importance of a fourth attachment group showing characteristics of both avoidance and ambivalence (Crittenden, 1985); in particular, fearful adults tend to endorse both avoidant and ambivalent attachment prototypes (Brennan et al., 1991)."[5] Fearful people (pleasers) desire connection to reduce their anxiety (like ambivalents) but avoid their own feelings and needs in relationships (like avoidants). There is disagreement about exactly how to classify this fearful individual.

Bartholomew and Horowitz (1991) suggest another approach. They also add a fourth category by dividing avoidant attachment into "fearful" and "dismissing" types. John Byng-Hall summarizes their views: "Avoidants with high self-esteem are categorized as dismissing; they emphasize achievement and self-reliance, maintaining a sense of self-worth at the expense of intimacy. In contrast, avoidants with low self-esteem are categorized as fearful; they desire intimacy but distrust others, avoiding close involvements that may lead to loss or rejection."[6] Although we do see fearful people's attempts to avoid rejection, we have difficulty seeing them as a type of avoidant because of their tendencies to pursue and seek closeness when fearful.

In his book *Loss: Sadness and Depression,* Bowlby identifies a fearful group as well. He describes three relational styles as follows: "In one such group affectional relationships tend to be marked by a high degree of anxious attachment, suffused with overt or covert ambivalence. In a second and related group there is a strong disposition to engage in compulsive caregiving.... In a third and *contrasting* group there are strenuous attempts to claim emotional self-sufficiency and independence of all affectional ties."[7] Bowlby goes on to say that people with these three types of affectional ties (relational styles) will have greater adverse reactions to loss. Bowlby believes the fearful group is related to the ambivalent group due to the anxiety that drives each style. He sees the self-sufficient (avoidant) as a contrasting style because these people reduce anxiety by disavowing their needs and do not pursue others. In observing our clients, we agree with Bowlby's view.

In this book, we included the "fearful" or pleaser style because we find that many people relate to this fearful pattern of attachment. In an attempt to simplify terms, we have adopted different labels for some of the styles, but they come from the original framework of this body of research. In this book, we have used the following labels: secure connector (secure), avoider (avoidant/dismissing), pleaser (insecure/fearful), vacillator (ambivalent/preoccupied), and chaotic—controller or victim (disorganized/unresolved). In observing our own marriage and our clients, we readily see all these groups. While the framework of our book is based on attachment research, our own experiences of working with couples has influenced much of our writing as well. We find these same groups in our seminars as well as in our work with clients.

Our purpose has not been to reflect all the current data on attachment theory, though we've tried to include as much of the supporting materials we leaned on as was feasible. We acknowledge we cannot accurately reflect every study and body of research, especially due to the differing views. We offer our heartfelt thanks to the researchers, psychologists, and authors who have helped make this book possible. Their work has changed lives—including ours—by transforming relationships and revolutionizing our approach to life and love.

Workbook

How to Get the Most Out of This Workbook

Whether it's a doctor's accurate diagnosis or a sudden revelation about a knotty problem, insight usually offers immediate comfort, but don't stop there. The important insight offered in *How We Love,* for instance, is merely head knowledge about the ways the experiences of our early years influence our adult relationships. And while the influences of our past can definitely help explain the difficulties we encounter in marriage, unless we're willing to commit to changing the areas of our lives that most need it, the information alone changes nothing.

Put differently, genuine change requires a commitment to growth. It means we will feel awkward, inadequate, and uncomfortable. It means we will have to work hard. It means we will have to fight against our resistance to change. The alternative, though, is to remain stuck right where we are in our relationships. And, folks, that is painful too. Either way, we'll experience discomfort and distress. Why not choose constructive discomfort? That's what we're offering in this workbook: the experience of constructive, beneficial discomfort! The trade-off of current uneasiness for the awkward pain of growth is the promise of future relief. In fact, in this book you will find hope for new levels of emerging security, trust, and intimacy in your marriage as well as healing from your injured love style. This love style, or imprint of intimacy, which was learned in your family of origin, has been controlling you for many years, and for most of us, it has adversely affected our capacity to successfully give and receive love.

The instruction in this workbook is all about improving your primary human relationship, your connection to your spouse. Although you'd certainly benefit from using this workbook on your own, we've intentionally designed it to be most useful for couples. There are also specific exercises for a group setting. Applying these insights in relationship is the only way to truly change how you love. Groups not only help you feel less alone in your struggles, they also provide encouragement and support as you hear other people's similar—and contrasting—experiences. Some questions may be distressing, so having your small group's support throughout this process will help you feel less overwhelmed. A small group can also encourage you to process your feelings and thoughts as you grow and change. The added bonus of accountability is that someone will know whether you complete the assignments and can help you persevere on the path of change.

You may find this workbook a bit different from others. Some pages—even some questions—will require more than a week to cover. That's okay! Give yourself the time you need to thoughtfully consider your answers. The time you spend reflecting on and evaluating your personal imprint, the core pattern of your marriage, and your progress toward change, is time well spent. Whether you work through this book with your spouse, a small group, or even alone, you will only grow and change according to the time and effort you put into answering the questions. There is much to discover about how you love, so be patient and know that real growth takes time. This workbook will be a good guide, but *you* are responsible for your own growth. We've intended for you to use this workbook along with a journal to record your thoughts and feelings as you interact with the questions. You may also find that you have different and surprising answers after you've gone through the exercises several times. That's a sign of growth!

If you are currently single, consider holding off on a new relationship until you can complete the exercises and develop the new habits in this workbook. Not only will you gain insights into your ability to choose an emotionally healthy mate, you will also acquire new levels of awareness that will help you become a better mate.

If your spouse is resistant to going through the material with you, forge ahead alone. In time, your new understanding and skills will have an effect upon your core pattern and will likely begin to gain your spouse's attention. Change yourself and see what happens.

Christian leaders take heart. Estimates show that one in three Christian leaders finishes well, yet the courage that brought you where you are right now will serve as you invest in these tools and learn to resist the gradual erosion of your marriage as you serve the Lord.

As you look intently at your past and present relationships, you may experience uncomfortable levels of emotional distress. If you feel overwhelmed and find yourself struggling to know how to handle your feelings, it is important that you call a professional therapist. As that person walks alongside you for a season, he or she will be familiar with the questions and personal reflection we have suggested in this book and will bring a measure of security to you and your spouse. There is also low-cost help available through local county programs, churches, and non-profit organizations. Our sincere hope and prayer is that you'll stay motivated to continually dig deeper into your past as you begin to see positive changes from your efforts. This book and workbook are our personal journey. Believe us, the work is worth it! Make the investment in yourself and your marriage so you can indeed *finish well.* God bless you on your journey!

Chapter 1

Why Every Marriage Gets Stuck

1. In chapter 1 we talked about nagging problems that grab our attention and keep us from getting to the roots of problems. Perhaps you are like us and have made symptoms the focal point of your efforts to improve your marriage. Describe some of the chronic irritations and patterns that remain unresolved.

2. We shared two truths in chapter 1. The first was that the close proximity of your partner triggers old feelings because you look to your spouse to meet some of the same needs your parents were supposed to meet. That means your marriage problems did not start in your marriage. What bothers you most about your spouse is undoubtedly related to painful experiences from his or her childhood or to the lack of training that would have prepared your mate and you to face the challenges of marriage. Without accusing or blaming, write down which of your spouse's attitudes or behaviors bothers you most.

3. What is your spouse's biggest complaint about you? Ask him or her if you're not sure.

4. The second truth in chapter 1 is this: you will never truly know yourself or your mate until you understand how each of you was shaped by your childhood experiences. Write about and discuss some key memories (especially relational hurts) that might relate to or have been the cause of the irritating traits you just wrote about.

   Now take some time to write your answers to the following questions. These answers may help you better determine what is at the root of your marriage problems.

5. Do you fight about the same old subject over and over? Identify the topic and describe the usual fight. What are each partner's behaviors and beliefs?

6. Jot down any insights about how childhood wounds may be at the root of the behaviors and beliefs that fuel repetitive problems. (If this is too challenging, don't worry, as there is help ahead.)

7. A great starting place for our journey is the prayer Jesus prayed for you in John 17. Look at verses 20–23. What does Jesus pray for you? Now list the three or four most important relationships in your life today. Evaluate each of these relationships in light of this prayer.

8. Read Psalm 139:23–24. "Wicked way in me" (KJV), "offensive way in me" (NIV), and "hurtful way in me" (NASB) is literally in the Hebrew, according to the NASB notes, "way of pain." This workbook will help you identify specific ways of pain that hinder the expression of love and unity in your relationships. What ways of pain do you see in yourself and those you are in relationship with (the people you listed in question 7)?

9. God is capable of using far more than this workbook to help you experience and manifest his love in your relationships. Consider writing a personal prayer based on the ideas expressed in these verses, asking God to reveal new insights about the ways in which you give and receive love.

To follow are some statements that will help you evaluate the strengths and weaknesses in your marriage. Both you and your mate can respond by writing after each sentence a *Y* for *Yes* or an *NI* for *Needs Improvement*. Then use the inventory as a springboard for discussion.

Acceptance

_____ My mate knows my strengths and weaknesses, and I am fully accepted in spite of my shortcomings.

_____ I know my mate's strengths and weaknesses and fully accept him/her in spite of the shortcomings.

_____ When I make a mistake, my mate forgives me.

_____ When my mate makes a mistake, I forgive him/her.

Safety and Communication

_____ I feel safe to discuss any subject with my mate.

_____ I feel safe to share my deepest feelings, even my negative emotions.

_____ I am honest with my mate.

_____ My mate and I discuss sexual problems as they arise in our relationship.

_____ I can effectively communicate with my spouse about areas of disagreement and conflict.

_____ We usually reach resolution or compromise when we disagree about a problem.

_____ I am aware of my feelings and needs, and I communicate them.

_____ I try to understand the feelings and needs of my spouse and then respond to the feelings and meet the needs.

_____ My spouse and I pray together.

Support and Respect

_____ I feel that my mate sees, values, supports, and respects my uniqueness as a person.

_____ My mate knows my gifts and talents and encourages me to use them.

_____ I know my mate's gifts and talents, and I encourage him/her to use them.

Nurture and Comfort

_____ I receive comfort from my spouse when I need it.

_____ My spouse is able to receive comfort from me.

_____ We show affection and touch each other without the closeness necessarily becoming sexual.

Individuality and Space

_____ I have interests, hobbies, and friends apart from my mate.

_____ My mate has friends, hobbies, and interests outside our relationship.

_____ My spouse supports my participation in these pursuits and sees them as a healthy complement to couple/family time.

_____ I support my spouse's participation in these pursuits and see them as a healthy complement to couple/family time.

Fun and Play

_____ I have fun with my mate.

_____ We have regular time alone without kids or business distractions.

____ We enjoy at least one recreational activity together.

____ We laugh together.

____ Most of the time we have an enjoyable sex life together.

Most of us have endured an annual review at work, that sometimes nerve-racking conversation during which our performance for the year is evaluated and ideas for improvement are discussed. A review can often spark important change, yet rarely do we take the time to do an annual review of the most important area of our lives: our marriages. But you've just reviewed your marriage as you've thought about many aspects of your relationship. Perhaps your list of items that need improvement is overwhelmingly long. If that's true, don't be discouraged before you even begin. Creating a healthy, satisfying marriage is worth the effort, and every step of growth moves you toward that goal.

One of the most important aspects of marriage—and a good habit to develop— is to have fun together as a couple. A mutual agreement to schedule date nights with the following guidelines can bring renewal and hope to a tired or taxed relationship.

GUIDELINES FOR FUN AND RENEWAL

- At the beginning of each month, schedule two date nights and put them on the calendar.
- Each partner is responsible for planning one of the dates. Decide when you mark your calendar who will plan the first date and who will plan the second.
- Date nights are for fun and enjoyment. *No problems will be discussed.*
- Use date-night conversations for praise, compliments, words of appreciation, and the sharing of good memories.

So get your calendars out now. Even if it's the middle of the month, plan a date—or even two.

Chapter 2

The Revealing Question You Need to Answer

In chapter 2, we asked you to think about childhood memories of being comforted, and we discussed the ingredients of emotional connection between parents and children. We also considered the importance of learning to become aware of what's inside our hearts and of having soul words to describe our experiences.

You may think you are already familiar with the topic and acquainted with all you need to know. However, since it's this imprint of intimacy that affects your capacity to give and receive love, we believe the following questions may improve your ability to determine your love style.

Before you begin reviewing your history, we want to acknowledge that some of these questions may be difficult to answer, so just do your best. Asking relatives for their memories and insights is sometimes helpful, but that's up to you. Also, reflecting on your childhood experiences might be painful as you recall specific events. We feel it is very important for you to have a safe place to discuss your responses to these questions. Ideally, we hope you will be able to talk with your spouse. If that isn't possible, we recommend that you join a support group in which you can share what you're learning and process the feelings that arise. If you feel depressed or overwhelmed, please get some individual counseling before you continue these workbook exercises.

1. Do you have a memory of being comforted? If so, describe the scene—who was comforting you, why you needed comfort, and how effective that person's comfort was. Then evaluate the comfort you received in light of the three critical ingredients of comfort found on pages 15–17 of *How We Love.*

2. What comfort did each parent offer you in the following categories? Be as specific as possible.
Touch and Affection
Listening to You Talk and Responding with Insightful Questions

Validating Your Feelings

Addressing and Resolving Conflict

3. List the immediate family members you were consistently around as a child. Start with the most influential caregiver in your life (usually a parent), the second most influential, and then on through the other significant figures from your childhood. Next to each person's name, write the following:
   - five descriptive words that reflect their personality and character
   - three soul words that describe what you most often felt in the presence of that person (see the soul words list at the end of this book)
   - your best memory of each person
   - your worst memory of each person

4. If you could change one thing about your most influential caregiver, what would it be? What traits, if any, about this person did you enjoy?

5. If you could change one thing about your second most influential caregiver, what would it be? What traits, if any, about this person did you enjoy?

6. Think about people other than your biological parents who influenced your life, such as stepparents or grandparents. If you could change one thing about them, what would it be? What traits, if any, about these people did you enjoy?

7. Describe how your family handled feelings as you were growing up. Focus on the emotions of anger, sadness, fear, jealousy, and joy. What did your family do to encourage or discourage the expression of a variety of feelings? Be specific.

8. Which feelings did your family allow and perhaps even encourage?

9. Which feelings were simply not allowed?

10. Was any family member allowed to express feelings that other members were denied? Be specific about the family member and the feeling(s).

11. Are you currently able to appropriately express a variety of feelings? Explain. Which feelings, for instance, are acceptable, and which are not? Who in your life is a safe person for you to share feelings with, and who is not?

12. In chapter 2, we talked about soul words. Did your parents enable you to develop the skill of talking about your feelings? If not, know that it isn't too late. What steps can you take to learn this skill now?

13. Did anything in your home make you feel unsafe when you were growing up? What did you do to protect yourself?

14. Did any family members have addictions? Who was addicted to what? In what ways did this addiction affect the family? What impact did the addiction have on you?

15. We live in an imperfect world, and no parent is perfect, so all of us bring issues into our marriages. Psalm 139, however, gives us a picture of connection that serves as a blueprint for intimacy. Read that psalm and underline the words and phrases that you find most significant. Why do you think you respond to those ideas?

God created us with a need for emotional connection with Him and with other people. It was His idea that we should desire love, and He satisfies that desire by lovingly reaching out to us, watching over us, and guiding us, and by giving us relationships with other human beings. God, however, is our perfect parent, but since none of us had a perfect earthly parent, it is hard for us to understand exactly what that description means. For starters, it means that God knows our heart of hearts; He is intimately acquainted with us. When we embrace such attentive love—a love that guides and protects—we can more easily avoid the paths that lead to pain.

Now, having spent time thinking about Psalm 139, write your own psalm or paragraph describing your relationship with your parents. You may want to begin with "Dear Mom and Dad." *But do not give it to them.* The goal is not to assign blame or seek amends but to take an honest look at the things that hurt us when we were younger so that we can grow and change. The purpose is to zero in on what your emotional connection with your parents was like and then set some specific goals for your relationship with your spouse. If you've struggled to accept and trust in God's love as well as your spouse's love, this exercise may help you begin to understand why.

After you've written your own composition to your parents, consider sharing it with your spouse. Also discuss with someone safe (ideally your spouse) the impact your experience with your parents has had on your ability to experience intimacy with God and with your spouse.

16. Take turns sharing what thought, insight, or workbook question was most meaningful from this chapter

Chapter 3

Imprints of Intimacy from Our First Lessons in Love

In the preceding chapter of the workbook, you began seeing your childhood experience in a realistic light. As you continue with that exercise, remember that any time you read something new, that idea might serve as a good springboard for discussion with your spouse. Also, if using soul words is new to you, talking about your reactions to and thoughts about what you read will give you opportunities to practice. You might also copy the list of soul words at the back of this book and hang it on your refrigerator as a handy reference.

Review the meaning and characteristics of *implicit* and *explicit* memories on page 26 of *How We Love*. Remember how Tina's implicit memories affected her relationships? You might be wondering, *How am I supposed to remember anything from the first three or four years of my life?* In fact, most people can't remember early trauma but may have been told stories about such events. All of us have plenty of explicit memories from later years to draw from, which is the focus of the workbook. One of the reasons we included the story about Tina is because some people have always known about events or circumstances that occurred in childhood but never considered their impact on the way they relate.

1. If you know about a traumatic event during the first four or five years of your childhood, write about feelings and responses you may have experienced in the space below. Do you experience similar feelings in your current relationships? What triggers them?

2. Do you identify with Lee's struggle? Why do you think people are resistant to looking at their pasts? Are you struggling with this as well? Write down some of your thoughts and share them with your spouse.

3. You have to know yourself before you can change yourself. Why can taking a realistic look at your past help you know yourself better?

EXTRAORDINARY CHALLENGES

Difficult circumstances—severe loss, childhood trauma, family crises—can disrupt the process of bonding with one's parents, especially if you didn't have any opportunities to talk about what happened or express your negative feelings. And unless you had many opportunities as a child to express what was on your heart, you will struggle as an adult to process stressful situations and manage the accompanying feelings.

If any of the experiences listed below were a part of your history and you *did* have many opportunities to be listened to and comforted, their negative impact was probably greatly reduced. If no one was available to listen to you or comfort you, though, the negative impact might be significant. Either way, write about your experience and the impact you think it has had on you.

The following list isn't exhaustive, and you may remember some events not listed below that had a big effect on your family. Whatever those circumstances, consider their impact on you, especially on your ability to form close connections with others. Afterward, take time to share your observations and feelings with your spouse and/or small group.

"My parent was ill, or a sibling had serious health problems."
When someone in the home suffers from a serious illness, it adds tremendous stress to the family unit and may limit the time and energy available for parenting.

"One of my parents died when I was growing up."
The death of a parent at any stage of a child's development is a horrendous trauma. What impact do you think this event had on your ability to form emotional connections with people?

"One of my parents was depressed or suffered from mental illness."

Brain damage, chemical imbalances, and psychological problems in a parent can negatively affect everyone else in the home. "Baby blues" are common after childbirth, but this usually dissipates within two weeks. However, a few new mothers experience more serious postpartum depression up to one year after childbirth. This is a serious condition that requires medical treatment and can definitely impact a family. (If you recognize symptoms of depression or mental illness in yourself or another family member, please seek medical help very soon. There are ways to alleviate suffering and stop the damage to your family, but you must choose to take action.)

"I've been told I was a fussy baby and cried all the time."

Some children are born with a hypersensitive nervous system and experience touch, sounds, lights, and smell as overwhelming, irritating, and overstimulating. As a result, they may have difficulty associating touch with pleasure and relief.

"My parent(s) had a hard time accepting my personality."

Parents may find they have personality conflicts with one of their children. (By the way, this kind of conflict seems to most often occur between the firstborn child and the same-sex parent.) Constant tension and discord can certainly impact bonding. Also, we've found that many adults who identify themselves as introverts believe they were not understood by their parents.

"I'm adopted."

Babies begin connecting to their mothers while they are still in the womb. They recognize their mothers' voices and even their intonations and rhythms. Although adoption is a wonderful alternative for mothers who are unable to keep their babies, it does interrupt the natural process of bonding.

"There were more than five kids in my family when I was growing up."

In very large families, parents are often consumed with meeting their children's basic needs. Consequently, Mom and Dad may be overwhelmed by the amount of work and therefore have little time to notice or attend to each child's emotional needs.

"My parents were busy all the time."

Perhaps you suffered from neglect, spent significant time in day care, or were largely raised by someone other than your parents.

"A sibling mistreated me."

Maybe an older brother or sister tormented you when your parents were not around. Perhaps they threatened you with serious consequences if you told your parents.

"I had medical problems when I was born or a serious illness as I was growing up."

Medical treatment during infancy or the preschool years can be problematic as children learn to associate touch with invasive and painful medical procedures. At times these children often feel great levels of distress that cannot be reduced by even the best parenting. (A high tolerance for pain is often an indicator of early physical or medical trauma.)

"I had learning problems in school."

Kids who struggle in school commonly experience a nightmare of anxiety, humiliation, and teasing in the classroom and on the playground. If, as an adult, you procrastinate about reading or deskwork, feel anxious in new situations, or are very sensitive to correction or criticism, you may have had a hard time in school.

4. Take time to think about and talk about memories from your early years. Use the soul words list to express the feelings you experienced during the memory you are describing. If you like, you might also try stretching out on the couch and putting your head in your spouse's lap as you share. Write down the memory and the words you used to describe it.

UNDERSTANDING THE ROLES WE PLAYED

Relational experiences from our childhoods become wired into our behaviors and beliefs, and this is how it happens: When we were young and events or people hurt us, we used certain strategies to protect ourselves from those painful experiences. Somewhere along the way, for instance, we learned to play certain roles in an attempt to lessen tensions in the family. Over time those roles became a part of who we are, and they often operate without our awareness. Just like old and familiar songs buried in the dusty attic of our minds, these childhood roles stay with us.

Children begin playing roles to gain attention, reduce disharmony, conform to parental expectations, or meet the needs of a parent. Look through the list below and see if any of these roles feel familiar.

- *Good Kid:* I made sure not to burden my parents.
- *Clown:* I used humor to reduce conflict and stress.
- *Invisible One:* I tried to avoid conflict and stress by hiding.
- *Perfectionist:* I attempted to avoid criticism or disapproval by doing things perfectly.
- *Hero:* I accomplished great things so my parents would be proud of me.
- *Confronter:* I was passionate about the truth no matter the consequences.
- *Scapegoat:* I took the blame for everything and everyone.
- *Surrogate Parent:* I had to take care of situations that were beyond my ability to manage well.
- *Surrogate Spouse:* I had to be there for one of my parents in his/her spouse's absence.

- *Black Sheep:* I was labeled the bad kid for acting out and doing my own thing.

As kids, we initially fill these roles to help our families function more smoothly. But they eventually stifle our development, requiring us to give up important aspects of our personalities and temperaments. Playing a role may mean having to relinquish significant aspects of who God created us to be. Furthermore, when we reach adulthood, these roles often continue to operate, stagnating our emotional and even spiritual growth.

5. If you played one of these roles when you were growing up, identify which one(s) and explain what need it may have met in your family. What did that role do for you? How did it increase or decrease your anxiety?

6. What evidence that you still play this role in adult relationships do you see in your life, if any? In what ways does this role hinder intimacy in your relationships now? Be specific. What do you think would happen in these relationships if you stopped playing this role?

7. Be teachable and ask your spouse for his or her sense of what roles you play in relationships with others. Write down the answer. How does playing each role make you feel? How might you feel if you stopped?

8. Share with your spouse or group members which point was most beneficial to you as you worked through chapter 3.

Chapter 4

Ideal Love Lessons: The Secure Connector

A few of us were blessed to have had parents who were attentive and in tune with us as we were growing up, and the result was a generally secure imprint. In chapter 4 of *How We Love,* we looked at the hallmarks of this imprint and its implications for adult relationships. We also discussed the comfort circle and how trust and respect develop in relationships between parents and their children. This chapter of the workbook will prompt you to give more thought to these ideas.

TRUST AND RESPECT

Trust is an essential part of a healthy emotional connection. When we develop the ability to trust from our early days, we become comfortable needing others, and we expect relationships to bring relief and comfort. Of course, this trust can be broken if we are betrayed, badly hurt, or abandoned.

1. Think about your reactions to the word *trust*. Describe those reactions. Then, on a scale from 1 to 10, evaluate how easy it is for you to trust people. What in your past has made it easy or difficult—or somewhere in between—to trust?

2. Do you have difficulty trusting people today? What childhood event(s) involving a family member or someone else taught you that not everyone— or anyone—is trustworthy?

3. Evaluate the level of trust in your marriage. What circumstances, situations, or even people seem to consistently erode that trust? What can you do to stand strong against those forces?

4. What specific actions or choices might increase your ability to trust your spouse?

If we learned to feel and deal—to successfully manage a wide range of emotions—as we grew up, our parents honored and respected us and our feelings. This is not the kind of respect demanded by an angry parent whose motto is "Do as I say and not as I do." True respect does not develop in that kind of family when everyone is playing by different rules. In fact, respect is an attitude that is best taught by example as opposed to being demanded or commanded.

5. Evaluate the level of respect members of your family had for one another as you were growing up.

6. Evaluate the level of respect in your marriage. Do you respect your mate? Why or why not? What impact do your childhood experiences of respect or its ab-sence have on your relationships, specifically on your ability to respect people?

7. Do you feel that trust and respect have to be earned? Why or why not?

8. What aspects of your spouse would you put in the category of Being Human (you trust that person even when he or she makes mistakes and

shows weaknesses). What aspects of your spouse would you put in the category of Must Change (you trust that person only after he or she changes)?

9. What childhood memories have you and your spouse shared with each other? Do you have new levels of understanding, empathy, and compassion for each other? What impact does this have on your ability to trust? Explain.

10. What was God's response when Peter broke Jesus's trust? Read Luke 22:54–62 and John 21:15–23 to get the whole story. What do you think God would do with you if you failed Him? What within you would cause you to have trouble restoring others who have broken your trust?

11. You probably know that God created us in His image, but have you considered that your *feelings* are part of God's creation? God, too, has emotions, so despite what you may have learned in your family growing up, emotions aren't bad. In fact, one reason feelings are so important is that they act as a signal telling us what we need. *If we don't know what we feel, we won't know what we need.* Are you willing to ask God to help you recover any emotions that have been suppressed or remain underdeveloped from your childhood? Take a look at the soul words list. Write the three feelings you most often express. List three feelings you rarely express. Write out a prayer about the emotions you are unable to feel or express.

12. When we have feelings and emotions, we have to learn to deal with them appropriately. Review the story about Susie in chapter 4 of *How We Love,* who was learning to feel and deal. Did your parents help you feel and deal? If so, what did they do? If not, what could they have done to help you develop this skill? What particular emotion, if any, is managing you rather than your managing it? Why do you think you struggle to manage this emotion?

13. Evaluate your level of self-care. What do you do to replenish yourself or fill your gas tank? If you don't know, what steps will you take to find out? What aspects of your marriage are being affected—for good or bad—by your ability or inability to take care of yourself? Be specific.

14. Were you able to truly be a child in your home growing up? Explain your answer and support it with evidence from your childhood. Did you have to

manage the emotions of one or both of your parents? If so, which emotion(s), and what role did that management lead you to assume?

15. What hallmarks of a secure love style do you feel you lack? (See the list on pages 48–49 of *How We Love*.)

16. What hallmarks of a secure love style do you possess? Does your spouse agree? If you have children, would they agree? If you aren't sure, ask them. (In doing so, you will foster an open atmosphere for growth in your home, and they will love you for it.)

17. Have you known people who seem to stay the same, people who have never changed or grown out of childhood defenses or roles? Why do you think they have remained stuck all their lives?

18. What behavioral change(s) do you see in yourself as you look back over the past year? Be specific. Ask those closest to you what growth and change they have observed in you. If you can't identify any areas, ask those closest to you what they would like to see changed in your life in the upcoming year.

SECURE-CONNECTOR ASSESSMENT

Below is a list of assessment statements that describes a secure connector. Put a check mark by any statement that describes you most of the time as you relate to your spouse. Then record your score below.

_____ I have a wide range of emotions and express them appropriately.

_____ It is easy for me to ask for help and receive from others when I have needs.

_____ I enjoy time with my spouse and also have friends and interests outside my marriage.

_____ I can say no to others even when I know it will upset them.

_____ I will initiate a difficult conversation in order to resolve a problem.

_____ When I want something, I can plan and wait in order to have it.

_____ When I make a mistake, I can recover easily and try again.

_____ I know when I'm wrong and I take responsibility for my actions or attitudes and apologize.

_____ I'm a hard worker and take my responsibilities seriously.

_____ I'm adventuresome and know how to play and have fun.

_____ I know I'm not perfect, and I give my spouse (and kids) room to have weaknesses.

_____ I am able to negotiate and offer compromises when my spouse and I disagree.

_____ I enjoy touch and am affectionate with my family.

_____ I give respect to each member of my family even when they annoy me.

_____ I'm comfortable with emotions and can offer comfort when someone is upset.

Score _____

(Ask your spouse if he or she agrees with your answers.)

Chapter 5

The Avoider Love Style

If you are working through this material in a group, we suggest one or two weeks for members to identify their love styles and to share what aspects of themselves placed them in that category. In subsequent weeks, members can then share responses to the questions within the chapter that most describes them. Allow members to go at their own pace and work on different questions as they go. All will benefit from hearing questions raised and challenges faced. Group feedback will be especially useful to those members still attempting to identify their particular styles.

And remember, these questions *cannot* be completed in a week. The goal of this workbook is to promote deep and lasting growth, and that takes time and effort. Uncovering the roots of your present difficulties can take many weeks, even months, but keep at it. If you feel resistant, that's often a sign that you're close. Be patient and allow yourself time to explore. Act on the suggestions for as long as it takes to see results. However, if an issue doesn't seem to apply to you, don't spend time there. Move on and try something else. Keep taking steps forward and allow yourself the necessary time to make healthy changes in how you love.

Most people imprinted to be avoiders make statements like the ones below. Even if you do not think this is your style, read the list and put a check mark by any statement you feel is often true for you. Tally your points at the bottom of the list.

AVOIDER ASSESSMENT

_____ It seems as if my spouse has a lot more emotional needs than I do.

_____ Events, remarks, and interactions with people that are upsetting to my spouse seem like no big deal to me.

_____ I don't have many memories from my childhood.

_____ I would describe myself as an independent, self-reliant person.

_____ I would rather do something alone than have a long conversation with someone.

_____ My spouse complains that I don't show enough affection.

_____ When something bad happens, I get over it and move on.

_____ I need my space in relationships and feel annoyed if someone wants to be with me a lot.

_____ I like to make decisions on my own.

_____ I feel uncomfortable when someone is very emotional, especially if I think I am supposed to help that person.

_____ In my family growing up, we all sort of did our own thing.

_____ I have siblings with whom I have little to no contact today.

_____ I have never felt particularly close to my parents.

_____ Nothing gets me too bothered or upset.

_____ I rarely cry.

Score _____

(Ask your spouse if he or she agrees with your answers.)

If you are imprinted to be an avoider, this chapter of the workbook is designed to help you grow. We also include a section for those in relationship with a person who has an avoider love style.

1. Read Psalm 69. Make a list of all the feelings described in this song. Circle any of the feelings that you have experienced in the last month.

2. Many times painful events prompt an individual to enter therapy. In fact, over the years, we have recognized that one way God uses painful circumstances in the lives of those imprinted to avoid is to bring their feelings back to the surface again. It is as though God is thawing feelings that were locked away long ago. We sometimes say to such clients or friends, "Perhaps God is using this upsetting event to give you back the feelings you rarely expressed as a child." What event in your life has God used or is currently using to give you back your feelings? Why is this an important gift to you? Consider, for instance, that we are to love God with all our hearts. Can you do that if you've had to deaden your heart to feelings?

   One of the most important growth goals for those imprinted to be avoiders is to learn to recognize what you are feeling and to expand your range of emotions. This skill is extremely important, because emotions are linked to needs, and—as we said earlier—if you don't know what you feel, you can't know what you need. We suggest posting the soul words list in a prominent place at home (taped to the remote control?). Also place a copy in your purse or wallet. As you encounter daily events, refer to the list and choose a word that might fit what you are feeling.

3. Looking at the list of soul words at the back of this book, which feelings are the hardest for you to experience or express? Which feelings, if any, do you find more accessible?

4. Reflect on the last time you cried. How old were you? Why did you cry? When, if ever, would tears have been appropriate but you found yourself unable to cry?

5. What happened—or may have happened—in your family growing up that caused you to stop feeling sadness? Journal and/or share with your spouse or group.

6. Do you have memories of being comforted as a child or adult? Share one or two. If you don't have such memories, what do you envision when you imagine someone offering you comfort? Journal and/or share these thoughts.

7. Remember Jack from chapter 5 of *How We Love*? He had few memories of childhood events. In what ways, if any, do you relate to his experience? Talk about your childhood memories—or lack of them—with someone. If no listener is available, journal either some key memories or specific characteristics of your parents that might explain your avoider love style. Do you remember experiencing emotions during those key memories you recalled? If so, what were they? If you don't remember any emotions, use the soul words list and write down any feelings that would be likely to occur in such circumstances.

Being able to express your childhood memories is important. So seek an opportunity to share your journaling with your spouse. If memories are few, ask siblings or relatives for their memories of you as a child. Even just one sentence from a person who knew you well can help you make sense of your feelings and responses as an adult. Looking at old family pictures may also spur memories.

Besides being unaware of their emotions, individuals with an imprint to avoid are often unaware of sensations in their bodies. So learn to become aware of how your body tenses when you encounter emotions. A tight chest, a clenched jaw, a constricted throat, crossed arms, concave shoulders, and especially constricted breathing are bodily responses we often see in our offices. You may also be unaware of smiling as you describe painful events, and that is a common defense to block pain. All these bodily responses operate outside of our conscious awareness. Noticing and reversing them will help allow emotions to surface. Ask your spouse or group members to tell you when they notice any bodily responses that you may not notice yourself. Their reflections and observations will help you learn about yourself, especially during the sharing of emotions. Your spouse or group members will begin to do for you as an adult what your family was unable to do when you were a child.

8. Are you up for a challenge? Make extended eye contact with your spouse or a group member. Try to lock gazes for one or two minutes. Notice the sensations in your body. What do you experience?

9. Close your eyes and try to imagine your mother's eyes. If they could talk, what would they say to you? Notice your bodily sensations as you do this. Jot down your thoughts and feelings or share your experience with someone you trust. Do the same with your father's eyes. Again, jot down your thoughts and feelings or share your experience with someone you trust.

If you want to be a better listener, especially when you're dealing with another person's difficult emotions or strong feelings, it's important for you to learn not to mentally detach and emotionally disengage. Be courageous. Move toward others when they are upset rather than becoming angry or withdrawing. The first feeling you encounter will probably be anxiety. Expect this—and be encouraged that at least you are feeling! Admit to the person you're with that you are anxious and do not know what to do but that you *will try* to help.

Ask the person if he wishes to vent or problem solve. If he needs to vent, simply say out loud what you observe. For example, "I see this makes you very upset" or "I see you are very mad about what the kids did." Saying what you see is not hard. If the person wishes to problem solve, ask what part of the problem he most needs help with. Offer to brainstorm possible solutions.

Keep a record of your attempts to stay engaged with others when they are emotional. Jot down the subject of the conservation and the date. If you are in a group setting, practice with members of the group. Remember that you are trying to learn a skill you didn't have the opportunity to develop as a young person. Be patient with yourself.

10. Attempt to listen to the feelings of others, then jot down details about what you experienced, including your emotions.

Another valuable exercise is to ask someone for help even if you don't think you need it. Focus on your emotional needs rather than on tasks and jobs. Notice when you feel stressed and ask for something by starting with, "I need…" For example, "I need to talk," "I need a hug," "I need to take a walk with you," or "I need some time alone with you." This will be difficult, so ask God to help you first recognize and then acknowledge your needs. This skill is crucial to growth. Make it your goal to share your needs at least once a day.

11. Write a brief summary of your efforts and feelings as you do this exercise.

12. Learning to include others in your thought and decision-making process is also crucial for closeness. Consult with another person, ideally your spouse, before you make a decision. Ask them for input before you finalize your plans. (Remember, people who are married to avoiders usually feel like they're in the dark.) Summarize your attempts here.

HELPING AVOIDERS

The following suggestions are not meant as a personal guide for how to reform the avoiders in your life. Instead, they are intended to help you better understand and connect with them. You must keep in mind that an injury has prompted their behavior, so have compassion for their struggles and fears about intimacy. Realize, too, that because they have such difficulty with appearing vulnerable, their struggle will not be visible on the surface. So take these suggestions slowly, one at a time. If you try to do everything in one week, you will overwhelm the avoider. Ask God to guide you as you make an effort to support anyone in your life who has the avoider imprint.

13. Before we get to the tips, list people in your life whom you suspect were imprinted to be avoiders. Then write a prayer asking God to give you more love and understanding for these individuals.

14. Describe a time when you felt angry with one of the people you just listed. What happened? What avoider behavior, if any, prompted or fueled your anger?

Next time you attempt to relationally connect with an avoider, try the following approaches.

Stay calm. Anger repels them and causes them to clam up, as do other intense agitated emotions. If you do get angry, try to express the hurt under your anger. Hopefully, avoiders will be less defensive then. Also, use a low tone of voice and wait patiently for a response. Keep in mind that past injuries have caused this pattern of avoiding, which they do with everyone. So, as much as possible, try not to take their behavior personally. Ask them if there is anything you can do to make it safer for them to open up. Remember, avoiders are awkward when it comes to feeling and communicating emotions. Since they never had opportunities as a child to describe or share their inner feelings and responses, this is new for them. Anger and impatience will send them crawling back into their caves. Wait after you ask a question; let them search for words. If a long time passes, say patiently and warmly, "I'm going to wait until you can put words to your feelings and thoughts. I want to understand."

Give them gentle feedback when they pull away. When the avoiders in your life detach, they may not even be aware of it. You might say, for example, "You seem very detached this evening" or "Could you try to share some part of your day that was stressful for you?" Keep a record of your attempts to draw out the avoider. Notice what works as well as what does not.

Tell them you want to understand their history. When the time seems right, ask them to describe memories of being alone, ignored, or unseen. Help them link feelings to the childhood events they describe (the soul words list can be very helpful). Also invite these avoiders to explore emotions of anger or sadness that could not be expressed in earlier years. Again, ask a question about their feelings and wait. It may take time for them to formulate their thoughts.

Don't discount small efforts. Avoiders often link feelings and needs to shame. As they slowly thaw from their detached state, they will feel very vulnerable, embarrassed, and uncomfortable. Compliment their efforts even if the steps seem insignificant to you. Write down the efforts you have noticed even if they are small. Also, in the space that follows, note the avoider's response to your praise and encouragement. Pray and ask God to help you be aware and ready to take advantage of opportunities for showing your appreciation for the avoider's efforts to connect.

If possible, help avoiders discover their wants and desires as well as interests or talents that were never acknowledged or developed. Avoiders often don't know what they want or desire, what they're interested in or good at, because they were rarely asked about such things when they were growing up. For example, after noting how visually oriented and observant one client was, I encouraged her to purchase some art supplies and express her emerging feelings with color, shapes, and textures. Her talent was incredible, and it came as a total surprise to her. She was reluctant to bring her drawings and paintings into my office to show me, but she did. Then she was bewildered by my true enjoyment and enthusiasm for her work. She had never experienced anyone being so interested in her or her talents.

Extend comfort through words and touch to the avoiders you are close to. Be aware, however, that avoiders (also known as detachers) will be uncomfortable and have trouble accepting tenderness. So expect an awkward response to your efforts, but keep trying. You might say something like, "You look upset and you probably want to be left alone, but come sit by me on the couch and let me put my arm around you." Be playful when possible: "Come here, honey. Even Superman needed Lois Lane." If the avoider is a male, make it clear that this isn't a sexual gesture but that you are offering nonsexual touch and nurture. Keep the two separate, because avoiders often believe that sex and physical intimacy are one and the same.

15. Write about your efforts to approach the avoider(s) in your life as outlined in the previous paragraphs. Make sure to describe the outcome.

Chapter 6

The Pleaser Love Style

Let's look at some statements that are often true for people imprinted to be pleasers. Even if you do not think this is your style, read the list below and put a check mark by any statement you feel is true for you *most of the time*. After you finish, tally your points.

PLEASER ASSESSMENT

____ I am usually the giver in relationships.

____ I am good at keeping the peace.

____ I find I am able to anticipate the needs of my spouse and meet them.

____ Sometimes I am dishonest in order to avoid conflict.

_____ I am afraid of making my spouse upset or angry.

_____ When there is conflict, I'll give in just to get it over with.

_____ I don't like to be alone.

_____ It really upsets me when I feel someone is mad at me.

_____ When someone requests my help, I have trouble saying no, so I sometimes find myself overcommitted and stressed.

_____ I had a very critical and/or angry parent, and I tried very hard to win his or her approval.

_____ Sometimes I get mad, but I usually don't show it.

_____ I had a parent who never stood up for himself or herself, but passively accepted poor treatment.

_____ When I sense others are distancing themselves from me, I try harder to win them back.

_____ I am on the cautious side; I definitely wouldn't call myself a risk-taker.

_____ I had an overprotective parent who worried a lot.

Score_____

(Ask your spouse if he or she agrees with your answers.)

Perhaps you identify with the pleaser. If so, we hope you are beginning to understand what may have created your imprint. And although such insight is helpful, nothing about us changes unless we choose to grow and practice new behaviors. This chapter of the workbook is going to help direct you along that path of growth.

First a quick observation. It is always amazing to us how many people with this love style are unaware of the anxiety that drives it. This is probably because they were apprehensive as kids and became so accustomed to this sensation that they no longer recognize it as anxiety. Other people with this pleaser imprint are more aware that they are indeed feeling anxious, but they tend to minimize it with statements like "I'm just stressed" or "I'm just concerned." So one of the first steps of healing, as obvious as this may sound, is to admit that your anxiety is high much of the time. Recognizing that you are anxious and fearful of people's responses is a gradual process and can take some time. After all, you may have lived with this anxious feeling for so many years that you don't see it for what it is.

1. If you relate to the pleaser love style, would you call yourself an anxious person? Why or why not? Ask God to help you be aware of when you are feeling anxious. List some recent times when you have noticed this feeling. Then, using a 1–10 scale, rate your general level of anxiety. What types of situations tend to increase your anxiety? What causes it to go down?

2. As we pointed out in the book, this pleaser imprint commonly occurs either when a child's parent is fearful and overprotective or when a parent is angry and critical. If you think you're probably a pleaser, with which of these two situations did you grow up? What details from your childhood experiences might have contributed to this imprint? We hope you have shared some of your family background with your spouse and/or group to help them better understand you. If you have not, take the time to do so.

3. A person's anxiety can block other feelings, especially sadness or anger. If you are a pleaser, do you remember sharing feelings of sadness or anger with one or both of your parents as you were growing up? If not, why not? If so, what was their response? As an adult, how do you deal with sadness? with anger? Do you hide these emotions or share them. Write about these two feelings in your own life.

4. In what ways do you assume the pleasing role in order to keep others from detaching or being angry with you? Give a few specific examples. Also, in what ways do you give in to others to reduce your own anxiety? Ask God to help you see what motivates your giving. Make some notes about your observations.

5. Constantly being in the giving role can keep you out of touch with your own feelings, because you are focusing on the feelings and needs of others. Use the soul words list and write the feelings you are most often aware of. Which emotions do you rarely feel? Why do you think those feelings are difficult for you to access?

6. Now think about yourself as a receiver. What is your response to a compliment? What is your general response to an offer of help? How often do you ask for something from your spouse? What do your answers to these three questions tell you about your ability to receive or how comfortable you are receiving?

7. An important growth goal for pleasers like you is to learn to tolerate other people being angry with you. What is your response when your spouse is angry in general? is angry with *you*? Do you tend to want to quickly fix the situation? If so, why? What do you think would happen if you just let your spouse be upset?

8. Read Psalm 51:6, Ephesians 4:25, and Colossians 3:9. What instructions and insights into what God values are given in these verses? Now read John 8:44 which explains why honesty is so important. Are you ever dishonest in order to avoid conflict? In what areas of your relationship with your spouse do you most struggle to be honest? Practice initiating honest conversations when you are upset or annoyed with someone rather than avoiding that conflict altogether. Each time make a note of your efforts. What happened, and what was happening inside you?

9. Now read Ephesians 4:26. What is this verse saying to you personally? What can you do to show your anger without sinning?

10. No one likes rejection, but pleasers tend to avoid it at all costs. Most of the time, speaking truth involves a cost—people experience discomfort. Read Luke 4:14–30 and John 6:53–66 and list some examples of the rejection Jesus experienced. In what ways might your behavior be different if you were able to face someone's anger or rebuff?

11. Being alone is sometimes hard for pleasers. Is it hard for you? Why do you think that is? What feelings do you tend to have when you're alone? Were there times you were alone as a child? What happened? Next time you're alone, get the soul words list and see if you can identify how exactly being alone makes you feel. Write about that experience.

12. Pay attention to your breathing. Tense, tight muscles that lead to shallow breathing increase anxiety. You can, however, teach yourself to relax and

breathe deeply. The first step is to notice what is happening with your body. (Shallow breathing, for instance, does not make your belly move.) Take several minutes right now to do so. Relax your forehead; make sure it's nice and smooth. No furrows allowed! Then relax your eyes and jaw. Soften your tongue all the way down your throat. Take a deep, slow breath. As you exhale, let your head drop forward and relax your neck and shoulders. Take five more slow breaths, letting each one move deeper into your belly. Now, as you sit in this relaxed position, pick a simple comforting word or verse and repeat it slowly several times. (If you begin to drool, you're definitely relaxed!) Wasn't that nice? Be good to yourself and do this five or six times a day. It only takes a minute or a minute and a half. Write what you noticed as you started this exercise and how you felt at the end.

13. When your spouse asks for space, time alone, or time with friends, how do you feel? Why do you think you feel that way? Also, do you tend to make your spouse feel guilty if he or she wants some time apart? If so, what exactly do you do and/or say? What impact do your words and actions have on your marriage?

14. Do you enjoy spending some time apart from your spouse? If so, what do you like to do, and why does it help your relationship? If you don't like to be away from your spouse, why do you think that is? What personal interests, hobbies, or activities—if any—do you enjoy that do not include your mate? If you don't have any, why is that? Write one thing you might enjoy if you gave yourself the opportunity to develop outside interests.

15. If you came from a home where you were overprotected, you may feel afraid to try new things. But we encourage you to take a risk and step out of your comfort zone. Think of something you would normally avoid doing and make specific plans to try it. It could be anything. The goal of this exercise is for you to get a taste of not letting fear hold you back from living life. Write what you will try. After you have taken this bold step, share with your spouse or group how the experience was for you.

16. Are decisions usually difficult for you? What types of decisions do you most often avoid? Make a decision—not necessarily a big one—on your own

without asking anyone for permission, advice, or reassurance. Flexing your muscles of independence in small ways like this will build your confidence. Write about your experience.

17. Do you have difficulty saying no when others request your time, attention, or help? Do you struggle with being overly committed? Do you feel that others take advantage of your generous nature? Perhaps you need to limit your giving by learning to say no. Write a simple, straightforward sentence expressing a limit (for example, "I can't help; my schedule is full.") and practice saying it out loud so you can hear yourself say the words. Write about when you actually use your sentence in a real situation. Remember, people are used to your always saying yes. Prepare yourself for a look of surprise or even some objection when you say no.

18. When pleasers want to control something, their goal is usually to keep their world predictable and safe. Carefully planning ahead and knowing what to expect can also lower their anxiety. In what areas of life do you see yourself being controlling in order to lower your anxiety?

19. Are you direct or indirect when you communicate? Why? And how does your spouse react?

20. People are generally more patient when they can see that you are making an obvious effort to grow. But being a bit more adventuresome and spontaneous may bring you face to face with your anxiety. Knowing that your effort will be worth it, write one specific thing you are willing to do that you have been reluctant to do. Plan ahead of time how you can best be supported. What will help you more—words of reassurance and encouragement, holding someone's hand, a hug, reminders to breathe, or something else?

Sometimes, in spite of your best efforts, your anxiety might continue to be overwhelming. If that's the case, don't suffer needlessly. Seek help from a medical doctor, preferably a psychiatrist who can prescribe medications that can recalibrate your brain chemistry. Some drugs that help with anxiety can be addictive, but many are not. Actually, drug and alcohol abuse are often people's attempts to self-medicate their anxiety. Let us reassure you that we have seen many, many lives transformed by the proper use of medication.

HELPING PLEASERS

Keep in mind that the primary difficult emotion for pleasers is anxiety. When they are pushed too far past their comfort zone, you will notice a reaction of some kind, and it will likely be anxiety based. Maybe your spouse has never identified his or her inner experience as anxiety. If this is true, the soul words list can be helpful during any discussion. It is especially hard for men to admit they feel anxious, scared, or insecure. It may take some encouragement and acceptance for them to open up and begin to have words for what is in their hearts. If your spouse can't identify his or her anxiety but you suspect it's there, write a prayer asking God to reveal this. Remember, God is usually more gentle and patient than we might be, so be willing to wait for an answer.

Develop compassion for the pleaser's anxiety by understanding the childhood experiences that contributed to this problem. Take time to ask about family memories and about the times they were scared, traumatized, teased, or overprotected. You may also need to explore the possibility of an overly critical or angry parent and the impact of that relationship in creating fear and anxiety. Finally, remember the question at the beginning of the workbook about what annoys you most in your spouse? One of my biggest complaints about Milan was that he was always asking me, "How are you?" After listening to him talk about his childhood memories, though, I understood why he felt so compelled to need to know my mood. My irritation was greatly reduced, and for the first time I began to feel compassion for his struggle. In light of my experience, I encourage you to make a note of what you learn about your spouse. Review those lessons when you find yourself feeling annoyed with him or her.

After pleasers have identified some of their childhood memories, *encourage them to explore feelings, such as sadness and anger, that may underlie their anxiety.* Also, regularly ask them directly how they are coping: "How is your anxiety level today?" Offer to hold and comfort pleasers as they become aware of the impact of the early years in creating an imprint of insecurity and fear. A man will sometimes be willing to stretch out on the couch and put his head in his wife's lap. This position communicates to a man, "You are the focus of my time and attention, and

I'm here to listen and care for you." At times you may begin to feel sympathy. Express those feelings and any others. Seeing your feelings can help pleasers pull their own feelings toward the surface.

When pleasers make an effort to face their fears, offer acceptance and reassurance. Tell them you will patiently support their efforts to overcome their worries. Your doing so shows them that you are not overwhelmed by their feelings, and it provides them with *containment,* a newfound sense of stability and safety, which will become a basis for their newly emerging security base.

Encourage pleasers to stretch beyond their comfort level. Develop a plan, for instance, that gradually promotes separation from you in amounts that are increasingly tolerable. Also engage with pleasers in new activities that will help them learn to be comfortable in the areas they fear. You will be helping them discover as adults what they missed as children—that they can conquer fear instead of giving in to it. Be patient and encouraging, yet firm. Pray for wisdom about when to push and when to be compassionate and tolerant.

21. Write about your efforts to approach the pleaser(s) in your life as outlined in the previous paragraphs. Make sure to describe the outcome.

Chapter 7

The Vacillator Love Style

Vacillators may identify with many of the statements below. But even if you don't think this is your style, read through the list and put a check mark next to any statements that remind you of yourself. Tally your points at the bottom of the list.

Vacillator Assessment

_____ I feel like no one has ever really understood what I need.

_____ I was instantly attracted to my spouse, and our early relationship was intense and passionate.

_____ I hope for more in my relationships than I get; I am often disappointed as time goes on.

_____ When my spouse tries to respond to my needs, I feel it is too little too late.

_____ I am a very passionate person and feel things deeply.

_____ I could list many times my spouse has hurt and disappointed me.

_____ I can really sense when others pull away from me.

_____ I want far more connection with my spouse than I have.

_____ I like the feeling of making up after a fight.

_____ When people hurt me long enough, I write them off.

_____ If my spouse would pursue me more often and more passionately, our relationship would be better.

_____ I don't like to be alone, but when my spouse is around, I feel angry and empty.

_____ My parent(s) still drive me crazy.

_____ Sometimes I find myself picking fights, and I'm really not sure why.

_____ I make it obvious when I'm hurt, and when my spouse does not pursue me and ask what's wrong, I hurt more.

_____ It seems I end up waiting for my spouse to be available and pay attention to me.

Score_____

(Ask your spouse if he or she agrees with your answers.)

The vacillator imprint is formed when a child is raised in a home where there is some connection and bonding, but it is sporadic, unpredictable, and governed by the mood of the parent rather than the needs of the child. Left in a constant state of wanting and waiting, vacillators grow up looking for consistent attention, yet they cannot trust others to truly provide it. They idealize new relationships and then feel angry and hurt when their high expectations are not met. They create a push-pull (I want you/I don't want you) feeling within relationships. They can feel madly in love one minute and then deeply hurt and hateful the next.

1. What parts of chapter 7 in *How We Love* did you relate to? What circumstances in your home growing up contributed to your vacillator imprint? Do you remember hoping and waiting for connection or attention? Describe one or two of those times. Did you experience abandonment? Explain the situation and note how old you were. Was one of your parents inconsistent or unpredictable? If so, describe how. List some disappointments you experienced during your growing-up years. Write down some key memories and the feelings that characterized those memories. Share these memories and feelings with your spouse or small group.

2. After contemplating the feelings prompted by the memories above, consider how often you experience these same feelings with your spouse. Write down any similarities between past feelings and present feelings.

3. Do you remember feeling sad or angry as a child? If so, what brought on the sadness? the anger? What did you do with these feelings, and what were your parents' reactions?

4. It is very important for you to both develop self-reflection skills and come to understand the origins of your imprint. After all, your expectations for relationships, as well as your reactions to people disappointing you, are fed by your childhood wounds. You must therefore acknowledge and accept that you probably have a strong desire to find a person who can relieve all your "bad" feelings by being close, staying engaged, and giving you lots of attention. The agitation and uncertainty you feel when this does not happen isn't new. You felt it countless times as a child. So continue to review childhood memories and ask God to help you identify the roots of your imprint. This exercise means taking the focus off your current relationships and everything people do to hurt or anger you. Instead, spend a season looking inward and asking God to reveal the wounds that drive your current feelings, behaviors, and reactions. That truth will begin to set you free. Write down the insights God brings you as you continue to pray this prayer.

5. More than people with any other love style, vacillators tend to idealize romance. They enjoy the intense early phases of a relationship when each partner is paying a lot of attention to the other. It can therefore be difficult for vacillators to make the transition to real life. They feel as though all the passion has gone out of the relationship, and it is harder to sense that excitement and love. As disappointment sets in, so does anger, and the vacillator may put pressure on the spouse to rekindle those original feelings, because the feelings of loss trigger painful memories. Has this dynamic occurred in your marriage or in other relationships? Describe.

6. Experiencing healing means you must recognize the ways your love style drives you to find the magical person who will make you consistently feel special and wanted so you will never again have to feel anxious about rejection or abandonment. Right now, though, list the important people in your life whom you are currently idealizing. Among those people may be a friend, pastor, boyfriend or girlfriend, or therapist, but you will most likely notice that you're listing fairly new relationships. Next, make yourself write three of each of these people's weaknesses and human limitations. Ask yourself why you need to see them as so wonderful and "all good." What do you feel when you see in black and white the faults and weaknesses of the people on your list?

7. You will have a tendency to devalue your long-term relationships and see little good in those people who have disappointed you. So right now list those people who have hurt you or let you down. Next to each person's name list three positive qualities. Make a point of telling those people what you appreciate about them. You may feel that you already do this, but tell them anyway.

8. Read Romans 12:9–21 and Hebrews 12:14–15. What is God saying to you through these scriptures about your relationships, present or past? What action steps is He prompting you to take? What could you do to make obedience to these verses more a part of your life? Be very specific. By the way, even if it is best for you to have no contact with someone, have you forgiven that person for hurting you? Explain your answer.

9. Write down some things you are currently angry about in your marriage. Then get out the soul words list and try to determine which emotions underlie your anger. Too often vacillators use vague words like *bad, yucky,* or *awful,* but those words don't readily identify a specific feeling. So, again, look at your list of things you are angry about and write down the specific feelings that are submerged under the anger.

10. When you feel angry in the future, remind yourself to identify what feeling is underneath the anger, and share that emotion with your spouse. Anger tends to repel others and make them defensive, but other feelings can invite openness and intimacy. So instead of saying, "I'm sick and tired of your promises to be home for dinner. Just don't bother coming home," express your sadness: "I'm sad you aren't coming home for dinner. I was looking forward to sharing some things about my day and hearing about yours." There are times when anger is appropriate, but it is also helpful to learn to communicate the more vulnerable feelings that underlie the anger. When you do, you have a greater chance of being heard. Write about your experience of communicating your anger differently or, even better, about communicating the feelings underneath that anger.

11. Vacillators have a keen awareness of closeness and distance in relationships. In the first part chapter 7 of *How We Love,* Lea described how she was watching and waiting, hoping her mom would again give her the kind of physical affection she had shown Lea in the hospital. Lea grew very proficient at reading her mom's moods to determine how likely it was that her desire would be fulfilled. In what ways does Lea's experience remind you of yourself? What gauging of other people's moods did you have to do when you were growing up? Write down some of your memories.

When you were a kid, you had to guess about what might happen. You had to completely rely on your own assumptions. So you learned to constantly read between the lines in an attempt to determine what to expect and how to respond. You may not even be aware of how much you still read body language and the moods and actions of others to determine whether you are wanted or unwanted, liked or disliked, accepted or rejected. To you, relationships are a guessing game, and your assumptions may or may not be accurate. In fact, the actions and reactions of others are not always about you at all, but you probably assume they are.

You will never know the truth about people's thoughts or feelings toward you until you learn to check your assumptions by directly asking them about your concerns. If, for instance, you don't feel comfortable in a certain situation, you may conclude that the other person has negative feelings toward you, but that simply may not be the case. So ask! (If the person does have some negative feelings, at least you will know for sure! And now you have a chance to address whatever issue is causing the feelings.)

Your feelings are real, but you may be imagining the other person's intentions or feelings. If you leave these imagined injuries unmanaged and unchecked, you may find yourself depositing them in the bank of bitterness and resentment, and that account accrues interest as you continue to make other deposits. Over time, your level of anger and bitterness will grow. Because those emotions can be so destructive, keeping short accounts and checking assumptions are critical for healthy relationships and personal growth.

12. Identify some recent assumptions you have made about situations or people that you believe are true, but are—now that you think about it—merely guesses. Next, share your assumptions with your spouse, friend, or group. How do you feel as you take this step? Ask for a hug if you need it, and don't be afraid to cry.

13. In the week ahead, ask God to help you be aware of your tendency to make assumptions and guesses as you interact with others. Verbally check any assumptions you notice. You might say, for example, "You seem distant. Did I do something to upset you?" or "I can tell you are sad. I need to know if it's about something I did." Make notes about these times when you check your assumptions.

A lot of indirect communication goes on in the childhood home of a vacillator. As Lea grew up, for instance, her mom would be mad at her dad. Her mom communicated her displeasure by leaving the house and spending time only with Lea. In one session Lea said her mom could pout for weeks and sometimes would even ignore Lea. Learn to recognize when you communicate in an indirect manner, and develop the ability to speak more openly and truthfully. In other words, say your feelings and thoughts rather than showing them.

14. In what situations and in what specific ways do you act out your feelings rather than talking about them directly? Write down some examples. Then write a direct statement that clearly communicates your thoughts and feelings. Your spouse isn't a mind reader, so practice saying your feelings rather than showing them. Note the results.

15. During an argument, do you tend to bring up the past? Sometimes vacillators have been flooded with so many hurts throughout the years that, when conflict arises, past pain surfaces and overwhelms the vacillator and then, because of that, the spouse as well. So when you are upset, focus on *one topic* without bringing up every complaint about past behavior. Share something you appreciate about your spouse as well as what has upset you. If at the time you cannot think of anything good about your spouse, realize that you have made that person "all bad" in your mind. Remember, every person, every day, every vacation, every church, every friend, every holiday—you get the idea—is both good *and* bad. Being balanced means we are aware of both the good and the bad at any given moment, even in the middle of an argument. Write the results of your efforts to stick to the topic and to share words of appreciation alongside your complaint.

If your level of reactivity remains high and seems impossible to manage, seek the help of a professional. Extreme mood swings or uncontrollable rage can indicate chemical imbalances in the brain that may be a result of early trauma, medical problems, or genetic predispositions. We have both been amazed at the positive impact proper diagnosis and treatment can have in promoting healing and health.

HELPING VACILLATORS

If you are married to a vacillator, the following suggestions may be helpful. Work on one of these at a time. Also, your spouse would probably appreciate being able to choose which one would mean the most to him or her.

Don't allow the vacillator to pull you into extreme all-or-nothing thinking. Hold to middle ground. Record your experiences of striving for balance.

One of the most common complaints we hear about vacillators is, "They are so reactive." And they are—but *keep in mind that painful childhood experiences are at the root of this reactivity.* Ask your mate questions about childhood experiences and explore how he or she felt at the time. You will probably discover that, under all that anger, is a great deal of unacknowledged anxiety and pain. As children, vacillators were probably unable to think or speak about their own internal experiences when they were upset or distressed. They are, however, often unaware of their early wounds or the absence of comfort in their homes during their formative years. Childhood photographs can be helpful in spurring memories. Note some of the things you discover that help you better understand your spouse.

The antidote for anger is grief. Angry individuals, however, block the more vulnerable emotions of sadness or fear with their anger. During a conflict, the vacillator's anger may turn into tears of total frustration, but those are quite different from tears of unadulterated grief over painful childhood experiences. Pray and ask God to reveal memories that are crucial to understanding current conflicts in your marriage. Sadness and tears are essential to healing. Be tender and comforting as you search for memories attached to your spouse's sadness and grief. Write what you learn from the times you do this.

When your spouse has an angry outburst, here's a way to handle it. Learn the following words for those times when your spouse—or any other vacillator you know—is angry and reactive: "I see how upset you are. I want to listen, and I *will* listen when you can calm down. Then you'll be able to tell me what hurt you before you got so angry." If the anger continues, repeat these statements several more times. If necessary, end the conversation by saying, "I am willing to listen when you are able to share your hurt feelings. Let me know when you are ready." Be faithful to your promise and give positive feedback when the vacillator is willing to make an effort. Afterward explain how much easier it is for you to listen and stay engaged when the tone of voice is soft and vulnerable instead of harsh and insulting. We suggest you stick with this approach even if you don't get good responses initially. Note your experiences.

It is difficult to be honest about your own shortcomings, because vacillators tend to do a lot of blaming. They see you as the problem and rarely admit their own contributions to any difficulties. This behavior can set up a pattern of blame, defense, and escalating anger, but you can break that pattern. *Humble yourself and agree when you know your spouse is making a valid point.* Also, know that times of mutual confession and prayer can be productive and healing. Write about a confession you made and the effect it had on the other person and the argument.

Be aware of the temptation to avoid conflict with vacillators by appeasing them or being dishonest. Some vacillators are married to passive spouses who take the road of least resistance, but that's not helpful or healthy. Instead, speak the truth in love and learn to set limits. Initially, this approach will make vacillators more agitated, but you will earn their respect—and keep your self-respect and dignity—by doing so. Note a time when you spoke the truth in love.

In calmer moments, when the agitation level is low, *gently explain to your spouse the effect of his or her anger and how it makes you feel.* Ask for input for ways you two could communicate in calmer, nonreactive ways. In the case of physical abuse or violence, call 911. Such swift action clearly sends the message that violence will not be tolerated.

As disappointment increases and problems multiply, the vacillator can devalue your marriage relationship and make you feel that you cannot do anything right. (If you lived with a critical parent, this may be a familiar and unsettling feeling for you.) When that happens, *solicit help from others to help you sort out which complaints are valid and to remind you of your positive attributes.* Also learn to directly ask the vacillator for positive feedback: "I'm willing to listen to your complaint, but it would really help me if you acknowledged some positive aspects of our relationship as well." Finally, ask your spouse to join you for coffee or a date with the specific purpose of sharing things you appreciate about each other. Write about how you felt—about yourself, your spouse, your relationship—after that time of appreciation.

16. Write about your efforts to approach the vacillator(s) in your life as outlined in the previous paragraphs. Make sure to describe the outcome.

Chapter 8

The Chaotic (Controller and Victim) Love Styles

We learned in chapter 8 of *How We Love* that a chaotic environment produces one of these two chaotic love styles. Relationships in such an environment are rarely safe and nurturing; instead they are destructive and dangerous. Some children respond by internalizing their anger and trying to be invisible; they become imprinted as victims and accept abuse quietly. Other children openly display their anger, especially when they are teenagers, exhibiting the controller imprint. As adults, victims will fearfully allow others to dominate them, while the angry victimizer will intimidate those who are weaker.

This chapter has two sets of statements. Even if you don't think either reflects your style, read through both groups of statements and put a check mark by any statement that is true for you most of the time. Tally your points at the bottom of the list.

Victim Assessment

_____ I grew up in a family with serious problems, such as outbursts of anger, violence, addictions, abuse, and neglect.

_____ I have to keep my mate from knowing certain things, because he or she would be angry.

_____ I have a history of being in or even staying in destructive relationships.

_____ I suffer with depression and/or anxiety, and that makes it hard for me to cope with life.

_____ I am loyal even when I realize others are probably exploiting me.

_____ For most of my life, I have felt unworthy and unlovable.

_____ A lot of the time my mind is far off, and I feel emotionally flat, detached, and disengaged.

_____ My parents had drug and alcohol problems.

_____ One of my parents was abusive and the other passive.

_____ I feel as though I functioned as the parent in my home when I was growing up.

_____ My spouse mistreats me, but I stay because it would be worse to be alone.

_____ I was physically, emotionally, or sexually abused during my childhood—or I saw these things happening to other people.

_____ I get nervous when things are calm because I know it won't last, so I'm always waiting for my spouse to get angry or critical.

_____ Sometimes I feel life isn't worth living.

_____ I don't let myself cry, because if I started, I'd never stop.

Score_____

CONTROLLER ASSESSMENT

_____ Growing up, I had an angry parent or sibling who threatened me, intimidated me, and/or was violent toward me.

_____ No one protected me from harm when I was growing up.

_____ My spouse does things behind my back.

_____ I feel angry when other people try to control me or tell me what to do.

_____ I have problems with alcohol, drugs, pornography, gambling, or overspending.

_____ My life is one problem after another, and that means constant stress.

_____ Sometimes I try to control my temper, but I feel too angry to stop raging.

_____ My spouse does things that make me jealous.

_____ I lose my temper a lot, especially at home, but my spouse (or kid) deserves it.

_____ I have hit or pushed my spouse—or I have come very close to doing so.

_____ I change jobs a lot.

_____ By the time I was a teenager, people knew not to mess with me.

_____ By the time I left home, some family members were afraid of me.

____ My spouse ignores me when I ask him or her to do things a certain way.

____ My spouse starts most of our fights, because he or she doesn't listen to
what I say.

Score_____

GROWTH GOALS FOR BOTH THE VICTIM AND THE CONTROLLER

The first steps of growth and healing almost always take place outside the home
in a counselor's office where victims as well as controllers can experience safety and
support for the first time in their lives. (That's why this chapter doesn't include
couples' exercises.) We share the following suggestions, however, in hope that they
can help get the healing process started.

As we have explained, chaotic homes tend to push individuals to one of two
opposite poles, resulting in two very different imprints. First we will look at goals
that could benefit both the victim and the controller. Then we will consider separate growth goals for each.

Whether you relate to the imprint of the victim or the controller, you first
need to acknowledge that you do have an injured love style. While this sounds
simple enough, it is not easy to do. After all, chaos and stress seem normal, because
that is the way life has always been. Also complicating your healing journey is the
fact that it is almost impossible to heal from these injuries without assistance, but
asking for help is probably a foreign concept to you. Nevertheless, you will most
likely have to seek outside help—and when you experience that safe, loving environment for the first time ever, you will begin to understand what you have been
missing all your life.

But where on earth can you find a safe place? First, pray and ask God to lead
you to the best resources for you. Then get on the phone and call churches in your
area to find out if they have recovery groups. If so, try one out. You can also look
for a Christian-based Twelve Step program. There are groups for kids, teens, and
adults—and for just about every problem imaginable. Since addictions are almost

a universal problem in chaotic homes, there is a dual benefit to selecting a Twelve Step group that addresses the types of issues with which you struggle. In such a setting, you can address your problems with addictions at the same time that you are learning to build honest, trusting, safe relationships. Additionally, Twelve Step groups provide each participant with a sponsor or mentor who is further down the road of healing and recovery. These groups are free and life changing, so there is no excuse for not seeking help. We have seen clients make amazing progress from getting involved in a support group.

List the churches and groups you can contact in an effort to find help and support.

Once you're in a supportive environment, you can begin to talk about your memories of early abuse and ask others to help you determine their effect on your current functioning as an adult. You need to learn how to identify and express your feelings as well as your needs. This will probably be a new experience, because your feelings have probably never been acknowledged or validated. Also, know that feelings of shame—common for people who have chaotic backgrounds—and humiliation only go away when you share your secrets and experience grace, acceptance, and love.

Counselors, support groups, or mentors will give you other opportunities to learn to receive comfort and compassion as they validate the painful effects of your childhood abuse. You probably have grief tucked deep down inside that had no place to go when you were little. Being able to finally grieve over the parenting, love, and acceptance you didn't receive as a child can be incredibly redemptive and healing. And slowly, over time, a new imprint begins to form in your soul, one that will replace the imprint of chaos, rejection, humiliation, and fear.

Finally, it's no surprise that people from chaotic homes can have serious difficulties in their marriages and relationships. The help that is required goes beyond the scope of this workbook. Our goal is to get you started on the road to healing by helping you acknowledge the problems and encouraging you to ask for the help you need.

GROWTH FOR THE VICTIM

The victim imprint is somewhat similar to the pleaser imprint, so you may find some questions in that section of the workbook helpful. But while pleasers are willing to put up with a lot, they draw the line at abuse. The victim, however, does not see the line and tolerates the intolerable.

If you are a victim, the first concern you need to address is that of safety. If you or your children are being abused, you need to find a shelter where all of you can receive safety, support, and counseling. Call and gather information so you have an idea what to expect in terms of the emotions you may feel and the protective steps that are needed to guard you against possible angry and dangerous responses from your spouse. You have probably lived for a while with the hope that things at home will get better. But usually the pattern keeps repeating itself, getting worse, not better. As long as fear keeps you frozen, it is impossible to begin the process of healing.

If fear of reprisal from the angry controller in your life is, in fact, preventing you from taking action, you must acknowledge the seriousness of the situation. Nothing in your marriage or your family life will change until you ask for help. Your tendency to minimize problems in your home and excuse your spouse's behavior keeps you from seeking assistance. Asking for help requires you, first, to realize that the situation is beyond your ability to change without help and then to admit that truth to another person—and God encourages us to speak the truth.

1. In what ways do you minimize the problems in your marriage? Give a few specific examples.
2. List some of the excuses you make for your spouse.
3. What do you do to cover and disguise the truth of what goes on in your home? In what ways, if any, are your public life and your private life different? Again, give a few examples.
4. What does your spouse do that makes you afraid?
5. Do you remember feeling that same way in your home growing up? What were you afraid of then?

6. When you were growing up, did you ever say "No!" or "Stop!" when someone was treating you badly? If so, was it difficult for you to confront them, and what happened? If not, what were you feeling?

7. Do you ever say "No!" or "Stop!" to your spouse? If not, what are you feeling? What do you wish for or ask God to do for you during these moments?

8. When you give in to your spouse's requests/demands, do you respect yourself? Why or why not? Does your spouse respect you? Support your answers with evidence.

Most people imprinted to be victims have difficulty saying no and taking firm action when they are mistreated. You will need to learn to set boundaries and make them stick.

9. What health problems, if any, are you dealing with? What do you think your body is telling you that you are refusing to acknowledge? If your symptoms could speak, what would they say?

Once you have found a safe environment, you will need to grow in your ability to enjoy periods of calm by learning to recognize and soothe your underlying anxiety. Detoxifying your mind and body from the adrenaline, anxiety, and constant stress it's used to will take time. Music, deep breathing, and relaxation exercises may help. Speaking words of comfort to the anxious "child part" inside you can also provide new messages of hope. You might, for instance, say, "It's okay to relax, because I'm learning how to keep you safe."

You may be afraid to get angry with your spouse, but you may find it harder to hold back those impulses with your children or pets. If anger is a problem, know that it won't get better until you get help. One caller to the *New Life Live!* radio show confessed to violently shaking her dog when she was upset, and she was worried about someday doing this to her child. We immediately confirmed that this was a likelihood and that she needed to get outside help to better understand and control her rage.

10. Do you struggle with anger when dealing with your children? Support your answer with specific scenes from your life.

11. If you are surprised by the intensity of the anger your children can spark in you, have you ever admitted this to anyone or attempted to get help? Explain. Do you see your anger as a character flaw or a result of your childhood experiences? Explain what you think the source of your anger is.

Some victims rarely feel angry with anyone, even their children. If this is true for you, we are going to make an educated guess that you probably struggle with depression, that you find it easier to be angry with yourself than with another person. You need to recover the feeling of anger if you were never allowed to express it as a child. Constructive anger, properly displayed, is essential to health and growth. The goal is not to eliminate anger, but to learn how to effectively communicate and deal with it. A display of controlled, productive anger should not set off fear in the people around you (as does a violent rage).

12. Do you struggle to express or even feel anger? Explain.

Have you ever witnessed someone display their anger appropriately? Jesus exhibited appropriate anger by being direct about infractions, adjusting his tone and intensity depending on the maturity level of the person(s), stating the truth that had been violated, not being demeaning, and telling the person(s) not to do it again. Further, Jesus expected people to become agitated and experience conflicted emotions, but He didn't try to protect them from feelings of guilt. He told them He loved them and that their sins grieved His heart. Yet He offered them restoration if they would comply with His request, and He gave them grace and mercy when they repented. When He restored them, He didn't hold a grudge.

13. What elements of Jesus's appropriate display of anger would you have liked to experience more of as a child? What aspects would you like to see more developed in your own behavior as a spouse and/or parent?

GROWTH FOR THE CONTROLLER

Considering the home in which you grew up, anger is an appropriate feeling for you to have. The trouble is, anger is probably the only emotion you feel, and it is probably directed at people in your life today who had absolutely nothing to do with making your life miserable when you were young. So what are you to do with all your anger?

We have only seen one thing really lower the level of anger, and that is having the freedom to grieve. Learning to *grieve* your childhood injuries and losses will give you a greater sense of peace, and the more you grieve, the less angry you will be. We have observed this over and over as we've worked with angry people. Grief and sadness are always blocked in chaotic homes, and anger can become a defense against feeling the hurt, especially for men. Furthermore, any vulnerable emotion is often associated with humiliation, shame, and dread. Reviving feelings of grief—definitely a vulnerable emotion—will take courage, time, and a safe person who is willing to listen.

14. Have you ever considered the idea that your anger blocks sadness and grief? What reasons for sadness and grief did you experience as a child? Why might you have chosen to feel anger rather than sadness?

15. Remember Doug in chapter 8 of *How We Love*? It was hard for him to remember or even guess what his feelings were during all the terrible things that went on in his home when he was a child. In what ways, if any, are you like Doug?

Eventually, as your anger and grief subside, you will be able to forgive the person or people who hurt you—even if they are no longer alive. Forgiveness can be defined as "letting the offender out of jail so that you can go free."

The flip side of forgiveness is beginning to take responsibility for the hurtful things you have said and done, to confess those words and deeds, and to ask forgiveness from those you have hurt. It is amazing how much healing can occur as we begin to confess our own shortcomings and sinful behaviors. Besides, such honesty, vulnerability, and transparency are the key character qualities that allow others to trust us and feel safe around us.

HELPING VICTIMS

If you are in a relationship with a victim, the following suggestions may be helpful.

Our goal is to *recognize that much of the fearful reactivity of victims is fueled by childhood injuries.* Politely request permission to ask them questions about their childhood experiences, exploring how they *felt* during those events. Remind them that they can stop or alter the conversation at any time. Under their fear and anger is a great deal of unacknowledged anxiety and hurt. As children, victims were unable to speak about their internal experiences when distressed. They often don't even recognize their early wounds or the absence of comfort.

One antidote to their fear and anxiety is appropriate anger and grief. People who are frozen in fear often block the more vulnerable emotion of sadness. As an essential component of healing, victims need safe places to learn to grieve the painful childhood experiences and shed tears. Ask God to reveal memories that are crucial to understanding current conflicts. Be tender and comforting as you explore memories attached to their sadness and grief.

Remember that because the *victim's prevailing emotion is fear, they will try to conform to their surroundings.* Invite them to speak their mind freely, assuring them that they are safe—they can express their own opinion and disagree with you. Role play with them (if they are willing), pretending you are a parent or other significant person who may have harmed them. Reassure them about their safety as needed.

Because victims have experienced a very disorganized environment growing up, *they will struggle to pull their thoughts together and formulate their words.* Give them time to answer, and don't put words in their mouth. Smile, use soft tones, let them know you understand this is difficult, and tell them to take their time. Treat them with complete respect.

Victims struggle with assertiveness and lack boundaries. Encourage them to set boundaries and learn to say no to demands and requests. Invite them to practice saying no aloud, and help them find and set areas of emotional safety. Let them know they can say no to you without harming the relationship.

Individuals with the victim love style have rarely had anyone acknowledge their positive attributes. They are in desperate need of praise and encouragement, even though they may have a hard time believing it. Let them know you believe in them and reinforce that they have worth and value. By doing so, you will help them experience a healthy new self-image. Be patient, as healing will take time.

HELPING CONTROLLERS

If you are in a relationship with a controller, the following suggestions may be helpful. Again, your safety is extremely important. So before attempting any of these suggestions, determine—with the help of your support system—both the safety of trying any intervention and the wisest timing for doing so.

Our goal is to *recognize that much of the reactivity of controllers is fueled by childhood injuries.* If you feel it is safe doing so, ask questions about their early experiences and, as they share memories, explore how they felt during those childhood events. Under all their anger is a great deal of unacknowledged anxiety and hurt. When they were children, people with this love style were unable to speak about their own internal experiences when they were upset and distressed. They often don't recognize their early wounds or the absence of comfort in their homes during their formative years.

Again, *the antidote to anger is grief.* Angry individuals block the more vulnerable emotions of sadness or fear with anger. Controllers need to learn to shed tears and grieve over their painful childhood experiences. The emergence of sadness and tears is essential to healing. So pray and ask God to reveal memories that are crucial to understanding current conflicts. Then be tender and comforting as you explore memories attached to their sadness and grief.

The most intense, unproductive fights often occur between partners with chaotic love styles. If you are married to a controller, you can change the dynamic by *refusing to talk until there is no yelling or insulting.* Learn the following mantra and repeat it often when anger erupts. Calmly make eye contact, and in a soft, caring voice say, "I see how upset you are. I want to listen. But it will be easier for me to listen if you stop yelling." If the yelling continues, end the conversation by saying, "I am willing to listen when you can stop yelling. Let me know when you're ready." Be faithful to your promise: listen when the yelling stops. Also, give positive feedback when the controlling individual makes an effort in this area. Explain how much easier it is for you to listen and stay engaged when the tone of voice is soft and vulnerable instead of harsh and insulting. As we do in our offices, be willing to talk about your own love-style injury and the fact that all of us are wounded.

Your humble confession will allow the shame, so prevalent in controllers, to be less intense. Such mutual times of confession can be productive and healing.

Be aware of the temptation to avoid conflict with controllers by appeasing them, trying to fix them, or being dishonest. Many of us are used to taking the road of least resistance, but that's not helpful or healthy. Instead, speak the truth in love and learn to set limits. Initially this approach can make controllers more agitated, but by doing so, you will earn their respect—and maintain your self-respect and dignity. Also, keep yourself safe. Taking yourself and your children to a safe place is a way of communicating limits. In the case of physical abuse or violence, call 911. Such swift action clearly sends the message that violence will not be tolerated.

Controllers have rarely had anyone acknowledge any positive aspect of their personhood. They are in desperate need of praise and positive words, even though they may have a hard time believing them. So persevere. Let those wounded adults know—again and again—why you love them.

Chapter 9

Identifying Your Love Style

1. Now that you have read detailed descriptions of each imprint, note below the imprint(s) that most accurately describe you. (You may see yourself as a combination of styles.) List the main beliefs and behaviors in your life that make you identify with the particular style(s). If you see yourself as a combination, which style causes the most problems in your marriage?
2. Which imprint best fits your spouse? List the behaviors and beliefs that caused you to choose that particular imprint for him or her. If you see your spouse as a combination, which style do you think causes the most problems in your marriage?
3. Do you and your spouse agree about which imprint best describes each of you? If not, which close friends could share their observations?

4. In what ways do you identify with the core of anxiety that lies at the heart of each of these love styles? At what point in your childhood can you first pinpoint that feeling of anxiety?

   Now take a moment to consider the common lies each love style believes:

   • *Avoider:* I don't need anyone.
   • *Pleaser:* I am responsible to maintain the happiness and well-being of others, because conflict and rejection are deadly and to be avoided at all costs.
   • *Vacillator:* My spouse is the problem in my marriage. There is nothing I can do to improve my marriage because my husband/wife won't change. I need my spouse to take away my bad feelings.
   • *Controller:* I have to control and intimidate in order to get what I want.
   • *Victim:* If I tried harder in my relationship, my spouse wouldn't get so angry.

5. As you come to better understand your imprint, you may be able to identify other distortions of the truth. For now, see if you can write a corresponding statement of truth for each of the lies (for all five love styles).

   Avoider

   Pleaser

   Vacillator

   Controller

   Victim

6. In the Bible, Satan is described as the "father of lies" (John 8:44). When God reveals a truth to us, we have an opportunity to recognize it and take control of our thought processes (see 2 Corinthians 10:3–6). Why does believing the truth make you free (see John 8:32)?

7. What lies about yourself and others do you need to recognize and then replace with truths?

8. What new truths about God, yourself, and others do you need to embrace?

9. What feelings, thoughts, and behaviors alert you that your negative love style is in control? (When you recognize these, then you can refute them.) For example, alerts to avoider behavior might be isolating yourself, detaching

emotionally, eluding eye contact, and being abnormally silent. Ask others to help you see when you are in the old pattern.

10. When two people with different love styles get married, predictable relational patterns occur. We will talk about these at length in the next section. Before you read on, try to identify the patterns within your marriage. Which patterns mentioned in *How We Love* do they match?

Group Exercises

11. Take turns sharing which imprint you identify with and why.
12. Address the spiritual implications of your imprint by discussing the beliefs that characterize your imprint that are distortions of the truth.
13. Talk about what kind of relational patterns might develop with the various combinations.

Chapter 10

The Vacillator Marries the Avoider

When avoiders marry vacillators, the vacillators tend to pursue the independent spouse. When the avoiders instinctively disengage and retreat, the vacillators feel rebuffed and abandoned, and their anger intensifies. Over time, the chase scene picks up both speed and intensity, leading these couples on a perilous roller-coaster ride.

1. What traits initially attracted you to your spouse?

For the Avoider

2. Do you feel as if you are constantly in trouble with your spouse? If so, what do you think you've said or done to be in trouble? Now think about your spouse's childhood history. In what specific ways was he or she disappointed by relationships in the past? Do you think your spouse could be feeling the

same way as he or she relates to you? What impact could this insight have on your relationship?

FOR THE VACILLATOR

3. When did you become disappointed with your spouse? When did you realize that he or she has trouble connecting? Now review your spouse's childhood and explain why he or she has trouble connecting. What impact could this insight have on your relationship?

4. When you are angry, what kind of behavior and words do you direct at your spouse? Ephesians 4:26 says, "In your anger do not sin" (NIV). In what ways, if any, do you sin when you are angry?

5. Now consider the possibility that your spouse is getting some of the anger that someone in your past deserves. Who might that someone be, and what could have prompted your anger?

6. Every time you are mad, stop and ask yourself, What is the hurt under this anger? Once you figure it out, communicate that sad, hurt feeling to your spouse rather than the anger.

FOR THE AVOIDER

7. Do you feel like you are walking on eggshells? Explain.

8. When your spouse gets angry, how do you feel inside? Do you remember having a similar feeling during your childhood years?

9. In an earlier question, your spouse was encouraged to learn to get sad, not mad. Tell your spouse you are willing to learn to comfort him or her, if he or she will work on the sad feelings. (Chapter 17 on engagement will help you do that.)

10. If you were willing to be less avoidant and allow your vacillator spouse's emotions, and if his or her anger diminished as a result, how might that change your negative marital dynamics? Would you be more inclined to be less avoidant? If so, in what ways?

FOR THE VACILLATOR

11. If you were to become less angry and critical of your avoider spouse, how might this change your negative marital dynamics? Would you be more inclined to control your vacillations? If so, in what ways?

FOR BOTH OF YOU

12. Review the workbook discussion of your particular imprint. Choose one growth goal to work on, and tell your spouse what it is. Write a prayer asking God to help you reach your goal.
13. If you're working with a group, share your growth goal with the members, and ask them to pray for you and hold you accountable.

Chapter 11

The Pleaser Marries the Vacillator

Vacillators idealize pleasers' giving natures and believe they have found their soul mates. All is well until the vacillators' idealized view is shattered by disappointment, and they become angry. The pleasers' fear of that anger causes them to try harder, but they lose a bit of themselves in the process. After years of living out this pattern, pleasers walk on eggshells and are passively resentful. The vacillators are still unhappy, sensing a connection based on fear and duty rather than passion.

1. From *How We Love,* is there anything in Peter and Shannon's story or Michael and Sandy's story in chapter 11 that you relate to? If so, what?
2. What traits initially attracted you to your spouse?

FOR THE PLEASER

3. Do you feel as if you are constantly in trouble with your spouse? If so, what do you think you've said or done to be in trouble? Now think about your

spouse's childhood history. In what specific ways was he or she disappointed by relationships in the past? Do you think your spouse could be feeling the same way as he or she relates to you? What impact could this insight have on your relationship?

FOR THE VACILLATOR

4. When did you become disappointed with your spouse? When did you realize that he or she has trouble connecting? Review your spouse's childhood and explain why he or she has trouble connecting. What impact could this insight have on your relationship?

5. When you are angry, what kind of behavior and words do you direct at your spouse? Ephesians 4:26 says, "In your anger do not sin" (NIV). In what ways, if any, do you sin when you are angry?

6. Now consider the possibility that your spouse is getting some of the anger that someone in your past deserves. Who might that someone be, and what could have prompted your anger?

7. Every time you are mad, stop and ask yourself, What is the hurt under this anger? Once you figure it out, communicate that sad, hurt feeling to your spouse rather than the anger.

FOR THE PLEASER

8. Do you as if you are walking on eggshells? Explain.

9. When your spouse gets angry, how do you feel inside? Do you remember having a similar feeling during your childhood years?

10. In an earlier question, your spouse was encouraged to learn to get sad, not mad. Tell your spouse you are willing to learn to comfort him or her. What frightens you about making this offer?

11. One more question about your reaction to your spouse's anger: Do you feel something inside other than fear, something like sadness and anger? Make an effort to be aware of feelings inside you besides anxiety and share them

with your spouse. If he or she gets upset, you'll be able to practice owning your feelings even if your spouse is agitated by your emotions. Journal about any feelings that have never come out before.

FOR THE VACILLATOR

12. How do you think it would change your negative marriage pattern if you worked on changing your love style? Describe how you would feel if your spouse were stronger and could engage with your painful emotions instead of just pleasing you. Are you willing to let him or her stand up and have more of a voice in the relationship? And what would you like your response to be if your spouse were to stand up to you? (Standing up to you is necessary before your spouse can engage with you in a healthy way.)

FOR THE PLEASER

13. How would your negative marriage pattern change if you worked on being honest and not always pleasing? Describe how you would feel if your spouse were less angry at you and took some responsibility for your negative love style.

FOR BOTH OF YOU

14. Review the workbook discussion of your particular imprint. Choose one growth goal to work on, and tell your spouse what it is. Write a prayer asking God to help you reach your goal.
15. If you're working with a group, share your growth goal with the members, and ask them to pray for you and hold you accountable.

Chapter 12

The Controller Marries the Victim

In this combination, usually controllers marry people with the weaker victim style. As the relationship begins, the roles feel strangely familiar and yet different, because both parties believe they have finally escaped their childhood homes. But it does not take long for controllers to become angry, possessive, and dissatisfied. When overwhelmed or threatened with a loss of power, the controller rages and intimidates. The victim, whose esteem was decimated long ago, believes he or she is at fault. Drugs, alcohol, and other addictive behaviors often find their way into this home as a means of soothing the constant anxiety everyone feels.

1. Is there anything in Bill and Carlie's story or Leslie and Paul's story in chapter 12 of the book that you relate to? If so, what?
2. If this is your marital combination, what things initially attracted you to your spouse?
3. What things about your mate have been the hardest for you to accept or live with?

One of the keys to changing this core dynamic is for the controller and the victim to learn to listen and offer comfort to each other about their painful childhood memories. Take time to listen and get to know the child inside your mate.

FOR VICTIMS

4. Do you feel you are constantly in trouble with, and disappointing to, your spouse? When you review your spouse's childhood history, how was he or she hurt or disappointed by relationships? How might your spouse's early experiences be fueling his or her anger now? It is important for you to realize the anger is not about you, even though it is probably directed at you now.
5. Do you feel like you are walking on eggshells? How does your spouse's anger make you feel inside? Do you remember a similar feeling from your childhood years? What events or people made you afraid?

6. Do you feel something inside other than fear, such as sadness, anger, shame, or something else? Journal about the feelings inside that have never really come into the light. Perhaps, at a later date, when you feel safer, you can share these feelings with your spouse.

If you haven't yet, you need to realize you can never be good enough to keep your spouse from getting angry. Write how your feelings might change if your spouse took responsibility for controlling his or her emotions. As you learn to resist the controller's black-and-white, extreme thinking, try to remember that this person was once a little child who felt overwhelmed and hopeless. You can have compassion; however, you cannot "fix" him or her. And if you feel threatened or fearful in any way, you need to seek professional counsel.

FOR CONTROLLERS

7. Do you display anger toward your spouse? How? Is it "out of bounds" when you consider the biblical guidelines in Ephesians 4:26?

8. Is your spouse getting some of the anger that someone in your past deserves? Every time you are mad, stop and ask yourself, What is the hurt under this anger? Communicate the sad hurt feeling to your spouse rather than the anger.

9. Have you ever considered that you make your spouse (and children) feel just like the abusive people in your childhood made you feel when you were young? Write about how you felt as a child when people were critical, mean, and angry. Does your anger cause the same feelings in others now?

10. Are you willing to deal with your anger instead of blaming others? Your core pattern cannot change until you accept how destructive this is to your marriage.

11. Would you respect your mate more if one day he or she was stronger and learned to have an adult voice and speak up to you? How does your mate's passivity fuel your contempt?

For Both of You

12. Commit yourself to one growth goal from the workbook for your attachment style that will begin to change this core pattern. Share your goal with your spouse. Write a prayer asking God to specifically help you with this goal.
Controller
Victim

Group Exercise

13. Share your growth goal with your group and ask them to hold you account-able.

Chapter 13

The Avoider Marries the Pleaser

Pleasers' insecurity causes yet another relational chase scene, yet instead of anger being the motivator, as it is with vacillators, fear drives pleasers into a relentless pursuit of the independent avoiders' attention. The pleasers' neediness irritates avoiders, and they move farther away. As the avoiders detach, the pleasers' anxiety and fear increase, so the chase intensifies. And the pattern continues.

1. What traits initially attracted you to your spouse?
2. Which of your spouse's traits are the hardest for you to accept or live with?

For the Avoider

3. Do you feel as if you are constantly being chased, pursued, or smothered by your spouse? What words and/or behaviors prompt those feelings? Do you feel that you are frequently disappointing your spouse? If so, explain.

4. Now think about your spouse's childhood history. In what specific ways was he or she disappointed by relationships in the past? Do you think your spouse could be feeling the same way as he or she relates to you? What impact could this insight have on your relationship?

FOR THE PLEASER

5. When did you become disappointed with your spouse? When did you realize that he or she has trouble connecting with you as an adult? Now review your spouse's childhood and explain why he or she has trouble connecting with people in general. Describe your thoughts and feelings about their childhood. What impact could this insight have on your relationship?

FOR THE AVOIDER

6. When you are angry, what kind of behavior and words do you direct at your spouse? Are you verbal and clear about your anger, or do you want to pull away and be quietly angry? Why do you think that's your way of being angry?

7. Consider the possibility that your spouse is receiving the anger that someone in your past deserves. Who might that someone be, and what could have prompted your anger?

8. Every time you are mad, stop and ask yourself, What is the hurt under this anger? Once you figure it out, communicate that sad, hurt feeling to your spouse rather than the anger.

FOR THE PLEASER

9. What are you anxious about in your marriage relationship? Do you find yourself trying to avoid rejection or keep your spouse close to you so that you feel better about yourself? What could be the roots of that behavior?

10. What do you feel when your spouse expresses the need for some time or space apart from you? Do you worry that, if you gave your spouse that space, he or she might never come back? What do you feel inside when you contemplate this? Again, what could be at the root of that concern?

11. When, if ever, have you felt sad that people moved away from you (either emotionally or physically)? Do you remember a similar feeling from your childhood years?

12. In an earlier question, we asked your spouse to learn to get sad rather than mad. Tell your spouse you are willing to learn to comfort him or her as well as be comforted when you are sad or scared. Does the idea of approaching your spouse in this way frighten you? Explain.

FOR THE AVOIDER

13. How would the core pattern (the repetitive conflict that you experience) in your marriage change if you worked on changing your love style? Be specific.

FOR THE PLEASER

14. How would the core pattern in your marriage change if you worked on changing your love style?

FOR BOTH OF YOU

15. Review the workbook discussion of your particular love style. Choose one growth goal to work on, and tell your spouse what it is. Write a prayer asking God to help you reach your goal.

16. If you're working with a group, share your growth goal with the members, and ask them to pray for you and hold you accountable.

Chapter 14

Other Challenging Combinations

THE AVOIDER-AVOIDER COMBINATION

As we said in the book, "Pleasant talk and shared interests cause two avoiders to enjoy spending time together. Since both individuals are independent and self-sufficient, they may be satisfied with less contact than most dating couples find satisfactory. Long-distance relationships are also more acceptable to this combination, and usually the level of emotional connection between this pair is somewhat superficial because it is familiar and comfortable. Also, since neither partner is comfortable with emotional displays, this relationship is often even-keeled; the couple experiences few ups and downs. Not surprisingly, feelings are rarely the topic of conversations, but intellectual discussions about subjects of mutual interest may be quiet deep. If both people are introverts, each will value and maintain space, solitude, and privacy."

The following questions are for both of you.

1. What traits initially attracted you to your spouse?
2. Which of your spouse's traits have been the hardest for you to accept or live with?
3. Does either of you feel as if the two of you are just roommates, friends, or acquaintances? If so, do you feel a sense of loss about this? Explain why or why not.
4. When, if ever, do you feel lonely in the relationship?
5. Do you find it hard to communicate your loneliness to your spouse? Explain your feelings.
6. When you are angry, what kind of behavior and words do you direct at your spouse? Are you verbal and clear about your anger, quietly resentful, or gruff and abrupt with your mate? Why do you think that's your way of being angry?

7. Now consider the possibility that your spouse is getting some of the anger that someone in your past deserves. Who might that someone be, and what could have prompted your anger?

8. Every time you are mad, stop and ask yourself, What is the hurt under this anger? Once you figure it out, communicate that sad, hurt feeling to your spouse rather than the anger.

9. How would your relationship change if each of you worked at changing your love style?

10. Review the workbook discussion of your particular love style. Choose one growth goal

   to work on, and tell your spouse what it is. Write a prayer asking God to help you reach your goal.

11. If you're working in a group, share your growth goal with the members, and ask them to pray for you and hold you accountable.

THE VACILLATOR-VACILLATOR, CONTROLLER-VACILLATOR, OR CONTROLLER-CONTROLLER COMBINATIONS

From the book: "In all three of these combinations, two people who both need control are marrying each other. The resulting core patterns are similar, so we will talk about all three combinations together. When a couple like this meets, there is often an immediate strong and passionate connection. The chemistry seems to be just right, and the intense good feelings are a welcome relief from the pain of the past. The relationship is all good as long as the idealization phase lasts. Then it goes downhill with the same intensity."

12. What traits initially attracted you to your spouse?

13. Which of your spouse's traits have been the hardest for you to accept or live with?

14. Both of these love styles have tendencies to anger. If you are a vacillator or a controller, what kind of behavior and words do you direct at your spouse when you are angry? Ephesians 4:26 says, "In your anger do not sin" (NIV). In what ways, if any, do you sin when you are angry?

15. Now consider the possibility that your spouse is getting some of the anger that someone in your past deserves. Who might that someone be, and what could have prompted your anger?

16. Every time you are mad, stop and ask yourself, What is the hurt under this anger? Once you figure it out, communicate that sad, hurt feeling to your spouse rather than the anger.

17. Think about your spouse's childhood history. In what specific ways was he or she disappointed by relationships in the past? Do you think your spouse could be feeling the same way as he or she relates to you? What impact could this insight have on your relationship?

18. Take turns, with open minds, to ask your spouse what he or she feels when around you?

19. How would your marriage change if each of you worked on changing your love style?

20. Review the workbook discussion of your particular love style. Choose one growth goal
to work on, and tell your spouse what it is. Write a prayer asking God to help you reach your goal.

21. If you're working with a group, share your growth goal with the members, and ask them to pray for you and hold you accountable.

Chapter 15

The Comfort Circle

While we can't control the way we were raised, we can control how we choose to live the rest of our lives. The key to having healthier relationships, and therefore a happier life, is escaping the gravitational field of our negative imprints of intimacy. Thankfully, that's what God's life-transforming power is all about. He is in the business of making us new creations and forming in us new relational imprints—if we let Him.

Extra Help in Breaking Your Core Pattern

1. Sometimes childhood roles can contribute to the core pattern of a marriage. In chapter 3 of the workbook, you identified roles you may have played in your childhood home. Which of these roles, if any, do you play in your marriage? In what ways have they influenced your core pattern?

   As we are growing up, we all adopt certain defenses to protect ourselves against conflict and relational pain. These defenses can be found listed in any basic psychology book and are common to everyone. Review the list below and put a check mark beside those that might be your preferences.

   _____ *Regression:* "If I am angry or hurt, sometime I act in childish ways. I pout, sulk, go to my parents' house, or have temper tantrums."

   _____ *Suppression:* "I distract myself a lot so I don't have to feel or deal with what is bothering me. I can practically erase unpleasant experiences."

   _____ *Withdrawal:* "When I'm hurt or upset, I physically leave, or I just go off in my own thoughts."

   _____ *Blame:* "Other people cause most of my problems. I act and feel the way I do because of them. If they would change, everything would be fine." (This is a very common choice.)

   _____ *Rationalization:* "It's easy to tell myself the wrong things I do aren't that bad when I compare myself to what most of the people in the world do wrong." (This choice is a close second after blame.)

   _____ *Devaluation:* "When I'm upset, I focus on the negative traits of others. Those traits are always more numerous and pronounced than my own."

   _____ *Intellectualization:* "I can analyze my way out of any feeling or emotion."

   _____ *Compensation:* "I feel the need to exaggerate my good points in order to hide any deficiencies."

   _____ *Denial:* "I refuse to acknowledge pain and problems and call it having a positive attitude."

   _____ *Replacement:* "When I'm feeling a negative emotion, I express the opposite in order to hide the truth."

_____ *Distraction:* "I avoid conflict or pain by filling the day with anything and everything."

2. Which of these behaviors and attitudes are surfacing in your marriage? What happened—or might have happened—during your childhood to cause you to develop these defenses? Write out your ideas.

Defenses block pain. In contrast, acknowledging and being willing to *feel* the pain reduces the need for protective armor. Processing pain and finding comfort and relief through relationships will leave us more open and free to relate to people, including our spouses, in nondefensive ways.

3. What is one specific response or action you can implement that might help you to begin to let go of your defenses the next time you find yourself using them?

4. It is difficult to change or let go of a behavior or attitude if we don't have an alternative behavior or attitude in mind. What attitude(s) or behavior(s) might *replace* your defensive postures? For example, if you use denial as a defense, what specific steps can you take when you notice you are in denial?

5. Sometimes core patterns surface when our spouses remind us of our parent(s) and we react in the same way without realizing what we're doing. (Some of these reminders might be referred to as "triggers.") Which of your spouse's expectations, behaviors, attitudes, or tones of voice, if any, remind you of one of your parents? Are you reacting to your spouse in the same way you reacted to your parent(s) when you were a child or teen? Be specific. Is your reaction part of a repetitive pattern in your marriage? If so, consider that your reaction might be connected to past experiences and why that truth is significant for your marriage relationship.

CORE PATTERN WORKSHEET

6. What repetitive fight or pattern of fighting, if any, do you experience in your marriage relationship? Describe it.

7. What events, feelings, behaviors, actions, expectations, or tones of voice trigger the pattern?

8. What are your behaviors in this pattern? What are your feelings and thoughts as you live out this pattern?

9. When you're living out this pattern, what beliefs are you acting on about yourself? about your spouse? about God?

10. What are your most intense feelings when this pattern occurs?

11. What message, expectation, behavior, attitude, or tone of voice when you relate to your spouse is similar to what you knew with your parent(s)? Explain.

12. When you were a child, how did you react to authority figures who were negative toward you? How do you react now when your spouse does something similar?

13. In what specific way(s) did this imprint, role, defense mechanism, behavior, or attitude help or protect you as a child? Did your role, for example, help improve your mom's mood or did your defense mechanism keep you from feeling your dad's anger?

14. When this pattern occurs, how does it hinder intimacy and the expression of love in your marriage?

15. Share your insights with your spouse or group.

16. Put a check mark beside the following myths and misconceptions about marriage that you identify with. Counter each one with a true statement— and know that the truth may not be what you want to hear!

_____ "You shouldn't have to work on *true* love."

_____ "Our positive attitude/motivation/skill/compatibility will keep us going."

_____ "Christians should just claim victory over their marriage problems."

_____ "I shouldn't have to change; my mate should love me just the way I am."

_____ "I keep trying to get my spouse to change, but he or she won't budge!"

_____ "I'd be happier with another person. I just know my soul mate is out there."

_____ "If the feelings are gone, there's no hope."

_____ "If I were honest with my mate, I don't think he or she could handle it."

_____ "When God decides to change my feelings, then I will change."

_____ "My spouse should know what I need and do it!"

17. Review the following reasons relational problems develop. Discuss the ones that have had the strongest impact on your marriage.

- inadequate modeling and teaching
- hurt and pain from your family of origin
- roles or defense mechanisms you learned in childhood that protected you then but now block and hinder intimacy
- a restricted range of emotions (feelings indicate needs, so if you don't know what you feel or if you only have a narrow range of emotions, you won't know what you need)
- wrong priorities (focusing too much on children or work/career to the detriment of your marriage)
- seasons of intense stress that push character weaknesses to the forefront
- a relationship in which conflict is not resolved in a healthy way; such conflict produces resentment, bitterness, anger, and the tendency to see your spouse as the problem

All the negative coping mechanisms we've just described are ways we miss the mark before a holy God. We all fail and have shortcomings that sabotage our relationships. When we do, we find ourselves outside His will for our lives, where we face problems and consequences that often make us miserable. The Bible calls this sowing and reaping. If you are in a group, discuss your thoughts as to how you have been outside God's will and in what ways you might be reaping what you have been sowing.

18. The way of healing and bonding is to reverse all of these wayward tendencies in your relationship with God and others. Look at the comfort circle on the next page and read the steps with your spouse. Is that person willing to go around the comfort circle with you? If not, are you willing to focus on yourself and begin to change and grow as an individual? If not, why not? Also, are you willing to take the role of listener for a while in order to try to draw out your spouse's thoughts and feelings about love, life, and the hope of change?

Before moving on to the next section, review the following key concepts about comfort:

- Important relationships are *dynamic,* not *static.* They are ever-changing and must be continually maintained.
- Every time you successfully complete a circle, you'll experience greater trust and security, a blossoming love, and the elevation of your relationship to a higher plane.
- When couples cannot go around this circle, their relationship steadily declines and deteriorates.

The Comfort Circle

1. Seek Awareness
of feelings and underlying needs.

4. Resolve
needs verbally and with touch,
seeking how and when needs
may be met in the future.

2. Engage
with feelings and
acknowledge needs openly.

3. Explore
the speaker's thoughts and feelings—
listening, validating, and concluding
with, "What do you need?"

Note: Completing the circle should bring relief—an increase in trust and feelings of connectedness. If hurtful action or inaction is experienced at any point in the circle, you should begin again.

19. When you were growing up, was any member of your family able to go around this comfort circle with you? If so, who? What impact did this connection have on you? If no one comforted you, at what point on the circle did your family get stuck? What impact has this lack of experience in comfort had on your ability to communicate in your marriage?

20. If you're in a group, take turns discussing your childhood experiences and what part of the circle will be most challenging for you.

As we said at the beginning of the chapter, we cannot change the state of a fallen and sinful world or our experience in it, but with God's help we can learn new attitudes and behaviors that will create a *new imprint of intimacy* within our minds and hearts—one that more closely resembles a healthy and secure love style. By starting new practices, leaving behind lies we've believed, and realigning our attitudes, we will learn to become bonded to those people who are most important to us. It is a conscious choice, and the effort required can feel like boot camp. In fact, in some ways it feels like we are growing up all over again. Know that growing in this way can have a dramatic impact on the level of intimacy in your marriage. The potential rewards are worth the effort.

Chapter 16

Seek Awareness

Healing and reconciliation can only begin when we are willing to take responsibility for our part in the unhealthy marriage dance. Husbands and wives usually blame each other. In fact, they are often blind to their own injurious imprints. We begin walking the path of acceptance, confession, and forgiveness when we admit before God and others the ways that our harmful imprints contribute to the problems in our marriages.

The starting point is simply becoming aware of a single thought or feeling in your mind and soul. It could be something that makes you happy or sad. It could be an emotion that is distressing or perhaps quite soothing. It might be a warm thought about your spouse, or it might be just the opposite. You might be irritated because of something he or she has done. Many people feel emotions but have no words with which to define those emotions for themselves, let alone to tell someone else about what they're feeling.

Use the soul words list to help you answer the following questions:

1. What are a few of the feelings on this list that you most often feel?
2. What feelings do you think your spouse most commonly feels?
3. What do you most rarely feel?
4. What feelings do you rarely see your spouse express?
5. What feelings would be most frightening for you to express? Why?
6. What feelings do you believe your spouse would have the most difficult time expressing?
7. What feelings would be most difficult to see or hear your spouse express? Why?
8. What do you wish you could feel more often?
9. What do you wish your spouse could feel more often? Why?
10. Pick three words from the soul words list to describe your current feelings about the following, then have a feelings talk with your spouse about your answers.

    marriage
    friendships
    job
    children
    church
    finances

11. What has answering these questions taught you about yourself? What feelings on the list would you not have identified if you hadn't seen them in print? Why would using this list on a regular basis help you become more aware of your feelings?
12. Draw two circles to represent the tanks described in the book. Label one *Fuel* and the second one *Pressure*. Draw a line to indicate how full each of

your tanks is right now. Then, next to each tank, list some things that would help fill the fuel tank or empty the pressure tank. Share your answers with your spouse.

13. When was the last time you filled up your spouse's fuel tank with praise or appreciation? What would help this encouragement happen more often? Write down some ideas and start acting today.

Group Exercise

14. What feelings on the soul words list are most often expressed in your group? Which emotions are rarely expressed? Which feelings do you wish members in your group would express more freely? What would have to happen for that kind of sharing to be safe?

15. This week ask different people how they feel about something. Listen to see if you get a feeling word or facts. If you get facts, ask again for a feeling. Note your experiences.

Extra Help with Triggers

16. After reading about triggers in the book, take a moment to think about anything you might consider a trigger. Then write a prayer asking God to help you better manage those areas of reactivity. If you're having trouble identifying your triggers, ask God to help you identify them.

17. In *How We Love* we suggested that, when you notice yourself feeling intense reactions to something or someone (even if others don't notice), you take a deep breath, settle down, and ask yourself three questions: (a) When have I felt this in the past? (b) Who was I with? (c) What soul words describe this intense reaction? Walk through that process now.

18. Which of your spouse's behaviors, attitudes, reactions, or tones of voice cause strong feelings in you?

19. When have you felt these same strong feelings in the past?

20. Who were you with when you felt these same intense feelings?

21. What soul words describe this intense reaction in the present? And to whom from your past would you like to be able to tell what you were feeling? Remember, we don't suggest that you actually say these words to family members.

22. Write a paragraph about the childhood experiences that underlie your triggers. If you can't think of anything, come back to this question later.

23. Your spouse's behavior may be genuinely irritating, but explain why your old injury causes your current feelings to be more powerful. What, for instance, did you do or not do with those feelings in the past?

24. Not focusing on your mate when you are triggered is hard, but we encourage you to do so by sharing with him or her the real origin of your pain.

25. Perhaps your spouse could be more sensitive in your trigger areas. What changes in his or her behavior and attitudes would soften, if not eliminate, your triggers? Write ideas about what might help and share them with your spouse.

If you find yourself getting angry at your parents as you consider the impact of the past on the present, remember that they entered marriage and parenting with their own childhood injuries and human shortcomings. So don't express your anger to them. Instead, role play. Have your spouse or a friend sit in for the parent or relative you are upset with and talk to that person in the present tense as though you were speaking to your relative.

26. At the end of chapter 16 on awareness in *How We Love*, we shared how people with each imprint might struggle to become aware of certain feelings. Read the section on your imprint. Do you agree with what we wrote? If so, write a growth goal to help expand your range of emotions. If not, explain why.

Chapter 17

Engage

Remember how Adam and Eve fearfully hid from God after disobeying him? Our natural tendency is to do the same—to hide in fear when we are troubled. Such shame, however, causes us to hold many thoughts and feelings within. Consequently, we suffer in silence as we isolate ourselves; we stay alone in our pain. God, however, tells us to step into the light of relationship and to bring our inner thoughts and feelings into community.

Many of us were not welcomed into relationships when our feelings were not positive. So we learned to be quiet. Now that we're adults, we either hold everything in, or we dump our feelings onto others in hurtful, blaming ways. But God calls all of us to lay aside our fears and shame and to engage with other people. This can be very hard to do, especially if we never had opportunities to do so or positive experiences when we were growing up.

So engagement can feel frightening, yet the goal is to bring the newly discovered feelings, thoughts, and reactions out from the hidden recesses of our souls and into the open light of relationship. God wants to engage with us and help us grow. He is in the business of mending our wounds and giving us a new song in our mouths (see Psalm 40:3). Marriage is one of the primary places where He shines His light on our childish ways in order to help us grow.

1. What were your feelings and responses as you read about Kay's response to her miscarriage in chapter 17 of *How We Love*?

2. What was your reaction to the poem "The Wall" on pages 231–32 in *How We Love*? In what details did you see yourself and/or your marriage?

3. Are you a better giver or a better receiver? Why do you think you're that way?

4. Are you a giver in your marriage? Rate yourself on a scale from 1 to 10. Write about a recent time when you noticed the needs of your spouse and worked on meeting them (engaging) without being asked.

5. When, if at all, did you recently notice a need but chose to ignore it in hope it would go away? Why do you think you responded that way?

6. Are you willing to sacrifice in order to meet your spouse's needs if it takes more time and effort than you expected? Or do you just give up when meeting a need gets too hard? Explain what might be the root of that behavior.

7. If your mate is unresponsive and unappreciative when you give to him or her, do you keep trying anyway? Why or why not?

8. Make it your goal to give to your spouse in one specific way this week. Note his or her reaction.

9. On a scale of 1 to 10, rate yourself as a receiver. Why do you think it is hard or easy for you to receive?

10. Are you open to having your spouse help you recognize your shortcomings? Will you allow him or her to expose an area of need? Why or why not?

11. Do you need your spouse only in superficial ways (tasks and duties), or do you reveal to him or her your deeper soul needs? Give evidence supporting your answer and explain why you share the needs you do.

12. When someone gives you a compliment, can you accept it? Why or why not?

13. Can you accept compliments, praise, or appreciation from your spouse if he or she also has a valid criticism in another area, or does the criticism cancel out the compliment? What do you think that is all about?

14. Will you admit your frailties to your spouse and confess to him or her that you need to be loved in your most unlovely places? Confessing our weaknesses and shortcomings makes room for our spouses to offer us the love we need.

15. When your spouse tries wholeheartedly to open his or her arms and heart to you, do you accept that love, or do you act based on your resentment for past mistakes and keep your mate at a distance? Explain your behavior as best you can.

16. Do you feel that your spouse is an enemy? If so, why? And if so, are you willing to draw up a truce? Tell them about it and ask them to start over with you. Write the results of your efforts.

17. Describe the most recent time you apologized or confessed your sin to your mate.

18. When you were growing up, how did your family handle apologies, mistakes, and hurtful behavior? In what specific ways has that childhood experience influenced you?

19. For what attitude or behavior do you need to apologize to someone? What's keeping you from doing so? Ask your spouse or a friend to support you by praying and holding you accountable. Then go apologize.

20. Evaluate the level of honesty in your marriage. Is it satisfactory? Why or why not? What steps would improve the level of honesty?

21. What do you fear about telling the truth? What do you think your spouse's reaction to the truth would be?

22. Some common secrets that spouses keep from each other are sexual struggles within the marriage or outside the marriage, matters of finances and spending, relationships outside the marriage that put the marriage at risk, addictions, and sharing with others things one mate has told the other in confidence. Are you keeping secrets from your spouse? What negative impact could that be having on your relationship? Consider the implications of having those secrets revealed. Would confessing or getting caught be better for your marriage? Perhaps you need to share your responses with someone like your pastor or a close friend before you share them with your spouse.

TIPS FOR ENGAGING WITH OTHER LOVE STYLES

Pleasers: Pleasers fear rejection. When you engage with pleasers, reassure them that your complaints don't mean you don't love them. Encourage them to be truthful with you. Tell them that even if you are hurt or angry, your marriage can and will survive. Also ask pleasers to speak directly about what is bothering them.

Avoiders: Don't take their distancing personally. They are just doing what they learned to do. Be patient with their efforts to put their feelings into words because this is a new experience for them. Ask them questions, and then be quiet and give them time to think. If you get only facts, ask them to use a feeling word so you can better understand their experiences. If avoiders engage with you and ask you to meet a need, realize what a huge step that was and appreciate their efforts.

Vacillators: Instead of avoiding engagement with vacillators, sit them down and tell them some things you love and appreciate about them. Touch them as you are sharing. Explain that the purpose of this engagement is for you to express your thoughts and feelings with them. If they bring up problems, promise to listen at another time—and be sure to keep your promise.

23. As long as we hide, nothing in us or our relationship can change. Write some topics you would like to tell the truth about. Why are you hiding each item you listed? What might be the long-term consequences of not telling the truth?

24. Are you taking charge of your own change and growth, or do you think your mate should just accept you as you are? Have you seen a weakness in your life but done nothing about it? What effect do you think that has on your spouse? Spend some time in prayer asking God to soften your heart so you will engage more fully with your mate and in your journey of growth. (You do want your marriage to improve, don't you?)

25. Think about the safety pyramid. Is anyone (ideally your spouse) at the top of your pyramid? Why or why not? If your spouse is not at the point of your pyramid, what would have to change for him or her to be a safe person for you?

continued

Controllers: Take a deep breath and approach controllers directly yet calmly. Remember that when threatened or intimidated, controllers feel the need to control. They do not have well-developed coping mechanisms, so stick with one topic, keep the number of words to a minimum, and give them time to formulate a response. Smile, touch, and reassure controllers that you will be patient with them if they engage in ways that also make you feel safe. If they start to become volatile, tell them you are taking a brief time-out while they think. Come back in a few minutes to finish.

Victims: Victims are scared when anyone approaches them in a direct manner. As you engage with them, smile and reassure them that you want to connect with them in a positive way. Use a calm, quiet voice and speak slowly and deliberately. If you can, sit in a position lower than they are (like on the floor if they are on a sofa). Don't stare at them; instead, avert your gaze and look at them directly only occasionally and for short periods. Tell them they can have all the time they need to formulate their responses. Keep the entire engagement short at first, because it will be uncomfortable for them.

26. Plan a fun date (follow the suggestions on page 12 of this book) and write about how it went.

27. Do you make an effort to learn from your spouse? Write about the last time your spouse's ideas changed your point of view. What strengths does your spouse have that complement yours?

28. At the end of chapter 17 on engagement in *How We Love,* we discussed how people with each imprint might struggle to engage. Read the section about your imprint. Do you agree with what we wrote? If so, write a growth goal for yourself about how you could be a better engager. If you see your struggle as different from what we describe, describe your experience. What could your spouse do that would help you engage more readily?

GROUP EXERCISE

Discuss the qualities you look for in people that make you willing to dialoging openly with them. Share with the group your own strengths and weaknesses in engaging with others, as well as one attitude or behavior you would like to improve in this area.

Chapter 18

Explore

God's desire is that we be "quick to hear, slow to speak and slow to anger" (James 1:19). Healing and growth can begin when we are willing to listen and learn the art of extended listening. This chapter will help you learn to listen attentively instead of reacting defensively.

God calls us to "speak truth each one of you with his neighbor, for we are members of one another" (Ephesians 4:25). When we obey this verse, we bring out into the open the inner truths we have become aware of. We risk bringing our thoughts and feelings into relationship. When we openly acknowledge our feelings—when we bring that truth into the light—healing begins. The festering, old

THE SPEAKER

Goal: to explore a topic in a way that minimizes defensiveness in the listener. We need to speak truth in an edifying way (see Ephesians 4:25–32).

Getting Started
- Clearly state your desire to talk about one specific topic (for example, "I need to talk to you about the monthly finances"). Don't hint ("Maybe we could spend some time together") and don't drop bombs ("Well, the bank is going to repossess the house this month").
- Check the listener's readiness to listen ("When would be a good time for you to discuss this?") and agree upon a time.

Tips
- Introduce the issue you'd like to discuss by talking about yourself, your experiences, and your feelings.
- Use *I* statements rather than *you* statements. "I am feeling sad that I didn't get to spend any time with you" will be more easily heard than "You are always busy and never have time for me." If you need to share something negative about the listener, start and end with a positive affirmation about him or her.
- If the listener is causing you to feel unsafe, share what is making you feel unsafe: "I am feeling unsafe because your tone of voice sounds disinterested and defensive."
- If you have a concern about how the talk might go, share that concern at the beginning: "I have something to share that is difficult for me. Please try to hear me out."
- Use soul words to explain your experience.
- Be honest. Pretending or minimizing is dishonest. Speak the truth in the most loving way you can.
- Be vulnerable. Try not to avoid pain or embarrassment that may be a part of sharing deep feelings.

If you get angry, take a time-out, but don't use it as a way to escape or avoid. Statements like this work well: "I'm getting so angry that I need to call a time-out so I can cool down. We'll continue this talk in ten minutes." Do not blame, accuse, or call the listener names.

thoughts and feelings that contaminate our souls are flushed out, allowing fresh new thoughts and feelings to occur.

Sadly, too many of us have souls that are like the Dead Sea: it has no natural outlet and cannot sustain life. When water can flow, a lake stays fresh and can sustain life. Our souls also need an outflow if we are to know life and vitality. Opening up our hearts and sharing our thoughts will start that much-needed cleansing flow.

THE LISTENER

Goal: to gain the speaker's perspective on a situation by asking questions about feelings, thoughts, and experiences (see James 1:19–20).

Getting Started
- Listen calmly. Don't defend yourself, argue, explain, or try to problem solve. You don't have to agree with what you are hearing in order to learn.
- Focus on the speaker's experience, *not* yours.

Tips
- Control defensiveness. Do not react. Pay attention to your nonverbal responses. Remember that when your defenses go up, the quality of your listening goes down. Know that you can listen with an open mind even if you disagree with what you're hearing. The speaker is a separate person with his or her own feelings, thoughts, personality, and family history. Your spouse's perspective is different from yours.
- Don't roll your eyes, sigh, groan, or respond in other ways that stop communication.
- Maintain eye contact and encourage the speaker to continue.

The Four Keys of Listening
1. Ask the speaker to stop periodically so you can summarize what you're hearing.

1. The Bible has so much to say about how we communicate. Look up the following verses and note what they say about your prayer and thought life as well as how you talk with others.

   Psalm 51:6

   Psalm 139:23–24

   Proverbs 16:23

   Proverbs 17:27

continued

2. Repeat in your own words what you heard, and check for accuracy.
3. Ask questions that will increase your understanding.
4. Respond with empathy: "I see what you are saying" or "I can see how you might feel that way."

Listening Questions

- Don't ask why. This is often accusatory and difficult to answer.
- "Tell me more. I want to understand." (Say this whenever you are stuck.)
- "How does that make you feel?" or "How long have you been feeling this way?"
- "Do you feel anything in addition to what you just shared?"
- "Are there other times you have felt this way? When was that?"
- "What are your hopes? your expectations? your desires?"
- "On a scale of 1 to 10, how strong is your feeling?"
- "I can tell you are really upset. Do you think something triggered these intense emotions?"
- "If you could share what you're feeling right now with someone in the present or the past, who would it be? What would you say to that person?"
- "Does what you're currently feeling remind you of an old or familiar feeling that you felt when you were growing up?"
- "What does you body feel like right now?"
- "What do you need?" (Use this as your closing question.)

Proverbs 18:2

Proverbs 19:19–20

Proverbs 20:5

Nehemiah 5:6–7

Ephesians 4:25–27

James 1:19–20

James 3:1–18

2. Pages 135–37 are summary sheets for the roles of speaker and listener. Make a copy of each and a copy of the soul words list too. Use these when you have a conversation with your spouse. They will help you stay on track.

Conversations about problems between you and your spouse are among the most challenging ones you'll face. So as you get used to the listener and speaker roles, pick a topic that does not involve negative feelings about your spouse. Childhood memories (good or bad) are a good choice, because your spouse will learn more about you as, together, you work your way around the circle. *The only way to learn this skill is to try it.* If the pace is slow, you are on the right track. There will be pauses as the listener thinks of good questions and as the speaker reflects on his or her thoughts and feelings. Choose one of the "Conversation Starters" on page 258 of *How We Love.*

3. If anger makes it difficult to communicate with your spouse, practice saying a time-out statement to each other when you are *not* having an argument. Note what happens the first time you actually use a time-out statement.

4. Is your spouse an introvert or are there introverts in your family? Ask introverts you know if they tend to feel interrupted and talked over in their conversations with people. When talking with introverts, make an effort to ask a question and wait for an answer, no matter how long it takes for them to answer.

5. Here is a fun exercise to help you and your spouse learn to validate each other even when you disagree. Sit with your spouse and take turns making statements that you know he or she will disagree with. The listener will practice validating the speaker's point of view even though they disagree. For example:

- "I can understand how you could feel that way."
- "From your perspective, your feelings make sense."
- "I would probably feel the same way if I were in your shoes."
- "It makes sense to me that you would feel…"

Sometimes people get flustered when their mates are emotional during conversations. A good way to react when your spouse shows emotions is simply to say what you see: "I can see you are really hurt" or "I can see how upset this makes you." Comments like this let your mate know you are aware of his emotions and in tune with his feelings.

Also, try to maintain gentle physical contact (like a touch on the knee) with the speaker during the conversation. This is especially important if the person is obviously distraught (such as crying). However, if the speaker is really angry (especially if angry at you), she may not want to be touched, so give her some space. If softening and tears begin to occur, ask her if you may touch her or hold her hand.

6. At the end of chapter 18, we discussed how people with each imprint might struggle to be listeners and speakers. Read the section about your imprint. Do you agree with what we wrote? Whether you agree or disagree, what do you find most challenging about being a listener? a speaker? Write down your growth goals.

GROUP EXERCISE

7. Have a volunteer couple go around the comfort circle while the rest of the group watches and offers feedback. This exercise can be a bit intimidating for all involved, but it is one of the best ways to grow in your listening skills.

Chapter 19

Resolve

The question "What do you need?" can elicit a wide variety of responses. Different people need different things to help them feel better, and the last point in the comfort circle is to identify your spouse's best choice.

After compassionate and extended listening, you are ready to ask, "What do you need?" Doing so takes the guesswork and stress out of trying to come up with something on your own. It eliminates having to read your spouse's mind (an impossible task), and it requires your spouse to define his or her own needs. When it's clearly communicated, your spouse's answer gives you a very high chance of successfully meeting that need.

1. In the book I (Milan) talked about an experience where I processed some feelings alone on an airplane and felt relief. What are some ways you find relief alone?

2. What unhealthy ways of making negative feelings go away do you have, if any?

3. Do you tend to problem solve before listening? Does your spouse? What is the other person's reaction to that attempt to help? What would each speaker find more helpful than problem solving? If you don't know, ask!

4. Below are some important ways that a couple can experience resolution with each other. As you read each one, evaluate yourself and your spouse according to the three assessments listed first.

   (a) *I often say this. / My spouse often says this.*

   (b) *I rarely say this. / My spouse rarely says this.*

   (c) *I should say this more often. / My spouse should say this more often.*

   Ownership: "I admit and own the problem, infraction, or mistake."

   Forgiveness: "I offer a well-thought-out request for forgiveness and a genuine apology."

   Expression of needs: "You know, I don't think I need anything right now. I just feel better having gotten that off my chest."

Reassurance: "I need to hear from you that things will be okay, that you will work on this, that you still really love me."

Agree to disagree: "While we still don't agree on this, I do feel like we understand each other's perspective."

Negotiation: "I need for us to find some middle ground or some kind of compromise."

Analysis and problem solving: "Would you help me figure out how to solve this recurring problem or fix this situation?"

Comfort and nurture: "Would you please hold me and comfort me?"

5. Are you able to apologize when you are wrong? If owning your mistakes and apologizing are hard for you, what impact on your marriage would developing these skills have?

6. Do you hold grudges and let resentments fester? Read Galatians 5:15, Ephesians 4:31–32, and Hebrews 12:14–15. What is the message for you?

7. When has God brought you comfort in a way you did not expect? Share an example or two.

8. Rate your ability to comfort your spouse. Describe a time when you feel as if you did well and a time when you could have done better.

9. Now rate your marriage in the area of nonsexual touch. What change, if any, would you like to see in this aspect of your relationship? Explain.

10. Remember Zach and Emily from chapter 19 of *How We Love*? What was your reaction to their story? Do you and your spouse have a hard time in the area of sexual desire differences? What did you think about Zach and Emily's compromise?

11. Comforter/Giver: Your goal as the comforter is to acknowledge and pursue your spouse when he or she is hurting, offer to be present both emotionally and physically, and validate the reality of his or her inner experiences through caring touch and support. How do you feel about offering to hold your spouse when he or she is hurting? What internal hesitation, if any, do you feel? What's that reluctance about, and what can you do to counter it?

12. Receiver: To receive comfort, you must first acknowledge and identify your feelings of pain. Then you must choose to be vulnerable and share this with

your spouse, asking him or her to hold and comfort you. How do you feel about asking your spouse to hold you when you are hurting? How do you feel about offering to hold your spouse when he or she is hurting? What internal hesitation, if any, do you feel? What's that reluctance about, and what can you do to counter it?

13. Which of the following common obstacles to giving and receiving comfort do you struggle with, if any? What can you do to remove those obstacles from your mind and/or heart?

- wanting and trying to fix the situation, problem solve, or troubleshoot
- impatience and an unwillingness to stop whatever you're doing to engage with another's emotions
- aversion to emotions; fear of feelings and tears
- you have never experienced comfort

14. In light of your answers to questions 11, 12, and 13, are you willing to try a holding time with your mate (see pages 272–78 of *How We Love*)? Why or why not? If you're up for it, first try holding time without talking. Hold your spouse for five minutes or so. Before you switch places, describe your experience as the giver or receiver of comforting touch. Then switch places and be sure to debrief afterward. (If you're new to this, it may help to write out your initial feelings rather than speaking them aloud.)

Remember the comfort question: can you recall being comforted as a child or adolescent after a time of emotional distress? If your answer was no, which is the answer most people give, then you never experienced the emotional connection that God intends for you. *Now is your chance* to learn comfort as the giver and receiver.

As you grow more comfortable with holding your spouse and being held by him or her, you can try to be available like that for each other when one of you is hurting. Learning to be with people in their pain and comforting them when they are upset brings about new, wonderful levels of bonding and connection. Life always has its stresses, and we need to learn how to comfort each other when we face difficulties.

15. What impact would your ability to comfort each other have on your sexual relationship? Which activity makes you feel most vulnerable: having sex, receiving comfort, or giving comfort? Did your answer surprise you? What do you think it means?

GROUP EXERCISE

16. Discuss your feelings about holding time. When you do, you'll learn that you aren't the only one who feels awkward trying something new.

Chapter 20

Seeing into Your Spouse's Soul

Discuss the following questions with your spouse and/or group as a way to help you solidify the growth you've experienced through the use of these books.

1. What idea, suggestion, or exercise in this book has been most helpful to you?
2. What have you found most challenging about reading the book and doing this workbook?
3. What is the most important thing you have learned about yourself in this process?
4. What is the most important thing you have learned about your spouse?
5. What were your thoughts and feelings about how you have learned to love each other in your worst places?
6. In what worst place of your character or past do you most need your spouse to love and accept you?
7. Every small step of growth changes how you love. How are you loving your spouse differently after reading this book? Be specific.

Changing How We Love

It has been nineteen short years since God brought into our lives the people who would help us uncover the roots of our marital struggles. We believe they were an answer to our prayer, one that has been spoken in our home more than any other. It consists of four simple words: "Lord, give us wisdom" (see James 1:5). It's a handy little prayer that fits into every day, because wisdom is needed for big and small things alike. One of our favorite passages is Philippians 1:9–10, which asks for a specific kind of wisdom:

> So this is my prayer: that your love will flourish and that you will not only love much but well. Learn to love appropriately. You need to use your head and test your feelings so that your love is sincere and intelligent, not senti-mental gush. Live a lover's life, circumspect and exemplary, a life Jesus will be proud of: bountiful in fruits from the soul, making Jesus Christ attrac-tive to all, getting everyone involved in the glory and praise of God. (MSG)

The writer of this passage isn't talking about trying harder to love. It's a request for a *greater capacity* to give and receive love based on deeper insight. Since mak-ing this our prayer, God has shown us more ways to better love each other than we ever expected.

We pray that *How We Love* and this workbook have been a guide to you and introduced you to a new dance of a deeper, richer relationship. Practicing these new steps that God designed will truly change how you love.

See www.HowWeLove.com to sign up for the free How We Love newsletter, free resources, a schedule of How We Love seminars, and much more.

Notes

Chapter 1

1. The imprint concept was originated by Bowlby and Lorenz as cited by Stephen J. Suomi, "Attachment in Rhesus Monkeys," in *Handbook of Attachment: Theory, Research, and Clinical Applications,* ed. Jude Cassidy and Phillip R. Shaver (New York: Guilford, 1999), 185.

2. See Robert Karen, *Becoming Attached: Unfolding the Mystery of the Infant-Mother Bond and Its Impact on Later Life* (New York, Warner, 1994) for an excellent summary, description, and history of attachment theory.

3. Walter Bauer and Frederick William Danker, *A Greek-English Lexicon of the New Testament and Other Early Christian Literature* (Chicago: University of Chicago Press, 1974), 901–902.

Chapter 2

1. Daniel J. Siegel, *The Developing Mind: How Relationships and the Brain Interact to Shape Who We Are* (New York: Guilford, 1999), 116.

2. T. Berry Brazelton and Bertrand G. Cramer, *The Earliest Relationship: Parents, Infants, and the Drama of Early Attachment* (New York: Addison-Wesley, 1990), 61–62.

3. Robert Karen, *Becoming Attached: Unfolding the Mystery of the Infant-Mother Bond and Its Impact on Later Life* (New York: Warner, 1994), 375.

4. Karen, *Becoming Attached,* 400–401.

5. For a chart describing and contrasting love styles, see John Byng-Hall, "Family and Couple Therapy: Toward Greater Security," in *Handbook of Attachment: Theory, Research, and Clinical Applications,* ed. Jude Cassidy and Phillip R. Shaver (New York: Guilford, 1999), 630.

6. A secure attachment base from childhood allows the adult to make healthier mate selection. See Karen, *Becoming Attached,* 383–84.

7. *Encarta World English Dictionary,* North American Edition, 2005, Microsoft Corporation. Developed for Microsoft by Bloomsbury Publishing Plc.

Chapter 3

1. Daniel J. Siegel. *The Developing Mind: How Relationships and the Brain Interact to Shape Who We Are* (New York: Guilford, 1999), 34, 42.

2. Siegel, *The Developing Mind,* 32.

3. Siegel, *The Developing Mind,* 29.

4. Siegel, *The Developing Mind,* 34.

Chapter 4

1. Regarding the parenting style of the secure child, "A secure family base allows family members to engage in conflicts, safe in the knowledge that care will not be threatened. As resolving conflict is a necessary aspect of authority, a secure family base supports functional authority systems. In turn, functional authority facilitates caregiving, especially when parents are setting limits (e.g., sending children to bed). Conversely, insecure family bases help to disrupt authority, and dysfunctional authority disrupts security." See John Byng-Hall, "Family and Couple Therapy: Toward Greater Security," in *Handbook of Attachment: Theory, Research, and Clinical Applications,* ed. Jude Cassidy and Phillip R. Shaver (New York: Guilford, 1999), 637.

2. The term *avoider* comes from the original attachment term *avoidant,* coined by Bowlby and Ainsworth. For further characteristics and descriptions, see Robert Karen, *Becoming Attached: Unfolding the Mystery of the Infant-Mother Bond and Its Impact on Later Life* (New York: Warner, 1994), 367–68, 388, 443; and Judith A. Feeney, "Adult Romantic Attachment and Couple Relationships," 364, and Byng-Hall, "Family and Couple Therapy," 628–29, in Cassidy and Shaver, *Handbook of Attachment.*

3. The term *pleaser* comes from an insecure attachment type that clearly shows tendencies toward pleasing and pursuing, tendencies that are born of fear-based insecurities. This fear-based type is noted in John Bowlby, *Attachment and Loss, Volume III: Loss: Sadness and Depression* (New York: Harper Collins, 1980), 202, 206; and Feeney, "Adult Romantic Attachment," 361–62, and Byng-Hall, "Family and Couple Therapy," 629, in Cassidy and Shaver, *Handbook of Attachment.*

4. The term *vacillator* refers to the classic ambivalent style and was so named by Bowlby and Ainsworth. See Karen, *Becoming Attached,* 368–69, 388, 443; and Feeney, "Adult Romantic Attachment," 364, and Byng-Hall, "Family and Couple Therapy," 628, in Cassidy and Shaver, *Handbook of Attachment.*

5. The term *controller* refers to the chaotic-disorganized-disoriented attachment style (Main and Hesse, 1990). See Roger Kobak, "The Emotional Dynamics of Disruptions in Attachment Relationships: Implications for Theory, Research, and Clinical Intervention," 34–35, and Karlen Lyons-Ruth and Deborah Jacobvitz, "Attachment Disorganization: Unresolved Loss, Relational Violence, and Lapses in Behavioral and Attentional Strategies," 532–33, in Cassidy and Shaver, *Handbook of Attachment.*

6. The term *victim* also arises from the chaotic-disorganized-disoriented attachment style. See Lyons-Ruth and Jacobvitz, "Attachment Disorganization," 543–46, 550; and Carol George and Judith Solomon, "Attachment and Caregiving: The Caregiving Behavioral System," in Cassidy and Shaver, *Handbook of Attachment,* 662–63.

Chapter 5

1. Robert Karen includes a helpful chart on parental influences contributing to this imprint in a child, in *Becoming Attached: Unfolding the Mystery of the Infant-Mother Bond and Its Impact on Later Life* (New York: Warner, 1994), 442.

2. Brian E. Vaughn and Kelly K. Bost cite a study by Kemp (1987) in which "avoidant cases were described by their mothers as temperamentally 'easier' than were cases classified otherwise," in "Attachment and Temperament: Redundant, Independent, or Interacting Influences on Interpersonal Adaptation and Personality Development?" in *Handbook of Attachment: Theory, Research, and Clinical Applications,* ed. Jude Cassidy and Phillip R. Shaver (New York: Guilford, 1999), 208.

3. Robert Karen concluded that avoidant children are the least likely to behave dependently upon others when they are injured or disappointed because they expect to be rejected when distressed. See *Becoming Attached,* 191.

4. Judith A. Feeney cites Hazan, Zeifman, and Middleton (1994) regarding avoidant individuals whom they found to be most likely to report involvement in "(one-night stands, extrarelationship sex, sex without love), as well as less enjoyment of physical contact," in "Adult Romantic Attachment and Couple Relationships," *Handbook of Attachment,* 371.

5. Robert Karen notes, "If someone grew up in a home where attachment needs were played down and considered babyish, feelings of grief are likely to be stifled and not worked through," in *Becoming Attached*, 385.

Chapter 6

1. Quoting Kunce and Shaver (1994), Judith A. Feeney notes, "Consistent with their need for the approval of others, preoccupied and fearful subjects reported high compulsive caregiving but low sensitivity," in "Adult Romantic Attachment and Couple Relationships," in *Handbook of Attachment: Theory, Research, and Clinical Applications*, ed. Jude Cassidy and Phillip R. Shaver (New York: Guilford, 1999), 370.

2. Jay Belsky, quoting Cassidy and Berlin (1994), notes, "Several investigations suggest that preoccupied mothers 'behave in ways that interfere with their child's autonomy or exploration,'" in "Modern Evolutionary Theory and Patterns of Attachment," in Cassidy and Shaver, *Handbook of Attachment*, 156.

3. Jude Cassidy, citing the studies of Easterbrooks and Goldberg, 1987; Howes et al., 1988; Main et al., 1985; Main and Weston, 1981, states the following: "These same studies indicate, however, that the most well-functioning individuals have two secure relationships, while the least competent children have none," in "The Nature of the Child's Ties," in Cassidy and Shaver, *Handbook of Attachment*, 16.

4. Regarding parenting styles that produce the pleaser imprint, John Byng-Hall speaks of the insecure ambivalent mother who draws the child into close proximity to meet her own needs with the resulting enmeshment creating a child who fails to go to school, will not go out to play, and is clingy. Byng-Hall also refers to the child who, in the family systems dynamic, plays the role of the conciliator (pleaser) between the tumultuous parental dyad, which, in his case study, was an avoidant father and an ambivalent (vacillator) mother. See "Family and Couple Therapy: Toward Greater Security," in Cassidy and Shaver, *Handbook of Attachment*, 631–32, 636.

5. Robert Karen notes, "Others, who display what appears to be an ambivalent or preoccupied attachment style, are hypervigilant about separations, likely to become anxious or even panicky when left, and to become overwhelmed by feelings of clinginess and impotent rage. They do not readily venture forth or take chances, for they do not believe their attachment needs will ever be met." See *Becoming Attached: Unfolding the Mystery of the*

Infant-Mother Bond and Its Impact on Later Life (New York: Warner, 1994), 386.

6. Referring to the work of Bartholomew and Horowitz (1991), Feeney comments, "The interpersonal problems of fearful individuals involve social insecurity and lack of assertiveness," in "Adult Romantic Attachment," in Cassidy and Shaver, *Handbook of Attachment*, 362.

Chapter 7

1. John Byng-Hall states, "Because the parent is only intermittently emotionally available, the child demands to be noticed." He also notes, in chart form, that the parent is: "Intermittently available" with the result that the child is: "Demanding and/or angry; attachment behavior overactivated." See "Family and Couple Therapy: Toward Greater Security," in *Handbook of Attachment: Theory, Research, and Clinical Applications,* ed. Jude Cassidy and Phillip R. Shaver (New York: Guilford, 1999), 628, 630.

2. Daniel Siegel notes two aspects of the parental style which contribute to an ambivalent child: "the state of the child is intruded upon by that of the parent" and the "parent rigidly defines the nature of the interaction," in *The Developing Mind: How Relationships and the Brain Interact to Shape Who We Are* (New York: Guilford, 1999), 293.

3. T. Berry Brazelton describes mothers who attempt to "repair" or compensate for their own "missed opportunities" in childhood by trying to create the ideal connection with their own children that they never had. See Brazelton and Bertrand G. Cramer, *The Earliest Relationship: Parents, Infants, and the Drama of Early Attachment* (New York: Addison-Wesley, 1990), 153–54.

4. Carol Magai comments on the work of Cassidy (1994) on attachment and emotional regulation: "Ambivalent attachment, which is associated with hypervigilance, is accompanied by affect enhancement or heightening," in "Affect, Imagery, and Attachment: Working Models of Interpersonal Affect and the Socialization of Emotion," in Cassidy and Shaver, *Handbook of Attachment*, 790.

5. Judith A. Feeney notes, in chart form, that ambivalents believe that "people have little control over their own lives," in "Adult Romantic Attachment and Couple Relationships," in Cassidy and Shaver, *Handbook of Attachment*, 364.

6. Feeney again observes that "ambivalent individuals are expected to show heightened awareness and expression of negative feelings, learned as a way of maintaining contact

with inconsistent caregivers," in "Adult Romantic Attachment," in Cassidy and Shaver, *Handbook of Attachment,* 358.

7. Feeney continues: "Ambivalent subjects, in contrast, preferred unqualified closeness, commitment, and affection, and tended to idealize their partners," in "Adult Romantic Attachment," in Cassidy and Shaver, *Handbook of Attachment,* 359.

8. Feeney, citing her own work and the work of others (Feeney, 1995; Feeney, Noller, and Hanrahan, 1994) says, "Preoccupied and fearful groups report greater anxiety over relationships than secure and dismissing groups," in "Adult Romantic Attachment," in Cassidy and Shaver, *Handbook of Attachment,* 362.

Chapter 8

1. Daniel Siegel notes that parents' rage produces terror within children. When that happens, parents are simultaneously the source of fear and the source of needs being met. See *The Developing Mind: How Relationships and the Brain Interact to Shape Who We Are* (New York: Guilford, 1999), 117.

2. According to Siegel, "Children with disorganized attachment tend to become controlling in their behaviors with others and may be hostile and aggressive with their peers," in *The Developing Mind,* 120.

3. Karlen Lyons-Ruth and Deborah Jacobvitz comment on the "bifurcation into punitive or caregiving stances that occurs among disorganized infants during the preschool period," in "Attachment Disorganization: Unresolved Loss, Relational Violence, and Lapses in Behavioral and Attentional Strategies," in *Handbook of Attachment: Theory, Research, and Clinical Applications,* ed. Jude Cassidy and Phillip R. Shaver (New York: Guilford, 1999), 549.

4. Siegel states regarding unresolved chaotic attachment, "This impairment reveals itself in the emotional instability, social dysfunction, poor response to stress, and cognitive disorganization and disorientation that characterize both children and adults in this attachment grouping," in *The Developing Mind,* 120.

5. Lyons-Ruth and Jacobvitz refer to Main and Solomon's (1986, 1990) descriptions of disorganized attachment and state that one of the characteristics is that of "freezing," in "Attachment Disorganization," in Cassidy and Shaver, *Handbook of Attachment,* 522.

6. Siegel comments, "Unlike the other forms of insecure attachment which are 'organized' approaches to the pattern of parental communication, this form of insecure attachment

appears to involve significant problems in the development of a coherent mind," in *The Developing Mind*, 109.

7. Lyons-Ruth and Jacobvitz note the arousal of strong feelings within the disorganized caregiver while tending an infant. See "Attachment Disorganization," in Cassidy and Shaver, *Handbook of Attachment*, 548.

8. Siegel notes that severe early emotional chaotic trauma can precipitate dissociative tendencies in which the victim's "explicit memory for traumatic experience(s) may be impaired," in *The Developing Mind*, 295.

9. Patrick J. Carnes speaks of need for high drama and adrenaline within those who are in chaotic relationships. See *The Betrayal Bond: Breaking Free of Exploitive Relationships* (Deerfield Beach, FL: Health Communications, 1997), 11, 87.

10. Siegel states that "psychiatric medications may be needed to help the brain achieve the capacity to regulate the flow of states of mind, through direct biochemical effects that alter the synaptic strengths determining the internal constrains of the system," in *The Developing Mind*, 295.

Chapter 10

1. Referencing the work of Fisher and Crandell, John Byng-Hall states, "Fisher and Crandell describe the D (avoider) and E (vacillator) pairing as producing a highly conflictual relationship in which the preoccupied partner (vacillator) is expressing most of the discontent, while the dismissing partner (avoider) sees the only problem with the relationship as the other's discontent. The preoccupied partner feels chronically deprived and abandoned, while the dismissing partner is disdainful of his or her dependency needs. As the preoccupied partner escalates the appeal to have dependency needs met, this escalates the dismissing partner's defensive response of distancing, which leads to subsequent pursuer-distancer escalations." See "Family and Couple Therapy: Toward Greater Security," in *Handbook of Attachment: Theory, Research, and Clinical Applications*, ed. Jude Cassidy and Phillip R. Shaver (New York: Guilford, 1999), 629.

2. Citing Johnson (1997), Byng-Hall states, "If one partner's cruelty is really a frantic protest against the loss of attachment, the other's withdrawal expresses the equally primordial urge to protect oneself when one's partner looks like a predator (p. 40). The approach-avoidance conflict is used to explain some of the dynamics observed." See

"Family and Couple Therapy," in Cassidy and Shaver, *Handbook of Attachment*, 637.

3. Carol Magai remarks about the common tendency for the vacillator and the avoider to seek each other out. See "Affect, Imagery, and Attachment: Working Models of Interpersonal Affect and the Socialization of Emotion," in Cassidy and Shaver, *Handbook of Attachment*, 791.

4. Magai notes that the avoider-vacillator combination is a much more common combination and that the avoider-avoider and vacillator-vacillator combinations are less common. See "Affect, Imagery, and Attachment," in Cassidy and Shaver, *Handbook of Attachment*, 791.

5. Judith A. Feeney comments that "attachment differences are stronger under conditions that seem to threaten the relationship," in "Adult Romantic Attachment and Couple Relationships," in Cassidy and Shaver, *Handbook of Attachment*, 373.

Chapter 12

1. Although this journal article is regarding children, we see the exact same pattern in an adult abusive relationship between controller and victim. Karlen Lyons-Ruth and Deborah Jacobvitz write, "Inherent in a model of unbalanced relationships is an asymmetry of power in which one partner's (attachment-related) goals or initiatives are elaborated at the expense of the other's. By definition, then, one partner is more helpless in the relationship and the other more controlling, whether the control is exerted through active aggression or through the more covert mechanisms of withdrawal, guilt induction, or self-preoccupation." See "Attachment Disorganization: Unresolved Loss, Relational Violence, and Lapses in Behavioral and Attentional Strategies," in *Handbook of Attachment: Theory, Research, and Clinical Applications*, ed. Jude Cassidy and Phillip R. Shaver (New York: Guilford, 1999), 549.

2. Lyons-Ruth and Jacobvitz provide a detailed discussion regarding the correlation of disorganized attachment patterns and violence between intimate partners. See "Attachment Disorganization," in Cassidy and Shaver, *Handbook of Attachment*, 545.

3. Lyons-Ruth and Jacobvitz note that people with disorganized attachment commonly identify with "either the aggressor or the victim position in an abusive relationship," in "Attachment Disorganization," in Cassidy and Shaver, *Handbook of Attachment*, 544.

Chapter 16

1. David Keirsey and Marilyn Bates, *Please Understand Me: Character and Temperament Types* (Del Mar, CA: Gnosology Books, 1984), 21.
2. Daniel Siegel discusses triggers as internal reactive mechanisms, in *The Developing Mind: How Relationships and the Brain Interact to Shape Who We Are* (New York: Guilford, 1999), 258–89.
3. Keirsey and Bates, *Please Understand Me,* 176–77.

Chapter 18

1. David Keirsey and Marilyn Bates, *Please Understand Me: Character and Temperament Types* (Del Mar, CA: Gnosology Books, 1984), 16.

Chapter 20

1. Mike Mason, *The Mystery of Marriage* (Sisters, OR: Multnomah, 1985), 195–96.

For Further Study: Attachment Theory

1. Robert Karen, *Becoming Attached: Unfolding the Mystery of the Infant-Mother Bond and Its Impact on Later Life* (New York, Warner, 1994), 146–64.
2. Karen, *Becoming Attached,* 216.
3. Quoted in Erik Hesse, "The Adult Attachment Interview: Historical and Current Perspectives," in *Handbook of Attachment: Theory, Research, and Clinical Applications,* ed. Jude Cassidy and Phillip R. Shaver (New York: Guilford, 1999), 421.
4. Judith A. Feeney, "Adult Romantic Attachment and Couple Relationships," in Cassidy and Shaver, *Handbook of Attachment,* 356.
5. Feeney, "Adult Romantic Attachment," in Cassidy and Shaver, *Handbook of Attachment,* 362.
6. John Byng-Hall, "Family and Couple Therapy: Toward Greater Security," in Cassidy and Shaver, *Handbook of Attachment,* 629.
7. John Bowlby, *Attachment and Loss, Volume III: Loss: Sadness and Depression* (New York: Basic, 1980), 202.

Bibliography

American Psychiatric Association. *Diagnostic and Statistical Manual of Mental Disorders*, 4th ed. Text Revision. Washington, DC: American Psychiatric Association, 2000.

Bauer, Walter, and Frederick William Danker. *A Greek-English Lexicon of the New Testament and Other Early Christian Literature.* Chicago: University of Chicago Press, 1974.

Belsky, Jay. "Modern Evolutionary Theory and Patterns of Attachment." In *Handbook of Attachment: Theory, Research, and Clinical Applications,* ed. Jude Cassidy and Phillip R. Shaver. New York: Guilford, 1999.

Bowlby, John. *Attachment and Loss, Volume I: Attachment.* New York: Basic, 1969, 1982.

———. *Attachment and Loss, Volume II: Separation: Anxiety and Anger,* New York: Basic, 1973.

———. *Attachment and Loss, Volume III: Loss: Sadness and Depression.* New York: Basic, 1980.

Brazelton, T. Berry, and Bertrand G. Cramer. *The Earliest Relationship: Parents, Infants, and the Drama of Early Attachment.* New York: Addison-Wesley, 1990.

Bretherton, Inge, and Kristine A. Munholland. "Internal Working Models in Attachment Relationships: A Construct Revisited." In Cassidy and Shaver, *Handbook of Attachment.*

Byng-Hall, John. "Family and Couple Therapy: Toward Greater Security." In Cassidy and Shaver, *Handbook of Attachment.*

Carnes, Patrick J. *The Betrayal Bond: Breaking Free of Exploitive Relationships.* Deerfield Beach, FL: Health Communications, 1997.

Cassidy, Jude. "The Nature of the Child's Ties." In Cassidy and Shaver, *Handbook of Attachment.*

Cassidy, Jude, and Phillip R. Shaver, eds. *Handbook of Attachment: Theory, Research, and Clinical Applications.* New York: Guilford, 1999.

Cloud, Henry. *Changes That Heal.* Grand Rapids, MI: Zondervan, 1990.

Encarta World English Dictionary © and (P) 2005 Microsoft Corporation. All rights reserved. Developed for Microsoft by Bloomsbury Publishing Plc.

Feeney, Judith A. "Adult Romantic Attachment and Couple Relationships." In Cassidy and Shaver, *Handbook of Attachment.*

George, Carol, and Judith Solomon. "Attachment and Caregiving: The Caregiving Behavioral System." In Cassidy and Shaver, *Handbook of Attachment*.

Hesse, Erik. "The Adult Attachment Interview: Historical and Current Perspectives." In Cassidy and Shaver, *Handbook of Attachment*.

Karen, Robert. *Becoming Attached: Unfolding the Mystery of the Infant-Mother Bond and Its Impact on Later Life*. New York: Warner, 1994.

Keirsey, David, and Marilyn Bates. *Please Understand Me: Character and Temperament Types*. Del Mar, CA: Gnosology Books, 1984.

Kobak, Roger. "The Emotional Dynamics of Disruptions in Attachment Relationships: Implications for Theory, Research, and Clinical Intervention." In Cassidy and Shaver, *Handbook of Attachment*.

Lyons-Ruth, Karlen, and Deborah Jacobvitz. "Attachment Disorganization: Unresolved Loss, Relational Violence, and Lapses in Behavioral and Attentional Strategies." In Cassidy and Shaver, *Handbook of Attachment*.

Magai, Carol, "Affect, Imagery, and Attachment: Working Models of Interpersonal Affect and the Socialization of Emotion." In Cassidy and Shaver, *Handbook of Attachment*.

Marvin, Robert S., and Preston A. Britner. "Normative Development: The Ontogeny of Attachment." In Cassidy and Shaver, *Handbook of Attachment*.

Mason, Mike. *The Mystery of Marriage: Meditations on the Miracle*. Sisters, OR: Multnomah, 1985.

Myers, Isabel Briggs. *Gifts Differing: Understanding Personality Type*. Palo Alto, CA: Consulting Psychologists Press, 1980.

Siegel, Daniel J. *The Developing Mind: How Relationships and the Brain Interact to Shape Who We Are*. New York: Guilford, 1999.

Suomi, Stephen J. "Attachment in Rhesus Monkeys." In Cassidy and Shaver, *Handbook of Attachment*.

Vaughn, Brian E., and Kelly K. Bost. "Attachment and Temperament: Redundant, Independent, or Interacting Influences on Interpersonal Adaptation and Personality Development?" In Cassidy and Shaver, *Handbook of Attachment*.

Weinfield, Nancy S., L. Alan Sroufe, Byron Egeland, and Elizabeth A. Carlson. "The Nature of Individual Differences in Infant-Caregiver Attachment." In Cassidy and Shaver, *Handbook of Attachment*.

Acknowledgments

We want to thank our friends and family for their loving support as we worked on this project. We are also grateful for the teaching and influence of Dr. Henry Cloud and Dr. John Townsend, as God used both of them to spark a new flame of hope within the hearts of a young, burned-out pastor and his wife. Their workshop, which we attended, was the basis for Henry's book *Changes That Heal.* To this day, it remains one of the most profound influences on our spiritual growth, healing, and maturity.

Thanks to Mick Silva, our editor and lifelong friend, who believed in our work and fought for us behind the scenes in publishing circles. We have known Mick since the day he was born, and we consider it a privilege to have benefited from his amazing talent as an editor.

To our agent, Don Pape who took a risk and believed in our story and in us.

To Steve Arterburn, who has shared his heart with us and invited Milan to become one of the hosts on his *New Life Live!* radio program. We appreciate the encouragement and support.

Case studies have either been used by permission or are a compilation of many people and experiences. Some readers may think, *They are talking about me!* You'd be amazed at how many people are in situations just like yours. You are not the only ones with your problems. We have been very careful, however, to protect all confidential information our clients have shared with us. Our clients become our teachers, and we thank them as well.

Last, and most importantly, we thank God, whose redemptive love is at the core of any healing that occurs this side of heaven. After years of deep pain, we've gained a profound appreciation for His sending Jesus to provide a way back to wholeness.